THE PROBLEMATIC SCIENCE

THE PROBLEMATIC SCIENCE

PSYCHOLOGY IN NINETEENTH-CENTURY THOUGHT

Edited by

William R. Woodward

and

Mitchell G. Ash

PRAEGER SPECIAL STUDIES • PRAEGER SCIENTIFIC

Library of Congress Cataloging in Publication Data

Main entry under title:

The Problematic science.

Includes index.
1. Psychology—History—19th century.
I. Woodward, William R.   II. Ash, Mitchell.
BF103.P76   150′.9′034   81–21080
ISBN 0-03-059363-8   AACR2

Published in 1982 by Praeger Publishers
CBS Educational and Professional Publishing
a Division of CBS Inc.
521 Fifth Avenue, New York, New York 10175 U.S.A.

© 1982 by Praeger Publishers

23456789   145   987654321

Printed in the United States of America

PREFACE

The purpose of this book is to bring together a representative sample of current scholarship in the history of psychology. The authors were given the theme, "psychology in the nineteenth century: international cross-disciplinary perspectives." Our hope was that the invitation of persons from a variety of national and disciplinary backgrounds would yield a volume that would set an example of quality research in this relatively young historical specialty. To our surprise and satisfaction, the responses to our rather vague prescription turned out to focus upon a single important issue: did psychology become autonomous, either intellectually or socially, in the nineteenth century? The consistently negative answer provided by these chapters poses a challenge to the reigning assumption that psychology was in some sense "liberated" either from parent disciplines or from external social concerns during its formative period.

This publication is a group effort in many ways. The conception of the project derives from historiographical discussions at the 1979 and 1980 meetings of the Cheiron society; the editors' collaboration resulted from similar discussions following the International Congress of Psychology at Leipzig in 1980. Preliminary versions of some of the essays were presented at the 1980 meeting of the History of Science Society in Toronto. We would like to thank each of the contributors for responding so enthusiastically to our invitation and for keeping to our various deadlines. Most of the contributions are parts of larger projects in preparation; we are deeply grateful to the authors for sharing their work in advance.

The editors would like to acknowledge the financial support of the National Institutes of Health (Grant LM 03492 from the National Library of Medicine) and the Fulbright-Commission, respectively.

The Alexander von Humboldt-Stiftung supported the work in its final stages in the form of a sabbatical fellowship to the senior editor. The Department of Psychology of the University of New Hampshire contributed facilities and work space, and the generous sponsorship of Professor Dr. Carl Friedrich Graumann of the Psychologisches Institut of the Universität Heidelberg and Professor Dr. med. Gundolf Keil of the Institut für Geschichte der Medizin at the Universität Würzburg enabled us to work together during the preparation of the final manuscript. We would also like to thank our editor, George Zimmar, who committed us to the project and then awaited its completion with singular forbearance.

Muriel Woodward and Christiane Hartnack did not prepare the index to this volume—it would probably have been finished much sooner if they had. Instead they helped us in other, more important ways; our gratitude for this cannot be expressed in words.

CONTENTS

LIST OF TABLES

LIST OF FIGURES

THE PROBLEMATIC SCIENCE

Introduction

Stretching the Limits of Psychology's History

William R. Woodward

This book is about the psychological thought of a bygone time. Our concentration on the nineteenth century is dictated by the fact that this is the period in which the possibility of psychology as a science first emerged. We hasten to add, however, that this possibility was not realized; psychology did not fully emerge as an autonomous discipline until the twentieth century. The problem of psychology's conceptual and institutional identity ultimately remained unsolved— hence the word "problematic" in the title. The much-debated question whether psychology became a science or a profession can thus be left open, pending our preliminary sketch of the conceptual foundations, the problematic emergence, and the intellectual interests and social conditions of psychology during this period.

The word "thought" in our subtitle is meant to arouse curiosity by its antiquarian flavor. For the purposes at hand, such a comprehensive term is needed. Thought is an appropriately nineteenth-century term, whereas "science" carries twentieth-century connotations of methodological rigor and disciplinary separateness that were foreign to the epoch. We wish especially to convey that psychology was not the prerogative of philosopher, physician, educationalist, or scientist, but the common endeavor of all these and more. Indeed, we regret that we have scarcely touched on psychology in the literary or popular thought of that time.

The authors gathered together here come from a variety of disciplines. Their case studies make no pretension of offering a complete or final interpretation of a person, epoch, or subject area. Neither individually, nor collectively, do they adequately survey the scope of "psychological thought." At best, they emphasize the nineteenth-century crosscurrents between disciplines and nations in the European–American cultural region. The remainder of this introduction will consequently be devoted to lightening the reader's task of synthesizing such varied styles, historiographic approaches, and technical topics by briefly situating each chapter in the historical literature and exposing the central issues raised in it.

PART 1

CONCEPTUAL FOUNDATIONS

The first part of this book deals with the conceptual foundations of nineteenth-century psychological thought in philosophy, biology, and physics. Each foundation grew into a tradition that cut across disciplinary lines, challenging existing categories of thought and leading to reformulations of discourse about mind. While never entirely separate, these traditions matured during the century to the point where controversies and ambivalent allegiances could take shape between them. Psychobiology, psychophysics, child psychology, social psychology, and anthropometry each stand for a fluctuating boundary of the new scientific discipline. This later, tenuous synthesis of the Kantian, Darwinian, and Fechnerian legacies constitutes what is loosely known as the "new psychology."

Our starting with Kant is justified by the overwhelming importance of his psychological and philosophical orientation for the later "new psychology," both inside and outside academe. David E. Leary places Kant's psychological thinking in the context of his thought as a whole and in the tradition of empirical and rational philosophy of mind since Locke and Leibniz. He also explains why Kant consigned psychology to the empirical disciplines, while denying that it could ever attain rational knowledge through the use of mathematics or experiment. He finds Kant's verdict that psychology could never become a science overruled by his own successors, who carried his thought forward to accept consciousness as the proper subject matter of psychology and natural science as the appropriate methodology from which to approach it.

Several shibboleths have been corrected in this chapter. Leary concedes that Kant was primarily a philosopher; therefore his pronouncements on psychology were concerned with the nature of the subject matter, its possible laws, and its proper methods. Misunderstandings have repeatedly arisen from his statements being construed as psychology. For example, the attribution of a perceptual theory of "nativism" to Kant distorts his central epistemological conception, that experience is a synthesis of rational concepts with empirical sensory material. Nor did Kant propose a theory of behavior, though he did expose the irreconcilable situation that we experience choice as free but conceive it as determined. To study Kant, as the psychological thinkers of the nineteenth century did, is to confront the limits of one's science.

Historically, the "back to Kant" movement in the latter part of the nineteenth century owed much to the post-Darwinian effort to save the human "will" from the deterministic implications of evolutionary naturalism. Psychological thinkers needed Kant to answer Darwin, or thought they did. In fact, they required at least a generation and perhaps a century to assimilate Darwin's own answer to determinism. This answer was not at all the ultra-individualistic assumption of a "nature red in tooth and claw." On the contrary, Darwin advocated a conception of the community good, and he saw this as the way out of the problems engendered by a theory of the selection of individuals.

The disjunction between Robert J. Richards' historiographic perspective on Darwin and his historical narrative is revealing of this delayed reception of Darwin's theory of man. It required the contemporary scientific fashion of "sociobiology" to arouse historical interest in what Darwin really said, and meant, by the concept of a "moral sense." This concept has been variously interpreted by the followers of Darwin in keeping with hedonism or with faculty psychology. In Richards' exposition we learn that Darwin simply construed the "moral sense" as an instinct, hence the functional equivalent of a bodily organ. As such, it was subject to natural selection. Here Darwin confronted two problems that were so intransigent that he pondered them from the 1840s until the publication of the *Descent of Man* in 1871. One problem concerned the social instincts of bee drones and worker ants, which do not reproduce and therefore seem to be exempt from natural selection. The other problem was that of altruistic behavior, which may not benefit the individual and mitigates against the selection of moral behavior in evolution. Given the historical context of natural theology in which Darwin lived and worked, he was not satisfied to make a statement about man until he had the solution—that natural selection occurs through competition between groups rather than between individuals, thus preserving the right of conscience in a naturalistic world.

At some level, however, the conservation of matter and energy had to pose a profound challenge for a science of man. The ability to appreciate this challenge was conditioned, in German lands at least, by *Naturphilosophie*. Akin to natural theology in Great Britain, philosophy of nature constituted a heterogeneous bequest of the Enlightenment ideal of natural order and the Romantic dream of exploring organic life and ultimately consciousness. It was a physicist steeped in *Naturphilosophie* who finally accepted the challenge to measure mental energy in terms of physical energy. His proposal has yet to be appreciated for what it was. Neither the panpsychist interpretation of William James and Harald Høffding at the turn of the century nor the positivist emphasis on the trappings of experimental science does justice to the serious integrative vision and the scientific scruples of Gustav Theodor Fechner.

Marilyn E. Marshall fills this gap in our historical understanding of just how Fechner reworked the science and religion of his day into an equation for mental measurement. Her historiographic technique is to contrast the public presentation of psychophysics with its actual origin. The book *Elemente der Psychophysik* in 1860 was delivered to a doubting public, above all to Fechner's friend, the physicist Wilhelm Weber, in a form calculated to convince by its rationale, methods, data, and philosophical underpinnings. The actual story recounted by Marshall is that very early in the 1820s Fechner began to prepare himself for his goal of discovering, and putting into mathematical expression, the mysterious unity of mind and matter. He therefore translated French physics textbooks and supplemented them with his own electromagnetic experiments. In this way, he acquired a firm grasp of experiment and the tool of mathematical calculus, which enabled him to construct a mental law relating conscious sensation to physical stimulus intensity and quality.

Joining all three conceptual foundations—philosophy, biology, and physics—was the central problematic of the new psychology, the status of consciousness and its emergent property of will. Lorraine J. Daston has given us a set of categories and a sense of the mixed allegiances to them among persons who, though they did not consider themselves psychologists, yet addressed psychological issues in a central way. It would not stretch her rubric too much to suggest that Kant's foundation was built on the dualistic metaphysical ontology of Descartes, and that it straddled the explanatory problem of determinism versus free will. By comparison, Darwin's foundation implied monism in metaphysics, while its adherents separated into supporters of emergentism and reductionism in the scientific explanation of mind and behavior by natural selection. Fechner's foundation combined a monistic metaphysics with a deterministic explanation of mind subject to physical energy. Although her presentation involves a different cast of characters, Daston's thesis revolves around the contention that such philosophical allegiances lent a problematic character to the domain of psychology in the Victorian period. The serious implications of this reexamination of the Cartesian legacy, linking dualism of substance with two kinds of causality, she suggests, were felt in the physical sciences and philosophy of science as well.

Daston's thesis and the supporting evidence of these chapters offer a challenge to the claim of Edmund Husserl, Alexandre Koyré, and Thomas Kuhn that the mental sciences failed to evolve their own categories of explanation and methods of exploration. Robert M. Young and Roger Smith have advanced a correlary of the argument for psychology's subservience to the physical sciences, and Brian Mackenzie similarly claims that behaviorism in this century adopted the language of physical science without the testable scientific constructs. Daston, in pitting a science of mind against a theory of will, acknowledges the scientific pretentions of psychology while also calling attention to the very real problems that its philosophical debates raised for other disciplines. Paradoxically, the reflection of psychology's problematic in physics, biology, and philosophy may provide the truer measure of its contribution to the conceptual foundation of science in the nineteenth century.

PART II
PROBLEMATIC EMERGENCE

The received view of the history of psychology is that its limits were established, both intellectually and institutionally, in the second half of the nineteenth century. The usual evidence cited is the founding of laboratories and journals, the production of scientific knowledge in the form of articles and books, the delineation of professional roles, and the achievement of disciplinary autonomy. The revisionist view mentioned at the end of the preceding section is critical of the claims of the would-be science and its evidence for professionalization. The real measure of a science, so the revisionists claim, is the construction of categories of explanation and methods of investigation appropriate to the subject matter. The psychologists, having borrowed their categories and methods from the natural sciences, were merely pursuing pseudoscience.

To a large extent, these two points of view can be regarded as complementary. The alternative view proposed here is that the historian seek to combine the evidential criteria for the achievement of both scientific knowledge and professionalization. One further proviso is in order, however. We must not assume that the criteria of today's science are the same as those of yesteryear. We shall discover, for example, that in none of the cases presented in this book is psychology held to be an autonomous discipline or an independent subject. Clearly it would be false to argue for either an emergence or a failed emergence; rather, the problematic emergence and gradual self-definition of one discipline among others will be our theme.

A case in point is psycho-physiology, which sprang from dual intellectual commitments to religion and science on the one hand and to social ideology and technical industrial needs on the other. As Kurt Danziger has shown, this small branch of medical psychology spawned a modest reformulation of the prevailing views of reflex physiology and human conduct. Over the course of several generations of British and Continental science, the sensorimotor reflex arc came to provide the paradigm for the explanation and treatment of behavioral malfunction. As will be seen elsewhere in this volume, social context conditioned the specific form assumed by this problematic. Carpenter's manipulation of human will to overcome alcoholism, in contrast to Laycock's manipulation of the social conditions of the vice, is one example drawn from British psycho-physiology of this cultural counterpoint.

Danziger's chapter treats the criteria of knowledge side by side with the criteria of professionalization in medicine. These criteria help us to understand the reasons for the failure of British psycho-physiology in comparison with German and French efforts in the same field. There was no model of experimental physiology in Britain from which problems of behavior and conduct could be studied. Furthermore, the basic intellectual interest was to reconcile the principles of automatic action with a purposeful divine order and human will. The underlying social need was to help individuals to adjust to the demands of an increasingly industrialized society. In cases where such adjustment failed, Victorian society needed its science to provide policies for the control of behavior believed to be abnormal or immoral.

Whether it is strictly possible to rise above social ideology in any field is a moot point; what does matter is genuine knowledge and its social function. By most standards, German sensory physiology was successful in both respects. It has never been called a pseudo-science, as was medical psychology, not to mention phrenology. Moreover, theoretical interest and experimental craft combined with an air of practical relevance, perhaps because the application of knowledge about the eye and ear was easy to imagine. Thus the position of Hermann Helmholtz, like those of his comrades Carl Ludwig, Emil DuBois Reymond, and Ernst Brücke, was consistent with the desire of the German lands before and after the abortive revolution of 1848 to promote "pure research" that would reap a social benefit and confer status upon their universities.

But institutional and medical-scientific legitimation for sensory physiology, as R. Steven Turner shows, worked against the disciplinary separation of psychology. The role of Helmholtz was mainly that of a foil for the new psychology. His methods and data were borrowed, even as his theories were replaced with more truly psychological ones. The psychology of psychophysics and perception of George Elias Müller and Carl Stumpf lay outside medicine, as did their careers. Thus theoretical debates over his mathematical analysis of the elements of color vision and spatial perception take on the character of symptoms of disciplinary shift. As chairs in philosophy went to persons with predominantly psychological interests, the primacy of consciousness and will began to be argued with increasing vehemence. Thus began an irreversible process of change toward disciplinary autonomy, in which psychology, philosophy, and medicine began to draw their limits more tightly than before.

Wilhelm Wundt and William James represent the subsequent generation, which allegedly established psychology in Germany and North America. Yet for neither of them was psychology an autonomous discipline. They were alike in more ways than they would have liked to admit. As voluntarist critics of Helmholtz, both increasingly emphasized the irreducibility of consciousness and the behavioral manifestations of mind. As encyclopedists, they both defined the limits of the program for psychology far more broadly than anyone had up to then. They were not known for their experimental prowess, and they did not succumb to the positivism of their generation. But they effectively parlayed their "psychologism" into a legitimation of the laboratory, the lectures, the graduate students, and the other institutional accoutrements of a formative discipline.

The manner in which both men fashioned programmatic theories of psychology within a larger disciplinary framework is of particular relevance for our reevaluation of the status of psychology circa 1890. They each maintained a commitment to the continuity of nature in the form of an evolutionary approach to mind. For Wundt, as shown in my chapter, the subareas of psychology led from the activity of the most primitive nervous system to the most advanced society. Where Wundt was enamored of natural selection and dropped it, James, Dewey, and Baldwin made it the key to the evolution of mind through pragmatism, instrumentalism, and genetic logic. Psychology was for them a fundamental discipline that spilled over into ethics, religion, and epistemology, while "leaking metaphysics at every pore." In its privileged status between philosophy and medicine, psychology was not the handmaiden but the queen of the sciences. By contrast, for students of the next generation, their positivistic metaphors of brain and behavior hardened into organicist and behaviorist ontologies. Here, at the very brink of the opportunity to become scientific, is where psychology became scientistic.

Psychoanalysis offers a curious culmination to the interdisciplinary context of psychology sketched here. It arose in closer proximity to the therapeutic branch of medicine, drawing on clinical case studies for its working evidence and couched in terms far less systematic or "scientific." For all that, it laid claim to be a science of the mind, and for good reason, as Frank J. Sulloway has shown in the book from which this chapter is derived. The programmatic features of Freud's theory—including infantile sexuality, fixation, regression, repression, and susceptibility to neurosis—are shown here to have deep roots in Haeckel's evolutionary biology, which was at the forefront of science around 1890. Within a matter of years, however, this speculative branch of embryology would be superseded by a new era of genetics, heralded by the work of Gregor Mendel and August Weismann. Sulloway is sharply critical of the subsequent institutional ideology, which came in most cases to regard psychoanalysis as a sacrosanct discipline open in the first instance to those schooled in the clinical art rather than, as was Freud, in neurology and brain anatomy. It is worthwhile to compare the consequences of this disciplinary shift toward autonomy with the rest of psychological thought.

Like the British psycho-physiologists, Helmholtz, Wundt, and James, Freud did not work in a scientific vacuum. He shared in the ideologies, both scientific and cultural, of his time, and he drew on the neurological and evolutionary science of his day. He did take greater risks, however. He left academia, wrote for an educated public, and espoused an unorthodox theory of sexuality in a society that was prudish in pretension if not in reality. Yet for him, too, the status of psychology was mixed; it was originally deterministic and biological, while later, through a mixture of motives both personal and professional, it came to be more psychological. Generalizing Sulloway's argument, we could say that the psychologism of the early twentieth century served to narrow psychological thought from its nineteenth-century interdisciplinary context and thereby to legitimate psychology as an autonomous discipline. The price of this narrowing and fragmentation was that psychology lost touch with other disciplines and became positivistic. This gain of autonomy and corresponding loss of interrelatedness to other disciplines was characterized by a proliferation of schools and specialties from this time forward to the first World War.

PART III

INTELLECTUAL INTERESTS AND SOCIAL CONDITIONS

Concurrent with nineteenth-century efforts toward an interdisciplinary identity for psychology, this wide gamut of specialties stretched the limits of the discipline still further. From the twentieth-century viewpoint of "systems and theories" textbooks, many of psychology's "problem areas" were born of this first generation differentiation process, into, for example, physiological, existential, social, child, and differential psychologies.

The chapters in this final part depict the sociocultural conditions that gave a distinctively national flavor to the development of these specialties. In Russia, the school around Sechenov taught and did research in a European mode; in Spain, progressive scholars introduced European ideas into Spanish culture through public instruction; in France, self-styled crowd psychologists placed theories of suggestion at the disposal of right-wing political groups; in Germany, an evolutionary theory of child development supported a middle course toward school reform; and in the United States, a Baconian approach to mental testing was conceived in the spirit of a progressive "search for order." The historiographic perspectives of the authors, including their political and scientific allegiances, provide critical reflections on the relations of past to present intellectual interests. Together, these chapters make a forceful statement about the close reciprocal relationship between intellectual interests and the social conditions of knowledge.

One form in which the sciences belong to society is the "invisible college." With this term Derek Price and Diana Crane have described the collective work of scientific communities—in particular, the networking and publishing practices by which scientists share knowledge and establish property rights. Akin to the invisible college is the "school"; its distinguishing feature is that it is visible rather than invisible. In this book Mikhail Grigorevitch Yaroschevskii has applied a three-part model of science as human activity to the school: (1) the logical movement of knowledge categories within a given science; (2) the personal knowledge and intrinsic motivation of the participants, especially the teacher in cooperation with students; and (3) the social-logical unit of the school, viewed as an integral part of Kuhnian normal science, rather than as a stage preceding it.

As described in Yaroschevskii's book, *Psychologie im 20. Jahrhundert* (1974, German translation 1975), the "Russian physiological school" that developed around Sechenov became a tradition extending forward through Bekhterev to Pavlov. The present chapter analyzes only the short-lived flourishing of the school as "research collective" between 1860 and 1865, a period that well illustrates the historiographic model above. Sechenov's book *Reflexes of the Brain* represents a category shift from the mechanical reflex to a homeostatic regulatory conception of reflex function. The followers of Sechenov at that time developed a high degree of motivation through his encouragement of both independent projects and collaborative research on interrelated problems. Their contest with a Swiss institute shows how divergent "categorical profiles" may nevertheless belong to the same "categorical network" of normal science. This historical illustration of a school is also interesting for what it implies about the organization of scientific activity in Europe today—the institute, the hierarchical and close-knit relationship of director to staff, and the competition for knowledge in an international scientific community.

Psychology need not be organized around scientific problems, however. The unifying features of psychology in Spain were, by contrast, religious and political. The traditionalism of a regime that, after 1868, did not tolerate non-Catholic humanists in the university system turns out to be the major social factor in the assimilation of the new psychology in Spain. As a consequence, the "two Spains," traditionalist and Europeanist, gave support to very different psychologies, of which only the latter is traced here by Helio Carpintero.

Worth noting is a political parallel in the present: the importation of European and American ideas into Spanish social science again, after a post-World-War-II period of authoritarian rule.

Rather than focusing on a short-lived research collective, Carpintero describes several generations of Spanish psychological thought. An eclectic period blending spiritualism with phrenology and neoscholasticism was rejuvenated in the 1860s by a Krausist psychology modeled on German *Naturphilosophie*. The expulsion of the Krausists from the university by a neo-Catholic alliance in 1868 led to the formation of a loose-knit school called the Free Institution of Education in Madrid in 1876. During this Restoration period, progressive intellectuals blended psychological interests with law, literature, social reform, education, medicine, and science, expressing their ideas in literary journals, books, public instruction, and the professions. The absence of a "mandarin" alliance between the academic and political life, at least as far as the progressives were concerned, may have spared the discipline much of the academic-mindedness of European and American psychologies of this period.

The exclusion of a group from a place in the academic establishment has other ramifications as well. In France, as in Spain, psychology became bifurcated to a large extent. While Jean Charcot, Hippolyte Bernheim, Pierre Janet, Alfred Binet, and Emil Durkheim all belonged to the university and medical communities, another group, known as the crowd psychologists and including especially Gustave Le Bon, worked outside it. They necessarily sought their social and institutional support in the popular press and in alliances with powerful social groups, particularly the military. Ironically, they received belated critical reception following World War I from the psychoanalyst Freud and the behaviorist Floyd Allport. But it is the nature of their implicit theoretical assumptions and their explicit ideological context that are the central focus of the chapter by Alexandre Métraux.

Métraux's essay is part of an effort by critical psychologists in Europe and America to shed light upon current theoretical inadequacies by exposing their historical roots. In this instance, the main argument is that the "social" psychology of crowds, and more recently of groups, has borrowed an "individual" paradigm from the theory of hypnotic suggestion. This argument contains a twofold critique. On the level of intellectual interests, the purpose is to reconstruct the implications of theory in order to expose its inadequacies, hence contributing to current theoretical discussion. On the level of social conditions, the contention is that political ideology led, and continues to lead, not only to theoretical contradictions but also to unwarranted selectivity in the attribution of irrational behavior to the unenfranchised classes.

The essays presented so far in this part of the book have focused on social factors in the construction of psychological thought. The remaining two chapters point to a feature of psychological thought in the nineteenth century that deserves greater emphasis—the use of psychological ideas for the purpose of social integration, and not only for the narrow professional reason of seeking greater knowledge and expertise. The field of educational theory and practice and the technology of mental testing were both supported in crucial ways by the theory and methods of the new post-Darwinian psychology.

A case in point is the use in Germany of Darwinian ideas to legitimize a frankly nationalistic educational theory. Siegfried Jaeger shows that the spokesman for child psychology at the University of Jena, Willian Preyer, lent his considerable influence to the justification of a middle road between classics-oriented and occupationally oriented education in the controversial school reform discussions during the 1880s and 1890s. Preyer borrowed heavily from Darwin's theory of natural selection, which he interpreted as encouraging competition and self-reliance in the education of the individual will toward the purposes of the nation, thus implicitly opposing the ethic of cooperation. Among his allies against the socialists was the Prussian economist and state secretary Hugo Thiel; on the socialist side stood another academician, the Marburg philosopher Friedrich A. Lange. Thus, in the universities of Germany, unlike those of Spain and France, both liberal and conservative political views were clearly represented. Regardless of political stance, academicians did play a role in the determination of educational policy; that they did so by appealing to allegedly scientific theories such as psychogenesis raises important questions about the responsibility of scientists in society.

An equally dubious scientific rationale was invoked by educationalists in the United States to justify a nationalist effort of a quite different sort. Here the social problem was the influx of immigrants; the solution was to turn to psychology to provide tests for those who should be accorded the privileges of education, jobs, and, later, military leadership. The idea for mental testing had also sprung from Darwinian soil. But the so-called "triumph of evolution" in America was quite bereft of explicit theory, so conspicuous in Germany. Instead, it was thought that the numbers should speak for themselves. This positivistic solution masked the real problem of the comparative disadvantage of minority ethnic groups in competing for a position in the social order.

The fact that the anthropometric mental tests of James McKeen Cattell failed is no reason to discount their importance. As Michael M. Sokal shows, they were a prototype for the tests to come, and they drew on both of the leading quantitative methods of the era, reaction time measurement from Wundt and anthropometry from Galton. What they lacked, as subsequent criticism showed, was both reliability and validity. They did not correlate with one another, and they did not measure what they were supposed to measure. Moreover, their significance was curtailed by their failure to even address the higher mental processes, and by the lack of a theoretical basis. When these faults were partly corrected by the next generation of testers, the technology of educational and vocational measurement was born. This applied psychology so captured the market place that academic psychology, with its glorified ideal of pure experiment, was to become and remain only a fraction of the discipline.

PROSPECTS FOR A REVISION OF THE PROFESSIONALIZATION THESIS

The basis is laid in this book for a substantial revision of the so-called "professionalization thesis" in the history of science with respect to the history of psychology. The professionalization thesis has consisted of the central assumption that all roads lead to the present state of the discipline, namely, as institutionally separate and intellectually autonomous. This book casts doubt on the assumption that an autonomous discipline of psychology emerged in the nineteenth century. Actually, the discipline manifested heavy interdependencies on the medical profession, the academic establishment, and society at large with regard to both institutional affiliations and intellectual interests. The story of its separation and differentiation belongs, if anywhere, to the twentieth century.

The opening part of this book raises serious questions about the nature and scientific legitimation of psychological knowledge. In its conceptual foundations, psychology borrowed heavily from philosophy, biology, and physics. To the extent that it took over a unique subject matter of conscious experience and volitional behavior, it posed conceptual problems for a science based on assumptions of a materialist ontology and deterministic explanation.

Evidently these scientistic assumptions would have to go. Indeed, spiritualism and indeterminism were restored to scientific legitimacy in the early twentieth century in both the psychological and the physical sciences.

The second part of the book casts serious doubt upon two traditional characterizations by historians of psychology. In the United States, the image of a Baconian endeavor to replace speculative with experimental knowledge has led to an unfortunate neglect of the ideological commitments and larger philosophies of man and science held by entire generations of nineteenth-century psychological thinkers. In Europe, meanwhile, the historian's image of a Cartesian endeavor to replace speculative with rational knowledge has contributed to a neglect of concrete experimental advances as well as of ideological views beyond one's own. Both lacunae indicate a need to stretch the categorical limits of psychology beyond the artificial boundaries set by such legitimating self-images, in order to encompass the broad expanse of world views, human problems, and systematic thought that belonged, and still belong, to this interdisciplinary field of knowledge and action.

Finally, the third part of this book reveals some of the social factors that buffeted psychological thinkers during this period. The medical research institute could succeed or fail in the quest for knowledge, depending on the social relationships of its members and on their communication with other schools. The psychologist in a nonacademic setting had to seek sources of intellectual and financial support in the community, be it literary, educational, legal, or military; and psychology, in turn, had a profound impact on society, as the examples of child psychology and mental testing show. Whether this impact has been a salutary one can best be judged from the perspectives both of the social needs and of the level of development of the scientific conceptions during the periods concerned.

In sum, at every level—philosophical, scientific, and social—the professionalization thesis requires revision insofar as it applies to the nineteenth century. The acceptance of the evidence here for a merger of theory and practice and of psychology with other disciplines should make the history of this discipline both more problematic, and more relevant, to fundamental human desires for self-knowledge and understanding of others than before.

I

CONCEPTUAL FOUNDATIONS

1

Immanuel Kant and the Development of Modern Psychology

David E. Leary

Few thinkers in the history of Western civilization have had as broad and lasting an impact as Immanuel Kant (1724-1804). This "Sage of Königsberg" spent his entire life within the confines of East Prussia, but his thoughts traveled freely across Europe and, in time, to America, where their effects are still apparent. An untold number of analyses and commentaries have established Kant as a preeminent epistemologist, philosopher of science, moral philosopher, aesthetician, and metaphysician. He is even recognized as a natural historian and cosmologist: the author of the so-called Kant–Laplace hypothesis regarding the origin of the universe. He is less often credited as a "psychologist," "anthropologist," or "philosopher of mind," to

Work on this essay was supported by the National Science Foundation (Grant No. SES-8008051). Different aspects of the story told here were previously discussed before the American Psychological Association, the Cheiron Society, the History of Science Society, and the Society for Social Studies of Science, and they were presented in the *Journal of the History of Philosophy* and the *Journal of the History of the Behavioral Sciences*. I am indebted to the editor of the latter journal for permission to use materials from one of these articles (see Note 7) and to William R. Woodward for helpful conversations in the course of my writing of this essay.

use terms whose currency postdated his time.[1] Nonetheless, the thesis of this essay is that Immanuel Kant laid the foundation for later developments in the broad field of inquiry that had already been labeled "psychology."

KANT'S BACKGROUND

The details of Kant's life are not important for the story we have to tell. To be sure, the social historical context of his life is not without relevance: not even Immanuel Kant could, or would have wanted to, escape the formative and directive influence of his time. The general social, political, and economic features of the late Enlightenment period, culminating in the French Revolution and its aftermath, provided a necessary backdrop against which Kant developed his philosophical, and indeed his psychological, point of view. At the same time, Kant's personal relationship to the tradition of religious Pietism was a significant factor in his willingness to consider the less-than-rational aspects of human functioning. Still, everything considered, by far the most relevant context for understanding his work is provided by the intellectual culture to which he belonged. For our present purposes, a brief discussion of the work of four representatives of this culture—Gottfried Wilhelm Leibniz (1646–1716), Christian Wolff (1679–1754), Johann Nicolas Tetens (1736/38–1807), and Alexander Gottlieb Baumgarten (1714–1762)—will reasonably portray the background of Kant's psychological deliberations.

Gottfried Wilhelm Leibniz, one of the other intellectual giants in Western history, set the scene for the development of a distinctive German tradition of thought. Although it was left for Wolff and others to establish fully the period of German Enlightenment, it was Leibniz who bequeathed many of its philosophical principles and posited a number of the doctrines that retained vitality throughout this period. Furthermore, the posthumous publication of Leibniz's works served to keep his thought alive and influential long after his death. Indeed, one such posthumous publication, Leibniz's *Nouveau Essais sur l'entendement humain* (New Essays Concerning Human Understanding) (1975), had a tangible impact on German thought and in particular on Kant. Originally written in response to John Locke's *Essay Concerning Human Understanding* (1690), and withheld from publication when Locke died in 1704, this treatise stimulated Kant's thinking by its postulation of a crucial distinction between sensibility and understanding, that is, between the "material" sensations received from the world and the "formal" classification of these sensations by the mind. The influence of this distinction was clearly evident in Kant's *De Mundi Sensibilis atque Intelligibilis Forma et Principiis* (Concerning the Form and Principles of the Sensible and Intelligible World) (1779), which was the dissertation Kant delivered upon his inauguration to the chair of philosophy at Königsberg. This work was not only the symbolic starting point of Kant's so-called "critical period," it was also an important manifestation of Kant's acceptance of the "Leibnizian" principle of the formative activity of the mind (as opposed to the much more passive empiricist-oriented model of the mind that Kant had been considering not long before).[2] From this time forward, Kant developed his own philosophy and psychology, going beyond the bounds proposed even by Leibniz.

As Kant went beyond the thought of Leibniz, he also went beyond that of Christian Wolff, whom Kant considered the intellectual "preceptor of Germany." Wolff made his historical mark by synthesizing many of Leibniz's ideas within a grand system that also included elements from other sources as well as his own original insights and doctrines. Although his system was important for many reasons, the portion of it dedicated to psychology is of primary interest to us. The major significance of this portion is its dualistic nature: Wolff divided his psychology into two parts. On the basis of this division, made in the early 1730s, two relatively separable traditions of psychology began to develop in Germany—the tradition of rational psychology and the tradition of empirical psychology. Although twentieth-century historians of psychology invariably trace these two traditions to the works of René Descartes and John Locke respectively, in point of fact it was Christian Wolff who first clearly distinguished, defined, and established rational and empirical psychology as separate fields of intellectual inquiry.

In his *Psychologia Empirica* (Empirical Psychology) (1732) Wolff defined empirical psychology as the science of what experience teaches us about the soul. In other words, he said, it is an inductive science that leads to empirical generalizations about the soul and its activities. In contrast, he argued in his *Psychologia Rationalis* (Rational Psychology) (1734), rational psychology is the science of all that is possible to the human soul (as opposed to all that has actually happened to it). It is a branch of metaphysics, a demonstrative science that provides necessarily true statements regarding the nature and essence of the soul. In short, it gives rational explanations for the facts accumulated in empirical psychology. Thus rational psychology completes empirical psychology; and conversely, empirical psychology (along with metaphysics and cosmology) is one of the foundations of rational psychology.[3]

The notable point here is that Wolff clearly distinguished two different kinds of psychology, one of them independent from philosophy and the other a branch of philosophy. Although Wolff's empirical and rational psychologies overlapped in practice far more than his theoretical definitions implied, Wolff did, in fact, stimulate the development of two traditions that became increasingly separable over time; as a consequence, when Immanuel Kant surveyed psychology a half century later, his critical assessment and reformulation of psychology took place within the context of this dualistic vision of psychology bequeathed to him by Christian Wolff.

Of course, by Kant's time, other authors had replaced Wolff as the authorities on empirical and rational psychology.[4] In the realm of empirical psychology (or *Erfabrungsseelenlehre*, as it came to be designated in Germany), the most important authority was Johann Nicolas Tetens. Among his major contributions, Tetens' espousal of a tripartite faculty psychology (or *Vermögenpsychologie*) was particularly relevant to Kant's psychological thinking. Although there were additional reasons for Kant's conversion to a three-faculty psychology, Tetens' empirical psychology was at least strongly corroborative, as reflected in the fact that his *Philosophische Versuche über menschliche Natur und ihre Entwicklung* (Philosophical Essays on Human Nature and Its Development) (1777) lay open before Kant as he was working out the fundamental concepts of his critical philosophy. The philosophical significance of this tripartite division of psychological faculties is most clearly evident in the similarly trifurcated presentation of Kant's thought in his three major works— the *Kritik der reinen Vernunft* (Critique of Pure Reason) (1781), *Kritik der praktischen Vernunft* (Critique of Practical Reason) (1788), and *Kritik der Urtheilskraft* (Critique of Judgment) (1790). As Kant himself tells us, the tripartite division of these works reflects the psychological division between knowing, willing, and feeling. Similarly, Kant relied on this threefold division throughout his own psychological work, as for instance in his *Anthropologie in pragmatischer Hinsicht* (Anthropology from a Pragmatic Point of View) (1798).[5] Nonetheless, despite this and other involvements with the doctrines of empirical psychology, Kant was keenly aware, as we shall see, of the limitations of this field of inquiry.

In the realm of rational psychology, perhaps the most important test for Kant—and for his subsequent critique of psychology—was found in Alexander Gottlieb Baumgarten's treatise on *Metaphysica* (Metaphysics) (1739). This very popular work which went through numerous editions, was used by Kant throughout his teaching career. Although the works of other authors offered additional materials, Baumgarten's text provided Kant with some of his best examples of the major lines of argument of late eighteenth-century rational psychologists. As was typical, these rational arguments led to confident assertions on the soul's ontological substantiality, simplicity, identity, and relation to the physical world, especially the body.[6] As we shall see, Kant, came to the conclusion that all these assertions, as well as any other assertions that might be made about the essential nature of the soul, were logically fallacious and inevitably groundless. As a consequence, he began the formal, published presentation of his views on psychology with a resounding denial of the validity of rational psychology. Soon after, he extended his critique to the problematic character of empirical psychology.

KANT'S CRITIQUE OF PSYCHOLOGY

The first installment of Kant's critique of psychology appeared in his famous *Kritik der reinen Vernunft* (1781). Among the many things that Kant attempted to accomplish in this work was a systematic critique of rational psychology, and not only that of Baumgarten: according to Kant, no attempt to ascertain the nature of the soul—or thinking subject—by means of rational analysis can possibly withstand criticism.[7]

Although Kant's specific arguments against the validity of rational psychology varied from the first to the second (1787) edition of *Kritik der reinen Vernunft*, his general argument remained the same and was quite simple. To know the nature of the soul, or the "I," he argued, is beyond the power of human reason. There can be no purely rational knowledge of the soul. All arguments about the soul's substantiality, simplicity, identity, and relation to the physical world ultimately begin with "the single proposition 'I think'."[8] And this proposition is empirical, not rational. It is based upon a posteriori experience rather than a priori reason, and experience can never provide a basis for a purely rational and certain proof of the nature of the soul. Just because there is an empirical "I" in every act of thought, for instance, does not prove that this "I" is substantial, or that it is identical from one thought to another, or that it is simple. Nothing about the essence of the "I" follows necessarily from its existence. And even granting, as Kant did, that there must be a noumenal "I" to account for the a priori possibility of knowledge, no attribute other than existence can validly be predicated of this "I." Any other attribute, such as substantiality, would be drawn invalidly from the realm of experience. Therefore, Kant concluded, since rational psychology is "a science surpassing all powers of human reason," there is nothing left for us "but to study our soul under the guidance of experience, and to confine ourselves to those questions which do not go beyond the limits within which a content can be provided for them by possible inner experience."[9] In other words, Kant concluded that psychology can only be an empirical science.

With this conclusion Kant was ready to enter the second phase of his critique of psychology, the phase in which he analyzed the scientific status of empirical psychology. He published the results of this critical analysis in the preface of his *Metaphysische Anfangsgründe der Naturwissenschaft* (Metaphysical Foundations of Natural Science) (1786), a work in which he elaborated his own "Newtonian" conception of natural science. It was against this same conception that Kant measured the possibility of a scientific psychology. Again his conclusion was negative: psychology—or "the empirical doctrine of the soul"—can never become "a natural science proper"; it can "never become anything more than a historical . . . natural doctrine of the internal sense." As a consequence, it can only provide "a natural description of the [phenomena of the] soul, but not a science [i.e., demonstrative knowledge] of the soul."[10]

The reason psychology could never become a "natural science proper" according to Kant was that it could not be based upon a priori principles and thus could not yield apodictic, or certain, knowledge. More specifically, psychology could not utilize mathematics, which provides the necessary means for the a priori construction of concepts in science. According to Kant, "in every special doctrine of nature only so much science proper can be found as there is mathematics in it." Mathematics is the "pure [a priori] part [of science], which lies at the foundation of the empirical part [of science]." In other words, all true science must have a rational as well as an empirical part. Experience provides the empirical data; mathematics provides the inherently rational relationships between these data. But psychology could never utilize mathematics, according to Kant, because its empirical data do not have spatial dimensions and therefore exist only in the single dimension of time. Therefore, "unless one might want to take into consideration merely the law of continuity in the flow of . . . internal changes," mathematics could not be applied to purely mental phenomena. As a result, psychology could "become nothing more than a systematic art . . .

never a science proper; for . . . [it is] merely empirical." By "merely empirical" Kant meant that psychology had to depend entirely upon an inductive, or a posteriori, collection of data. Such a procedure can never yield apodictic knowledge because it contains no a priori, necessary elements. Instead it can lead only to tentative "laws of experience."[11]

The designation of psychology as "merely empirical" did not mark the end to Kant's critique. In the same preface to the same work he said that not only is psychology "merely empirical," it is not even a good empirical discipline. Psychology suffers, Kant pointed out, "because in it the manifold of internal observation is separated only by mere thought, but cannot be kept separate and be connected again at will." In brief, psychology cannot control its phenomena; it cannot be "experimental." Furthermore, psychology suffers from the poor quality and restricted range of the observations that are available to psychologists. On the one hand, "the [act of] observation itself alters and distorts the state of the object [i.e., the mental phenomenon] observed"; on the other, "still less does another thinking subject submit to our investigations in such a way as to be conformable to our purposes." Thus, psychologists can only report on their own mental phenomena, and even then they cannot be completely accurate in their reports.[12]

Such was the negative part of Kant's critique of "merely empirical" psychology. Psychology, in short, could never become a truly rational science, based upon mathematics and yielding necessary truths, nor could it become an experimental science. Kant could see no way to change this verdict, but he did see a way in which psychology could at least become a better empirical science. Therefore, in the third and final stage of his critique of psychology, Kant advocated the reformation of empirical psychology. Psychology should, he said, make use of a different methodology, a so-called "anthropological" methodology based upon observations of the external rather than internal sense. He set forth this thesis in his *Anthropologie in pragmatischer Hinsicht* (1798), claiming that psychology, although remaining "merely empirical," could become more useful to humanity if it would forsake its traditional introspective method and begin to make systematic observations of men and women "in the world" as they behave and interrelate with their fellow citizens. Such knowledge of "human nature" as can be gathered in this manner, and supplemented by "travelling, or at least reading travelogues" (as Kant avidly did), and by such "auxiliary means" as the study of "world history, biography, and even plays and novels," could be distilled, Kant said, into "laws of experience" that would assist men and women in the course of their lives. Knowing better how humans tend to behave and how they tend to react to certain behaviors, individuals could make better choices about their own best course of action. This was a sufficient justification, in Kant's opinion, for developing an empirical psychology based upon external rather than internal observations.[13] On this positive and prophetic note, Kant's critique of psychology came to an end.

KANT'S PSYCHOLOGICAL DOCTRINES

In view of Kant's recommendation of external observations in psychology, it is ironical that his own psychology, as presented in the *Anthropologie* as well as in other works, relied so heavily on traditional introspectionist data. In fact, the entire first part of the *Anthropologie* (by far the larger of its two parts) was concerned with the classification and discussion of mental phenomena. Furthermore, the positive psychological doctrines that resulted from Kant's analyses of mental life had as great an impact on subsequent psychological thought as did the essentially negative conclusions of his critique of psychology. The nature of these positive psychological doctrines can be discussed in relation to three issues: the sources of knowledge, the nature of the mind (or ego), and the nature and functions of the psychological faculties.

In reviewing the background to Kant's thought, we noted that Kant was stimulated at a crucial point in his intellectual development by Gottfried Wilhelm Leibniz's distinction between sensibility and understanding. Though true, this does not mean that Kant accepted the orthodox, Leibnizian interpretation of this distinction. To Leibniz, as to Christian Wolff, sensations—including what we call perceptions—are merely confused, indistinct thoughts; and, conversely, thoughts are merely sensory representations that have been clarified by rational analysis. Kant rejected this blurring of the distinction between sensibility and understanding and established a radical separation that proved to be both stimulating and problematic for later philosophers and psychologists: for Kant, sensations and thoughts were two distinctly different kinds of things.[14]

Kant was also influenced by the Leibnizian doctrine that the forms of knowledge are innate, whereas the content of knowledge must be acquired through experience. Kant's acceptance of this doctrine reflected his agreement with Leibniz's contention that ᴐme sort of synthesis of rationalism and empiricism was necessary.

In applying Leibniz's distinction between form and content to his own radical distinction between sensibility and understanding, however, Kant once again went beyond the Leibnizian–Wolffian view of cognition. According to Kant, both sensibility and understanding, since they represent separate mental functions, must have their own formal—as well as contentual—characteristics. The senses, he concluded in his inaugural dissertation (1770), apprehend individual, concrete things, whereas the understanding takes these individual apprehensions and represerts them in terms of abstract concepts. Although the specific content of sensation comes from the outer world through the senses, our sensibility is such that we grasp this content, always and automatically, according to the formal characteristics of time and space. These characteristics, Kant contended, are supplied by the mind; they are in no way a part of the sensory content of our knowledge. Kant referred to the products of sensibility as "intuitions." Intuitions, by their nature, are always sensible. Concepts, on the other hand, are intelligible and are the product, not of intuition, but of thought, or understanding. Thought transforms intuitions by the spontaneous and instantaneous application of such purely intellectual categories as possibility, existence, necessity, substance, and cause. The result is the generation of knowledge, properly so called.[15]

This brief review of Kant's doctrine of the dual sources of knowledge leads us very naturally into a discussion of his doctrine about the nature of the mind, or ego. It should be apparent by now that for Kant the mind is fundamentally and irrevocably active. It participates in the production of action. As we have seen in the previous section of this essay, Kant did not believe that it is possible definitively to describe the transcendental, or ultimate, nature of the mind, but he did contend that the existence of the "I" (or ego) is guaranteed, since it is the necessary "formal condition" that makes possible "the logical unity of every thought."[16] Whereas the ego in and of itself cannot be an object of thought, some of its attributes can be known, Kant said, insofar as the ego is "the vehicle of all concepts."[17] Indeed, the very existence of our concepts presupposes the activity of the mind, and in particular the mind's capacity of instantaneous apperception. For Kant, apperception referred to the special type of synthesis that is brought about by the faculty of thought, or understanding. As we have seen, Kant did not agree with the empiricists who felt that higher mental phenomena, such as concepts, are merely the final products of a random and essentially passive process of association of sensations. He could not conceive how disparate sensations could, by chance, come to adhere in a unified, structured manner. Instead, he viewed concepts as the basic, original "givens" of consciousness. Their existence, he said, rather than the existence of unorganized and thus meaningless sensations, is primary. We are first aware of unified states of mind; we secondarily analyze these states of mind into their elements. We never know these elements except as abstractions from our concepts. This was the reasoning behind Kant's doctrine of the primary "unity of consciousness."[18]

If his analysis of the nature of "pure reason," or knowledge, convinced Kant that the ego is both active and unitive, his analyses of both "practical reason" and "judgment" served to corroborate this emphasis many times over. As is commonly recognized, Kant's consideration of the application of reason in the realm of daily affairs was the culmination of his thought, and his discussion of the purposive character of "judgmental" thought and action put the finishing touches on the architectonic structure of his system of thought. The human person in action, freely making decisions and choosing his or her behavior, is the ultimate image of the human being that Kant wished to propose and defend. We shall return to this topic when we discuss Kant's doctrine of the will, a doctrine that profoundly influenced the subsequent development of German philosophy and psychology and had a definite impact on philosophers and psychologists in other countries.

The final aspect of Kant's psychological thought that we shall review concerns his doctrine of the mental faculties. This doctrine is intertwined with the topics we have already considered, namely, Kant's theory of the sources of knowledge and his view of the nature of the mind. It is also intertwined with the legacy of pre-Kantian empirical psychology, as we have seen in our discussion of the background to Kant's thought. Despite this connection with previous psychological doctrines, however, we should not underestimate the extent of Kant's originality. Although Johann Nicolas Tetens and several others had already laid the foundation for a thoroughgoing tripartite analysis of mental activity, they had not distinguished the faculties of knowing, willing, and feeling quite so clearly and definitively as Kant was about to do. Nor had they given a clear rationale for the relationship between these various faculties. As a result, it was Kant, not they, who must be given credit for firmly establishing the tradition of tripartite functional analysis, a tradition that was to have a fundamental influence on later philosophical and psychological thought.[19]

On the level of philosophical analysis, Kant distinguished three cognitive faculties—understanding, reasoning, and judgment. He discussed each of these faculties in turn in his three major works, namely, in *Kritik der reinen Vernunft* (1781), *Kritik der praktischen Vernunft* (1788), and *Kritik der Urtheilskraft* (1790), respectively. Implicit within these works, and explicit in his lectures on psychology and in his *Anthropologie in pragmatischer Hinsicht* (1798), were the three psychological faculties of cognition, desire, and feeling. Although he maintained a strict logical distinction between the philosophical and psychological levels of analysis, Kant himself indicated the consonance between his philosophical and psychological doctrines in the introduction to his *Kritik der Urtheilskraft*: the psychological processes of knowing, desiring, and feeling, he said, are directly related to the actual operation of the a priori faculties of understanding, reasoning, and judging.[20] It was the third of these faculties—feeling, or judging—that constituted Kant's most obvious addition to the tradition of functional analysis, but his treatment of the other two faculties was no less novel.

The faculty of knowing, as we have already seen, operates on two levels, the lower level dealing with sensibility and the higher with conceptual understanding. In addition to the process of sensory intuition that we have already discussed, Kant maintained that there is a second lower cognitive process. This process, which he called imagination, can take place even in the absence of immediate sensation. It can either produce new sensuous images or reproduce images of former intuitions. In the latter process, Kant conceded, the mind is more passive than active, being governed by habits of association; but in the former process the mind is much more active and creative. In either case, higher cognition builds upon the work of the imagination in the same way that it completes the process of sensory intuition, that is, by categorizing the images formed by the lower faculty. As in the case of intuitions, the product of the categorization of images is conceptualization, or ideas. Thinking with ideas is, for Kant, simply one of the powers of the mind.[21]

All this mental activity presupposes, for Kant, the a priori capacity of apperception and the existential fact of the unity of consciousness. Kant did not, however, limit his psychological vision to the realm of consciousness. In opposition to the empiricists, he endorsed the existence of unconscious ideas. Indeed, his discussion of the "degrees of consciousness" had notable historical consequences. In addition, Kant discussed various cognitive "deficiences" and "talents." Among the deficiencies he discussed mental illness, particularly—though not entirely—as it reflects the improper working of the rational mind; among the talents he discussed wit and the nature of genius.[22]

In his treatment of practical reason, or the will, Kant wanted to demonstrate the basic freedom of the human person: so much so, in fact, that Kant's voluntarism is commonly considered the central nerve of his entire philosophical system. Given this fact, the central irony of Kant's thought is that, although he posed a brilliant argument for the a priori freedom of the human being, he was equally adamant in his insistence that this freedom is a function solely of the practical reason, or will, and can never be comprehended by pure reason, or understanding. After all, as Kant had previously argued in the *Kritik der reinen Vernunft*, one of the basic categories of comprehension is causality. Human beings necessarily comprehend antecedents and consequences as causes and effects: our minds simply work that way.[23] As a result, since every act—even every free act—occurs in the context of a sequence of events over time, complete comprehension will always involve the specification of cause–effect relations. By arguing that these cause–effect relations are the product of mental analysis and do not necessarily describe the true state of nature, Kant was able to leave room for freedom in the world of human affairs. But this same argument also led him to present two diametrically opposed images of the human being—as free and as determined.

The image of the human person as free, which, as we have said, was the ultimate image that he wished to propose and defend, was presented by Kant in the *Kritik der praktischen Vernunft*. His argument for this freedom was completely philosophical, based on a logical analysis of the necessary prerequisites for moral life. The image of the human person as determined was presented in his *Anthropologie*, where he spoke not of a transcendental will but of the related psychological faculty of desire. According to Kant, in the context of actual empirical conditions, the "choices" of human beings are always preceded (and thus appear to be determined) by human appetites, inclinations, passions, habits, and instincts. Going one step further, Kant followed his own earlier advice to empirical psychologists and observed humans "externally," noting, classifying, and correlating their behavior with certain visible characteristics, sexual types, nationalities, racial origins, and human qualities. His conclusions, published in the second part of the *Anthropologie*, were consistent with his conviction that understanding—including psychological understanding—must necessarily be formulated in causal terms.[24]

Since freedom, the ultimate characteristic of human nature, is beyond the cognitive grasp of the human mind, it followed for Kant that the perspective of psychology must necessarily be incomplete, or limited. Empirical psychology can only provide tentative knowledge of the conditions of human choice, no more. Only the philosophical analysis of the practical demands of reason can reveal human freedom. About the psychodynamics of that freedom nothing can be said. In fact, to speak of the psychodynamics of freedom would be a contradiction in terms. Thus, in essence, Kant viewed the will as a noumenal reality behind the appearances of sense, knowledge, feeling, and appetite. Although this view is explicitly nonpsychological, Kant's doctrine of the will was to have broad repercussions within German psychology—as well as within philosophy—in the nineteenth century.

Kant saw the third psychological faculty, that of feeling, as intermediate between knowing and desiring, just as he saw judgment, its transcendental cognitive analog, as intermediate between understanding—that is, pure reason—and reason—that is, practical reason, or will. The most basic feelings, according to Kant, are pleasure and pain. Furthermore, pleasure and pain may be either sensuous, intellectual, or moral. Sensuous feelings accompany intuitions and imaginations; intellectual feelings accompany concepts or ideas; and moral feelings accompany desires. The significant point is that, although Kant made an analytic distinction between knowing, desiring, and feeling, he denied that the various phenomena of these faculties exist in isolation from one another. Cognitive intuitions, images, and concepts, as well as moral desires, are all attended by affective components. This analysis is quite different from that of Leibnizian psychology in which feelings are only confused ideas. According to Kant, even a clear idea is associated with an affective pleasure or pain.[25]

This interrelation of the various types of psychological phenomena is further illustrated by Kant's analysis of the phenomena of aesthetic taste. This special type of feeling, which he considered "partly sensuous, partly intellectual," fascinated Kant, and he investigated it at length because it implicitly involves processes analogous to, and substitutive for, both cognition and volition. On the one hand, like cognition, it involves a process of judgment, though not a strictly rational judgment. Instead it involves the kind of judgment that is passed by the feelings: a judgment of whether something is agreeable or disagreeable, a pleasure or pain. On the other hand, like the determinations of the will, these noncognitive judgments—that is, pleasures and pains—possess motivational powers. They can obstruct both the clarity of understanding and the resolve of the will, and they can thus lead to the commission of behaviors opposed by the will. Yet the feelings can also be enlisted in the service of morality if the feeling of pleasure is associated with the idea of the good and thus helps the will toward its proper object. Therefore, Kant hoped that the arts and literature would arouse beneficial feelings that would motivate human beings to make proper moral choices. At the same time, however, he did not think that the feelings could be of service to the cognitive processes. Indeed, he thought that these processes, to function properly, must be disturbed by the feelings as little as possible. In espousing this doctrine, Kant revealed that he had not entirely abandoned the intellectualism of Leibniz and Wolff. Feelings, he thought, are apt to become pathological and ought not to be left untended.[26]

Still, despite this contention, Kant clearly felt that all the psychological faculties continually interact. In fact, it is important to end this discussion of the three faculties by emphasizing that Kant did not mean to reify these faculties into metaphysically distinct entities. Although he did argue that the cognitive processes of understanding, reasoning, and judging are in principle distinct, Kant asserted that these faculties are as essentially related as the three steps of a syllogism. And, on the psychological level, Kant insisted that knowing, desiring, and feeling are continuously intertwined. Thus he conceived the three faculties as various aspects of the unitary functioning of the mind.[27] For better or worse, the philosophers and psychologists who came after him tended to focus on one or the other of these aspects and tried to recast the Kantian heritage by subordinating the other parts of that heritage to this single aspect. Often this meant taking one of Kant's faculties as fundamental and treating the others as somehow dependent upon, or derivative from, it. But even so, in accepting Kant's analysis as the framework for further discussions of mental activity, even those who opposed the very notion of a tripartite faculty psychology remained within the field of Kant's influence.

KANT'S HERITAGE

In the ferment of thought that occurred in Kant's wake, idealism came to the fore and dominated philosophical speculation in Germany for half a century. The major idealists—Johann Gottlieb Fichte (1762-1814), Friedrich Wilhelm von Schelling (1775-1854), and Georg Wilhelm Friedrich Hegel (1770-1831)—took their points of departure from the work of Kant, though they were among those who emphasized different aspects of his thought and developed forms of metaphysical idealism that far exceeded the narrow bounds of Kant's critical idealism. As regards the critique of psychology, however, they were in perfect agreement with Kant's contention that psychology is not, and cannot become, a true science. Like Kant, they regarded psychology as a "merely empirical" science; but, unlike Kant, they believed that this tentative preliminary science could be transformed and completed by philosophical thought. In many ways, then, they revived the spirit of earlier rational psychology, disregarding Kant's strictures about the limits of rational analysis. Nonetheless, in the course of their philosophical work they helped to propagate many of Kant's psychological doctrines, primarily through the publications of their psychologist disciples.[28]

The central focal point of Kant's thought was his analysis of the innate structure and functioning of the human mind. Even during Kant's lifetime, Karl Leonhard Reinhold argued persuasively that the Kantian concern about the nature of the mind—or, as Reinhold preferred to call it, "consciousness"—should be the fundamental issue for philosophy. The systematic description, or "phenomenology," of consciousness, he said, should be the immediate task of the post-Kantian generation.[29] Toward this end, Reinhold founded one of the most vital centers of Kantian thought at the University of Jena. Even before Kant's death in 1804, Reinhold's pupils and colleagues—including Fichte, Schelling, and Hegel—were already establishing the phenomenology of consciousness as the basic topic in German philosophy.

Fichte's elaboration of the concept of consciousness led him to an idealistic view of consciousness as an ever-active, striving ego, which is ultimately manifested as will.[30] His basic principles of egoism, activism, and voluntarism, deduced originally as principles of Absolute Reality, were used in psychological analyses by a number of his followers, including G. E. A. Mehmel and Karl Fortlage.[31] They also influenced Hermann von Helmholtz, particularly as regards his historically important theory of the active role of the mind in perception.[32] And when Wilhelm Wundt characterized his psychology as voluntaristic in nature, he clearly indicated the extent to which his "New Psychology" was premised on an acceptance of the Fichtean revision of traditional Leibnizian intellectualism.[33] Corroborated by the philosophies of Schopenhauer and Nietzsche, this new voluntaristic temper had a broad impact on the psychological thinking of the late nineteenth century. It is apparent that Sigmund Freud, among many others, was affected by this general movement of thought, especially insofar as certain evolutionary and dynamic conceptions were grafted onto it.

Schelling's considerations of consciousness led him to discussions of the unconscious as a necessary antecedent and corollary of consciousness as well as to discussions of the concepts of personality and genius. It also led him to propagate *Identitätsphilosophie*, or the philosophy of identity, which espoused the Spinozistic doctrine that mind and body are but two aspects of the same reality.[34] When applied to psychology, this doctrine suggested that the nature and activity of the mind is reflected in the structure and functioning of the body. This proved to be a fruitful suggestion. Not only did it inspire the psychological investigations of Karl Friedrich Burdach, Karl Gustav Carus, and others, it also stimulated the development of psychophysics by Gustav Theodor Fechner, the person most often credited with bringing actual measurement into the realm of psychology.[35] As Fechner himself admitted, the inspiration of his groundbreaking study of the relationship between conscious experience and physical stimulation came from the *Naturphilosophie* of Lorenz Oken. Oken, in turn, had been inspired by Schelling.[36] Thus, psychophysics, one of the major foundations of modern psychology, is historically rooted within the conceptual framework of post-Kantian idealism.

Schelling also introduced a strong genetic, or developmental, emphasis into the thinking of his followers. This led to the publication of books such as Gotthilf Heinrich von Schubert's popular *Geschichte der Seele* (History of the Soul) (1830) and Karl Gustav Carus's *Psyche: Zur Entwicklungsgeschichte der Seele* (Psyche: Toward a Developmental History of the Soul) (1846).[37] Carus's work was particularly significant because of his position as a comparative anatomist and physiologist. As early as 1831, in his *Vorlesungen über Psychologie* (Lectures on Psychology), Carus combined his genetic approach to psychology with a scientific knowledge of the physiological development of the nervous system. Later, taking the logic of the philosophy of identity and of the genetic principle one step further, Carus made a major contribution by espousing, and developing, comparative psychology, that is, the study of the historical development of consciousness through the animal kingdom, leading up to man.[38] Since his work was based largely on physiology, he also contributed to the development of physiological psychology.

Hegel had a more highly developed and formalized psychology than either Fichte or Schelling. He presented this psychology as part of his *Philosophie des Geistes* (Philosophy of Mind) (1830).[39] Among the many notable aspects of this psychology is its reliance on, and reverence for, Aristotle's psychology. This helped to spark a revival of Aristotelian studies in Germany, a revival that, especially through the teaching of Friedrich Adolf Trendelenberg, had a profound impact on Wilhelm Dilthey, Franz Brentano, and other notable contributors to the development of psychological thought.[40]

Another important aspect of Hegel's view of psychology was his conviction that psychology describes, and can only describe, the empirical conditions and experiences of the mind. In this, of course, he was in agreement with Kant. Going beyond Kant, however, he argued that the study of the "subjective" mind can and must be transcended, just as the individual mind itself is transcended, and develops beyond mere sense-dependence, by its immersion in a larger "objective," or group, mind. In other words, the study of the "I" must be followed by the study of the "we," which, in turn, leads to the study of the Absolute Mind. The important point is that Hegel formalized an insight that was implicit in the work of Johann Georg Hamann, Johann Gottfried Herder, and others: the social level of analysis, he claimed, transcends that of the individual. Beyond that, he prescribed the study of the social, or objective, mind by means of its products, such as language, law, custom, and myth. This Hegelian doctrine was an important influence upon the development of the social psychological perspective, especially as formulated in *Völkerpsychologie* (cultural, or "folk," psychology). Although he denied any direct influence by Hegel, Wilhelm Wundt was working a field prepared by Hegel when he spent several decades writing his multivolumed *Völkerpsychologie* (1900–20). Clearly, he agreed with Hegel when he claimed that the higher mental processes, involving the truly human, symbolic aspects of experience, can only be understood within a social context, using a nonexperimental methodology. In reaching this conclusion, Wundt lent his considerable authority to a distinction developed by the neo-Kantians of the latter part of the nineteenth century, namely, the distinction between psychology as a natural science (or *Naturwissenschaft*) and psychology as a social science (or *Geisteswissenschaft*). This distinction was to have particular significance in the late-nineteenth and twentieth centuries.[41]

One other notable aspect of Hegel's psychology was its development of the principle of self-actualization. In the Hegelian scheme, the fullness of development is reached only by participation in the Absolute, which Hegel's disciples often described by using the "mythological" concept of "Personality." This notion of actualization as a process leading toward the establishment of personality began an historical tradition of thought that led through Kurt Goldstein and Carl Gustav Jung to contemporary humanistic psychology. The correlative development in the Fichte-inspired voluntarist tradition led to a focusing on the development of "character," as eventually seen in the work of Wundt and Freud.[42]

Hegel's was the last of the major idealist systems, and it dominated the philosophical scene in Germany through the 1830s and even beyond. Among his followers were the psychologists Johann Eduard Erdmann, Leopold George, Carl Ludwig Michelet, Johann Georg Mussmann, Franz Vorländer, and Karl Friedrich Rosenkranz.[43] The work of Erdmann, published into the 1880s, shows the resilience of this tradition of thought. Although the works of these Hegelian psychologists are rather diverse, one common characteristic was their reliance on dialectical analysis, as propagated by Hegel. In several respects, their analyses presaged those of recent so-called dialectical psychologists. These latter individuals, however, typically refer to Karl Marx, or to various Russian psychologists such as S. L. Rubinstein, as the inspiration of their work.[44] Nonetheless, Hegelian dialectics is the historical foundation of their work.

For all their variations on the theme of consciousness, we can summarize the influence of the idealists on the development of psychology rather succinctly: (1) They made "consciousness" the primary subject matter, and problem, of psychology. As we have seen, Fechner developed psychophysics under the influence of the idealist thesis that consciousness is correlative with physical reality. Similarly, Wundt defined the subject matter of his new experimental, or "physiological," psychology as "the manifold of consciousness."[45] Although the empirical and experimental procedures that he proposed for the investigation of the lower forms of consciousness came from the natural scientific tradition, the object of study was clearly from the idealist tradition. Thus, both Fechner and Wundt, the two reputed founders of modern psychology, belonged to a broader intellectual tradition that developed in mid-to-late-nineteenth-century Germany, that is, the tradition of *Idealrealismus*. Participants in this tradition, including also Rudolph Hermann Lotze and Wilhelm Dilthey, attempted to combine the essential insights of both idealism and realism while avoiding the exclusive dogmatism of either. (2) Related to the issue of consciousness, the idealists spread a concern about the nature and development of the ego, personality, will, and character. The egoism and voluntarism thus sponsored had broad consequences in subsequent psychological thought. (3) The idealists emphasized the uniqueness and preeminence of the social psychological level of analysis. The antiindividualistic temper of their work clearly influenced the development of *Völkerpsychologie* and helped to increase the general sensitivity regarding the historical–cultural context of personality development. This latter sensitivity was reflected in the psychological histories of Dilthey and others. Even Freud's sensitivity to the social context of personality development can be seen as a part of this idealist heritage.[46] (4) In addition to inspiring psychophysics and encouraging special methods for social psychological analyses, the idealists also had an impact on the development of genetic and comparative methodologies. Although the empirical rigor of later studies was usually missing in their work, they did prepare the way conceptually for these later studies. The idealist notion of "the history of consciousness" was implicated in many of the early works of the first generation of scientific psychologists. Wundt's *Vorlesungen über die Menschen- und Thierseele* (Lectures on the Human and Animal Mind) (1863) are instructive in this regard since they exemplify how Darwinian thought was often assimilated in Germany through an essentially naturalized idealist framework.[47]

Despite these important contributions, it is nonetheless true that the idealists opposed the development of psychology as an autonomous discipline, and especially as a scientific discipline. In this respect, as regards the development of modern scientific psychology, a different group of post-Kantians was instrumental—the group of post-Kantian empirical philosophers composed of Jakob Friedrich Fries (1773–1843), Johann Friedrich Herbart (1776–1841), and Friedrich Eduard Beneke (1778–1854). Each member of this group clearly expressed his allegiance to Kant and his disagreement with idealism; each of them also went beyond orthodox Kantianism in order to "complete" Kant's system of thought. What characterized their work as a group was its consistent empiricism, even if this was supplemented at times by rational analysis and metaphysics. Although each of them also helped to propagate some of Kant's constructive doctrines, it was their development of the general conception of an autonomous, scientific psychology that constituted their major contribution as a group. Ironically, they based their thinking in this regard on Kant's critique of psychology.[48]

When Kant specified that psychology could never become a true science because it could not utilize any a priori notions, any mathematics, or any experimental techniques, he inadvertently proposed a prescription for those who wanted to develop psychology into a scientific discipline. Following Kant's direction, Fries argued that psychology can evolve a set of rational concepts to guide its theoretical work; Herbart devised a mathematical psychology, even if an ill-fated one; and Beneke proposed a set of experiments and ardently advocated the establishment of a truly experimental psychology.[49] Successively building on the work of their predecessors and keeping an eye on Kant's definition of science, these three thinkers developed the conception of psychology to the point where subsequent experimental physiologists, such as Wilhelm Wundt, were inspired to call their research—and perhaps more importantly to think of their research —as "psychology." Certainly it was not inevitable that Wundt and others would conceptualize their work in this way. (Hermann von Helmholtz, for instance, had not done so.) Theirs, after all, was a kind of psychology unlike that which had preceded it—except in the minds of the three empirical philosophers who had provided a conceptual foundation and who had argued for a scientific psychology. It was therefore fitting that, in the 1860s, the term Beneke had coined twenty years before—namely, the "New Psychology"—came to designate the work of Wundt and his contemporaries.[50]

In essence, we have traced the development of two traditions of thought, both preceeding from Kant and both leading to the psychology of the late-nineteenth and twentieth centuries. From the idealist line of development came the conception of the proper subject matter of psychology as well as certain theoretical and methodological orientations. From the empiricist line came the general definition of natural scientific psychology. In combination, and together with the judicious adoption of research, methods, and theory from the field of sensory phsyiology (which was also influenced by the Kantian heritage, as for instance in the work of Johannes Müller and Hermann von Helmholtz), these lines of development ushered in a new period in the history of psychology. In this new period the Kantian heritage was apparent in even more ways than we have already noted: The Kantian doctrine of sensibility, with its stipulation of the innate forms of time and space, led to the so-called "Kant–Müller–Hering–Mach–Stumpf line of descent" that propagated the law of specific sense energies and the theory of nativistic space perception.[51] The Kantian doctrine of intelligibility had, among its long-range effects, the setting of the theoretical context for the Würzburgers' declaration of "the rules of consciousness." The Kantian doctrines of apperception and the unity of consciousness likewise influenced the thinking of Wundt and others and advanced the theoretical tradition leading up to the work of the Gestalt psychologists. Similarly, as regards the concept of the unconscious, Kant's doctrine influenced Herbart, Schopenhauer, Nietzsche, and von Hartmann and, through them, Freud. Finally, as regards the relative autonomy of feeling, Kant's doctrine influenced the turning away from an overemphasis on reason and ideas in psychology. Together with his concern about practical reason, or the will, this helped to bring about a broadening of the empirical, conceptual, and theoretical range of psychology.

In addition, Kant's heritage extended far beyond the borders of Germany. In the latter part of the nineteenth century, French philosophy was dominated by Kantian thought, with subsequent effects on the developmental psychology of Jean Piaget. Likewise, British philosophy was deeply influenced by German idealism later in the century, and the influence of Kant was reflected in the activistic self-psychology of James Ward. Even earlier in the century, the influence of Kant was felt within the British psycho-physiological tradition through the impact of Johann Friedrich Blumenback upon the thinking of Thomas Laycock. Furthermore, there is good reason to suppose that the distinction between logic and psychology, so critical in the development of psychology in Britain, was influenced by Kantian thought.

Just as striking was the influence of Kant in the United States, which was evident early in the nineteenth century in the work of Frederic Rauch and Laurens Hickok and was reflected later in the work of Charles Peirce and William James. Often Kant's influence was indirect as well as direct: William James and George Trunball Ladd, like many of their British counterparts, were deeply influenced by the Idealrealistic Kantianism of Rudolph Hermann Lotze. In addition, James was also influenced at a critical point and in a critical way by the French neo-Kantian Charles Renouvier. James's subsequent emphasis upon the will as well as his fundamental conception of the active, "interested" mind are the direct consequences of these encounters with Kantianism. Slightly later, G. Stanley Hall, Josiah Royce, James Mark Baldwin, John Dewey, and George Herbert Mead were influenced in essential ways by German idealism. The dialectical modes of thought implicit in so much of their work would be inexplicable without their early contact with the idealistic branch of the Kantian heritage. Another mediated path of influence, which reached the United States only in the twentieth century, ran from the neo-Kantian Wilhelm Dilthey through Eduard Spranger to Gordon Allport, to the field of personality psychology, and eventually to Humanistic Psychology.[52]

CONCLUSION

Although these latter brush strokes are very broad, they should provide a general picture of the extent to which Kant laid the foundation for subsequent psychological thought. One final aspect of Kant's heritage, perhaps its central aspect, should be indicated once again at the conclusion of this essay. This aspect represents the major problem that Kant bequeathed to posterity. He did not invent this problem, but he did give it a poignant expression, and it underlies his entire system of thought. Simply stated, it is the problem of the place of the will in a deterministic world. In broader terms, this is the traditional problem of "man's place in nature"; in psychological terms it is the problem of the accommodation of "consciousness" to scientific method. Kant himself saw an irreconcilable difference between these pairs of concepts—between will and world, "man" and nature, mind and science. Later psychologists sought to reconcile these differences by either eliminating or changing the definition of one of these terms—as the behaviorists and humanists have done, to "consciousness" and "science" respectively—or by devising a practical compromise between them—as Fechner, Wundt, and many of their successors have done. The historical record shows that none of these solutions has worked for very long. The borders and territory of "consciousness"—including its putative extensions into unconsciousness—have never been mapped in a way that is satisfying for two consecutive generations.

Kant himself might have pointed out that the problem is innate rather than accidental. The attempt to submit a subject matter developed with the idealist tradition to the scrutiny of methods often taken from the naturalist tradition is bound to be frustrated. As capitulatory as it may seem, the conclusion of Hugo Münsterberg, a neo-Kantian as well as a student of Wundt and director of the Harvard Psychological Laboratory between 1892 and 1916, is consonant with Kant's own opinion: there may simply be two ways of looking at the world of human experience, as free and as determined. Freedom can be seen as a practical fact; determinism as a fact of knowledge.[53] The alternatives to accepting this dualistic point of view may be either the continuation of one-sided dogmatisms and temporary compromises, or the establishment of an entirely new tradition of thought, in which both subject matter and method are conceived anew. In any case, until we are fully aware of the extent to which we continue to stand on the foundation that Kant laid two hundred years ago, we may not see the choice that faces us.

NOTES

1. Kant was primarily a philosopher, not a psychologist. Yet he was deeply interested in psychology and spent a considerable amount of time reading, thinking, teaching, and writing about it. For more than twenty years, beginning about 1773, Kant offered a lecture course on psychology, or "anthropology."— See Immanuel Kant, *Die philosophischen Hauptvorlesungen Immanuel Kants,* ed. A. Kowalewski (Hildesheim: Georg Olms, 1965), pp. 55-385.—As we shall see, he eventually published a book based on these lectures in 1898. In addition, he wrote a number of essays bearing on psychological topics.—(Among others, see I. Kant, "Versuch uber die Krankheiten des Kopfes" (1764), in *Kants Werke,* repr. of Prussian Academy edition (1902), 9 vols. (Berlin: de Gruyter, 1968), 2:257-72; and I. Kant, "Von der Macht des Gemuths durch den blossen Vorsatz seiner krankhaften Gefuhle Meister zu sein," which is Part III of *Der Streit der Facultäten* (1798), in *Kants Werke,* 7:95-116.)—Furthermore, his three major philosophical works are redolent with psychological implications. In fact, throughout the nineteenth century, Kant's philosophical doctrines were often given psychological interpretations.—See, for example, Edward Franklin Buchner, "A Study of Kant's Psychology," *Psychological Review* Monograph Supplement No. 4 (1897):1-208; and J. B. Meyer, *Kant's Psychologie* (Berlin: Hertz, 1870).— Whatever philosophical distortions this may have caused, it did not necessarily lead to a misreading of Kant's psychology. As Kant himself pointed out, there is a very close relationship between his philosophical and his psychological doctrines, even though he rigorously defended the distinction between the philosophical and psychological levels of analysis. In the following essay, we shall utilize Kant's philosophical works, as did many of his followers, in order to round out our understanding of his psychology. By keeping an eye on Kant's explicit psychological doctrines, we shall avoid the dangers of inferential interpretation, while gaining an understanding of the "expanded" version of Kant's psychology that had an impact on his contemporaries and later disciples.

2. G. W. Leibniz, *New Essays on Human Understanding,* trans. & ed. P. Remnant and J. Bennett (Cambridge: Cambridge University Press, 1981); Immanuel Kant, *De Mundi Sensibilis atque Intelligibilis Forma et Principiis* (1770), in *Kants Werke,* 2:385-420. Leibniz actually responded to Pierre Coste's French version of the fourth edition of Locke's *Essay,* entitled *Essai philosophique concernant l'entendement humain* (Amsterdam: Schaltz, 1700).

3. Christian Wolff, *Psychologia Empirica* (1734) and C. Wolff, *Psychologia Rationalis* (1734), in his *Gesammelte Werke,* ed. Jean Ecole, 52 vols. (Gildesheim: Georg Olms, 1962-74), Part II: vols. 5 & 6 respectively. See also Robert J. Richards, "Christian Wolff's Prolegomena to Empirical and Rational Psychology: Translation and Commentary," *Proceedings of the American Philosophical Society* 124 (1980): 227-39.

4. See Max Dessoir, *Geschichte der neueren deutschen Psychologie,* rev. 2d ed. (Berlin: Duncker, 1902), pp. 165-209; and Robert Sommer, *Grundzuge einer Geschichte der deutschen Psychologie und Aesthetik von Wolff-Baumgarten bis Kant-Schiller* (Wurzburg: Stahel, 1892).

5. Johann Nicolas Tetens, *Philosophische Versuche uber die menschliche Natur und ihre Entwicklung,* 2 vols. (Leipzig: Weidmann, 1777); Immanuel Kant, *Critique of Pure Reason,* trans. N. K. Smith, unabridged ed. (New York: St. Martin's, 1965); I. Kant, *Critique of Practical Reason,* trans. L. W. Beck (Indianapolis: Bobbs-Merrill, 1956); I. Kant, *Critique of Judgment,* trans. J. H.

Bernard (New York: Hafner, 1972); and I. Kant, *Anthropology from a Pragmatic Point of View*, trans. M. J. Gregor (Hague, Nijhoff, 1974).

6. Alexander Gottlieb Baumgarten, *Metaphysica*, 7th ed. (Halle: Hemmerde, 1779), especially pp. 292-329. Other materials for Kant's critique came from the works of Martin Knutzen, Moses Mendelssohn, and Hermann Samuel Reimarus.

7. Much of the following materials is taken with permission from David E. Leary, "The Philosphical Development of the Conception of Psychology in Germany, 1780-1850," *Journal of the History of the Behavioral Sciences* 14 (1978): 113-21, where references to some of the secondary literature on Kant's psychology can also be found.

8. Kant, *Pure Reason*, p. 329.

9. Ibid., p. 353.

10. Immanuel Kant, *Metaphysical Foundations of Natural Science*, trans. J. Ellington (Indianapolis: Bobbs-Merrill, 1970), p. 8.

11. Ibid., pp. 6-8. Regarding mathematics and the a priori construction of concepts, see Kant, *Pure Reason*, pp. 575-85, and I. Kant, *Prolegomena to Any Future Metaphysics* (1783), trans. L. W. Beck (Indianapolis: Bobbs-Merrill, 1950), pp. 28-32.

12. Kant, *Metaphysical Foundations*, p. 8.

13. Kant, *Anthropology*, pp. 4-5.

14. Kant, *De Mundi*, pp. 392-98.

15. See ibid., especially pp. 398-410, for the basic development of these ideas; Kant, *Pure Reason*, pp. 65-91 and 102-19, for a more complete elaboration; and Kant, *Anthropology*, pp. 9-97, for a purely psychological rendition.

16. Kant, *Pure Reason*, pp. 130-38 (A), 143 (A), 146 (A), 153 (B), 331, and 362 (A). A indicates the text of the 1781 edition; B, the revised text of the 1787 edition; no letter, an unrevised passage.

17. Ibid., p. 329.

18. Regarding apperception and the unity of consciousness, see ibid., pp. 133-50 (A), 151-59 (B).

19. See Lewis White Beck, *Early German Philosophy: Kant and His Predecessors* (Cambridge: Harvard University Press, 1969), pp. 497-98.

20. Kant, *Judgment*, pp. 32-34.

21. Regarding intuition, imagination, and conceptualization, see Kant, *Pure Reason*, pp. 65-91; 132-33 (A); 111-15; and Kant, *Anthropology*, 21-26, 32-40; 44-50, 53-62; 69-73, respectively.

22. Regarding unconscious ideas, cognitive deficiencies, and cognitive talents, see ibid., pp. 16-18; 73-89; 89-97, respectively.

23. Kant, *Pure Reason*, pp. 111-15.

24. Kant, *Practical Reason*, passim; and Kant, *Anthropology*, pp. 120-93.

25. Regarding the faculty of feeling, see ibid., pp. 99-117; regarding the association of cognition and feeling, see ibid., p. 89.

26. Regarding aesthetic taste, see Kant, *Judgment*, pp. 37-81, and Kant, *Anthropology*, pp. 107-15; regarding the need to control feeling, see Kant, *Practical Reason*, pp. 77-78.

27. Regarding the three cognitive faculties as related steps of a syllogism, see Kant, *Pure Reason*, pp. 176-77; regarding the systematic relationship of the various faculties, see Kant, *Judgment*, especially pp. 3-15 and 32-34.

28. For a more complete discussion of the idealists' view of science and their impact on psychology, see David E. Leary, "German Idealism and the

Development of Psychology in the Nineteenth Century," *Journal of the History of Philosophy* 18 (1980): 299-317.

29. Karl Leonhard Reinhold, *Versuch einer neuen Theorie des menschlichen Vorstellungsvermögens* (Jena: Mauke, 1789) and K. L. Reinhold, *Ueber das Fundament des philosophischen Wissens* (Jena: Mauke, 1791).

30. Regarding his basic doctrines, see Johann Gottlieb Fichte, *Ueber den Begriff der Wissenschaftslehre* (1794), in J. G. Fichte, *Gesamtausgabe*, ed. R. Lauth and H. Jacob, 12 vols. (Stuttgart-Bad Cannstatt: Frommann, 1965), 1: bk. 2, pp. 107-72 and 249-451; regarding the application of these doctrines to human affairs, see Fichte, *Addresses to the German Nation*, trans. R. F. Jones and G. H. Turnbull & ed. G. A. Kelley (New York: Harper, 1968).

31. See, for example, G. E. A. Mehmel, *Versuch einer vollständigen analytischen Denklehre, als Vorphilosphie* (Erlangen: Walther, 1803) and Karl Fortlage, *System der Psychologie als empirischer Wissenschaft aus Beobachtung des innern Sinnes*, 2 vols. (Leipzig: Brockhaus, 1855).

32. See R. Steven Turner, "Hermann von Helmholtz and the Empiricist Vision," *Journal of the History of the Behavioral Sciences* 13 (1977): 48-58.

33. See Kurt Danziger, "Wundt's Theory of Behavior and Volition," in R. W. Rieber, ed., *Wilhelm Wundt and the Making of a Scientific Psychology* (New York: Plenum, 1980), pp. 89-115.

34. Friedrich Wilhelm von Schelling first developed his philosophy of identity in his *Vorlesunger über die Methode des akademischen Studiums* (1803), the revised third edition of which appears in *Schellings Werke*, ed. M. Schröter, 13 vols. (Munich: Beck und Oldenbourg, 1929-59), 3:229-374. Regarding his early system of thought, see his *System des transcendentalen Idealismus* (1800), in *Shellings Werke*, 2:327-634.

35. Karl Friedrich Burdach, *Das Seelenleben* (Stuttgart: Balz, 1836); Karl Gustav Carus, *Vorlesungen über Psychologie* (Leipzig: Fleischer, 1831); Gustav Theodor Fechner, *Element der Psychophysik*, 2 vols. (Leipzig: Breitkopf und Hartel, 1860).

36. See William R. Woodward, "Fechner's Panpsychism: A Scientific Solution to the Mind-Body Problem," *Journal of the History of the Behavioral Sciences* 8 (1972):367-86, especially p. 385.

37. Gotthilf Heinrich von Schubert, *Geschichte der Seele*, 2 vols. (Stuttgart: von Gotta, 1830); Karl Gustav Carus, *Psyche: Zur Entwicklungsgeschichte der Seele* (Pforzheim: Flammer und Hofmann, 1846).

38. Karl Gustav Carus, *Comparative Psychologie*, 2 vols. (Leipzig: Voss, 1842) and K. G. Carus, *Vergleichende Psychologie oder Geschichte der Seele in Reihenfolge der Thierwelt* (Vienna: Braumüller, 1866).

39. Georg Wilhelm Friedrich Hegel, *Philosophy of Mind*, trans. W. Wallace, with *Zusätze*, trans. A. V. Miller (Oxford: Clarendon, 1971), Section I: Mind Subjective, especially pp. 179-240.

40. See, for example, Gershon George Rosenstock, *F. A. Trendelenberg: Forerunner to John Dewey* (Carbondale, Ill.: Southern Illinois University Press, 1965).

41. Wilhelm Wundt, *Völkerpsychologie*, 10 vols. (Leipzig: Engelmann, 1900-20). For a discussion of Wundt's view of *Völkerpsychologie* and an overview of the shifting fates of natural and social scientific psychology since Wundt's time, see David E. Leary, "Wundt and After: Psychology's Shifting Relations with the Natural Sciences, Social Sciences, and Philosophy," *Journal of the History of the Behavioral Sciences* 15 (1979):231-41.

42. The history of the related notions of self-actualization, personality, and character has yet to be written.

43. Johann Eduard Erdmann, *Grundriss der Psychologie* (Leipzig: Vogel, 1840); Leopold George, *Lehrbuch der Psychologie* (Berlin: Reimr, 1854); Carl Ludwig Michelet, *Anthropologie und Psychologie* (Berlin: Sander, 1840); Johann Georg Mussmann, *Lehrbuch der Seelenwissenschaft* (Berlin: Mylius, 1827); Karl Vorlander, *Grundlinien einer organischen Wissenschaft der menschlichen Seele* (Berlin: Müller, 1841); Karl Friedrich Rosenkranz, *Psychologie* (Königsberg: Bornträger, 1837).

44. See, for example, Klaus F. Riegel and George C. Rosenwald, eds., *Structure and Transformation: Developmental and Historical Aspects* (New York: Wiley, 1975).

45. Wilhelm Wundt, *Principles of Physiological Psychology*, vol. 1, trans. from rev. 5th German ed. (1902) by E. B. Titchener (New York: Macmillan, 1910), p. 11.

46. Freud's relation, either direct or indirect, to the idealist tradition has not been adequately explored. Even granting the influence of the hysterico-hypnotic, bioevolutionary, and physico–dynamic traditions, it would be remarkable if a person as culturally sensitive as he could have developed notions of the ego, id, and superego—and adopted a historical mode of analysis as well as a doctrine of psychophysical parallelism—without incurring some sort of debt to the egoism, voluntarism, social psychological perspective, geneticism, and identicalism of the idealist philosophy that permeated so much of the nineteenth-century thought.

47. Wilhelm Wundt, *Vorlesungen über die Menschen- und Thierseele*, 2 vols. (Leipzig: Voss, 1863).

48. I have discussed the contributions of Fries, Herbart, and Beneke at greater length in my "Philosophical Development," pp. 116-19.

49. Jakob Friedrich Fries, *Neue Kritik der Vernunft*, 3 vols. (Heidelberg: Mohr und Zimmer, 1807) and J. F. Fries, *Handbuch der psychischen Anthropologie oder der Lehre von der Natur des menschlichen Geistes*, 2 vols. (Jena: Cröker, 1820-21); Johann Friedrich Herbart, *Psychologie als Wissenschaft, neu gegründet auf Erfahrung, Metaphysik und Mathematik*, 2 vols. (Königsberg: Unzer, 1824-25); Friedrich Eduard Beneke, *Lehrbuch der Psychologie* (Berlin: Mittler, 1833). Regarding Herbart's contribution, see David E. Leary, "The Historical Foundation of Herbart's Mathematization of Psychology," *Journal of the History of the Behavioral Sciences* 16 (1980):150-63, which documents the positive influence of Kant on Herbart's innovative work.

50. Friedrich Eduard Beneke, *Die neue Psychologie* (Berlin: Mittler, 1845).

51. The phrase is from Edwin G. Boring, *A History of Experimental Psychology*, rev. 2d ed. (New York: Appleton-Century-Crofts, 1950), p. 249.

52. To document all the statements made in the last three paragraphs would require far more space than can be allotted to a footnote, or even a series of footnotes. Some of the statements are noncontroversial and are corroborated by a readily available secondary literature. Others are more controversial, but they are precisely the ones for which there is little or no adequate secondary literature. Their documentation would therefore require a discursive analysis with a complete referencing of primary sources and unpublished materials. As a result, I find it expedient to defer documentation to another occasion.

53. See, for example, Hugo Munsterberg, *Psychology and Life* (Boston: Houghton Mifflin, 1899), especially pp. 1-34.

2

Darwin
and the Biologizing
of Moral Behavior

Robert J. Richards

History at its best is, as Horace said of poetry, *dulcis et utilis*. It delights when the past is unexpectedly captured with similitude. And it can usefully prepare us to deal with contemporary problems— at least, many historians have thought so. The history of Darwin's theory of evolution is, I believe, particularly instructive, since the basic framework of his conception still supports contemporary biology and a number of the psychological and social sciences. Many of the difficulties with the theory, recognized by Darwin and his critics, have not faded, but still invest present science. Current controversies, then, might more easily be assessed, perhaps even partly resolved, in light of their origins. For at the beginning, motivations

An earlier version of this paper was read at a joint meeting of the History of Science Society and the Philosophy of Science Association, Toronto, October, 1980; it was also presented at the regular meeting of the Chicago Group for the History of the Social Sciences, University of Chicago, autumn, 1980. To members of this latter society, I am grateful for their generous and loud criticism. I am also in debt to the staff of the Manuscript Room of Cambridge University Library and of the Library of the American Philosophical Society for their considerate and prompt service. This research was supported by N.I.H. grant PHS 5 SO7 RR-07029-12 and by a grant from the Spencer Foundation.

tend to fall into bolder relief, and issues are usually formulated more simply. In this chapter, I would like to direct an historical analysis to a modest but controversial proposal made by Edward Wilson, in his book *Sociobiology*, that "scientists and humanists should consider together the possibility that the time has come for ethics to be removed temporarily from the hands of the philosopher and biologicized."[1]

Wilson's suggestion has provoked humanists and scientists alike to something less than a cool reflection on such a possibility. They have generally reacted in a way similar to that of an earlier thinker, who also confronted the impending invasion of the moral philosopher's domain by the Darwinian biologist. In the preface to his play *Back to Methuselah*, George Bernard Shaw observed:

> . . . you cannot understand Moses without imagination nor Spurgeon [a famous preacher of the day] without metaphysics; but you can be a thorough-going Neo-Darwinian without imagination, metaphysics, poetry, conscience, or decency. For "Natural Selection" has no moral significance: it deals with that part of evolution which has no purpose, no intelligence, and might more appropriately be called accidental selection, or better still, Un-natural Selection, since nothing is more unnatural than an accident. If it could be proved that the whole universe had been produced by such Selection, only fools and rascles could bear to live.[2]

There are, I suspect, three principal reasons for the response of humanists like Shaw. First, they regard the evolutionary interpretation of moral behavior to imply physical determinism, the idea that human action follows directly from mechanical causes. But mechanical causation, they urge, renders purposeful behavior a sham and is simply insufficient to produce the nuances of moral judgment. Those of a more sophisticated taste suggest a second reason. They believe they have detected a logically vulgar inference, the derivation of moral imperatives from scientifically factual statements, a lubricious slide from an *is* to an *ought*. These two philosophical demurs usually lead to a third reason for objecting to an evolutionary construction of ethics. It is the historical objection that Darwin unwittingly infused his theory with the political assumptions of *laissez-faire* English liberalism and the hedonistic selfishness of Benthamite utilitarianism and that this has hopelessly infected any evolutionary analysis of morals.[3]

I would like to consider seriously the proposal that it is time to biologize ethics. I will proceed by taking up the three objections just mentioned, but in reverse order and with principal focus on the historical complaint. That is, I will first examine in some detail the development of Darwin's theory of the evolution of moral behavior. This examination will, I think, reveal the scientific and moral appropriateness of the evolutionary perspective and put the two philosophical objections—about mechanical causation and logical failure —in a light that makes them appear far less formidable.

DARWIN'S EARLY THEORIES OF INSTINCT AND MORAL SENSE

In one of his excursions into the history of science, Loren Eiseley remarked that "man was not Darwin's best subject."[4] Eiseley saw Darwin as constantly trying to escape the bedevilment of metaphysicians, with their talk of reason, morals, and the nature of God and man. It is true that Darwin often enough deprecated his own abilities in the profounder sciences, so one might be persuaded to take him at his word.[5] The opinion is easily formed that, to adapt Hobbes' characterization of Descartes, had Darwin kept to beetles, worms, and orchids, he would have been the best biologist in England, but his head did not lie for philosophy. This, I think is a mistaken evaluation of Darwin's accomplishment, and it overlooks his abiding interest in the nature of moral behavior.

Instinct as Inherited Habit and Mechanism of Change

Darwin's *Diary*, kept during his five-year voyage on the Beagle (1831–36), records countless observations, not only of the geology and zoology of South America and Australia—his professional mandate—but also of the customs and behavior of the human inhabitants. Darwin's upbringing sensitized him to the moral environment through which he passed. He stood affronted by the ignorant, vengeful, and indolent Brazilians, who possessed "but a small share of those qualities which give dignity to mankind."[6] Darwin judged that the Spaniards' genocidal war against the Indians would leave the country "in the hands of white Gaucho savages instead of copper-coloured Indians. The former being a little superior in civilization, as they are inferior in every moral virtue."[7]

When Darwin returned from his trip around the world, he began to elaborate a theory that embraced not only the proposition that the anatomical structures of species were transformed over time, but the belief that their behavioral structures and their mental and moral faculties were modified as well. In his early notebooks, Darwin developed the idea that behavior displayed determinate patterns and that these forms, no different from the architecture of the jaguar's foot or the anteater's proboscis, were heritable and changed through generations. But behavior had this added feature in his early speculations: it also functioned as the mechanism of anatomical adaptation.

In his second and third *Transmutation Notebooks*, kept between February and September of 1838, Darwin worked out his mechanism for species change.[8] He supposed that habits an animal might adopt to cope with a shifting environment would, during the course of generations, slowly become instinctive, that is, innately determined patterns of behavior. Instincts, in their turn, would gradually modify the anatomy of an organism, adapting it to its surroundings. In Darwin's summary: "According to my view, habits give structure, therefore habits precede structure, therefore habitual instincts precede structure."[9]

Prior to having read Malthus, who turned him to thoughts of population pressure, Darwin regarded behavior as the chief agent of species transformation. Even after late September of 1838, when the idea of natural selection had begun to ripen and he had, as he recalled in his *Autobiography*, "a theory by which to work,"[10] he did not give up the hypothesis that instincts resulted from ingrained habits. As late as December 1840, when he read John Fleming's *Philosophy of Zoology*,[11] he appears to have retained use-inheritance as the primary explanation of instinct. This is the clear implication of an annotation he made in his copy of Fleming's book:

> The individual who by long intellectual study acquires a habit, & can perform action almost instinctively, does that in his life time which suceeding generations do in acquiring true instincts: Instinct is a habit of generations—each step in each generation being intellectual—for in lower animals [there is] intellect.[12]

Similar annotations can be culled from other books Darwin was reading in 1839 and 1840.

By 1842, however, in an essay that sketched out his maturing theory, he brought the principle of natural selection, in recognizable form, to explain behavior.[13] Yet he did not give up the idea that inherited habit could also produce instincts. This was a conviction Darwin clearly retained in the *Origin of Species* and never abandoned.[14]

The Moral Sense

During his five-year voyage, Darwin experienced the extremes of moral behavior, from the almost endemic venality of the South American gauchos to the frequent nobility of the Indians whom they slaughtered. Each of the different societies he lived in appeared to have its distinctive code of behavior. which often as not repelled the young Englishman. Yet even within the diversity, Darwin detected common attitudes about right and wrong conduct. As with other aspects of his developing species theory, he began to excavate and organize this sedimented experience only after serious reading. At about the time he edged toward an initial formulation of natural selection, during the summer and early fall of 1838, he was also busy tracing out a theory of the moral sense. Three books in particular helped him along the way: Harriet Martineau's *How to Observe: Morals and Manners*, James Mackintosh's *Dissertation on the Progress of Ethical Philosophy*, and John Abercrombie's *Inquiries Concerning the Intellectual Powers*.[15]

Darwin met Harriet Martineau, the essayist and radical social critic, in 1838, at a dinner party given by his brother Erasmus. Her intellectual charms bedazzled the young naturalist, but no less the other eminent minds of her widening circle, which included the irascible historian Thomas Carlyle, the great amateur scientist and Chancellor of the Exchequer Henry Lord Brougham, and the leading geologist of Britain Charles Lyell. Darwin reported to his grandmother that Miss Martineau "has been as frisky lately as the Rhinoceros" at the zoological park. He confided his gratitude that Martineau was "so very plain," lest his brother, who "has been with her noon, morning, and night," succumb to more than her intellect.[16] Probably the family tie and his own encounter seduced Darwin to read her newly published book, *How to Observe: Manners and Morals*.

In her little tract, Martineau emphasized the varieties of morally sanctioned behavior found in other times and places. Men of an earlier age, for instance, estimated their virtue by the number of enemies killed, while a British gentleman recognized the dignity in saving life. Those who acknowledge a universal moral sense for right action must be puzzled, she reflected, that "there are parts of this world where mothers believe it a duty to drown their children; and that Eastern potentates openly deride the king of England for having only one wife instead of a hundred."[17] Men, she concluded, lacked any innate sense of what behavior was morally enjoined or what condemned.[18]

Darwin reacted to Martineau's thesis as a natural historian might. He judged the variability of conscience in the many races of man no more unusual than the variety of instincts displayed by different breeds of dog. Mere variability, as he observed in his *M Notebook* (1838), did not mean that moral behavior lacked an innate foundation.[19]

Darwin's response to Martineau, while expressed in categories of the naturalist, derived support from a mainstream of British moral philosophy, as interpreted by Mackintosh in his *Dissertation on the Progress of Ethical Philosophy*. Like Butler, Hutchinson, and Hume—philosophers whose theories he analyzed—Mackintosh believed that human nature came equipped with a moral sense for right conduct. He allowed that external circumstances were probably necessary to educate the moral faculty; thus we could expect variation of moral behavior in different societies, as well as a progressive development of higher moral standards over time. Nonetheless, mere learned associations could not, he argued, produce the special connections between particular acts and feelings of obligation.[20] Though Mackintosh gave associative learning a role in honing the moral sense, he did not regard moral action as ultimately selfish, that is, as motivated by anticipations of pleasure with which such behavior might have become associated.[21] Men, rather, gave spontaneous approval to virtuous acts; they immediately tried to secure the well-being of their children; they despised cowardice and meanness—they did all this without the kind of hedonistic accounting required to estimate possible rewards to oneself. To get clear on this point and to separate his system from that of the great pleasure-calculator Jeremy Bentham, Mackintosh made what he believed to be a critical distinction for moral theory: that between the *moral sense* for right and wrong and the *criterion* of moral behavior.[22] Our immediate repugnance for vicious acts is quite different, he maintained, from subsequent estimations of their consequences. We instinctively perceive murder as vile. And in a cool moment of rational evaluation, we can also weigh the disutility of murder. But these processes are not the same. For Mackintosh, then, utility—or the greatest happiness principle—was, indeed, a basic criterion for measuring behavior; it simply did not function as an immediate motive for behavior.[23]

There was, however, a tender spot in Mackintosh's analysis. He could not satisfactorily explain the coincidence of the moral motive and the moral criterion. Why was it that what men did from moral impulse, without reflection, happened to be what subsequent evaluation using the moral criterion might sanction? Why did a nonrational sentiment and a consequent rational judgment always seem to agree?

Darwin perceived that Mackintosh had no adequate account for this constant conjunction. He found that his own theory of behavior gained proportional strength as it could explain in this instance—and in several others—what Mackintosh ultimately took for granted.

Darwin's early theory of moral behavior, as well as its mature expression in the *Descent of Man*, can best be understood, I believe, as a biologizing of Mackintosh's ethical system. Darwin set out to give, in natural-historical and evolutionary terms, an account of the faculties and relationships he found described in Mackintosh's *Dissertation*.[24]

The central nerve of Darwin's theory, which sustains its parts, is the proposal that the moral sense be regarded as an instinct. The bare suggestion itself was hardly original. The Reverend William Paley, in his *Moral and Political Philosophy*, which Darwin had to get up for his exams at Cambridge, considered the likeness of moral sense to animal instinct, although he rejected the comparison.[25] The importance of Darwin's proposal lay in the enriched notion he had of instinct and its genesis. The more he followed the analogy between instinct and the moral faculty, the more exact he found the fit. The social instincts of animals, like the moral impulses of men, were unselfish and natural affections. The mother bird, for instance, acts instinctively to protect her young and provide for their welfare. Moreover, both moral sense and the social instincts function to bind a society together. In Darwin's judgment, "society could not go on except for the moral sense, any more than a hive of Bees without their instincts."[26] Thus moral acts of men and social instincts of animals had the qualities of being innate, disinterested, and socially unifying.

The similarity of moral sense to instinct led Darwin to construct a wonderfully ingenious explanation for the faculty of conscience, complete with its reprimanding pang and insistent call to duty. He distinguished two kinds of instinct: those immediately impulsive instincts, such as a sudden flare of anger, for instance; and the more calmly persistent social instincts, which kept a mother bird patiently tending her brood. Often enough, however, these instincts came into conflict—when, for example, a hen would be momentarily overcome by the sight of a migrating flock and abandon her young. Now, Darwin hypothesized, if the reprobate mother possessed sufficient intellect to recall the situation of her chicks, she would be uncomfortable, uneasy in spirit; she would once again feel the unrequited urgings of social instinct. A rational animal in such circumstances would confess a troubled conscience. In Darwin's view, all that was necessary to turn social instinct into the voice of conscience was a mind somewhat greater than that possessed by animals. Conscience so conceived, of course, would become progressively more sensitive over generations as both greater intellect and advancing civilization acted to sharpen the focus of instinct on more finely graded objects. This was the hypothesis that congealed in Darwin's reflections in early October, 1838, a few days after he had read Malthus.[27]

In a 14-page manuscript on Mackintosh's ethical system, composed in the spring of 1839, Darwin amplified his account of conscience.[28] He reiterated that the insistent character of social instincts, which formed the very ribs of man's social being, should be regarded as equivalent to the moralist's *ought*. After all, he observed, we say a hound ought to point, since that is part of its instinctive nature; just so, we think a father ought to care for his children because of the natural bond of parentage. Yet Darwin did not let moral obligation rest solely on instinctive feeling. In the 1839 manuscript, he adumbrated a kind of rule-utilitarianism, which supposed one gradually learned that the momentary pleasures of passion did not outweigh the more constant satisfactions of the social instincts. The habit of following such rules, Darwin appears to have believed, brought a distinctive feeling of moral obligation, one more refined than the elemental urgings of social instincts alone. It also imbued conscience with a greater rational character and so helped explain how children advanced beyond their primitive moral condition.

Darwin did not regard his theory as postulating a selfish or vulgar utilitarianism, one that assumed that men usually acted in moral situations so as to maximize their own pleasure. Insofar as the promptings of conscience were equivalent to the urgings of instinct, the agent would respond immediately and without calculating the possible pleasurable consequences of action. And even if one learned of the quiet pleasures associated with satisfying conscience, the habit of acting conscientiously would itself become virtually automatic, such that good acts would again be performed without thought of possible rewards to oneself.

Perhaps the most impressive feature of Darwin's early theory of moral behavior was the way it biologically united the psychology of moral sense with the normative criterion of utility. Darwin worked out the account in a series of notes kept from late 1838 through the spring of 1839.[29] He proposed that the moral instincts of the individual tended to agree with the criterion of utility, the greatest good for the greatest number, because only those instincts that generally benefited past generations would be inherited. Now Darwin at this time did not argue that such instincts had been inherited through natural selection, though he had already formulated the principle several months before.[30] Rather, he still found sufficient the mechanism of inherited habit, which, as he noted in May, 1839, "fully explains the cementation of habits into instincts."[31] Useful behaviors would be cemented into the hereditary substance of animals because, as useful, such behaviors would have been practiced frequently, so producing instincts in succeeding generations. Darwin thus proposed the law of utility, the criterion of moral judgment, as also that law governing the acquisition of instinct:

> *On Law of Utility* Nothing but that which has beneficial tendency through many ages could be acquired, & we are certain from our reason, that all which (as we must admit) has been acquired, does possess the beneficial tendency. It is probable that becomes instinctive which is repeated under many generations . . . & only that which is beneficial to race, will have reoccurred.[32]

Those behaviors occurring most constantly would be the conjugal, parental, and social habits—the glue of human and animal societies. Hence Darwin's solution to Mackintosh's problem:

> Two classes of moralists: one says our rule of life is what *will* produce the greatest happiness.—The other says we have a moral sense.—But my view unites both / & shows them to be almost identical / & what *has* produced the greatest good / or rather what was necessary for good at all / *is* the / instinctive / moral sense. . . . In judging of the rule of happiness we must look *far forward* / & to the *general* action / —certainly because it is the result of what has *generally* been best for our good *far back*.[33]

Moral instincts, that is, social instincts, would agree with the common good of the species, because only those acts generally beneficial would be passed on as instincts.

Moral Freedom and Biological Determinism

Darwin realized that a biological explanation of thought and behavior implied that organisms acted under law, that they were not free. Free will could only be equivalent to chance: "I varily believe," he remarked in his *M Notebook*, "free will & chance are synonymous. Shake ten thousand grains of sand together & one will be uppermost, so in thoughts, one will rise according to law."[34] Now there is a certain tension, as philosophers like to put it, between the belief that man can make unfettered moral decisions and the belief that his thoughts fall out like marbles from a bag. Insofar, however, as Darwin meant his moral theory to be descriptive, explaining how people actually come to ethical decisions and perform moral acts, there really is no conflict between the theory and the conviction that mind is sheerly a biological product. But Darwin also regarded his moral system as leading to ethical imperatives.

He sketched out what was to be a persistent view of the relationship between moral choice and biological determinism in a gloss on a passage from Abercrombie's *Inquiries Concerning the Intellectual Powers*, which he read in late summer of 1838. The Scots philosopher had argued that the moral law, when clearly understood by the agent, coerced his judgement, so that he had to choose according to its dictates. Even in the moral realm, freedom—except as ignorance—did not exist. The idea of determined action under law struck a resonant cord in Darwin, and in the margins of his copy of Abercrombie he penned in his reaction:

> If believed—pretty world we should be in—But it could not be believed excepting by intellectual people—if I believed it—it would make as one difference in my life. for I feel more virtue more happiness—Believers would [mate] with only good women & pay attention to education & so put their children in way of being happy. It is yet right to punish criminals for *public* good. All this delusion of free will would necessarily be from men feeling power of action. View no more improbable than there should be sick & therefore unhappy men. What humility this view teaches. A man [three words illegible] with his state of desire (neither by themselves sufficient) effect of birth and other accidents. Yes but what determines his *consideration*? his own previous conduct—& what has determined that? & so on—*Hereditary* character & education & chance. According to all this ones disgust at villain ought to be is nothing more than disgust at one under fowl disease.[35]

Darwin understood that the doctrine of determinism, if believed, would unsettle the mass of men; but he also recognized that only men of reflection would take it seriously. Most men, because of their feelings of executive agency, would remain deluded in believing themselves free. But for those who carefully considered the doctrine, Darwin thought they would see in it a kind of grandeur. For the doctrine counseled reasoned treatment of those committing crime, not blind revenge. Vice, the theory implied, was a disease, due to hereditary disposition, environment, and chance—influences anyone might fall victim to. Yet for the person persuaded of the transmutational view of morals, he would take care to select a healthy—morally healthy—mate, so that his children would be given the best chance to escape sin. Moreover, a man would see to the proper education of his children, since habits acquired during early life would become as instincts, indeed, for his lineage they might actually become instinctive. This view quickened a man to his responsibilities to future generations.

Darwin did not attempt to resolve the dilemma of the moralist who also believes in determinism. But this does not force us to dismiss his theory. At one level it remains a plausible bit of social anthropology. There are, however, considerations compatible with the Darwinian perspective that mitigate the tension between an evolutionary construction of moral behavior and the acceptance of authentic ethical imperatives. These considerations will be offered in the last section of this chapter.

PROBLEMS FOR THE THEORIES OF
SOCIAL INSTINCT AND MORAL SENSE

By 1842, Darwin had come to apply the principle of natural selection to instinct. He thought instinctual patterns resulted from nervous structures, which, like other anatomical structures, were heritable and varied. Since certain variable patterns of behavior would undoubtedly give an animal an advantage over its competitors, instincts were subject to natural selection.

From 1843 to 1868, when he began work on the *Descent of Man*, Darwin faced two sets of problems in applying selection theory to behavior. Solutions for these were required for an acceptable evolutionary theory of morals. The first arose while he was reading, in 1843, William Kirby and William Spence's *Introduction to Entomology*.[36] The difficulty involved the natural selection and evolution of the social insects; and Darwin thought it so acute that, as he later confessed, it struck him as "fatal to my whole theory."[37] He outlined the problem in annotations to his copy of Kirby and Spence. It was simply this. Social instincts are displayed conspicuously by social insects, especially bees and ants. The bearers of the most marvelous of these instincts are neuter workers. But natural selection preserves individuals having beneficial traits, so that their offspring inherit them. Worker bees and ants leave no offspring. Natural selection thus seems precluded as an explanation for their instincts.[38]

Darwin did not immediately recognize the implications of this difficulty for his moral theory; in the two decades prior to the publication of the *Origin of Species* in 1859, his (recorded) thoughts seldom turned to problems of human evolution. Nonetheless, since he conceived the moral impulse as a species of social instinct, he would have to solve the puzzle of the worker insects in order to be able, in the *Descent of Man*, to introduce natural selection into his moral theory.

Darwin worried about the problem of social instincts for a long time. In a manuscript dated June, 1848, he spelled out the difficulty, tried a few solutions, but finally left off. For the moment he thought it intractable.[39] As late as 1848, therefore, he confronted a problem he regarded as fatal to his whole theory of descent by natural selection.

Other manuscript evidence, as well as internal evidence from Darwin's *Big Species Book*,[40] the abridgment and continuation of which is the *Origin of Species*, show how he eventually arrived at the answer we now take for granted.[41] The solution, of course, is that the unit of selection is not the individual, but the entire nest or hive of insects—natural selection operates on the community of related members. It is what we would call kin-selection. The resolution of the difficulty gave Darwin not only a way of dealing with the evolution of the social instincts and, not incidentally, removing a critical objection to his theory, but it also furnished a key to two further problems that arose during the decade after publication of the *Origin of Species*.

The first difficulty was suggested in 1865 by Darwin's cousin Francis Galton, in his essay "Hereditary Talent and Character,"[42] and was reiterated by William Greg three years later in an article entitled "The Failure of Natural Selection in the Case of Man."[43] Both Galton and Greg observed that in advanced civilizations, where the social instincts were well developed, sympathy and fellow-feeling prevented the natural elimination of the less intellectually able and the morally deficient. With the finely honed sensitivity of the Scots gentleman, Greg offered the case of the Irish as cautionary:

> The careless, squalid, unaspiring Irishman, fed on potatoes, living in a pig-sty, doting on a superstition, multiplies like rabbits or ephemera:—the frugal, foreseeing, self-respecting Scot, stern in his morality, spiritual in his faith, sagacious and disciplined in his intelligence, passes his best years in struggle and in celibacy, marries late, and leaves few behind him.[44]

With the protection provided by well-developed social feeling and sympathy, retrograde types, such as the Irish, simply could not be pruned back by natural selection. For Darwin, the difficulty resided in how to explain the evolution of moral sense beyond its first primitive stages; since, as soon as the social instincts became effective in groups of proto-men, natural selection should be thrown out of gear.

A second problem, which Darwin also recognized, was even more poignant: moral behavior was frequently harmful to the person exercising it. After all, the man who jumps into the stream to save the drowning child might himself drown. But even in benign circumstances, moral acts do not usually benefit the agent. Hence, they would seem to escape the discriminating hand of natural selection.

This was the kind of objection lodged against natural selection by no other than Alfred Wallace, the cofounder of the principle of natural selection. It marked an abrupt reversal of opinion for Wallace. In 1864, he wrote an essay showing how the mechanism of selection could explain man's distinctive traits, including the moral sense.[45] Darwin admired the piece, but was shocked several years later, when Wallace changed his mind. Some curious events caused Wallace to see things differently. In 1866, he hosted a series of seances in his home to test the reality of spiritualistic phenomena. He engaged the services of a Miss Nichol, a medium whose divine performances quickly convinced him. At one sitting, with the lights extinguished and hands held tight around the table, the very rotund Miss Nichol suddenly disappeared. When the lights were struck, she was found in her chair on the center of the table. To all assembled, she appeared to have floated up like a hot-air balloon. Events such as this persuaded Wallace and a host of nineteenth-century intellectuals that the destiny of man was governed by higher spiritual powers.[46] Spirits seemed a better explanation than natural selection for the evolution of human capacities, such as the moral sense, which had no obvious utility for the individual. When Darwin learned of Wallace's new faith, he wrote to his friend expressing the hope "that you have not murdered too completely yours and my child."[47]

THE DESCENT OF MAN

In the *Descent of Man*, begun in 1868 and published in 1871, Darwin tackled these two problems, that of natural selection ceasing to operate in social groups and of the disutility of altruistic behavior. For their solution he brought to bear his model of the evolution of the social insects. He argued that closely related anthropoids, proto-men, would be united into small social groups by the bonds of social instincts. And while moral behavior *within* the group would offer an individual no conspicuous advantages, in competition and warfare *between* groups, the more self-sacrificing and socially cohesive would have the edge. Those groups that by chance displayed more well-developed social—that is to say, moral—instincts would be more likely to survive and pass on their traits. Hence the general level of moral behavior would continue to increase. The unit of selection, as in the case of the social insects, would be the community, the group of more-or-less closely related individuals.[48]

The use of the model originally formed to account for instinct in the social insects also allowed Darwin to explain how moral acts that reduced the fitness of the individual exhibiting them might yet have evolved. Moral instincts would evolve in small communities of related individuals—if they gave the group an advantage and thus helped preserve the closer relatives of the individual, who were likely to have the same trait. Darwin, of course, did not have the means of calculating the Hamiltonian risk–reward ratios and the required degrees of consanguinity, but the basic idea that grounds contemporary sociobiology is there.

In laying out the supposed course of the evolution of conscience, Darwin elaborated his earlier analysis. In the *Descent*, he erected a four-stage model of the evolution of the moral sense.[49] In the first stage, well-developed social instincts would evolve to bind individuals into social groups, that is, potential units of selection. Secondly, for conscience to appear, creatures would need to develop sufficient intelligence to recall past instances of unrequited social instincts. The third stage would arrive when social groups became linguistically competent, so that the needs of individuals and society could be codified in language and easily communicated. In the fourth stage, individuals would acquire habits, actions of honor and etiquette that had no survival value but were characteristic of advanced societies. These, Darwin felt, would be learned anew at mother's knee by each generation; though in time such practices might become instinctual, not through natural selection, of course, but through inherited habit.

Darwin had to modify this last stage as a result of some objections raised by his cousin Hensleigh Wedgwood. Wedgwood sent Darwin a manuscript in which he analyzed his cousin's moral theory.[50] His strongest objection was directed at Darwin's view that instinctual urges were the foundation of our peculiar sense of moral obligation. Darwin responded to the objection in the second edition of the *Descent of Man* by reiterating an idea formulated earlier, namely, that in the ontogenesis of conscience, individuals learned to avoid the nagging persistence of unfulfilled social instinct by implicitly formulating rules about appropriate conduct.[51] Such rules put a rational edge on conscience and themselves, in the form of habits, might also in time become instinctual. Darwin suggested that in this way the voice of duty acquired its special piquancy.

Darwin's theory of moral sense was taken by some of his reviewers to be but a species of utilitarianism—a charge renewed by critics of our day.[52] Darwin himself, however, thought he had taken careful steps to distinguish his view from that of Bentham and Mill. Individuals, he emphasized, acted instinctively to avoid vice and seek virtue—no calculations of benefit were involved. Pleasure may be our sovereign mistress, but some human actions, Darwin believed, were indifferent to her allure. Moral behavior, moreover, was, as he conceived it, altruistic—it enhanced the vigor and health of the group, not the individual. Finally, he pointed out that the criterion of morality in his system was not the general happiness, but the general good, which he interpreted in terms of vigor, health, and survival of the group; subjective feelings of pleasure were simply not the measure.[53] This was no crude utilitarian theory of morality.

In the *Descent*, Darwin highlighted what he thought one of the strongest supports for his theory. With it he could explain what other moralists merely assumed: he could explain how the moral criterion and the moral sense were linked. That is, he was able to account for the coincidence between behavior motivated by a spontaneous moral impulse and behavior sanctioned by the criterion of morality. These two were joined by natural selection. Behaviors that tended to promote the survival of the group would have been selected and become instinctive. Those moral behaviors men actually exhibited, by reason of their social instincts, in a cool hour of evaluation could also be recognized as falling under the criterion of promoting the greatest good, which, in fact, was the standard according to which social instincts were naturally selected. Darwin believed that as civilization advanced, men would gradually expand their moral perception to include others outside their immediate social group. A rational appreciation of what it means to be human would concomitantly evoke an instinctive response to those so characterized, enfranchising them with moral rights.[54]

Unlike the many corpses that litter the history of science, a fair number of Darwin's ideas still live. The new synthetic theory, not so new any more, wedded the principle of natural selection to Mendelian genetics to yield the framework of contemporary biology. I think Darwin's theory of the evolution of moral conscience is another aspect of his thought that is still very vital. The phylogenetic stage analysis of conscience finds rough confirmation both in general theoretical considerations and in ontogenetic studies of the development of conscience, studies such as those of Kohlberg, Loevinger, and Piaget.[55] Moreover, the theory offers a resilient solution to the perplexity of justifying a fundamental moral criterion: Darwin was able to derive both particular moral *oughts* from *is's*, as well as showing why the moral criterion of regarding the common good demands our allegiance.

DARWINISM IN MORALS

Darwin's accomplishment in this regard has gone unrecognized, perhaps because few would suspect that the Shrewsbury biologist had created a theory providing solutions to the kinds of profound problems that sorely challenged moral philosophers such as Hume, Kant, and Moore. Certainly one might righteously pass over a conception that appears merely to embody a vulgar utilitarianism and to be guilty of a deadly sin of moral logic, the affirmation of whatever is, ought to be. And who could take seriously an ethical theory that inconsistently postulates nonrational instincts as causes of moral—that is, rationally responsible—acts? Yet, I think we have seen that Darwin's theory is not quite Benthamism biologized. I would like briefly now to attempt to shrive the theory of these supposed logical faults and to indicate the kind of sound foundation to ethics it does furnish.

First, does Darwin's theory commit the naturalistic fallacy of deriving an *ought* from an *is*? There are two distinct ways in which an evolutionary ethics might so lapse. It might represent the current state of our evolved society as ethically sanctioned, since whatever is, is right; or it might identify a certain trend in evolution, one in which, for example, the physically disabled are selected against, as the criterion for justified action against, in this case, the interests of the congenitally disabled. But Darwin's moral theory prescribes neither of these alternatives. It does not specify a particular social arrangement as being best; rather, it supposes that men will seek the arrangement that appears best to promote the community good. The conception of what constitutes such an ideal pattern will change through time and over different cultures. Nor does the theory isolate a particular historical trend and enshrine that. At one time in our prehistory, for instance, it might have been deemed in the community interest to sacrifice virgins, and this ritual might in fact have contributed to community cohesiveness and thus have been of some evolutionary advantage. But the theory does not justify thereafter the sacrifice of virgins, only acts that, on balance, appear to be conducive to the community good. As the rational capacities of men have evolved and presumably continue to do so, the ineffectiveness of such superstitious behavior has become obvious. The theory maintains that the criterion of morally approved behavior will remain constant, while the conception of what particular acts fall under the criterion will continue to change.

If evolutionary processes have stamped higher organisms with the imperative to serve the community good, does this mean that ethical decisions are coerced by irrational forces—that men, like helpless puppets, are jerked about by strands for the DNA? Hardly. There are three considerations that should defuse the charge that an evolutionary construction of behavior implies the denial of authentic moral choice. First, though evolutionary processes may have resulted in instinctual urges to regard the welfare of the community, is this not a goal at which careful ethical deliberation might also arrive? Certainly some moral philosophers have thought so. Moreover, an extrinsic, evolutionary account of why men generally act according to the community good does not invalidate a logically autonomous argument that concludes that this same standard is the ultimate moral standard. Consider the similar case of mathematical reasoning. Undoubtedly we have been naturally selected for an ability to recognize the quantitative aspects of our environment. Those proto-men who failed to perform simple quantitative computations (such as, for example, determining the closest tree when the saber-tooth charged) have founded extinct lines of descendants. A mathematician who concedes that his brain has been designed, in part at least, to make quantitative judgments need not discard his mathematical proofs as invalid, based on a crippled judgment. Nor should the moralist.[56] Second, the standard of community good must be intelligently applied. Rational deliberation must discover what actions in contingent circumstances lead to enhancing the community welfare. Such choices are not automatic but the result of improvable reason. Finally, the evolutionary perspective indicates that external forces do not conspire to wrench moral acts from a person. Rather, man is ineluctably a moral being. Aristotle believed that men were by nature moral creatures. Darwin demonstrated it.

Now what important problems in moral philosophy does the theory solve? The chief one is the meta-ethical justification of an ultimate moral principle. The most serious difficulty that ethical systems confront, as Allen Gewirth observes,[57] is the justification of their highest principle, whether that principle be the golden rule, selfish pleasure, divine commandment, or the community good. For one can always ask, Why ought I act according, say, to the golden rule? Within most moral systems, there is no answer for a question of this kind, since it requires appeal to some more ultimate principle, which itself will then demand justification.

Now in the face of this difficulty, that of justifying the cardinal principle of the system, moral philosophers have generally resorted to one of three strategies. They might, with G. E. Moore, proclaim that certain activities or principles of behavior are intuitively good, that their moral character is self-evident. But such moralists have no ready answer to the person who might truthfully say, I just don't see it; sorry. Nor do they have any way of excluding the possibility that a large number of such people exist or will exist. Another strategy is akin to that of Kant, which is to assert that men have some authentic moral experiences, and from these an argument can be made to a general principle in whose light their moral character is intelligible. But this tactic, too, suffers from the liability that men may differ in their judgments of what actions are moral. Finally, there is the method employed by Herbert Spencer.[58] He asks of someone proposing another principle—Spencer's was that of greatest pleasure—to reason with him. The outcome should be—if Spencer's principle is the correct one—that the other person will find either that actions he regards as authentically moral do not conform to his own principle, but to Spencer's, or that his principle reduces to or is another version of Spencer's principle. But here again, it is quite possible that the interlocutor's principle will cover all the cases of action he describes as moral, but will not be reducible to Spencer's principle. No reason is offered for expecting ultimate agreement.

All three strategies suppose that one can find near-universal consent among men concerning what actions are moral and what principles sanction them. Yet no way of conceptually securing such agreement is provided. And here is where Darwin's theory obliges: it shows that the pith of every man's nature, the core by which he is constituted a social and moral being, has been created according to the same standard. Each heart must resound to the same moral cord, acting for the common good. It may, of course, occur that some men are born deformed in spirit. There are psychopaths among us. But these, the theory suggests, are to be regarded as less than moral creatures, just as those born severely retarded are thought to be less than rational creatures. But for the vast community of men, they have been stamped by nature as moral beings. Darwin's moral theory, therefore, shows that the several strategies used to support an ultimate ethical principle will, in fact, be successful, something they themselves cannot guarantee. And what they will successfully show, of course, is that the ultimate principle is the community good.

NOTES

1. Edward O. Wilson, *Sociobiology* (Cambridge: Harvard University Press, 1975), p. 562.

2. George Bernard Shaw, "Preface," *Back to Methuselah* (London: Penguin Books, 1961; first published in 1921), p. 44.

3. Ashley Montagu, in *Darwin, Competition and Cooperation* (New York: Schuman, 1952), p. 32, gives expression to what has become a commonplace: "The truth is that Darwinian biology was largely influenced by the social and political thought of the first half of the nineteenth century, and that its own influence took the form of giving scientific support in terms of natural law for what had hitherto been factitiously imposed social law." For other explicit assertions of this interpretation of Darwin's theory, see: Bertrand Russell, *Religion and Science* (New York: Holt, 1935), pp. 72-73; Eric Nordenskiold, *The History of Biology* (New York: Tudor, 1936), p. 477; Marvin Harris, *The Rise of Anthropological Theory* (London: Routledge and Kegan Paul, 1968), pp. 108-25.

4. Loren Eiseley, *Darwin and the Mysterious Mr. X* (New York: Dutton, 1979), p. 202.

5. In his *Autobiography*, ed. Nora Barlow (New York: Norton, 1969), Darwin credited himself with the ability to sustain a line of thought—"for the *Origin of Species* is one long argument from beginning to end" (p. 140)—but not with a penetrating intellect that could deal with abstract matters: "My power to follow a long and purely abstract train of thought is very limited; I should, moreover, never have succeeded with metaphysics or mathematics" (p. 140). Jacques Barzun, in *Darwin, Marx, Wagner*, 2nd ed. (New York: Doubleday Anchor, 1958), p. 74, shares Darwin's own estimate: "Darwin was a great assembler of facts and a poor joiner of ideas."

6. Charles Darwin, *Diary of the Voyage of H. M. S. "Beagle,"* ed. Nora Barlow (Cambridge: Cambridge University Press, 1933), p. 76.

7. Darwin, *Diary*, pp. 172-73.

8. Darwin's *Transmutation Notebooks* have been transcribed by Gavin de Beer, *Bulletin of the British Museum (Natural History), Historical Series* (1960-67), 2:27-200; 3:129-76.

9. Darwin, *Second Transmutation Notebook*, ms. p. 171 (de Beer, pp. 102-3). For an account of Darwin's early theories about evolution, see: David Kohn, "Theories to Work By: Rejected Theories, Reproduction and Darwin's Path to Natural Selection," *Studies in History of Biology* 4 (1980):67-170; Robert Richards, "Influence of Sensationalist Tradition on Early Theories of the Evolution of Behavior," *Journal of History of Ideas* 40 (1979):85-105.

10. Darwin, *Autobiography*, p. 120.

11. Darwin left a record of the books he read and the periods during which he read them. See the transcription of these lists by Peter Vorzimmer, "The Darwin Reading Notebooks (1838-1860)," *Journal of History of Biology* 10 (1977):107-52.

12. Darwin's annotation is in his copy of John Fleming, *Philosophy of Zoology*, 2 vols. (Edinburgh: Constable, 1822), 1:242-43. Books from Darwin's library are preserved in the Manuscript Room of Cambridge University Library.

13. Darwin's "Essay" of 1842 and an expanded version written in 1844 were published posthumously by Francis Darwin in *The Foundations of the Origin of Species* (Cambridge: Cambridge University Press, 1909). Darwin's slow transition from a use-inheritance explanation of instinct to a selectionist explanation is described in Robert Richards, "Instinct and Intelligence in British Natural Theology: Some Contributions to Darwin's Theory of the Evolution of Behavior," *Journal of History of Biology* 14 (1981):193-230.

14. For example, in describing domestic instincts in the *Origin of Species* (London: Murray, 1859), p. 216, Darwin retained a role for inherited habit: "In some cases compulsory habit alone has sufficed to produce such inherited mental changes; in other cases compulsory habit has done nothing, and all has been the result of selection, pursued both methodically and unconsciously, but in most cases, probably, habit and selection have acted together."

15. Harriet Martineau, *How to Observe: Manners and Morals* (New York: Harper, 1838); James Mackintosh, *Dissertation on the Progress of Ethical Philosophy* (Edinburgh: Adam and Charles Black, 1836); John Abercrombie, *Inquiries Concerning the Intellectual Powers*, 8th ed. (London: Murray, 1836). Edward Manier, in his continuously interesting *The Young Darwin and His Cultural Circle* (Dordrecht: Reidel, 1978), briefly describes the views of Martineau, Mackintosh, and Abercrombie.

16. Charles Darwin, "Letter to Granny (Mrs. Wedgwood), 1838." The letter is on microfilm at the American Philosophical Society, 496.1.

17. Martineau, *How to Observe*, pp. 29-30.

18. Ibid., p. 33.

19. Charles Darwin, *M Notebook*, ms. pp. 76-6, transcribed by Paul Barrett in Howard Gruber, *Darwin on Man* (New York: Dutton, 1974), p. 279.

20. Mackintosh, *Dissertation*, pp. 254-61.

21. Ibid., pp. 192-93, 385, 400.

22. Ibid., pp. 62-67.

23. Ibid., pp. 355-61.

24. Darwin was explicit about this motivation in the *Descent of Man*, 2 vols. (London: Murray, 1871), 1: p. 71: "This great question [of the moral sense] has been discussed by many writers of consumate ability; and my sole excuse for touching on it, is the impossibility of here passing it over; and because, as far as I know, no one has approached it exclusively from the side of natural history. The investigation possesses, also, some independent interest, as an attempt to see how far the study of the lower animals throws light on one of the highest psychical faculties of man."

25. William Paley, *Moral and Political Philosophy* (1785), in *The Works of William Paley*, new ed. (Philadelphia: Woodward, n.d.), p. 30.

26. Charles Darwin, *Old and Useless Notes*, ms. p. 30, transcribed by Barrett, in Gruber, *Darwin on Man*, p. 390.

27. Darwin's theory is developed in his *N Notebook*, ms. pp. 2-4, transcribed by Barrett, in Gruber, *Darwin on Man*, pp. 329-30. The example of the mother bird abandoning her young is taken from *Descent of Man*, 1:90-91.

28. The manuscript is included among the bundle of notes labeled by Darwin *Old and Useless Notes,* ms. pp. 42–55 (Gruber, pp. 398–405).

29. Ibid., (Gruber, pp. 382–405).

30. Manier, in *Young Darwin,* p. 146, assumes that Darwin used the principle of natural selection in his early theory to explain the evolution of the moral sense. Manier's effort to place the young Darwin in his cultural and historical context is consumately skillful and illuminating; although, on this issue, I believe the evidence is clearly against him. See also Richards, "Instinct and Intelligence in British Natural Theology."

31. Darwin, *Old and Useless Notes,* ms. p. 48 (Gruber, p. 401).

32. Ibid., ms. p. 50 (Griber, p. 402).

33. Ibid., ms. p. 30 (Gruber, p. 390). Slashes enclose words Darwin inserted.

34. Darwin, *M Notebook,* ms. p. 31 (Gruber, p. 271).

35. Darwin's annotations appear in Abercrombie, *Inquiries Concerning the Intellectual Powers,* pp. 202–3.

36. William Kirby and William Spence, *Introduction to Entomology,* 2nd ed., 4 vols. (London: Longman, Hurst, Rees, Orme, and Brown, 1818).

37. Darwin, *Origin of Species,* p. 236.

38. Darwin's annotations occur in Kirby and Spence, *Introduction to Entomology,* 2: 55, 513, and back flyleaf. I have described Darwin's struggles with this difficulty in Richards, "Instinct and Intelligence in British Natural Theology."

39. Darwin's four-page manuscript is in container-book #73, held in the Manuscript Room of Cambridge University Library. I have transcribed it in Richards, "Instinct and Intelligence in British Natural Theology," pp. 220–21.

40. Charles Darwin, *Natural Selection: Being the Second Part of His Big Species Book Written from 1856 to 1858,* ed. R. C. Stauffer (Cambridge: Cambridge University Press, 1975).

41. I have described the way he arrived at the solution in Richards, "Instinct and Intelligence in British Natural Theology."

42. Francis Galton, "Hereditary Talent and Character," *Macmillan's Magazine* 12 (1865):157–66; 318–27. Galton (p. 326) cautioned: "One of the effects of civilization is to diminish the rigour of the application of the law of natural selection. It preserves weakly lives, that would have perished in barbarous lands. . . . In civilized society, money interposes her aegis between the law of natural selection and very many of its rightful victims. Scrofula and madness are naturalized among us by wealth."

43. [William Greg], "On the Failure of 'Natural Selection' in the Case of Man," *Fraser's Magazine* 78 (1868):353–62. Greg also regard civilization as disrupting that "righteous and salutary law which God ordained for the preservation of a worthy and improving humanity" (p. 358).

44. Greg, "On the Failure of 'Natural Selection,' " p. 361.

45. Alfred Wallace, "The Origin of Human Races and the Antiquity of Man Deduced from the Theory of 'Natural Selection,' " *Anthropological Review* 2 (1864):153–87.

46. Wallace described these seances in *A Defense of Modern Spiritualism* (Boston: Colby and Rich, 1874). Malcolm Kottler provides the most detailed and persuasive account of Wallace's conversion to spiritualism and of its effect on his theory of human evolution. See M. Kottler, "Alfred Russell Wallace, the Origin of Man, and Spiritualism," *Isis* 65 (1974): 145–92.

47. Charles Darwin, "Letter to Wallace, March 27, 1869," in James

Marchant, *Alfred Russell Wallace: Letters and Reminiscences*, 2 vols. (London: Cassell, 1916), 1:241.

48. Darwin, *Descent of Man*, 1:159-61;

49. Ibid., 1:72-73.

50. Hensleigh Wedgwood's manuscript is in container-book #88 at Cambridge University Library.

51. Charles Darwin, *Descent of Man*, 2nd ed., in *Origin of Species and Descent of Man* (New York: Modern Library, 1936), p. 486.

52. John Morley, "Mr. Darwin on Conscience," *Pall Mall Gazette* 13 (April 12, 1871), 1358-59. See also authors listed in note 3 above.

53. Darwin, *Descent of Man*, 1:97-98.

54. Ibid., 1:97-104.

55. This argument sketch supposes that the biogenic law of ontogeny recapitulating phylogeny has some validity. Most evolutionists agree that it does—when properly interpreted. See Stephen Gould, *Ontogeny and Phylogeny* (Cambridge: Harvard University Press, 1977). E. Turiel describes various stage theories of moral development and considers the proposal that such sequences might be genetically controlled. See his "The Development of Moral Concepts," in *Morality as a Biological Phenomenon*, ed. Gunther Stent (Berkeley: University of California Press, 1980), pp. 109-23.

56. C. Fried makes a similar argument for the autonomy of moral argument in "Biology and Ethics: Normative Implications," in *Morality as a Biological Phenomenon*, pp. 186-95.

57. Alan Gewirth, *Reason and Morality* (Chicago: University of Chicago Press, 1979), p. 2.

58. Herbert Spencer, *The Principles of Ethics*, 2 vols. (Indianapolis: Liberty Classics, 1977; originally published in 1893), 1:66.

3

Physics, Metaphsyics, and Fechner's Psychophysics

Marilyn E. Marshall

Historical treatments of Fechner's *Elemente der Psychophysik* (Elements of Psychophysics) (1860) tend to emphasize either the philosophical origins of the psychophysical idea or the scientific ideas on which the arguments of the *Elemente* rest.[1] From the former orientation, Boring was led to characterize Fechner as inadvertant founder of the science of psychophysics because of his predominantly philosophical motives.[2] Ellenberger, following the lead of Wundt, referred to Fechner as epigone *Naturphilosoph* for the same reason. Paradoxically, although the philosophically oriented accounts have pointed to the origin of Fechner's double aspect view to *Naturphilosophie*, they have not shown how Fechner, on philosophical premises, might have arrived at his *Fundamentalformel* (Fundamental Formula) of 1851.[3]

Scientifically oriented historical accounts have analyzed the ideas with which Fechner justified his psychophysical notion in the

Parts of this paper were presented under the title "Echoes of physics in Fechner's psychophysics" in a symposium at the October, 1980, meetings of the History of Science Society in Toronto, Ontario. The research was supported by a grant from The Social Sciences and Humanities Research Council of Canada; the manuscript was read and discussed in several drafts by my colleague, R. A. Wendt, to whom I am grateful.

Elemente of 1860, and they have either argued or left the impression that scientific ideas also played a major role in the inception of the *Fundamentalformel.*[4] Furthermore, these authors have concentrated on the scientific microconcepts (physical atomism, conservation of physical energy, E. H. Weber's Law) employed by Fechner, while his general scientific assumptions have remained, in the main, unexamined.

The view of the *Elemente* as philosophically inspired is buttressed in the historical literature by the notion that Fechner metamorphosed from physicist into philosopher as a creative byproduct of his recovery from a disabling illness (1839-43). My first task is to show that Fechner's philosophical concerns did not first emerge in the 1840s; nor did his scientific concerns cease then. In a second section I will illustrate the active role of the qualitative mathematics of *Naturphilosophie* in the nascent phase of development of Fechner's *Fundamentalformel,* suggesting also that certain of the scientific concepts that became all-important in Fechner's justification for psychophysics, though evident in the context of discovery, were probably not indispensable to it. In section three I will show that the *Elemente* was explicitly designed to inaugurate a new science, and to stand or to fall on experimental evidence independent of metaphysical stance; further, that certain important general characteristics of the psychophysics can be identified with those of the physics of Germany's *Vormärz* period. In conclusion I will suggest that these characteristics, particularly Fechner's abstract hypothetico-deductive approach and his scientifically radical view of consciousness, may have sparked much of the controversy that followed the publication of the *Elemente.*

THE INTERTWINING TRAJECTORIES OF PHILOSOPHY AND SCIENCE, 1820-49

In 1820, as a disillusioned and atheistically inclined medical student at Leipzig,[5] Fechner read and was enchanted by Lorenz Oken's *Lehrbuch der Naturphilosophie* (Textbook of Natural Philosophy).[6] Three years later he habilitated, and earned the right to teach, hoping to become a professional philosopher in the Schelling-Oken mold. Fechner's *Habilitationsschrift, Praemissae ad Theoriam Organismi Generalem* (Premises toward a General Theory of Organisms),[7] betrays his ties with the post-Kantian idealists in their search for system, for unity of knowledge. His aim was a metaphysics from which the principles of all sciences could be deduced, and his approach was through an analysis of ideas, the basic units of understanding. Fechner's *Praemissae* derived from Hegelian, Schellingian, and Herbartian ideas; at the age of 23 he was now convinced that a single law prevailed throughout the universe and its individual parts, that one path to the discovery of this law was through the description of natural objects using mathematical equations, and that the phenomena of body and mind run in parallel. When we see that Fechner also played here with the possibility of construing the relation between quantitative and qualitative change logarithmically, we recognize in the *Praemissae* a significant prefiguration of his psychophysical law.[8]

But Fechner's plans to become a professional philosopher were thwarted by mundane financial pressures, and in 1824 he began a series of translations of French scientific works, including the *Précis elémentaire de physique expérimentale* (Elementary Textbook of Experimental Physics) of Jean-Baptiste Biot.[9] Biot's ideas changed Fechner's life; they made him dissatisfied with the pure speculation of his recent *Habilitationsschrift*, and they led him to a career in science.

Fechner had an excellent scientific model in Biot, who had been the first protégé of Laplace, and the senior member of the younger generation of the Society of Arcueil which carried out a conscious and concerted program to transform a largely qualitative, expository French physics into a rigorous mathematized discipline.[10] And Biot's publications were influential in propagating these new standards of precision, experimental rigor, and quantification.[11] Fechner's translation of 1824 was of the third edition of Biot's *Précis*.

Biot's inspiration led Fechner to a voluntary apprenticeship in natural science through a voluminous series of translations of journal articles and books by the younger generation of French scientists and through a self-imposed regimen of study of the mathematics of Cauchy and Poisson. In spite of a ruefully admitted personal weakness in mathematics, Fechner, like other German scientists of his generation, got from the French his basic knowledge of mathematical physics, the conviction of the power of mathematics as an essential feature of progressive experimental science, and a penetrating look at the fruits of innovative, precise, experimental methodology.

The extent to which Fechner embraced the ideals expressed by Biot is illustrated in his major contribution to experimental physics, *Maasbestimmungen ueber die galvanische Kette* (Measurements of the Series of Galvanic Cells, 1931).[12] This work, a verification of Ohm's law in 135 experiments, was a conscious and successful attempt to bring greater precision and quantification to work on galvanism. Fechner's experiments were models of precise measurement, experimental control, and consciously objective reporting, which distinguishes them from other contemporary researches on the galvanic circuit.[13] The *Maasbestimmungen* is also of interest because, as strongly as it was modeled on the values of Arcueil, and as much as it drew concretely on the innovative methodology of Biot's French physics, it did not reflect Biot's rejection of theoretical systems in the guidance of research.[14] The antitheoretical bent of French scientists in the generation following Biot differs from that of Fechner's generation in Germany and resembles the concrete inductivism of the older German physics against which Fechner and his contemporaries revolted. In contrast, Fechner's *Maasbestimmungen* has been described as an "extended example of the self-conscious use of the hypothetico-deductive method."[15]

Fechner's feverish translation output declined significantly after 1831. The years 1832 and 1833, which led up to his marriage to Clara Volkmann and to his professorship in physics at Leipzig, saw Fechner complete three volumes on experimental physics, two on inorganic chemistry, and one on organic chemistry; he was also occupied with articles on electricity and the editorship of a new pharmaceutical journal. Simultaneously, Fechner accepted the editorship of a household encyclopedia, which proved financially and psychologically disastrous. Its first volume appeared in 1834, the eighth and last in 1838; the successive volumes mark a decline in Fechner's energy reserves and an approach to the illness of 1840 to 1843 that would end his professional career as physicist.[16]

While Fechner was occupied with laboratory studies on the frontiers of electricity and becoming a leading figure in the reform of German science, he was also preoccupied with philosophical questions. This was not unusual in the second decade of the nineteenth century, when German science and philosophy frequently occupied the same minds. German scientists of Fechner's generation were inspired generally in their drive for unity of knowledge and inspired specifically in placing priority on theorizing by the speculative *Naturphilosophien* which their elders had rejected but to which the younger men were, on the whole, friendly.[17]

Fechner kept alive the intellectual flame of *Naturphilosophie* throughout his career as physicist in a series of quasi-satirical works, the first of which was published in 1824. Fechner's insistence on the difference between philosophical and scientific enterprises is, however, indicated by the use of the pseudonym, Dr. Mises, for his speculative work, and it was explicit in his reflections on *Naturphilosophie*: "Science . . . does not lie along this path."[18] He was by turns critical of the failings and struck by the promise of *Naturphilosophie*, which was ". . . a noble wine which should not be drunk by those whom it makes too gay," but it also operated in the conviction that in any science worthy of the name, "everything must be subsumed under one principle."[19]

The essays of the *Stapelia Mixta* (Various Carrion Flowers) of 1824 and the *Vergleichende Anatomie der Engel* (Comparative Anatomy of Angels) of 1825[20] show Mises-Fechner groping toward the unifying principle for which he had thirsted in the *Praemissae*. For example, he explored the possibility of finding such a principle in the geometric symbol of the circle:

> Mind is a circle whose radii (mental activities) are set from a mid-point (reason) to the periphery (the senses and outward limits of mind) within a larger circle (the external world of the senses), extending in its effects, however, over the periphery into the larger circle. While in reverse, the larger circle concentrates against the periphery and itself sends radii of its effects through the periphery to the midpoint.[21]

From this model of mind–environment interaction, Fechner extended the metaphor of the circle to a quasi-cosmological, religious view of the universe as a series of nested wholes: an organism's essence lies in the mutual relationship between its inorganic parts, such that each part exists and is effective only in the whole, and the whole in its parts; likewise, the state is a higher-level whole containing individual organisms as parts; humanity is a yet higher-level whole; so the earth, the solar system, and so on infinitely.[22]

In addition to the derivative (Schelling–Oken) nature of Fechner's "cosmorganic" view, the one characteristic of his arguments that deserves emphasis is that his ubiquitous use of geometry and algebra[23] was purely symbolic, schematic, analogical. He was unconcerned with measurement, and he explicitly identified the analogical form of his arguments with *Naturphilosophie*.[24]

The *Stapelia Mixta* also shows Fechner confronting two visions of the universe, the one material and dead, the other spiritual, conscious, and alive. Fechner painted horrific pictures of the universe as a monstrous, dead, mechanical system of interlocking levers, of the world as an imitative "ghost of life," and of death as the brutal annihilation of self-identity.[25] He could accept none of these conclusions, which he drew from materialism. On the other hand, he was well aware of the fragility of an alternative (all-besouling) hypothesis which gives ". . . the stone the same right as plants and animals."[26]

There was in Fechner's Gothic musings a felt paradox between the necessity of viewing the world as mechanism (to satisfy the requirements of science) and viewing the world as consciousness (to justify his idealistic premises and his moral-religious convictions). His search for a unifying symbol may be interpreted as a search for a clear expression of Schelling's identity (double-aspect) theory, which he was never quite able to find in Schelling.[27]

Dr. Mises' *Das Büchlein vom Leben nach dem Tode* (Little Book on Life after Death) of 1836 was prepared during Fechner's first years as *Ordinarius* in physics.[28] Here, he added to his symbol of mind-environment interaction, to the notion of a universe of nested wholes, and to the double aspect view, a developmental-genetic schema for the human soul, again following a dominant (historical) theme of Schelling. His purpose in the *Buchlein* was to argue for moral conduct in this life on the ground that the pleasurable or painful consequences of behavior do not end with death but must be dealt with in a continuing and developing life after death.

Fechner's illness forced him to resign his chair in physics, a position in which he had felt himself constantly frustrated because of his limitations as mathematician. The recuperative phase of the illness, from 1843 to the end of the decade, provided the leisure, free from major financial strain, to give serious attention to the philosophical problems with which, since the *Praemissae*, he had dealt in the patchworks of Dr. Mises.

Two books published in this decade under Fechner's own name represent elaborations of his earlier philosophical themes. *Ueber das höchste Gut* (On the Highest Good) of 1846 argued that the greatest possible material and spiritual pleasure for oneself and others forms the true morality. His *Nanna, oder ueber das Seelenleben des Pflanzen* (Nanna, or about the Soul Life of Plants, 1848) laid the groundwork for a serious metaphysics of all-besouling.[29] In this work, Fechner's opposition to one-sided materialistic reductionism (the nightmare of Dr. Mises' earlier works) is evident in explicit criticisms of Matthias Schleiden, coauthor of the cell theory. Schleiden's public response to *Nanna* was vehemently negative and he thought Fechner muddled.[30]

Muddled or not, the mind that conceived *Nanna* also produced its most significant contribution to theoretical physics in this decade. In 1845 Fechner published an atomic theory of electricity, a masterpiece of integration, in which he subsumed both Faraday's induction effects and Ampere's laws of electrodynamics.[31] This article provides another example of Fechner's heuristic use of theory, but it is most important as an occasion for showing the close relationship between Fechner and Wilhelm Weber in the 1840s. It was this Weber, the able mathematician, who, just one year later, turned the ideas discursively presented by Fechner into a mathematically elaborated and epoch-making atomic theory encompassing electrostatics, electrodynamics, and electromagnetic induction.[32]

The social proximity of the two men promoted Weber's rapid use of Fechner's ideas and Fechner's eventual reliance on Weber as a sounding board for his developing psychophysical notion. Between 1843, when Weber assumed Fechner's chair in physics at Leipzig, and 1849, when he returned to Göttingen, they met weekly at the "Fechner circle," a social gathering that regularly included the three brothers Weber.[33] By 1849 Fechner had again turned his mind to the application of mathematics to organic processes, and his conversations with Wilhelm Weber, whose refrains in physics were measure and measurement, contributed directly to certain of these ideas.[34]

THE BIRTH OF PSYCHOPHYSICS: 1850–59

Fechner hit upon his principle of mathematical psychology while working on his vast *Zend-Avesta* (1851), a defense of the double-aspect view. He marked October 22, 1850, as the day on which, abed in the morning, he suddenly saw that the functional relation between mental and physical might be construed logarithmically.[35] This is a generalization to all mental and physical events of empirical relationships which had been observed in special settings since 1760 and, notably, by Fechner's teacher and friend, E. H. Weber.[36] But the route to the insight of 1850 was not through E. H. Weber's work. It was, rather, through an attempt to represent the basic relationship of body to mind by the schematic use of mathematics. Fechner had explored this approach in the *Stapelia Mixta* of 1824 and he clearly still found it congenial.

Fechner required a symbol for his conclusion that body is a physical manifold of elements to which mental unity corresponds.[37]

In the *Zend-Avesta* he found this symbol in the unit arithmetic series where successive numerals represent the manifold of observable physical elements and the "unobserved" unit constant represents mental unity.

Fechner carried the analogy further to illustrate the relation of physical to lower and higher mental processes.[38] In the physical series 1 2 4 7 11 . . . the differences between successive numbers change, but these changing differences themselves form a new series (1 2 3 4 5 6 . . .) representing lower mental processes, a physical manifold corresponding to, but relatively simpler than, the physical. Implicit in the second series, in turn, is hidden a yet higher mental process, that of identity.

The relationship between the geometric and the arithmetic series of this example is logarithmic, illustrating the form of E. H. Weber's fraction: $(1 - 2)/1 = (2 - 4)/2 = (4 - 7)/3 = k = -1$. Fechner was silent on this point in the *Zend-Avesta*, but he later claimed that the mathematical series suggested to him that he attempt to find an expression for the real dependent relationship of mind and body:

> . . . the scheme of geometric progressions led me . . . through an uncertain chain of thought to make the relative increase in the physical kinetic energy . . . the measure of the increase in the related mental intensity.[39]

This insight gained Fechner the beginning of a firm conceptual basis for the relationship of body and mind in the individual and of spirit and matter in the entire realm of existence.[40] It allowed him to write his *Fundamentalformel* of 1851: $d\gamma = K\, d\beta/\beta$ where $d\gamma$ is an absolute change in the intensity of mental activity (γ) accompanying the relative change ($d\beta/\beta$) in the kinetic energy of bodily activity (β).[41] *The Maasformel* (Measurement Formula) was achieved by integration, so that the total amount of mental intensity is represented by a sum of relative increments of the corresponding physical energy, starting with the physical value when the physical is at zero:[42] $\gamma = \log \beta/b$ where $b = \beta$ when $\gamma = 0$.

Fechner did not bring the data of E. H. Weber to bear on the verification of these formulae in 1851. He knew Weber's work as well as he knew him personally, and he had referred to Weber's *Tastsinn und Gemeingefühl* (Sense of Touch and Common Sense, 1846) in a previous section of *Zend-Avesta*, but he did not mention Weber's name in introducing this formula in which (to us, but apparently not to Fechner) the Weber constant was so clearly implied.[43]

Though appearing to ignore E. H. Weber, Fechner was exceedingly prompt in bringing his new "immense perspective" to the attention of the brother, Wilhelm Weber, asking for his opinion and expressing the hope that his idea might be a scientifically "happy" one. This Weber replied in December, 1850, that though the basic idea was correct and discerning, the degree to which it would advance science would depend on whether the notion could be supported by facts and on whether it would lead to the discovery of new facts.[44]

Two points can be made in summary of Fechner's route to the *Maasformel*. First, the formula was argued neither upon the basis of what Fechner would himself eventually label "Weber's Law" nor upon any other systematic empirical facts. Although we may be content to assume that E. H. Weber's work influenced Fechner at some level of consciousness, the Weber fraction appears *de novo* in Fechner's *Zend-Avesta*. Secondly, the uncertain thought process that precipitated *Fundamentalformel* did not rest on a concern for measurement: "The task did not present itself at first at all as a matter of finding psychic measurement. . . ."[45] It rested on a continuation of Fechner's ubiquitous drive for satisfactory symbolic representation of his most cherished philosophical conviction, the double-aspect view of mind and body.

Fechner referred to the *Maasprinzip* of the *Zend-Avesta* as a babe in diapers.[46] Between 1851 and the *Elemente* of 1860, he sought to clothe this babe with facts:

> Psychic measurement, which was found in the course of this task, has been made the basis for a theory of these relations (between the physical and the psychical) which is indisputably the more suitable and sounder course.[47]

The introductory and historical sections of the *Elemente* document this search for facts thoroughly; here, we need only point to the dramatic dissonance between the format of the eventual *Elemente* and the natural history of the development of the measurement principle in Fechner's mind. The developmental sequence began with Fechner's insight of 1850 and the theoretical postulation of the *Fundametal-* and *Maasformel*. The next decade saw Fechner searching for validating facts and for reliable facts deducible from them, using a hypothetico-deductive methodology true to his form as physicist in the *Maasbestimmungen* of 1831, using his own skills in laboratory research, and mining the experimental work of others. It was late in the game, while his cherished formulae ". . . still hovered, as it were, in the air,"[48] that Fechner saw in the data of E. H. Weber the facts that Wilhelm Weber had urged him to find,[49] and with them the possibility of mental measurement in practice.

The path that led to the psychic measurement principle was opposite to that presented by Fechner in the *Elemente*. This is a tripartite work, appearing in two volumes. The first part is concerned with establishing the principle of psychic measurement discursively and with presenting methods, laws, and experimentally derived data relevant to the proof of what Fechner there calls Weber's Law (outer psychophysics). The *Fundamental-* and *Maasformel* do not appear until the beginning of Volume II, in a mathematical elaboration yielding new, hitherto untested deductions from the formulae. The implications of the facts and the mathematical derivations for inner psychophysics and for the mind–body relation in general are in the third part (the developmental starting point).

The effect of this format is that implicitly the reader is invited to construe Fechner's formulae as inductively derived best fits to empirical data points, which they patently were not. Wilhelm Weber's insistence that the scientific fate of psychophysics would depend on corroborating facts may have had much to do with the format that gave priority to E. H. Weber's Law and its validation. And Fechner, whose philosophical extravaganzas, *Nanna* and *Zend-Avesta*, had been received by the scientific—and philosophical—community with strained disbelief, would naturally stress those aspects of psychophysics that could be presented from an empirical platform.[50]

To argue that philosophical ideas and methods were necessary to the development of psychophysics is not to say that they were sufficient. Our discussion of the birth of psychophysics must now turn briefly to two scientific ideas that appeared in tandem with Fechner's postulation of the principle of 1851.

Fechner first used the idea of kinetic energy conservation (*Erhaltung der lebendigen Kraft*) in the *Zend-Avesta* of 1851, referring to the law as indisputable and valid for particular organisms as well as for the whole world of which they are parts.[51] But Fechner did not mention Helmholtz, and he may well have been referring to the earlier idea of the conservation of kinetic energy of Legrange, or to the even earlier conceptions of the conservation of *vis viva* dating from Leibnitz.[52] We have no direct evidence that in 1850 Fechner was aware of Helmholtz's publication of 1847,[53] and we have some indirect evidence that it was not to Helmholtz that Fechner referred in 1851: in 1860 Fechner clearly distinguished between the law of the conservation of kinetic energy (the rubric of 1851) and the more general law of the conservation of energy (incorporating both kinetic and potential energy forms), attributing the latter to Helmholtz.[54] Furthermore, when in 1849 Fechner published a paper arguing the possibility of universal deterministic law,[55] he mentioned neither Helmholtz nor conservation, which we would expect him to do had they been in his conceptual focus; conservation of energy was an example *par excellence* of what Fechner was arguing for. Certainly, if Fechner was aware of Helmholtz's coup in 1850, its immediacy would have provided motivational fuel for his own increasingly concerted search for universal law. Fundamentally, however, it is irrelevant to our purpose whether it was the Helmholtzian law to which Fechner referred. After all, Conservation of energy was "in the air" long before 1847, and, if Kuhn is correct, the idea was at least partially mediated by the *Naturphilosophie* so beloved of Fechner.[56]

A significant question is whether Fechner's formulae of 1851 were conceivable without the notion of kinetic energy conservation. That a particular stimulus value can be transformed into psychical energy does not require the notion, but, as Lowry insists, the idea that one can write an equation expressing the relation between the two is consistent with it. Recall, however, that as early as 1824 Fechner had played philosophically with the idea of a logarithmic function relating quality to quantity. When we also recognized that Herbart, in 1824–25, had already used exact mathematical equations to describe psychological dynamics on a simple equilibrium model, we see that a law of physical energy conservation was not strictly necessary to Fechner's *Fundamentalformel*.[57]

Lowry maintains that without conservation Fechner would never have seen the connection between his philosophical vision and the measurement of outer psychophysics.[58] While this may be so, we suspect that the connection was made after 1851. Fechner's relatively late recognition of the relevance of E. H. Weber's (outer psychophysical) law suggests that this is so. Certainly Fechner's focus in 1851 was on inner psychophysics: $d\beta$ referred to change in the kinetic energy of bodily activity, not of external stimulus energy.[59]

We do know that Fechner mentioned Helmholtz by name in connection with the conservation of energy in 1855 in his *Ueber die physikalische und philosophische Atomenlehre* (On the Physical and Philosophical Doctrines of Atoms);[60] and just as he eventually based his psychophysics on Weber's law, the *Elemente* of 1860 is based thunderously on the "great principle" of Helmholtz.[61] In summary, though Helmholtz is a fundamental authority for the elaborated *Elemente*, a Helmholtzian influence on the inception of the formulae of 1851 appears unlikely, although the evidence for the precedence of the concept of kinetic energy conservation is indisputable.

Fechner's atomic theory of electricity of 1845 was clearly based on a commitment to physical atomism, and the *Maasformel* of 1851 offers evidence of atomistic thinking: on one side of the equation is the integration of discrete quanta of physical energy, on the other the integration of quanta of sensation. Even so, such an argument directly entails only a commitment to the idea that in the mind, as in the physical world, a whole is an organized sum of parts. Thus, atomism was consistent with Fechner's arguments of 1851, but whether the *Maasformel* depended directly on physical atomistic assumptions remains uncertain. Schreier argues that physical atomism is a necessary "hidden" assumption of the formula, but he bases his arguments on Fechner's *Atomenlehre* of 1855.[62] However, one significant link between Fechner's treatment of physical atoms and sensations does appear in 1851 in a footnote to his *Maasformel*:

> The mental intensity of an element is a mathematical fiction which has no other meaning than to provide for the calculation of a relationship which occurs in a system of elements; for a sensation of perceptible magnitude cannot belong to a particle of either infinitely small space or time.[63]

Four years later, in his *Atomenlehre*, Fechner insisted that the physical atom be viewed, likewise, as hypothesis, as a conceptual tool, a convenient picture, having significance only in the number and interrelatedness of verifiable phenomena explicable and deducible from it.[64]

The first part of the *Atomenlehre* is a presentation of scientific fact and theory felicitously explained by assuming the physical atomistic model. In a new theme for Fechner, the second philosophical part contains the argument that although physics, with science in general, owes nothing to metaphysics, the contrary is not so. Metaphysics has everything to learn from science and should be built on it. And the *"einfache Atomenlehre"* of this section provides a philosophical extension of scientific atomism. Fechner concludes that atomism viewed as scientific construct is not necessarily allied with either materialism or idealism. Yet, though science uses atoms purely as constructs, philosophy, which is concerned with essences, can usefully make guesses about their nature. Fechner's simple atoms, described in detail by Molella,[65] are ultimate, indivisible, extensionless entities, mathematical Boscovichian points, whose motions are bound and unified organically by universal God-given law. This law, in turn, is characterized by forces of attraction and repulsion.

At least since 1845, Fechner had seen physical atomism prevailing in science as the best available working model.[66] He may have hesitated to ground his mathematical principle of 1951 more explicitly in physical atomism because he had not yet provided a conceptual link for his public between physical atomism and his philosophical–religious views. As the possibility of mental measurement in practice appeared more and more likely during the 1850s, the necessity for such a link would become evident. And Fechner's philosophical atomism of 1855 can be viewed as an attempt to show that science on the one hand, and philosophy and religion on the other, could both work without essential contradiction within the atomistic scheme. Life after death, in this context, became a continuation (conservation) of a unique part of a singular universal psychophysical process. The *Atomenlehre* is thus an essential bridge between the long-developing Fechnerian philosophy and the materialistic world view, and an essential groundwork for the elaborated psychophysics; therein, mind remained the citadel of human spirituality viewed from within the organismic unity of individual or of universal (God's) consciousness. But mind is ontologically identical with, and therefore empirically functionally interdependent with, what we conceive as physical reality.

The balance of evidence presented above suggests that Boring and others, while failing to appreciate the functional role of Fechner's qualitative mathematics, have correctly construed the inception of psychophysics as an act from philosophical conviction. An equation of mental and physical processes expressed their essential identity symbolically. The fact that atomistic thinking and the concept of kinetic energy conservation also appeared in Fechner's exposition of 1851 suggests that while the practical solution to the problem of mental measurement (via E. H. Weber's law) came to Fechner relatively late in the period between 1851 and 1860, the possibility, in principle, of mental measurement through correlated physical energy changes was coincident with his insight of 1850.

ECHOES OF PHYSICS
IN FECHNER'S PSYCHOPHYSICS OF 1860

Recognizing that philosophy played a major role in Fechner's discovery of 1850, the *tour de force* that he presented to posterity ten years later is nonetheless fundamentally a scientific one. When Fechner realized the possibility of mental measurement, he brought his entire hard-won arsenal of French and German physics to bear on the self-conscious construction of a new science, psychophysics. This is revealed in several macrocharacteristics of the *Elemente*, three of which are described here: its program, its public positivism, and its treatment of psychophysical processes as constructs.

Fechner described his psychophysics as the exact science of the relationship between mind and body. It was to be exact as in physics, having its basis in experience, connecting the facts of experience mathematically, and discovering measures of relevant phenomena when such were not already available.[67] I take these as echoes of the program of Arcueil and as evidence that his founding of the science was far from inadvertent.

Fechner's vision was of a precise scientific treatment of all aspects of psychophysics, yet he saw the work of 1860 as provisional, as ". . . but the paltry beginning of a start";[68] its deliberate arrangement in steps that increasingly depart from the safety of empirical evidence for deductively rich principles of greater generality shadows his *Atomenlehre* of 1855 in its transition from the scientific to the speculative. Yet the empirical portion of the work is a goldmine of precise research reportage on the model of his *Maasbestimmungen* of 1831.

It is significant that Fechner viewed the *Elemente* as a research progress report.[69] The ultimate criteria of the success of the work for Fechner lay, consequently, not in the support for the laws that he himself demonstrated therein, but in two other characteristics transplated from the German physics he had helped to reform. He argued that the work would stand or fall on the generative function served by the theory, in the degree to which it would provide testable ideas that would not have occurred otherwise; and in its public verification, the degree to which its ideas ultimately would gain the support of the exact investigations of the finest specialist scholars.[70]

Philosophy is the key to Fechner's discovery of the formulae of 1851, and the third part of the *Elemente* contains Fechner's view of the implications of psychophysics for metaphysical questions, just as the second part of his *Atomenlehre* provided a metaphysical extension of physical atomism. Yet the public position of the *Elemente*, which supplies the justification for his principle of measurement, is as deliberately a-metaphysical as was Fechner's stance in the *physikalische Atomenlehre:*

   . . . this investigation does not propose to take a position in the controversy about the basic relation of body and mind, which divides materialists and idealists.[71]

Fechner described his own double-aspect view as but one of many possible opinions that may serve to unify the factual relations between body and mind. Psychophysics, however:

> . . . refers to the physical in the sense of physics and chemistry, to the psychical in the sense of experiential psychology without referring back beyond the phenomena in any way to the essence of the body or of the mind in the metaphysical sense.[72]

In the mathematical equation Fechner found an expression for the parallel relation between mental and physical phenomena, which allowed him to remain neutral on the direction of their interdependence.[73] The symmetry of a mathematical function allows the prediction of y from x or x from y without imputing a causal relationship between them. Fechner saw mind and body not in causal relationship at all, but in a relation of simultaneity.[74] Yet, inevitably, his methodology led him to make his approach from the dependence of mind on body, because the measurement of psychical could be obtained only as dependent on the physical.[75] It is in this sense that Fechner speaks of the psychic having its "basis" in the physical, of the physical "underlying" the psychical. And his methodological materialism is unrelenting:

> All of nature is a single continuous system of component parts acting on one another, within which various partial systems create, use, and transmit to each other kinetic energy of different forms, while obeying general laws through which the connections are ruled and conserved.[76]

Given that all natural (including organismic) processes can be reduced to the motions of particles, they can always be measured in principle, if not in practice, indirectly if not directly. Mind is a part of this natural process, thus:

> . . . the law of the conservation of energy is a law for the conservation of the universe, and it is no misfortune that the mind is bound to feel, to think, or to will within the limitations of this law.[77]

The main implication of the universality of the law of the conservation of energy for Fechner was that higher mental activity as well as sensory activity, the activity of the mind as a whole and in detail, is subject to quantitative determination.[78]

Whether the organism is responding to external stimuli or acting on the external world, it is necessary, argued Fechner, to assume the mediation of the body. "Psychophysical" is the word Fechner coined to stand for physiological bodily processes immediately accompanying psychical events. These may be studied through outer or inner psychophysics, depending on whether the focus is on the relation of the mental to the body's external aspects, or to "those internal functions with which the psychic are closely related."[79]

Fechner treated inner psychophysical processes as he treated physical atoms—as constructs. He admitted ". . . their nature may still be quite unknown," but the assumption of their existence is necessary to ". . . the constancy or lawfulness of the relationship of body and mind."[80] Fechner's dilemma was that too little was known of central neural processes to permit a direct attack on inner psychophysics, and he was forced into an indirect assessment of them, as in the indirect measurement of the "impalpable" electricity. He argued that since neurological processes must mediate between stimulus and sensation, if lawful relationships are found between sensation and stimulus (outer psychophysics), these must include lawful relationships between stimulus and inner physical activity.[81]

In summary, we may say of the common presumptions of Fechner's physical and psychophysical science, first, that psychophysical processes and atoms alike were hypothetical constructs whose significance resided in their scientific utility: in their research-generative function and in their function as synthesizing bridges between phenomena hitherto conceived separately. Their utility lay in their amenability to confirmation by experiment. This required that precise testable hypotheses be put in the form of mathematical expressions relating variables whose empirical referents were measurable. Second, whether speaking of the atoms of the scientists or of the psychophysical processes of the scientist, Fechner eschewed essential definitions. Science can and should proceed from a study of phenomena, unencumbered by metaphysical considerations. Third, whether speaking of physical atoms or of mental events, Fechner was speaking of the same world. Science was searching for laws of the greatest generality, and these applied to all of nature, physical and psychological. Atoms and sensations alike were bound by universal law.

TOWARD AN EVALUATION
OF THE RECEPTION OF FECHNERIAN PSYCHOPHYSICS

We would expect Fechner, the physicist, to carry the most salient of his scientific presumptions to the novel problem of psychophysical measurement. That he did so, however, is not trivial. First, it shows as inadequate the assumption that after his major illness, Fechner the physicist changed into Fechner the *Naturphilosoph*. Psychophysics was inspired by philosophical passions, and philosophical thinking was essential in the context of discovery. Yet the salient features of psychophysics in the context of justification are not those of *Naturphilosophie* except in the interesting sense that the drive for theoretical unity that set the German physics of the *Vormärz* apart from the French and from the older indigenous tradition may be seen to have its roots in the unitary outlook of romantic philosophy. The *Elemente* was not written by a man who had abandoned physics for speculation but by a physicist who imposed the integrative vision of *Naturphilosophie* as well as the quantitative experimental rigor of physics on the most disparate of processes.

Secondly, the macrocharacteristics of physics echoed in the *Elemente* may lie at the heart of certain differences between Fechner and the younger generation of philosophers and scientists who forged the new psychology in the next quarter of the century. Reactions to certain of the microconcepts used by Fechner suggest this is so, and they invite scholarly study. For instance, Fechner chose to use the calculus to represent the relation between changes in physical stimulation and mental intensity. To the concrete-minded in his audience this implied that some psychological significance must be associated with infinitely small increments in sensation, and objections were raised that this was absurd in spite of Fechner's warning that psychic elements were convenient mathematical fictions. Similarly, the possibility of negative sensations was inherent in the *Maasformel*. The objection was raised that negative (subthreshold) sensations could have no phenomenal significance.[82] The critical concept of threshold was itself an abstract, statistically defined concept in Fechner's hands. Indeed, he used the concept of negative sensations to deduce the increasing probability of stimulus detection as one approaches threshold from below.

Of great interest to the student of the history of psychology is Fechner's insistence that all lower and higher mental processes are bound by the positivistic principle of the conservation of energy. For Fechner's younger colleague and the founder of experimental psychology, Wilhelm Wundt, would differ by proposing a psychological causality unbounded by energy conservation.[83] This suggests that the relation between Fechner's scientific presumptions and those of the psychology he is said to have influenced deserves closer study. Certainly much of Fechner's scientific platform had more in common with that of the positivists who repudiated Wundt than with that of Wundt himself.[84]

Finally, when Fechner searched in vain for a knowledge of the central nervous system that would permit a direct attack on inner psychophysics, he did not find this information, partly because the biophysicists working on the explanation of biological process in physical–chemical terms showed little interest in the brain and spinal cord. Culotta took this as evidence that biophysicists did not conceive of higher mental functioning in materialistic terms; and he supported this view with an analysis of their treatment of consciousness, showing that no biophysicist defined consciousness physically or chemically, tending rather to draw the outer boundary of their science where consciousness begins.[85] Culotta identified their separation of consciousness from the subject matter of science with the Schellingian idealist tradition, and used it as a means showing the longevity of the romantic influence on German science; consciousness was seen as a source of unity in nature, as a "hallowed cultural concept," but also as a scientifically unassailable one; biophysicists accepted this part of the romantic ideological heritage while rejecting its formal metaphysics.[86]

In this context, Fechner is seen to share a common ideology with the biophysicists rather than being philosophically out of step with other scientists of the 1860s. He shared with them an ametaphysical stance in his science of psychophysics, and he shared also the romantic ideal of unity of knowledge.

But the radical in Fechnerian thought, that which separates him from the idealistic ideology of Schelling and appears to separate him also from his scientific contemporaries, is Fechner's insistence that higher mental activity as well as sensory activity is subject to scientific determination, that the mind thinks, feels, and wills, always within the limitations of the law of the conservation of physical energy. In this important respect, Fechner appears less the epigone *Naturphilosoph* than his contemporaries in biophysics who, ironically, are often regarded as the radicals of nineteenth-century science. Consequently we anticipate that the controversies that ensued over his psychophysics may be understood in terms of resistance to the idea of consciousness as scientifically assailable, as well as in terms of the strictly scientific merits or shortcomings of the provisional *Elemente*.

NOTES

1. Gustav T. Fechner, *Elemente der Psychophysik* (Leipzig: Breitkopf & Hartel, 1860).

2. See particularly Edwin G. Boring, "Fechner: Inadvertent Founder of Psychophysics," *Psychometrika* 26 (1961):3-8; Henri Ellenberger, *The Discovery of the Unconscious: The History and Evolution of Dynamic Psychiatry* (London: Allen Lane The Penguin Press, 1970), p. 216; *Brett's History of Psychology*, ed. R. S. Peters (London: George Allen & Unwin, 1962), p. 580; Robert I. Watson, *The Great Psychologists from Aristotle to Freud* (Philadelphia & New York: J. B. Lippincott, 1963), p. 214; J. R. Kantor, *The Scientific Evolution of Psychology* (Chicago: Principia Press, 1969), Vol. 2, p. 293.

3. In Gustav T. Fechner, *Zend-Avesta oder ueber die Dinge des Himmels und des Jenseits: Vom Standpunkt der Naturbetrachtung* (Leipzig: L. Voss, 1851), pp. 374-75.

4. See particularly Helmut Adler's introduction to Gustav T. Fechner, *Elements of Psychophysics*, tr. Helmut Adler (New York: Holt, Rinehart and Winston, 1966), pp. xix-xxvi; Richard Lowry, *The Evolution of Psychological Theory* (Chicago & New York: Aldine Atherton, 1971), pp. 90-109; Wilhelm Schreier, "Über historische Wurzeln von Fechners Psychophysik," in *Zur Geschichte der Psychologie*, ed. Georg Eckardt (Berlin: VEB Deutscher Verlag der Wissenschaften, 1979), pp. 61-71; Lothar Sprung & Helga Sprung, "Gustav Theodor Fechner—Wege und Abwege in der Begründung der Psychophysik," *Zeitschrift für Psychologie* 93 (1978): 439-54.

5. Biographical details in this paper are taken from Johannes E. Kuntze, *Gustav Theodor Fechner: ein deutsches Gelehrtenleben* (Leipzig: Breitkopf & Härtel, 1892) and from Kurt Lasswitz, *Gustav Theodor Fechner* (Stuttgart: Fr. Frommans Verlag, 1910); a Fechner bibliography by Rudolph Müller appears in the Wundtian edition of Gustav T. Fechner, *Elemente der Psychophysik* (Leipzig: Breitkopf & Härtel, 1889).

6. Lorenz Oken, *Lehrbuch der Naturphilosophie* (Jena: Frommann, 1809-11); for a general discussion of the tradition of *Naturphilosophie* see Gerhard Hennemann, *Naturphilosophie im 19. Jahrhundert* (Freiberg: K. Alber, 1959).

7. Gustav T. Fechner, *Praemissae ad theoriam organismi generalem* (Lipsiae: Staritii, 1823).

8. For an extended discussion of this work and its implications for psychophysics, see Marilyn E. Marshall, "G. T. Fechner: Premises toward a General Theory of Organisms (1823)," *Journal of the History of the Behavioral Sciences* 10 (1974):438-47.

9. Jean-Baptiste Biot, *Lehrbuch der Experimental-Physik*, Volumes 1 and 2 tr. Gustav T. Fechner (Leipzig: L. Voss, 1824). The translation is of the third edition of Biot's *Precis elementaire de physique experimentale* (Paris: Deterville, 1824).

10. For a superb discussion of the work at Arcueil see Maurice Crosland, *The Society of Arcueil: a View of French Science at the Time of Napoleon I* (London: Heinemann Educational Books, 1967).

11. Eugene Frankel, "J. B. Biot and the Mathematization of Experimental Physics in Napoleonic France," *Historical Studies in the Physical Sciences* 8 (1977): 33-72.

12. Gustav T. Fechner, *Maasbestimmungen ueber die galvanische Kette* (Leipzig: F. A. Brockhaus, 1831).

13. For an extended discussion of these characteristics of the Maasbestim-mungen in the context of German physics see Kenneth Caneva, "From Galvanism to Electro-dynamics: the Transformation of German Physics and Its Social Context," *Historical Studies in the Physical Sciences* 9 (1978): 63–159.

14. Frankel, "J. B. Biot," p. 72. For the antitheoretical bent of mid-nineteenth century French physics see also R. Fox, "The Rise and Fall of Laplacean Physics," *Historical Studies in the Physical Sciences* 4 (1974):89–137.

15. Caneva, "From Galvanism," p. 116.

16. Gustav T. Fechner, ed., *Das Hauslexikon* (Leipzig: Breitkopf & Härtel, 1834–38). For an autobiographical account of the illness, see Kuntze, *Gustav Theodor Fechner*, Chapter 5.

17. An extensive account of Fechner's role in the reform of German physics can be found in Kenneth Caneva, "Conceptual and Generational Change in German Physics: The Case of Electricity, 1800–1846," Ph.D. dissertation, Princeton, 1974; for the interplay between philosophy and science, see also T. S. Kuhn, "Energy Conservation as an Example of Simultaneous Discovery," in *Critical Problems in the History of Science*, ed. Marshall Clagett (Madison: University of Wisconsin Press, 1959), pp. 321–56; Arthur Molella, "Philosophy and Nineteenth-Century German Electrodynamics: The Problem of Atomic Action at a Distance," Ph.D. dissertation, Cornell, 1972; Charles Culotta, "German Biophysics, Objective Knowledge, and Romanticism," *Historical Studies in the Physical Sciences* 4 (1974):3–38; L. Pearce Williams, "Kant, *Naturphilosophie* and Scientific Method," in *Foundations of Scientific Method: the Nineteenth Century*, ed. R. N. Giere and R. S. Westfall (Bloomington and London: Indiana University Press, 1973), pp. 3–22.

18. From Kuntze, *Gustav Theodor Fechner*, p. 40.

19. Dr. Mises, *Stapelia Mixta* (Leipzig: L. Voss, 1824), pp. 125, 128.

20. Dr. Mises, *Vergleichende Anatomie der Engel: Eine Skizze* (Leipzig: Baumgartner, 1825).

21. Mises, *Stapelia Mixta*, p. 120. Fechner's verbal picture, if drawn, resembles the interactive model of system-environment relations illustrated by Mario Bunge in *Causality* (Cambridge: Harvard University Press, 1959), p. 126, except that Bunge schematizes the two wholes as asymmetric and irregular with respect to each other, while Fechner would insist on circularity and concentricity. For a discussion of Fechner and the notion of Platonic (spherical) perfection, see Marilyn E. Marshall, "Gustav Fechner, Dr. Mises, and the Comparative Anatomy of Angels," *Journal of the History of the Behavioral Sciences* 5 (1969): 39–58.

22. Mises, *Stapelia Mixta*, pp. 136–37.

23. Ibid., p. 148.

24. Ibid., p. 123.

25. Ibid., pp. 72–73, 34–38.

26. Ibid., p. 71.

27. Fechner, *Zend-Avesta*, Vol. 2, p. 351.

28. Dr. Mises, *Das Büchlein vom Leben nach dem Tode* (Dresden: Ch. F. Grimmer, 1836).

29. Gustav T. Fechner, *Ueber das höchste Gut* (Leipzig: Breitkopf & Härtel, 1846); *Nanna, oder ueber das Seelenleben der Pflanzen* (Leipzig: L. Voss, 1848).

30. For discussion of Schleiden's response to Fechner see William Wood-ward, "Fechner's Panpsychism. A Scientific Solution to the Mind-Body Problem," *Journal of the History of the Behavioral Sciences* 8 (1972):367–86. For

Fechner's reply to Schleiden see Gustav T. Fechner, *Professor Schleiden und der Mond* Leipzig: A. Gumprecht, 1856).

31. Gustav. T. Fechner, "Ueber die Verknüpfung der Faraday'schen Induktions-Erscheinungen mit dem Ampere'schen elektrodynamischen Erscheinungen," *Annalen der Physik und Chemie* 64 (1845):337–45.

32. Wilhelm Weber, *Elektrodynamische Maasbestimmungen* (Leipzig: Weidmann'sche Buchhandlung, 1846).

33. K. H. Wiederkehr, *Wilhelm Eduard Weber. Erforscher der Wellenbewegung und der Elektrizität 1804–1891* (Stuttgart: Wissenschaftliche Verlagsgesellschaft, 1967), pp. 114–15. See also Kuntze, *Gustav Theodor Fechner*, pp. 242–43.

34. Gustav T. Fechner, "Die mathematische Behandlung organischer Gestalten und Processe," *Berichte ueber die Verhandlung der Königlich sachsischen Gesellschaft der Wissenschaften zu Leipzig* 1 (1849): 50–64.

35. Fechner, *Elemente*, Vol. 2, p. 554.

36. Ernst Heinrich Weber, *De pulsu, resorptione, auditu et tactu* (Leipzig: Koehler, 1834; "Der Tastsinn und das Gemeingefühl, "In *Handwörterbuch der Physiologie*, ed. Rudolph Wagner (Braunschweig: Viewig, 1846), Vol. 3, pp. 481–588.

37. Fechner, *Zend-Avesta*, Vol. 2, p. 330. For a discussion of J. F. Herbart's earlier insistence on the unity and simplicity of mind, see John T. Merz, *A History of European Scientific Thought in the Nineteenth Century* (Gloucester, Massachusetts: Peter Smith, 1976), Vol. 2, 497 ff.

38. Fechner, *Zend-Avesta*, Vol. 2, p. 337.

39. Fechner, *Elemente*, Vol. 2, p. 554.

40. Fechner, *Zend-Avesta*, Vol. 2, p. 373.

41. Ibid., Vol. 2, p. 374.

42. Ibid., Vol. 2, p. 375.

43. Ibid., Vol. 2, p. 368.

44. Fechner quotes Wilhelm Weber's letter in *Elemente*, Vol. 2, pp. 557–58.

45. Ibid., Vol. 2, p. 559.

46. Fechner, *Zend-Avesta*, Vol. 2, p. 386.

47. Fechner, *Elemente*, Vol. 2, p. 559.

48. Ibid., Vol. 2, p. 556.

49. Ibid., Vol. 2, p. 558.

50. Fechner's care was not misguided. Even after Helmholtz had deleted the philosophical introduction to his famous paper on the conservation of energy, it had been refused publication in the leading journal of physics, *Annalen der Physik*, on the grounds that it was mathematical and thus smacked dangerously of *Naturphilosophie*. See Leo Königsberger, *Hermann von Helmholtz* (Oxford: Clarendon Press, 1906), tr. Frances Welby, p. 43; see also note 53.

51. Fechner, *Zend-Avesta*, Vol. 2, p. 379.

52. For references to the eighteenth-century conception of *vis viva*, see L. L. Laudan, "The *vis viva* controversy, a post-mortem," *Isis* 59 (1968):131–43. For later antecedents of Helmholtzian conservation see Yehuda Elkana, *The Discovery of the Conservation of Energy* (Cambridge: Harvard University Press, 1974).

53. Although as physicist we might expect Fechner to have been aware of the publication, Merz, *A History*, Vol. 2, pp. 114–15, refers to the fact that Helmholtz's document generally attracted little attention at first because the "reigning school of natural philosophers in Germany discouraged theoretical deductions" as leaning toward *Naturphilosophie*, because mathematical reason-

ing was accessible to only a few scientists, and because of the ambiguity still inherent in the term "force."

54. Fechner, *Elemente*, Vol. 1, p. 34.

55. Gustav T. Fechner, "Ueber das Causalgesetz," *Berichte ueber die Verhandlung der Königlich sächsischen Gesellschaft der Wissenschaften zu Leipzig* 1 (1849): 98-120.

56. Kuhn, "Energy conservation."

57. David E. Leary, "The Philosophical Development of the Conception of Psychology in Germany, 1780-1850," *Journal of the History of the Behavioral Sciences* 14 (1978):113-21; "The Historical Foundation of Herbart's Mathematization of Psychology," *Journal of the History of the Behavioral Sciences* 16 (1980): 150-63.

58. Lowry, *The evolution*, p. 95.

59. Fechner, *Zend-Avesta*, Vol. 2, p. 374.

60. Gustav T. Fechner, *Ueber die physikalische und philosophische Atomenlehre* (Leipzig: H. Mendelssohn, 1855).

61. Fechner, *Elemente*, Vol. 1, p. 34.

62. Schreier, "Ueber historische Wurzeln," pp. 67-68.

63. Fechner, *Zend-Avesta*, Vol. 2, p. 374.

64. See Caneva, "From Galvanism," pp. 116-17, for an analysis of Fechner's hypothetico-deductive style, which, in the *Atomenlehre*, appears in a form generalized to all science.

65. Molella, "Philosophy," pp. 40-70.

66. Fechner had been aware of the controversy over atomism probably since his student days under L. W. Gilbert who, in 1811, had published the first critical and historical review of atomic theory in German. The themes of this controversy (Cartesian corpuscularism vs. Kantian dynamism; empirical-chemical vs. theoretical-physical atomism) were found repeatedly in the physics and chemistry of the literatures Fechner had translated. Fechner himself wrote several original articles employing both chemical and physical atomism, and among the original Fechneriana in the second German edition of Biot's *Précis* was an atomic treatment of the structure of matter.

67. Fechner, *Elemente*, Vol. 1, p. v.

68. Ibid., Vol. 1, p. ix.

69. Ibid., Vol. 2, p. vii.

70. Ibid., Vol. 1, p. ix.

71. Ibid., Vol. 1, p. xi.

72. Ibid., Vol. 1, p. 8.

73. Ibid., Vol. 1, p. 8.

74. Gustav T. Fechner, *In Sachen der Psychophysik* (Leipzig: Breitkopf und Härtel, 1877), p. 66.

75. Fechner, *Elemente*, Vol. 1, p. 9.

76. Ibid., Vol. 1, p. 26.

77. Ibid., Vol. 1, p. 36.

78. Ibid., Vol. 1, p. 55.

79. Ibid., Vol. 1, pp. 10-11.

80. Ibid., Vol. 1, p. 11.

81. Ibid., Vol. 1, p. 12.

82. For surveys of criticisms of the *Elemente*, see Boring, *A History*, pp. 289-94; Edwin G. Boring, *Sensation and Perception in the History of Psychology* (New York: Appleton-Century-Crofts, 1942), pp. 44-45; William R.

Woodward, "A Case Study in Scientific Revolutions: Kuhn, Popper, Lakatos, and Psychophyiscs." Unpublished ms. presented at the 86th Annual Convention of the American Psychological Association, at Toronto, Canada, August, 1978; Constantin Gutberlet, *Psychophysik: Historisch-Kritische Studien ueber experimentelle Psychologie* (Mainz: Kirchheim, 1905), pp. 194–221.

83. So little regard did Fechner have for processes purely psychological that when Wundt confided his fond plans for the founding of a psychological laboratory, Fechner wryly told him that the work of such a laboratory would surely not take many years to complete. In Wilhelm Wundt, *Erlebtes und Erkanntes* (Stuttgart: Kröner, 1920), p. 304.

84. See Kurt Danziger, "The Positivist Repudiation of Wundt," *Journal of the History of the Behavioral Sciences* 15 (1979): 205–30.

85. Culotta, "German Biophysics," pp. 24–27.

86. Ibid., p. 26.

4

The Theory of Will
versus the Science of Mind

Lorraine J. Daston

When the British psychologist James Sully addressed the Neurological Society on "The Psycho-Physical Process in Attention" in 1889, he could assume that he and his audience were "agreed upon the possibility of a true science of psychology, or, if the expression is preferred, physiological psychology, which proceeds by bringing together as closely as possible the results of subjective and objective research."[1] A survey of the late nineteenth- and early twentieth-century psychological literature in Britain and the United States bears out Sully's identification of "scientific" (or "new") with physiological psychology, although the terms encompassed several variations on the physiological theme.[2] Moderates of Sully's stamp hoped to reconcile the "old" (pejoratively known by its critics also as the "metaphysical" or "spiritual") psychology that depended on the subjective testimony of introspection with the allegedly

I would like to thank David Leary and William Woodward for their comments on an earlier version of this paper (delivered at the American Psychological Association meetings in September, 1980) and Gary Hatfield for his criticisms of subsequent drafts. Deborah Johnson corrected several errors of fact and interpretarion.

objective methods of physiological observation. Extremists on both sides of the debate argued for more monistic approaches that granted priority of method and subject matter to either mind or brain. But almost all combatants would have concurred that Sully's topic, the nature of the intertwined problems of volition and the associated process of attention, lay at the heart of the controversy. As G. F. Stout remarked in his review of Henry Maudsley's materialistic treatment of the issue, "The metaphysical stronghold is the freedom of a spiritual will; if once this airy citadel be carried, the champions of 'high mental philosophy' will be able to hold out no more."[3]

The discussions of volition that thus dominated turn-of-the-century British and American psychology took on a significance that dwarfed the theoretical interest of the will per se in contemporary psychology. Not only were the traditional foundations of ethics and jurisprudence placed in jeopardy;[4] the scientific future of psychology itself seemed to hang in the balance. This paper treats the second aspect of the controversy over volition.[5] I propose to examine the contemporary conceptions of scientific method and explanation that made current theories of volition apparently incompatible with a truly scientific psychology. By situating the debate within a more general methodological context, I hope to shed light not only upon a central concern of British and American psychology at the turn of the century, but also to explore the ways in which the controversy over volition within psychology threatened the philosophical foundations of the natural sciences in general.

THE CHALLENGE OF THE SCIENCE OF MIND

Philosophers and historians of science interested in the development and application of views on scientific method and explanation have generally confined their studies to the natural sciences.[6] To the extent that they have considered the reflections of social scientists on such issues, they have tended, with some justice, to regard these as self-conscious borrowings from the natural sciences. Although opinions diverge concerning the wisdom of such imitation, no one doubts that social scientists of every stripe are notoriously preoccupied with establishing the scientific credentials of their disciplines. But the historical and philosophical interest of such science-envy has been assumed to be at best parochial, restricted to the social sciences themselves, and at worst derivative, since discussions among social scientists about the nature of science per se seem pale reflections (or ludicrous caricatures) of analyses best conducted firsthand, that is, upon the natural sciences.

Yet the most serious challenges to late nineteenth-century views of science—its characteristic scope, methods, explanations, and assumptions—came from the fledgling social sciences, and especially (in Britain and the United States) from psychology. The debate over the rights of psychology as a member of the confraternity of sciences is a venerable one, and one whose reverberations extend beyond psychology proper. The late nineteenth-century controversy over the prospects for a "science of mind" in Britain and the United States challenged not only the aspiring science of psychology, but also the philosophical framework for science that had been the legacy of the Scientific Revolution. Within psychology, the question of volition polarized the discipline into factions deeply divided over questions of the legitimate methods, forms of explanation, and even subject matter of the discipline. These divisions in turn called into question the philosophical precepts that had guided natural scientists since the seventeenth century.

I will argue that the ultimate implications of the paired metaphysical and methodological revolutions that had inaugurated the new science of the seventeenth century were not spelled out until the latter half of the nineteenth century, and that the occasion was the science of mind rather than that of matter. Proponents of the "new psychology" (or rather, new psychologies, in the plural) and spokesmen for the more established sciences disagreed sharply over the precise character that such a science might assume, and the conflict among these factions revealed inherent instabilities such as mind/body interaction in the program that Descartes and others had charted for the natural sciences in the seventeenth century and thereafter. Peculiarly psychological subjects, particularly the theory of volition, also undermined contemporary treatments of scientific explanation by John Herschel, John Stuart Mill, William Whewell, and William Stanley Jevons. At stake was not only the possibility of a science of psychology, but the conception of science itself.

The special status of psychology with respect to four central issues in nineteenth-century Anglo-American philosophy of science made it the pivot around which far-reaching discussions of scientific method and explanation turned: Cartesian dualism, reductionism along the lines of the primary/secondary quality distinction, methodological objectivity, and causal determinism (in either the strong sense of necessary connection or the weak sense of constant conjunction). Preliminary to an examination of how the new psychology pitted these philosophical commitments against one another, I will briefly outline each position.

THE PHILOSOPHICAL BACKGROUND
TO THE NEW PSYCHOLOGY

According to Descartes, created substances were of two kinds, and two kinds only, "corporeal or thinking," or body and soul.[7] Each substance dictated its own standards for study: the natural sciences treated brute, passive matter from the sole standpoint of "the figure, motion and magnitude of each body, and examined what must follow from their mutual concourse according to the laws of mechanics";[8] while the active, perceiving, willing soul remained intractable to such mechanical descriptions. Descartes claimed the existence of free will to be the first and foremost of our self-evident innate notions, and identified it as that which ultimately distinguished man from machines, rendering him worthy of praise or blame; "For we do not praise automatic machines although they respond exactly to the movements which they were destined to produce, since their actions are performed necessarily."[9] Whereas all the phenomena of nature could be likened to a machine, the soul, and especially its noblest attribute, the will, resisted the simile.

Although Descartes premised this system upon interactions between these two ontological realms, the precise nature of these contacts between mind and matter was only sketched. As concerns the mediation of the human soul and body, Descartes located their point of intersection at the pineal gland in the brain, whose movements corresponded in one-to-one fashion with perceptions in the soul and which conversely could be "diversely moved by the soul, or by such other cause, whatever it is" to mobilize in turn the bodily machine.[10] At the level of natural phenomena, Descartes evidently relied upon incessant divine participation ("intervention" hardly does justice to such unremitting labor) or human action to imbue inert matter with motion.[11] In fact, action in the world machine precisely paralleled action in the bodily machine, in both cases stemming from the external exercise of divine and human volition.

These problematic but essential points of contact between mind and matter saddled Descartes' successors with a double dilemma: the two tiers could not be collapsed one into the other since they were ontologically incommensurable, nor yet could they be sealed off completely from one another, since the soul registered perceptions transmitted through the body, and the body (and the world) were literally animated by the active will. The unity of scientific explanations suffered on two counts: first, because psychology, the study of mind, had been defined out of the purview of the natural sciences;[12] and, second, because the sciences of matter (without pyschology) could not be ontologically self-sufficient. Although a third layer of "active principles" and "forces" was eventually interpolated between passive matter and active mind to permit God to retire to a more managerial role in creation, the categories used to describe activity in both the world and bodily machines were nonetheless imported wholesale from the vocabulary of mind, particularly of volition.[13]

A second Cartesian legacy also left its impress upon late nineteenth-century British and American debates over the scientific prospects of psychology. Descartes, along with several other seventeenth-century writers, including Galileo and Locke, had distinguished the primary qualitites of shape, size, and motion from the secondary qualities of color, taste, smell, etc.[14] The rationale for and inventory of primary qualities varied from author to author, but the epistemological claim that primary qualities resembled the elements of reality and secondary qualities merely represented them determined a characteristic form of reductionist explanation in post-seventeenth-century natural science. The raw material of experience was carefully sifted into primary and secondary qualities, and the latter correlated with—and thereby reduced to or explained by—the former.

The primary/secondary quality distinction presented late-nineteenth-century psychologists with an ambiguous model of scientific explanation. The most obvious strategy identified mental events with secondary, neural events with primary qualities and performed the materialist reduction.[15] However, there were other possibilities, including not only the idealist obverse but also the reduction of certain elements of consciousness (such as attention, feelings of pleasure or pain) to others that were deemed to be more fundamental.[16] Still others rejected the primary/secondary quality distinction outright as inimical to any psychology that purported to take the data of consciousness seriously.[17] The very breadth of the spectrum of opinions on this topic indicates its centrality in contemporary views of scientific explanation. Just as mind/matter dualism contradicted the equally entrenched precept of a unified scientific explanation[18] in the case of psychology, so the primary/secondary quality distinction collided with militant empericism, again in the context of psychology.[19]

Psychology, with its inherently subjective content, also challenged the dictum of objectivity. Although at least arguably empirical, the data of introspection could not satisfy the requirement of direct intersubjective confirmation.[20] Psychologists attempted various compromises to accommodate data to method, ranging from the behavioral (for example, the universal language of facial expressions) to the neurological.[21] Defenders of introspection for their part understood that this "special method or instrument" would sharply demarcate psychology from the natural sciences.[22]

Finally, psychology threatened to undermine the concept of causation, viewed either as necessary connection or merely uniform succession, which served as a demarcation criterion for nineteenth-century philosophy of science. That is, determinism of some description was thought to be a precondition for the scientific treatment of phenomena. The very possibility of science was predicated upon a manifest orderliness in events, which John Stuart Mill elevated to the principle of the uniformity of nature, in contrast to a random congeries of phenomena. Early in the century, volition became closely identified with chance in the epistemic interpretation of probability championed by Laplace, Quételet, and De Morgan. Briefly, both free will and chance came to be viewed as apparent disruptions of the causal order, and therefore as kindred classes of events. Both posed problems for thoroughgoing determinists like Laplace, and it was natural that they should be assimilated into one another. At least three distinct readings can be extracted from nineteenth-century discussions of chance concerning the opposition of chance and necessity: chance as a figment of our ignorance concerning the necessary laws that must obtain;[23] chance as the absence of purpose in contrast to the "blind" fatalism of necessity;[24] and chance as a varying, perturbing cause coincidentally superimposed upon a uniformly acting cause to create statistical spread.[25]

The first and third usages exposed volition as a glaring anomaly in scientific explanation, particularly after the principle of the conservation of energy seemed to plug all leaks in the natural world; while the second provided proponents of more traditional views on the spontaneity of will with ammunition for their cause. Given this tangle of ambiguities, discussions of the bearing of chance and necessity upon the psychological theory of volition often obscured more than they illumined. As in the cases of Cartesian dualism, the primary/secondary quality distinction, and the requirement of objectivity, debates over causation in psychology served to dramatize tensions inherent in nineteenth-century views of scientific explanation and of chance. Although these tensions also surfaced in other contexts, nowhere did they emerge so starkly as in the controversy over the new psychology.

The overlapping implications of these four issues obliged the participants in the debate over the new psychology to blend appeals to metaphysical, explanatory, and methodological precepts in their arguments. However, it will be helpful for the sake of clarity to distinguish these various levels of analysis with examples drawn from the controversy itself. Metaphysical claims concerning the ultimate constitution of the world—the bedrock reality, so to speak—were based upon the Cartesian dualism in which mind and matter each possessed a distinctive causal structure. Nineteenth-century materialists rejected dualism, but they retained the Cartesian assumption that material processes were marshaled into an inexorable causal chain. Explanatory criteria could thus dictate metaphysical allegiances: if strict determinism was reckoned indispensable to an acceptable scientific explanation and determinism was furthermore linked exclusively to the domain of matter, then a materialistic psychology was at a distinct advantage among rival accounts. Standards for a satisfactory explanation might also be keyed to intelligibility: one might prefer primary qualities as fundamental units of explanation on the grounds either that the former were more transparent to the understanding or that the reductionist form of such an explanation satisfied some principle of intellectual parsimony.[26] Finally, methodological criteria such as the possibility of public access to evidence might enter into the evaluation of the scientific merit of a theory. While one could imagine metaphysically neutral methodological criteria, in practice the demand for objective observations favored theories with a materialist bias. In principle, nerves were more intersubjectively accessible than thoughts.

Psycho-physiology held out the promise of reconciling psychology to the combined demands of these metaphysical, explanatory, and methodological precepts. Proponents of the new psychology of psycho-physiology proclaimed it to be a true *science* of mind, shifting the traditional alliance of psychology with logic, metaphysics, and ethics to one with physiology. Many currents swelled this tide. In France, Auguste Comte's positivism upheld the unity of the sciences on both historical and explanatory grounds, relegating psychology to biology and dismissing introspection as a vestige of a more primitive stage of scientific development.[27] Wundt's pioneering research in psycho-physiology made Germany the center for the alliance Comte had envisioned between the two disciplines, and the work of Johannes Müller, Pierre Flourens, Marshall Hall, Hughlings Jackson, and others built upon and internationalized the endeavor.[28] Investigations of hypnotism and somnambulism straddled distinctions between voluntary and involuntary actions. Philosophical materialism, propounded with missionary zeal by Ziehen in Germany, Ribot in France, and Maudsley in Britain, also lent support to those who hoped to colonize psychology as a subdiscipline of physiology. Research conducted by Ferrier and Broca on cerebral localization of higher mental functions applied further pressure to mind/matter dualism. In the hands of Herbert Spencer and Darwin himself, evolutionary biology alloyed with the old associationism and the new physiology entered the lists as yet another candidate for a true science of psychology.[29]

Yet one should not leap to the conclusion that it was particular discoveries in the newly thriving areas of psycho-physiological and evolutionary research that compelled late-nineteenth-century thinkers to reconsider the possibilities for a science of mind. For although studies of reflex action and cerebral localization made some headway during this period, even the boldest proponents of the view that "movements of particles of organized matter are causes or universal concomitants of all mental processes" admitted that neurological proof was not forthcoming. Neurological mechanisms posited for mental phenomena like attention and volition relied principally or exclusively upon analogical reasoning.[30] Indeed, the analogy proceeded at two levels: at the theoretical level, the neurological mechanism in question apparently possessed the same global properties —and these properties were often quite global, for example, tension and subsequent resolution—as the mental process to be explained; and at the metaphysical level, mind in general and will in particular were to be subordinated to the hegemony of causal—and therefore by implication physiological—explanations.

It was the metaphysical level of analogy that stiffened the conviction of those who spun out these neurological hypotheses that future research would vindicate them. Henry Maudsley, in his provocatively titled *Physiology of Mind*, argued from the sweeping assumption of the "continuity of nature" against those who demanded more concrete assurances that psycho-physiology was the long-awaited science of mind.[31] Although critics as influential as William James might angrily object that "It is really monstrous to see the *prestige* of 'science' invoked for a materialistic conclusion which, were they only used for spiritualistic ends, would be hooted at as unscientific in the extreme,"[32] the prestige, if not the "concrete facts" James demanded, undeniably rested on the material, mechanistic side of the Cartesian divide. And it was this prestige, rather than any hard results, which prompted T. H. Huxley and others to anoint psycho-physiology as the true science of mind, and to wave aside the mind itself as a mere byproduct of brain.

That fact that very different brands of "scientific" psychology joined forces in the campaign against consciousness, volition, introspection and the other distinctive aspects of mind suggests that the battle was waged more at the metaphysical than at the factual level. Although both associationists like Alexander Bain and evolutionists like Spencer did graft some muscular physiology onto their theories, it was not a penchant for specifically physiological explanations that united the new "scientific" approaches to mental life. What psycho-physiologists, associationists, and evolutionists all shared was chiefly a belief that the expanding empire of deterministic scientific explanation was synonymous with intellectual progress, and that the category of mind, conceived as self-determining ego, posed the most formidable obstacle to that advance. Each school, however, attacked this metaphysical impasse from a different angle, and the resulting theories agreed in little more than the elimination of the will and in manifestos proclaiming the superior scientific merit of each. I will analyze three major lines of attack—associationism, physiological reductionism, and psychophysical parallelism—and the counterattacks these provoked.[33]

ASSOCIATIONISM AND THE THEORY OF WILL

Associationism was already a venerable psychological tradition both in Britain and in France by the middle of the nineteenth century.[34] With its mechanical overtones (atomistic ideas attracted or repelled one another), associationism had always harmonized well with prevailing physical theories of the same bent. Nineteenth-century associationists, most notably James Mill and Alexander Bain, infused new life into the theory by borrowing eclectically from more recent physiological findings. Bain's *On the Study of Character* (1861) reflected the influence of the cerebral localization doctrines of phrenology; later works, such as *Mental and Moral Science* (1868), incorporated recent findings in physiology.[35]

Bain's conception of the aims and methods of mental science and the role of volition within that science marked a turning-point in the debate. Like his eighteenth-century predecessors, Bain took the data of introspection as his departure point, but he sought to generalize this data into a more scientifically respectable form in two ways: first, by correlating mental processes with hypothetical neural or muscular motions; and, second, by correlating internal states with external conduct. Despite the fact that such correlations varied even for individuals over time and that the motions of the brain had yet to be mapped, Bain insisted that these in principle observable states would supply psychologists with a common measure for thoughts, feelings, and volitions: "The only solution of the difficulty is . . . [to] accept identical objective marks, as showing identical subjective states." Bain's own survey of the limitations of this assumption even for a single individual suggested that it was a concession to method rather than to fact.[36]

Bain's treatment of will amply demonstrates the hybrid nature of his associationism, which blended psychological "effort" with physiological "energy." It also displays the stamp of the dominant nineteenth-century models of scientific explanation, the theories of evolution and energy. Indeed, Bain's theory of volition precisely paralleled the biological theory of evolution in its structure. A burst of spontaneous "energy" stored up from food and sleep impels the organism willy-nilly into action of an entirely undirected sort; the resulting pleasure or pain forges associations between the act and its consequences. Here, the spontaneous explosion of bodily energy corresponded to the random variation of mutation, selected for or against by the environmental pressure of pleasure or pain. In this blundering, trial-and-error fashion, the child converts originally arbitrary, involuntary acts into a repertoire of voluntary conduct to be summoned up on command. This command invokes no impetus of undetermined will, however, but only a weighing of motives born of remembered or anticipated pleasure or pain. The undifferentiated energy of volition automatically responds to the levers of pleasure and pain without any intervention of the active subject:

> No formal resolution of the mind, adopted after consideration or debate, no special intervention of the 'ego', or the personality, is essential to this putting forth of the energy of retaining on the one hand, or of repudiation on the other, what is felt to be clearly suitable, to the feelings or aims of the moment.[37]

Viewed in terms of the methodological prohibitions that encumbered mental science, Bain's theory is a curious compromise. While he accepted the testimony of consciousness as the proper subject matter of psychology, he insisted that introspection must be broadened by publicly observable concomitants, however speculative the connection between the two. Although he laced his explanations liberally with physiology, Bain nonetheless couched his explanations in psychological terms: pain and pleasure were ultimately feelings, not neural tremors. Yet some mental entities were evidently more real than others. The experiences of pleasure and pain were primary, but the equally vivid experiences of deliberation, choice, and effort counted only as a kind of secondary quality to be explained in terms of pleasure and pain: "So that 'effort' really means the muscular consciousness accompanying voluntary activity, and more especially in the painful stages."[38] Mind and matter remained distinct, but they somehow interacted through vaguely specified exchanges of energy. Moreover, Bain had emasculated mind by rendering will automatic, thus depriving mind of its characteristic features of activity, purpose, and choice. Here was a science of mind in its objective method and determinist explanations, but one in which mind was all but unrecognizable.

Hugo Münsterberg, the German psychologist who later directed Harvard's pyschological laboratory, supplied associationism with a more systematic scientific rationale. By clarifying issues that Bain had left nebulous, Münsterberg's psychology became the most daring statement of the new science of mind. Münsterberg's views are especially interesting, since although he was the foremost spokesman for a reduction of volition to a "complex of sensations" and of Wundt's apperception to reflex action,[39] he also considered himself to be a champion of Fichtean idealism against scientific naturalism. In order to reconcile these polar positions, Münsterberg was obliged to draw sharp distinctions between psychological theory and the reality it purported to describe and explain.

Münsterberg attracted the attention of American and British pyschologists with his attempts to account for all psychological phenomena in terms of mechanistic laws of association describing the inexorable succession of one discrete mental state by another. Münsterberg readily admitted that such descriptions betrayed the inner experience of the continuity of consciousness and the teleology of will, but he contended that scientific psychology made no pretense of dealing with mental reality, but only with abstractions from that reality. Like physics, psychology belonged to the class of "objectifying" sciences that describe necessary sequences of events artificially excised from the flow of experience and decomposed into elements. In contrast, "subjectifying" sciences such as history aimed at interpretation, appreciation, and understanding and embraced the "ethical and practical reality" of the will.[40]

Münsterberg had thus redrawn the Cartesian boundary to split the original category of mind in two, one part preserving activity and will but belonging to interpretive history rather than explanatory science, the other methodologically indistinguishable from the material universe studied by physicists. In so doing, he advanced his own version of the primary/secondary quality distinction for psychology between the atomized abstractions of scientific psychology and the actual flow of consciousness. Yet despite his claim that any genuine science of psychology must "objectify" private mental states into communicable abstractions, Münsterberg inverted the seventeenth-century hierarchy. For Descartes, it had been the primary qualities that figured as units of scientific explanation and counted as fundamental, and the secondary qualities of tint, timbre, texture, and so forth that were discounted as epiphenomenal. For Münsterberg, the will of daily experience and history was in fact metaphysically primary, in opposition to its "unreal transformation" by scientific pyschology. In effect, Münsterberg had driven a wedge between explanatory and metaphysical units: what was primary for the purposes of rendering a scientific explanation was only secondary for the purposes of a faithful account of the psychological reality to be explained. Hence, Münsterberg repeatedly berated his critics for misunderstanding his claims for that psychology:

> My critics ought to show that my analysis of the psychological data of the will is incorrect, and, instead of that, they only show that the analysis of the psychological facts is not a description of the real will. But who in the world has pretended that it is? . . . if you want it as an object of psychology, that is, of the science which describes and explains mental life, you must transform mental life into a set of objects and substitute in that service the psycho-physical personality for the real center of subjective functions.[41]

However, Münsterberg's critics were probably correct in their suspicions that once the active, self-determining will had been banished from the domain of science, no amount of ontological glorification would redeem it. For in British and American, if not continental, intellectual circles, "scientific" had come to mean "true." As A. E. Taylor remarked in his review of the first volume of Münsterberg's *Grundzüge der Psychologie* (Principles of Psychology, 1900) in *Mind*, the opposition was not so much between the objectifying sciences of interpretation and understanding, but rather "between science, which can only describe with more or less concreteness, and the intuition of the poetic genius who 'understands'."[42] Exalted as poetry might be, it could not carry the conviction of science. Taylor further protested that Münsterberg had committed himself too narrowly to physics as his model science, for biologists were able to invoke teleological explanations for adaptation and survival without being branded unscientific. Taylor voiced the fears of many of his colleagues when he suggested that Münsterberg had sacrificed "the real facts of mental life" to a petty consistency of method, complaining that "the elimination of all teleological concepts amounts to much more than 'transformation' of real mental life into a form suitable for scientific analysis; it is much more like a new creation of a fanciful world of non-human automata."[43]

In the eyes of Taylor, James Ward, Andrew Seth Pringle-Pattison, G. F. Stout, and others, Münsterberg's objectifying psychology had retained the contents of consciousness as the subject matter of scientific pyschology only as an absurd caricature. Mind without active will was simply not science. Attempts to distinguish between primary and secondary mental phenomena foundered for lack of any criterion that did not smuggle in the old dichotomy between purpose and mechanical law at some other point. Most psychologists were willing to tolerate some abstraction in the service of scientific explanation along the Galilean–Newtonian model, but many objected to abstractions that seemed to denature mental phenomena altogether. Because they lacked the mathematical framework that had guided such idealizations in the physical sciences, psychologists accused one another of imposing arbitrary simplifications. As long as associationist accounts dealt with introspective evidence only partially correlated with behavior or physiology, the difficulties of dualism persisted, since introspective experience seemed to testify unequivocally to the existence of an undetermined will. Heterogeneously mental and material explanations could only reintroduce the problem of mind/brain interaction at other points.

PSYCHOPHYSICAL PARALLELISM, CONSCIOUS AUTOMATISM, AND THE THEORY OF WILL

T. H. Huxley, the flamboyant biologist and popularizer of the new theories of evolution and physiology, set out to cut this Gordian knot with the radically homogeneous hypothesis of conscious automata. In his 1874 Presidential Address to the British Association for the Advancement of Science, Huxley revived Descartes' mechanistic physiology but went Descartes one better. Whereas Descartes had stretched the model of reflex action to include all nonhuman organisms as automata and so subject to mechanical laws resembling those that governed inanimate matter, Huxley suggested that consciousness itself was an automatic function. Because Descartes had considered consciousness to be the sine qua non of mind and thus beyond the ken of mechanical explanation and yet classed physiology with the sciences of matter, he had been compelled to take the counterintuitive position that animals lacked any consciousness whatsoever. When a dog yelped upon being kicked, it was not expressing the sensation of pain but only reacting automatically: a reflex arc reflected the stimulus of the kick into the responding yelp without any intervention of feelings. Huxley abandoned this implausible artifice by granting consciousness or at least sensitivity to animals. But in so doing he did not relinquish Descartes' mechanical program for animal physiology, and therefore he made consciousness itself automatic. Defying what he called the "drum ecclesiastic," Huxley did not hesitate to extend the label of conscious automata from frogs, the source of the bulk of the evidence for his hypothesis, to humans.

Yet Huxley no more denied the existence of mind and the distinctive experiences of consciousness and volition that attested to it than the associationists had. Unwilling to join the ranks of the thoroughgoing materialists and enough of an introspective empiricist to acknowledge at least the appearance of mind, Huxley resorted to the hypothesis that mental states were the "symbols" of brain states. The causal arrow pointed in only one direction, from the brain state that was the "invariable antecedent" of each mental state. Huxley was hardly more explicit about the neurological details of the "special apparatus" that coordinated sensations, emotions, thoughts, volitions, and so forth with the brain states they purportedly symbolized than Descartes had been concerning the analogous apparatus in animals. But Huxley was able to cite the responses of galvanically stimulated decerebrated frogs and studies of somnambulism resulting from brain injuries in support of his neo-Cartesianism and to refurbish Descartes' rough-hewn model of reflex action with the latest findings on sensory/motor pathways. It was primarily consistency of method and explanation rather than new evidence that recommended Huxley's hypothesis.

With consistency paramount, Huxley attacked the anomaly of volition. While he conceded the existence of the feeling of volition, Huxley refused to grant it the special status Descartes and his successors had accorded it. Like all other states of consciousness, volition was "immediately caused by molecular changes in the brain substance." Here was an extreme version of the primary/secondary quality distinction: the seventeenth-century metaphysics had dis-

carded the bulk of our sensations as at best mere signs of an underlying reality of mathematized properties but had certified at least
these perceptions of size, shape, velocity, and configuration as the
unvarnished truth. Moreover, some internal sensations, such as the
intuition of clear and distinct ideas or the sense of effort accompanying
willing, enjoyed an immediate self-evidence at least as compelling as
any external sensation. Huxley tolerated no such exceptions. *All*
conscious states were merely signs, bound to the real order of things
by ties possibly as arbitrary as those that link words and things and
just as impotent as words to affect the things they signify. In particular, Huxley emphasized that "the feeling we call volition is not the
cause of the voluntary act, but the symbol of that state of the brain
which is the immediate cause of the act."[44]

Here, then, were the new metaphysical foundations for a science
of mind indistinguishable in method and mode of explanation from
the sciences of matter. But these very foundations made such a
science superfluous. If states of mind simply signified states of brain,
it was at best circuitous and redundant to study the former at all,
and at worst to confuse the study of words with that of the world
they described. Given a choice, brain states were methodologically
preferable to mental states, for the former were, in principle at least,
observable. Psychology would be better absorbed by neurophysiology.
Psychologists such as James Sully might protest that neurophysiology
without psychology would be unable to define its subject matter—
did the neural quiver in question correspond to a throbbing pain,
a mathematical deduction, or a moral choice?—but they could not
invert the hierarchy of explanation unless they rejected Huxley's
metaphysics outright.[45] So long as brain states *caused* mental states,
psychology would remain at best an ancillary science—a kind of
natural history of the mind—which ceded the ultimate explanation
of the phenomena it described to neurophysiology.

While it seemed to offer an escape from Huxley's physiological
imperialism, the doctrine of psycho-physical parallelism was really no
more than a variation on the same metaphysical theme. The mathematician William Kingdon Clifford, like Huxley a controversial
polemicist for scientific naturalism in Britain, sympathized with
Huxley's aim to unite the sciences of physical, animate, and conscious
phenomena within a single explanatory framework. Clifford agreed
that physiology would bridge these last two realms. However, he
deepened the abyss between the realms of matter and mind in
response to Huxley's claim of a one-way causal arrow between
brain and mental states. Clifford could no more countenance this
interaction than he could the reverse influence of mind upon brain,

which jeopardized the principle of the conservation of energy. Convinced that mind and matter were categorically immiscible, Clifford fell back on Malebranche's occasionalism, minus the occasions. According to the doctrine of psychophysical parallelism, mental and physical facts "are on two utterly different platforms—the physical facts go along by themselves, and the mental facts go along by themselves. There is a parallelism between them, but there is no interference of one with the other."[46] That volition might span the two platforms struck Clifford as "neither true nor untrue, but nonsense." Presumably, Huxley's hypothesis that brain generated mind was equally nonsensical, thus implying that psychology could maintain its disciplinary independence vis à vis physiology.

However, Clifford's psychophysical parallelism also threatened the self-sufficiency of psychology in just the way that Huxley's conscious automatism had. Once a complete correlation of observable physical facts (in this case, brain states) and inaccessible mental states had been posited, the methodological preference for the former asserted itself. Moreover, if Hume's view of causation as merely constant conjunction were also assumed, Clifford's parallelism was indistinguishable from Huxley's physiological reductionism. Clifford himself recognized the explanatory implications of his parallelism, observing that ". . . the fact that mind and brain are associated in a definite way, and in that particular way that I have mentioned, affords a very strong presumption that we have here something which can be *explained*; that it is possible to find a reason for this exact correspondence."[47] Although it was conceivable that brain might be explained in terms of mind, the possibility of observing the former together with the causal gaps in the latter made brain the inevitable explanatory substratum. Psychology would thus give way to neurophysiology.

THE DEFENSE OF WILL

The associationists had resolved the anomaly of mind by transforming it beyond recognition, the proponents of the hypothesis of conscious automatism by making it irrelevant. All invoked the principle of the continuity of nature and the precepts of the scientific method; none thought it possible to reconcile the Cartesian concept of mind with Cartesian dictates for science. Their critics, many of them sympathetic to or active in psycho-physiological research but insistent upon the prerogatives of a more traditional psychology, were willing to sacrifice the seventeenth-century conception of science in order to hold fast to the seventeenth-century conception of mind. By staking their claims on the testimony of immediate experience, they hoped to drive a wedge of empiricism between mechanistic determinism and science per se. Henry Sidgwick summed up the full force of this appeal to mental experience against the "almost overwhelming cumulative proof" for determinism, which he deemed to be "more than balanced by a single argument on the other side: the immediate affirmation of consciousness in the moment of deliberate volition."[48] Although all of the defenders of the traditional theory of volition ultimately based their case on introspective empiricism, their strategies varied widely. The most naive of these defenders of mind retreated to an unintelligible double-aspect theory; their more sophisticated allies appealed to a new philosophy of science.

W. B. Carpenter, author of the emblematically titled *Mental Physiology* (1874) and eminent psycho-physiologist, was perhaps the most enthusiastic convert to Fechner's double-aspect theory, which considered mind and matter as two aspects of a single world-stuff viewed from different perspectives. Just as a curved surface appeared convex or concave depending on the angle of vision, so the metaphor went, so phenomena seemed psychological or physiological. However striking the analogy, Carpenter's monism did little in practice to mend the contradictions between what Carpenter admitted to be the guiding principles of his treatise: "that of the dependence of the Automatic activity of the Mind upon conditions which bring it within the *nexus* of Physical Causation; and that of the existence of an independent Power, controlling and directing that activity which we call Will. I can only say that both are equally true to my own consciousness. . . ."[49] It was the conviction carried by his own conscious experience that prompted Carpenter to attack what he perceived as the one-sided materialism of the determinist camp, which singled out physical facts "as the only thing with which science has to do," and whose overweening metaphysical pretensions led them to dismiss as " 'nonsense' the doctrine (based on the universal experience of mankind)" of the efficacy of the will.[50]

Although Carpenter's alternative metaphysics won few adherents (the physicist John Tyndall tartly inquired "Why should the phenomena have two sides?"), his appeal to the "universal experience of mankind" found hearty echoes among psychologists, physiologists, and philosophers who could not second Huxley's identification of scientific progress with "the extension of the province of what we call matter and causation, and the concomitant banishment from all regions of human thought what we call spirit and spontaneity."[51]

All conceded that some abstraction from experience was a prerequisite to scientific explanation but protested that in banishing will the determinists had eliminated the phenomena altogether. Their version of psychology without will was as impoverished as celestial mechanics would be without planetary motion.

Primary/secondary quality distinctions could be drawn among the givens of consciousness itself, as well as between mind and brain. Volition figured both as a secondary quality, as in Bain's attempts to explicate it in terms of the root feelings of pleasure and pain, and as a primary quality, depending on the expositor. Edward Franklin Buchner defended volition as a "scientific datum" on the grounds that it was universal, definite, and typical of all conscious processes and therefore counted as a primary quality for psychology: "Volition is ready and able to explain in a psychological manner, rather than being in need of explanation itself."[52] Significantly, Buchner grounded his retention of volition as a primary quality on a claim of disciplinary autonomy—it would be as absurd to import the methods of psychology into physics as the reverse—and on fidelity to the psychological "facts." Although he sided with their opponents, he understood the force of Huxley's and Clifford's criticisms well enough to pose the problem in these terms: "Does the ability of psychology to continue to exist as a 'science' depend upon its attitude towards the facts of a volitional quality?"[53]

More sweeping attempts to save the typically pyschological phenomena abandoned any form of the primary/secondary quality distinction whatsoever. Those who decried the new psychology as "in the strictest sense incredible"[54] on factual grounds found a credo in James Ward's *Encyclopedia Britannica* (ninth edition) article on "Psychology." Like Carpenter, Ward had been trained in physiology as well as psychology, but, again like Carpenter, he insisted upon the irreducible quality of conscious experience. According to Ward, that experience is dominated by the conscious, willing, active self, the psychological phenomenon *par excellence.*[55] Science must admit a pluralism of methods in order to do justice to the variety of its subject matter; hence pyschology could hardly be reproached with the fact that its explanations did not resemble those of physics. And the differences between the two disciplines were indeed profound: Ward was willing to jettison the strict determinism of matter and the objectivity of method in his science of mind. While the physicist rightly screened out not only his personal idiosyncrasies but any and all subjective elements from his observations, the psychologist was constrained to study the mind per se, and the mind qua individual mind.[56] Enmeshed in the concrete particulars of mental experience, Ward's psychologist would realign the science of mind with common sense, which Ward apparently believed to be uncontaminated by metaphysics. Ward's solution to the metaphysical quandary bequeathed to psychology by Descartes was to abolish metaphysics altogether:

> To make the language of science metaphysical is like working a wedge with the thick end foremost; nor is this all, but the contents of the science are affected by it, some are perverted and some are lost. And here by the way it is time to insist that not those who retain the concepts of matter and mind, but those who reject them are the persons who impede the progress of science with metaphysical non-entities.[57]

Ward's rejection of metaphysics in favor of common sense—or rather his transfiguration of the old metaphysics *into* common sense —represents at once the most conservative and the most radical solution to the turn-of-the-century dilemma of the science of mind: the most conservative, because it retained almost all of the Cartesian dualist ontology; the most radical, because it redefined scientific method and scientific explanation in order to do so. Ward tailored the method of psychological science to its traditional subject matter and thus abandoned determinism, objectivity, and any form of the primary/secondary quality distinction. While Ward did not wholly exclude physiological and comparative methods from psychology, he insisted upon the priority of introspective psychology grounded upon "the facts and analogies of our own experience."[58] By enthroning common sense, Ward broke with the post-seventeenth-century tradition of scientific reductionism.

But even if the proponents of the new psychology had conceded the primary/secondary quality distinction to the voluntarists, the strict nineteenth-century conception of causal connection or even constant conjunction would have been a stumbling block to scientific theories of will. Views among philosophers on the necessity of the causal bond ran the gamut from William Whewell's contention that our conviction that all events have a cause was as "rigorously necessary and universal" as our knowledge of mathematical truths,[59] to John Herschel's belief that our concept of cause stemmed from "our own immediate consciousness of effort,"[60] to William Stanley Jevon's probabilistic definition of cause as "the group of positive or negative conditions which, with more or less probability, precede an event."[61] Although it may have been a matter of heated philosophical dispute, the distinction between necessary connection and constant conjunction was largely an academic one for scientists: the chain of causation could be forged from invariable antecedents as well as from necessary ones. Neither weak nor strong versions of determinism could be reconciled with the belief "that in mental acts there is free will—in short, self-causation."[62]

Consequently, those ambitious to extend universal determinism to all phenomena often assimilated free will to chance, the one viewed as an apparent discontinuity in the moral order, the other as an apparent gap in the physical order. Laplace underscored the purely subjective character of both interpretations: objectively speaking, rigid causation prevails everywhere, always. Only the overwhelming complexity of certain events in the natural sciences (such as the toss of a coin) and almost all cases in the moral sciences created the illusion of indeterminacy and made probability theory an indispensable tool.[63] Antivoluntarists such as Maudsley were quick to exploit the analogy in the case of volition, claiming "the right and proper opposite of *necessary* is not *free*, but *fortuitous* or contingent; the contingency or chance lying not in the absence of determination but in the presence of unknown determinants."[64] Laplace's disciple, the Belgian statistician Quételet, developed the analogy with respect to social phenomena in the aggregate, arguing that as the number of instances increased, irregularities disappeared. Just as chance variations in, for example, a large number of meteorological observations did not obscure general trends, so "the greater the number of individuals, the more individual will disappears and the series of general facts dependent upon causes predominates...."[65] To compare free will to chance, either as a figment of human ignorance concerning the true filiation of causes or as a perturbation ultimately swamped by the operation of constant, uniform causes effectively removed it from the sphere of serious scientific investigation.

Earlier writers such as Bain had at times loosely inserted volition in the causal sequence with a vague reference to exchanges of energy between mind and brain. The rigorous formulation and popularization of the principle of the conservation of energy by Helmholtz and others eventually put an end to such nebulous claims and exiled volition still further from the realm of reputable science. It became a byword among antivoluntarists that traditional claims on behalf of free will violated not only the metaphysical dictum of universal, uninterrupted causation but also the established physical principle of the conservation of energy.[66] In other words, conservation of energy strengthened the hand of those who viewed the physical world, including brain and body, as a closed, self-sufficient system to be explained thoroughly in its own terms.

Given that physics occupied the apex of the hierarchy of sciences, only an accredited insider could challenge the hegemony of determinism in the physical sciences in order to make room for the traditional view of will. If the challenge succeeded, the unity of the sciences and volition might both be salvaged. James Clerk Maxwell attempted to reconcile the principle of the conservation of energy to the theory of volition by weakening determinism in both the natural and moral spheres and by suspending the "metaphysical doctrine" that like causes produce like effects in special "singular" cases. Maxwell suggested that certain systems, physical as well as mental, were unstable, such that infinitesimal perturbations occasionally produced effects out of all proportion to the cause. Perfect accuracy could guarantee predictions even in such precarious cases, but because all human knowledge is only approximate, our predictions are invalidated. Moral as well as physical systems exhibited stability—hence the success of statistical predictions with respect to large numbers of individuals, or of inferences drawn for persons of "confirmed character." Maxwell compared the operation of free will to Lucretian atoms "which at quite uncertain times and places deviate in an uncertain manner from their course."[67]

Maxwell retained the Laplacean link between chance and free will and the subjective interpretation of lapses in determinism as artifacts of limited human knowledge. However, he urged that, short of divine omniscience, such lapses were incorrigible and, moreover, extended their sphere of action to include physics as well as psychology and sociology. Volition was simply one example of a much larger class of unstable systems in which infinitesimal variations produced palpable effects; it therefore lost its anomalous scientific status. In order to salvage free will, Maxwell was willing to relinquish both the metaphysical position of strong determinism and the methodological guide of like causes, like effects, even for physics. He endorsed Balfour Stewart's suggestion that both stemmed from a distorted emphasis upon stable systems in physics and unstable ones in psychology, thus artificially heightening the contrast between the two disciplines.[68] Maxwell, in contrast to Ward, upheld the ideal of a unified science but was willing to prune the claims of causal determinism in physics in order to accommodate volition in psychology.

For the most part, however, psychologists accepted the image of physics that the physicist Maxwell had discarded. William James' vision of a science of psychology conformed for the most part to the determinist model of the scientific naturalists, and he eagerly anticipated "a *causal* account . . . of the laws yet unknown of the connexion of the mind with the body," as he wrote the dubious Ward.[69] However, James took sharp exception to what he considered to be the unfortunate tendency of the naturalists to exalt metaphysical preference with the title of "science." James' response to Huxley's hypothesis of conscious automatism was fully as violent as Carpenter's or Ward's, but he chose a biological rather than a metaphysical or methodological strategy, and one which turned his adversaries' favorite weapons against them.

James launched his rebuttal to Huxley, Spalding, and the rest with a distinction between two "faiths," the one "scientific" (a label James used here with a certain irony), the other commonsensical. While scientists subscribed to the likes of the conscious automaton hypothesis out of an "aesthetic" demand for homogeneous descriptions and explanations, their opponents maintained the efficacy of consciousness and will for equally aesthetic reasons. Since neither viewpoint could therefore be vindicated or vitiated a priori, James proposed that the issue be adjudicated by an appeal to "circumstantial evidence." The evidence James had in mind was evolutionary and neurological and therefore acceptable to the "scientists." If consciousness was no more than the superfluous byproduct of brain, what, James queried, could be the advantage to the organism possessing both mind and brain? James attempted to show that the brain of higher animals owed its admirable flexibility to its complex, "hair-trigger" organization, a complexity that rendered its responses a precarious, risky affair.

Here James had adroitly replaced the determinist bogey of an arbitrary will with the menace of a "happy-go-lucky, hit-or-miss" brain. The function of consciousness, he argued, was to load the neural dice in favor of choices that promoted the organism's survival. Nor could Bain's pleasure/pain selection mechanism dispense with the need for such a helmsman of the higher brain: first, pleasure and pain need not be respectively associated with biologically advantageous and disadvantageous conduct (inebriation was one of the many exceptions to this correlation); and, second, pleasure and pain can only serve as effective goads to action if the efficacy of consciousness is acknowledged, since they are, after all, only feelings.

On the basis of this argument, James awarded the decision of the common sense faction, albeit on a provisional basis. He recognized that new facts might reveal ways in which the dice might be neurologically loaded so that the complex brain reacted appropriately on a statistical basis, over the long run. However, James emphasized his allegiance to "concrete facts," in contrast to the metaphysical hubris of the "scientists," concluding with this empiricist's rebuke:

> When a philosophy comes which, by new facts or conceptions shall show how particular feelings may be destitute of causal efficacy without the genus Feeling as a whole becoming the sort of *ignis fatuus* and outcast which it seems to-day to so many "scientists" (lothly word!), we may hail Professors Huxley and Clifford as true prophets.[70]

True to his word, James continued to grapple with the methodological allure of the determinist model. The James–Lange theory of emotions posited that outward physiological expressions of emotion were a necessary condition of the feelings themselves, but James stopped short of admitting such physiological expressions to be a sufficient condition. Similarly, he clung to a theory of volition based upon selective attention, although he was sensible to the appeal of psycho-physiology and conceded that the link between stable ideas and the muscular movements they apparently triggered was still entirely "mysterious."[71]

Eventually, James declared the problem of will to lie outside the purview of psychology and the personal choice between "this whole goodly universe" implied by voluntarism and the "world without a purpose of mechanical philosophy" to lie beyond the reach of empirical evidence. James himself opted for voluntarism, but he did so on avowedly ethical rather than scientific grounds. Although his later speculations on a philosophy of "pure experience" seemed to eschew all ontologies that differentiated and rank-ordered raw experience as falsifications, James never developed the implications of such views for the science of mind.

James represents a compromise position in the controversy over the new psychology. Sensitive to the requirements for scientific explanation and method in psychology and yet reluctant to sacrifice the traditional understanding of volition to this end, he ultimately banished the problem from psychology altogether. By placing will *hors de combat*, he implicitly conceded the point that the explanatory and methodological scheme of the sciences of matter could not be applied to the science of mind without either mind or science giving way. John Tyndall's fear that "we are here, in fact, upon the boundary line of the intellect, where our ordinary canons fail to extricate us from our difficulties,"[72] lent force to James' expedient of relegating will to ethics. By the early decades of this century, the category of will had all but disappeared from the mainstream psychological literature.

THE LIMITS OF SCIENTIFIC NATURALISM

But the controversy over the science of mind concerned more than psychology. Varied as late-nineteenth-century British and American responses were to the impasse of mind versus science, all were obliged to address the status of the will, and the position of this problematic concept in any given theory of the period offers a reliable index to the author's philosophical—and arguably ethical—priorities. Moreover, the struggle to tailor psychology to scientific specifications, as these were then understood, pushed contemporary conceptions of scientific explanation and method to their limits. In particular, the conflict between determinism and the seemingly incontrovertible mental experience of spontaneous willing raised the possibility that there were as many scientific methods as disciplines and revealed a contradiction between the paired precepts of universal causation and empiricism that had jointly guided scientific naturalism. Issues raised by the new psychology compelled not only psychologists but natural scientists and philosophers as well to uncover contradictions, make forced choices, pursue unsuspected implications, and clarify positions concerning the nature of science in general. In some cases, this reexamination contributed to new views of the natural as well as of the moral sciences: witness the advent of radical empiricism in the work of Mach and others[73] and Maxwell's retreat from strict determinism even in physics.

Judged in terms of the next generation of psychological theories, these attempts to ransom the will at the price of a new philosophy of science ultimately failed. The category of volition has an antique ring to most psychologists today, who have by and large subscribed to rather old-fashioned views of scientific method and explanation. In the turn-of-the-century controversy, the theory of will became the common target of an attack launched by several different schools within British and American psychology. Indeed, opposition to (and exclusion of) any traditional account of volition was the hallmark of all of the various competing "scientific" psychologies of the period—and arguably their only point of unanimity. These critics of the older theory of will did not submit new evidence (although they used old evidence to new ends) but relied instead on a battery of metaphysical and methodological arguments that stretched contemporary philosophy of science to the breaking point. If the unity of the sciences were made paramount, Cartesian dualism would have to be sacrificed; if strict determinism were upheld, (introspective) empiricism would suffer; if psychology were to adopt a primary/ secondary quality distinction with respect to states of mind and brain—or simply among states of mind—would volition count as primary or secondary? The theory of will thus undermined post-seventeenth-century natural science at its foundations. The furor over the new psychology did not merely register the birth pangs of a new science; it also marked a serious attack on the reigning conception of science itself.

NOTES

1. James Sully, "The Psycho-Physical Processes in Attention," *Brain* 13(1890):145-64, on p. 145.
2. For example, evolutionary and associationist psychologies were allied with psychological psychology in both content and method.
3. G. F. Stout, "Review of *Body and Will* by Henry Maudsley," *Mind* 9 (1884):135-41, on p. 136.
4. See Henry Sidgwick, *The Methods of Ethics* (London: Macmillan, 1874), Ch. 5, for a discussion of the ethical and legal implications of the debate.
5. I have discussed the first in my article, "British Responses to Psycho-Physiology, 1860-1900," *Isis* 69(1978):192-208.
6. And within the natural sciences, the physical sciences have commanded the most attention, although historians and philosophers of biology have recently asserted the claims of the life sciences to separate but equal treatment: see, for example, David L. Hull, "Philosophy of Biology," in *Current Researches in the Philosophy of Science*, ed. Peter D. Asquith and Henry E. Kyberg, Jr. (East Lansing: Philosophy of Science Association, 1979), pp. 421-35.
7. René Descartes, *Principles of Philosophy* (Principles LII-LIV), in *Philosophical Works*, ed. and trans. Elizabeth Haldane and G. R. T. Ross (Cambridge: Cambridge University Press, 1931), v. 1, pp. 240-41.
8. Ibid., (Principle CC), p. 296.
9. Ibid., (Principles XXXIX; XXXVII), p. 234.
10. Descartes, *Passions of the Soul* (Article XXXIV), in *Philosophical Works*, v. 1, p. 347.
11. Gary C. Hatfield, "Force (God) in Descartes' Physics," *Studies in History and Philosophy of Science* 10(1979):113-40.
12. For a general discussion of the impact of this exclusion on psychology, see Robert M. Young, "Scholarship and the History of the Behavioral Sciences," *History of Science* 5(1966):1-51.

13. Roger Smith, "Physiological Psychology," *History of Science* 11 (1973):75-123.

14. Descartes, *Principles* (Principles CLXXXVIII; CXCVIII), pp. 284; 295. See also Locke, *Essay Concerning Human Understanding* (Book 1, Ch. 8, 8-10), ed. Alexander Campbell Fraser (New York: Dover, 1959), v. 1, pp. 169-71. For Descartes and Locke, secondary qualities refer to the "powers" of primary qualities to produce sensations in us, not to the ideas themselves.—See Reginald Jackson, "Locke's Distinction between Primary and Secondary Qualities," in *Locke and Berkeley*, ed. D. M. Armstrong and C. B. Martin (Notre Dame: University of Notre Dame Press, 1968), pp. 53-77.—The nineteenth-century authors discussed in this paper generally regarded the distinction as one between notions that resembled the actual state of the world (primary qualities) and those that merely represented it (secondary qualities).

15. See, for example, Henry Maudsley, "The New Psychology," *Journal of Mental Science* 46(1900):411-26, especially p. 417.

16. See Alexander F. Shand, "Attention and Will: A Study in Involuntary Action," *Mind* n.s. 4(1895):450-71, especially p. 459, for a critique of such attempts.

17. Sully, *Outlines of Psychology* (London, Longmans, Green, & Co., 1884), Preface.

18. This principle was often expressed as one of causal parsimony, as in Isaac Newton, "Rules of Reasoning," (Rule I), in *Mathematical Principles of Natural Philosophy*, trans. Andrew Motte and Florian Cajori (Berkeley, California: University of California Press, 1962), v. 2, p. 398.

19. See Paul Tibbetts, "The Doctrine of 'Pure Experience': The Evolution of a Concept from Mach to James to Tolman," *Journal for the History of the Behavioral Sciences* 11(1975):55-66, for the application of radical empiricism to psychology.

20. This criterion assumed increasing importance in late nineteenth-century discussions of scientific method in which "objectivity" blurred into "impartiality." See, for example, Karl Pearson's discussion of the civic importance of the "scientific habit of mind" in *The Grammar of Science*, 3rd ed. (London, A. and C. Black, 1911), Ch. 1.

21. Alexander Bain presents arguments of both sorts in "The Feelings and the Will, Viewed Physiologically," *Fortnightly Review* 3(1866):575-88.

22. Sully, *Outlines*, Preface.

23. Pierre Simon Laplace, *Essai philosophique sur les probabilités*, 5th ed. (Paris: Bachelier, 1825 [1814]), p. 3.

24. This usage is at least as old as Aristotle's opposition of final and necessary causes (e.g. *Generation of Animals*, 755a, 23-25); see William Paley, *Natural Theology*, ed. John Ware (Boston: Gould and Lincoln, 1857 [1838]) for a version influential in the nineteenth century.

25. Adolphe Quételet, *Sur l'homme et le développement de ses facultés, ou Essai de physique sociale* (Paris: Bachelier, 1835), v. 1, pp. 4-5; 12; 18.

26. See, for example, Gottfried Wilhelm Leibniz, "On the Elements of Natural Science," in *Philosophical Papers and Letters*, ed. L. E. Loemaker (Dordrecht: Reidel, 1969), pp. 277-90.

27. Auguste Comte, *Positive Philosophy*, ed. and trans. Harriet Martineau (London: J. Chapman, 1853 [1830-42]), v. 1, pp. 458-62.

28. E. G. Boring, *A History of Experimental Psychology* (New York: Century, 1929), Chs. 15-16.

29. Robert M. Young, *Mind, Brain, and Adaptation* (Oxford: Clarendon, 1970), Ch. 5.

30. See, for example, H. Charlton Bastian, "On the Neural Processes Underlying Attention and Volition," *Brain* 15(1892):1–34.

31. Henry Maudsley, *The Physiology of Mind*, 3rd ed. (London: Macmillan, 1876), p. 49.

32. William James, "Are We Automata?" *Mind* 4(1879):1–22, on p. 21.

33. I have chosen to exclude evolutionary psychology from this account because it consisted largely of associationist psychology rejuvenated by physiology, so far as the issue of volition was concerned.

34. See Young, "Association of Ideas," *Dictionary of the History of Ideas*, ed. Philip P. Wiener (New York: Charles Scribner's Sons, 1973), v. 1: 111–18, for a historical sketch of associationism.

35. Young, *Mind*, Ch. 3.

36. Bain, *The Emotions and the Will*, 3rd ed. (London: Longmans, Green, and Co., 1875 [1859]), pp. 37–38.

37. Ibid., p. 376.

38. Ibid., p. 421.

39. See Boring, *History*, pp. 334ff. for an account of Wundt's theory of apperception.

40. Hugo Münsterberg, "The Psychology of the Will," *Psychological Review* 5(1898):639–45.

41. Ibid., p. 641.

42. A. E. Taylor, "Review of Hugo Münsterberg, *Grundzüge der Psychologie*, Band i, " *Mind* n.s. 11(1902):227–46, on p. 231.

43. Ibid., p. 243.

44. Thomas Henry Huxley, "On the Hypothesis that Animals are Automata and Its History," *Fortnightly Review* 22(1874):555–80, on p. 577.

45. Sully, *Outlines*, p. 4.

46. William Kingdon Clifford, "Body and Mind," *Fortnightly Review* 22(1874):714–36, on p. 728.

47. Ibid., p. 734.

48. Sidgwick, *Ethics*, p. 51.

49. William Benjamin Carpenter, *The Principles of Mental Physiology* (New York: D. Appleton & Co., 1874), pp. ix–x.

50. Carpenter, "On the Doctrine of Human Automatism," *Contemporary Review* 25(1875):397–416, on p. 398.

51. Quoted by Henry Calderwood, "The Present Relations of Physical Science to Mental Philosophy," *Contemporary Review* 16(1871):225–38, on p. 232.

52. E. F. Buchner, "Volition as a Scientific Datum," *Psychological Review* 7(1900):494–507, on p. 507.

53. Buchner, "Volition," p. 496. See also Edward Thorndike, "What is a Psychical Fact," *Psychological Review* 5(1898):645–50, on p. 648.

54. Andrew Seth Pringle-Pattison, "The 'New' Psychology and Automatism," *Contemporary Review* 63(1893):555–74, on p. 566.

55. James Ward, "Psychology," *Encyclopedia Britannica*, 9th ed. (New York, 1886), v. 20:37–85, on p. 39.

56. Ward, " 'Modern' Psychology: A Reflexion," *Mind* 18(1893):54–82, on pp. 72–73.

57. Ward, *The Relation of Physiology to Psychology* (London, 1875), p. 13.

58. Ward, "On the Definition of Psychology," *British Journal of Psychology* 1(1904):3–25, on p. 25.

59. William Whewell, *The Philosophy of the Inductive Sciences, Founded Upon Their History* (London: J. W. Parker, 1840), v. 1, p. 159.

60. John Herschel, *A Preliminary Discourse on the Study of Natural Philosophy*, Cabinet Cyclopaedia ed. (London: Longman, 1840 [1830]), p. 198.

61. William Stanley Jevons, *The Principles of Science: A Treatise on Logic and Scientific Method*, rev. ed. (London: Macmillan and Co., 1887 [1874]), p. 226.

62. Hevons, *Principles*, p. 223. Even proponents of constant conjunction versions of causation such as John Stuart Mill insisted that the "law of universal causation" was the "main pillar of inductive science." See John Stuart Mill, *A System of Logic*, 8th ed. (New York: Harper, 1881 [1843]), pp. 236–37.

63. Laplace, *Essai*, p. 136. Laplace himself dismissed free will as an "illusion" of the internal sense, comparable to the illusion of colors produced by the external sense of vision, in an unpublished manuscript fragment titled "De l'idée de pouvoir," preserved in the Dossier Laplace, Archives de l'Académie des Sciences, Paris.

64. Maudsley, *Body and Will* (London, 1883), p.36.

65. Quételet, *Sur l'homme*, v. 2, p. 247.

66. See, for example, Clifford, "Body," p. 728; and Maudsley, "The New Psychology," *Journal of Mental Science* 46(1990):411–26, on p. 417.

67. James Clerk Maxwell, "Does the Progress of the Physical Sciences Tend to Give Any Advantage to the Opinion of Necessity (or Determinism) over that of the Contingency of Events and the Freedom of Will?" (11 February 1873), in Lewis Campbell and William Garnett, *The Life of James Clerk Maxwell* (New York: Kargon, 1970 [London, 1882]), p. 441.

68. Ibid., p. 444.

69. James, letter to James Ward, 1 November 1892, William James Correspondence, Houghton Library, Harvard University.

70. James, "Automata," p. 22.

71. James, "What the Will Effects," *Scribner's Magazine* 3(1888):240–50, on p. 246.

72. John Tyndall, "Science and Man," *Fortnightly Review* 22(1877): 593–617, on p. 607.

73. Erwin N. Hiebart, "The Genesis of Mach's Early Views on Atomism," in *Ernst Mach, Physicist and Philosopher*, ed. Robert S. Cohen and Raymond J. Seeger, Boston Studies in the Philosphy of Science, 6 (Dordrecht: Reidel, 1970), pp. 96–98.

II

PROBLEMATIC EMERGENCE

5

Mid–Nineteenth-Century British Psycho-Physiology: A Neglected Chapter in the History of Psychology

Kurt Danziger

OVERVIEW

The British psycho-physiology of the mid-Victorian period constitutes an almost forgotten chapter of the history of psychology. This is not altogether deserved. In terms of the line of development that psychology was to take later in the nineteenth century, the psycho-physiologists of this earlier period can be seen to represent the most advanced psychological thought of their time. Several of them continued to be regarded as authorities almost to the end of the century, and their formulations often set the stage for later developments, especially in late-nineteenth-century American psychology.

For many twentieth-century historians of psychology, the Victorian psycho-physiologists were under a cloud because of their great weakness in matters of technique. In particular, they completely missed the bus with regard to experimentation and quantification. Perhaps the relative insignificance of Britain as a psychological power in the twentieth century also made it easier to ignore its former importance.[1] The eclipse of this period was not total. Two figures, Alexander Bain and Herbert Spencer, have always been remembered. But much of the reorientation of the field with which they are credited was due to a new set of interests that they shared with a number of their early contemporaries. What was involved was a new recognition of the relevance of biological or physiological perspectives for psychology. Rather than constituting a world apart, the mind was now to be viewed in terms of its place in nature.

The first context for the emergence of the new perspective was a medical one, and medical writers continued to be its main representatives for many years. For this reason, and because their role in the history of psychology has so often been overlooked, this chapter will focus on these medical contributions. During the third quarter of the nineteenth century, the context for the generation of psycho-physiological ideas in Britain was largely provided by medical discourse. This discourse had its roots both in scientific and in social developments. Advances in the anatomy and physiology of the nervous system gave the discussion something to work with. But certain social changes made it necessary.

By the middle of the century the transformation of medicine into a unitary profession, with pretensions to a scientifically based practice, was nearly complete.[2] Until the early nineteenth century, the physicians, who formed a tiny medical elite, were able to exert their psychological authority over their wealthy clients by virtue of their gentlemanly humanistic education. In the industrial society that succeeded this period, a much larger number of practitioners had to serve a growing middle class that expected their physicians to bring a knowledge of natural processes to bear on their health problems. Medical education was rationalized and given a systematic natural scientific basis. At first, a strict dualism between the physiological and the moral level was maintained. This is still quite evident in the 1830s, for example in Prichard's distinction between moral and physical insanity and in Marshall Hall's rigid division between reflex and voluntary functions.[3] But medical men were being drawn into the management of psychological disorders on an increasing scale. The 1840s were a period during which the human toll of primitive industrial capitalism became impossible to ignore. It was a period of social violence and political confrontation, a period during which the medical profession was increasingly mobilized to make its contribution to combating psychosocial evils such as mass alcoholism. Psychiatric institutions began to play a more important social role; they were expanded and made more effective vehicles for the control of certain forms of social deviance. Rationalized programs of care and a more careful observation of patients replaced the older, more haphazard methods. Psychiatric issues received more consideration in the courts.[4]

Such was the general background out of which a new interest in medical psychology developed. In 1847, the Sydenham Society made an exception to its policy of republishing medical classics by bringing out a translation of a contemporary Austrian text on medical psychology "on account of," as the editor explains, "the great interest which medical psychology at this time excites."[5] This book appears to be the first published in Britain to use "Psychology" in the title. Indigenous textbooks on medical psychology were published by Noble in 1853 and by Bucknill and Tuke in 1858.[6] The 1850s saw the appearance of books in this area at a rate that was not to be equaled for the rest of the century. In 1854, Sir Benjamin Brodie, a medical adviser to the Queen and a President of the Royal Society, published two volumes, entitled *Psychological Inquiries*, in which he advocated a new science of Psychology for which "the observation of the physiologist must be combined with those of the moral philosopher."[7] Two years earlier Sir Henry Holland had published his *Chapters on Mental Physiology* a book noteworthy for the emphasis it placed on involuntary factors in mental life.[8]

These works are worthy of note, more as an indication of a general tide of medical interest in such questions than because of any profound or lasting contribution they made. Some other works that formed part of the same tide deserve more detailed consideration. The new concerns began to find their way into medical texts devoted to more general issues. In particular, W. B. Carpenter, Professor of Physiology at the Royal Institution and Examiner at the University of London, added a large section on physiological psychology to the fourth edition of his widely used *Textbook of Human Physiology*, which appeared in 1852. This section was further elaborated in the fifth edition of 1855 and eventually expanded into a separate book that did not appear until 1874.[9] This latter work went through four editions of its own and was republished in America as late as 1891. William James quoted it extensively in his *Principles of Psychology*. Here we are dealing with work that proved to be of more than local and ephemeral interest. Carpenter's ideas carried weight, and their influence is apparent in other works of the period.[10]

The monopolistic claims of the newly established scientific medicine on the remaining areas of quackery played their role in fueling the interest in medical psychology. While Carpenter's interest was first aroused by the role of psychiatry in the criminal justice system and by the problems of alcohol and drug intoxication,[11] he was moved to a major engagement with psycho-physiological issues by a wave of public interest in spiritualist demonstrations that affected England around 1850.[12] At this time, the perennially renewed public interest in topics such as animal magnetism, somnambulism, table-turning, and spirit rapping had been given a boost by the new fad of "Electro-Biology" or "Odylism" promoted by the books of a certain Baron von Reichenbach and by well-publicized demonstrations of two of his American popularizers. Carpenter applied himself to the task of showing that none of these phenomena constituted a threat to the claims of a naturalistically oriented medical theory, because the latter could account for them on its own terms. The elaboration of his psycho-physiological theories was a direct result of this endeavor. In this respect Carpenter was following in the footsteps of James Braid, another medical authority of the time who had begun to apply himself to the naturalistic explanation of mesmeric phenomena a few years previously.[13] Braid's invention of the term "hypnosis" has won him a permanent place in history texts. However, his work belongs not only to the special history of hypnosis but was very much a part of the more general current of psycho-physiological interest that affected British medical theory at the time. His works of the early 1850s, dealing with such topics as the "physiology of fascination," "human hybernation," and "electro-biology" show this general interest clearly enough.[14]

The names of Braid and Carpenter are the only ones among the mid-century psycho-physiologists that are likely to evoke a faint nod of recognition in the modern reader. However, it was not they who were the most original minds in this group. That distinction must go to Thomas Laycock, Professor of Medicine at the University of Edinburgh from 1855, and before that a lecturer at a medical school that existed at York. At the latter Laycock had a loyal pupil who was soon to overshadow his erstwhile teacher—the neurologist Hughlings Jackson. A paper published by Laycock in 1845 and entitled "Reflex Functions of the Brain,"[15] was a kind of cock's crow announcing the impending rise of the whole psycho-physiological trend, though its ideas were expressed with an awkwardness, characteristic of its author, that caused him to be widely misunderstood. He followed this with numerous papers in medical journals and with his magnum opus, *Mind and Brain*, in 1860. Unlike the other medical psycho-physiologists in Britain, Laycock came under the influence of German *Naturphilosophie*, having obtained his medical degree at Göttingen. His writings shared some of the metaphysical obscurity of his German counterparts, but in the breadth of his scholarship[16] and in his profound appreciation of the problem of the place of mind in nature he was unique among his medical countrymen.

A layman who hovered on the fringes of the psycho-physiological tide shared Laycock's ties to German philosophy. This was J. D. Morell, an educationist, who was well acquainted with the current medical psychological literature and who, in his *Elements of Psychology* of 1853,[17] attempted to incorporate its approach in an eclectic philosophical framework, largely of German origin. For Morell, Mind is an objective teleological principle present in all living nature. There is a continuous development of forms of organic action from the most primitive to the most advanced, not only in the scale of living species, but also in the life of the human individual. On this basis Morell projects a new kind of Psychology: "In this way mind comes to be viewed as an organic unity, developing successive powers like every other organism; and the science of mind, no longer standing alone, takes its place in the regular series of the natural sciences, depending for its data upon the results of those which have gone before."[18]

Morell was the first of a number of nonmedical writers who shared the basic problematic of the medical psycho-physiologists while analyzing its implications in a more philosophical manner. G. H. Lewes, an admirer and biographer of Goethe, wrote extensively on psycho-physiological issues,[19] presenting a curious mixture of ideas derived from *Naturphilosophie* and Comtean positivism. For Lewes, every action of the nervous system had both a physical and a mental side. Consciousness and voluntariness were matters of degree and did not involve separate entities such as Mind and Will. Even spinal reflexes involved a degree of mental organization. Lewes performed experiments on the behavior of spinal frogs, but he remained an amateur without academic credentials. However, his works were well known at the time and formed an important contribution to the later stages of the psycho-physiological trend.

Such fundamental concerns of *Naturphilosophie* as the problem of the place of mind in nature and the concept of a scale of natural-mental development also find their echoes in the writings of Herbert Spencer, who discovered them through his early perusal of Coleridge.[20] Certainly, Spencer's *Principles of Psychology* (1855) shares some of the direction of interest that was characteristic of the psycho-physiologists of the time. The same is true of Alexander Bain's *The Senses and the Intellect* of the same year. Bain not only introduced his psychological text with a section on the nervous system (and thereby started a now venerable tradition), but he also attempted to provide a hypothetical physiological basis for the way in which the sensation of pleasure strengthened associations. His physiologizing of the classical associationist mental philosophy was very much in the spirit of the psycho-physiological trend of his time. Both Bain and Spencer also picked up some of their early notions from phrenology, which was the immediate precursor of psycho-physiology. But Bain, Spencer, and phrenology will not be considered further in this chapter as they have been adequately dealt with in readily available secondary sources.[21] It needs to be recognized, however, that the relatively well-known psychological contributions of both these authors share common interests with the core group of psycho-physiologist discussed here. The general psycho-physiological problematic was not the special preoccupation of any one individual but rather the product of a rather specific social constellation. Because of their special professional interests, medical writers were particularly likely to be drawn into this problematic, but because of its general significance nonmedical varieties of psycho-physiology were by no means excluded.

THE CENTRAL FIGURES:
LAYCOCK AND CARPENTER

The most economical way of considering the content of the psycho-physiological theories of this time is to concentrate on the two most important medical contributors, Laycock and Carpenter. Other contributors tended to repeat ideas to be found in the writing of these two, often in a more confused and eclectic jumble. Also, Laycock engaged Carpenter in a running dispute that superficially involved a question of priority but actually expressed a fundamental conflict about how to conceive of the psycho-physical relationship. Laycock and Carpenter exemplify two poles of the psycho-physiological movement: One pole that was grounded in an essentially monistic view of mind in nature derived from *Naturphilosophie*, and another pole that kept entirely within the dualistic framework of a conventional British empiricism.

Both Laycock and Carpenter built on the principle of reflex functioning that had been established by Marshall Hall (and others) when they were medical students.[22] The physiology of the 1830s and 1840s had made a rigid distinction between reflex functioning attributed to the level of the spinal cord and brain stem and the totally different mode of functioning of the cerebral hemispheres, which were the seat of the mind. The gulf between psychology and physiology was profound, and the activity of the soul remained beyond the reach of physiology. The psycho-physiological period began when Laycock, followed later by Carpenter and others, attempted to explore the application of the concept of reflex function to higher levels. Here it must be noted that what both Hall and the psycho-physiologists were talking about was the notion of reflex *function*, not the concept of *the* reflex. This latter concept was a product of the German mechanistic physiology of the 1840s and 1850s[23] and played no role in the British psycho-physiology of that time.

To the physiology of Hall, of Flourens, of Johannes Müller, with its rigid division of fundamentally different levels of neuro-physiological function, Laycock opposed a point of view founded on the principle of *continuity*:

> the structure and functions of the nervous system in all animals are subject to the same laws of development and action: that a continuous and harmonious whole is formed out of the multitudinous and disjected parts; and that varied and dissimilar as they appear, each may be made to illustrate the other.[24]

This leads to

> the general principle, that the ganglia within the cranium being a continuation of the spinal cord must necessarily be regulated as to their reaction on external agencies by laws identical with those governing the functions of the spinal ganglia and their analogues in the lower animals.[25]

Laycock rejected the then-prevailing dualism that created a complete hiatus between movements governed by the principle of reflex action and voluntary action governed by totally different, psychological, principles. The nervous system, which controlled all action, was not several different systems but a single system governed by one set of fundamental principles that were most simply demonstrated in reflex action. There were no sharp breaks in the laws governing different levels of the activity of living organisms, only continuous gradations:

> The automatic acts pass insensibly into the reflex, the reflex into the instinctive, the instinctive are quasi emotional, the emotional are intellectual. This gradation of structure and function observed in the nervous system, is observed also with reference to all other structures of his body. Man is as the head of a vast ascending scale of animal life. . . .[26]

The metaphysical ideas that formed the background for Laycock's conception were those of "the great chain of being," a teleological model of the interconnectedness of different levels of life. In due course he developed an elaborate philosophy of nature in which Ideas act in and through nature and not in opposition to it.[27] He always emphasized the teleological aspect of vital processes, and this gave a characteristic coloring to his interpretation of the principles of reflex action:

> The fundamental principles of motor reflex action are these: That there is an apparatus so contrived as to place the individual in relation with the external world, and receive impressions from it in such a way that, whatever in the external world is good for the organism, is sought after and secured, if possible; and whatever is injurious is avoided or repelled, if possible; secured or repelled automatically and mechanically, without the intervention of any sensation, feeling, thought, volition, or act of conscious mind whatever.[28]

It is clear that Laycock transformed Hall's very specific and circumscribed reflex function into a general principle governing the behavior of human and animal organisms. In doing this he became the first nineteenth-century theorist to break through the conventional dualistic explanations based on the distinction between voluntary and involuntary action. He was able to do this by generalizing certain features of the concept of reflex action and dropping others. What he generalized were the following features: (1) Reflex action mediates between the organism and its environment (this is the generalized form of the sensorimotor scheme); (2) reflex action involves an in-built purposiveness—it functions in terms of the law of organismic self-conservation; (3) reflex action is automatic—conscious processes play no causal role in it. What Laycock dropped was the tie to a specific anatomically localizable nervous structure. In its generalized form reflex action became characteristic of all levels of the nervous system, including that level which was regarded as the source of voluntary action. Instead of a sharp break between voluntary and involuntary, between human and animal action, Laycock emerged with a common set of principles that formed the basis of both human and animal behavior and of all levels of human behavior.

The importance of this development should not be underestimated. For the first time we encounter the conception of universal principles of behavior in a recognizably modern form. There had been certain eighteenth-century attempts that pointed in a similar direction, but they had perforce to be almost entirely speculative and were therefore easily forgotten or misunderstood. Laycock's approach was still quite speculative, but he had more solid ground under his feet than his predecessors. He could use the established fact of reflex action in a paradigmatic sense, that is, as a concrete example of a set of principles that he claimed to be of general relevance. These principles could then be used to understand hitherto puzzling phenomena such as somnambulism, hysteria, impulsive insanity, and bizarre religious behavior. Of course, Laycock's principles of reflex action were extremely general, and their concrete application raised a lot more questions than it answered, but significantly it was Laycock who inaugurated systematic lectures on medical psychology (at Edinburgh)—he did have the rudiments of a system where before there had only been a catalogue of observations.

What his contemporaries found most difficult to understand and accept was Laycock's treatment of mental processes. He rejected the notion of a mind or will that was independent of the nervous system and could play on it like a player on a piano. He stressed that consciousness was a property, not a thing. It was a property of certain nervous processes, but it was not itself a causal agent. The nervous processes went off in terms of their own causal relationships, and consciousness, the subjective experience of sensation, volition, and so forth, was merely a "coincident" property. But Laycock was not a materialist. Like the German philosophers whom he followed, he did not equate mind and consciousness. Mind was objective, not subjective, and it manifested itself in the order of nature. So the teleological arrangement of nervous processes was itself an expression of Mind, though not of course mind in the sense of a subjective consciousness. Neurophysiological processes have their mental aspects, and at a certain level of organization these aspects develop the additional property of consciousness. The doctrine of a purposive spiritual side to natural processes enabled Laycock to achieve that reconciliation between scientific and religious interests that most of his contemporaries sought to achieve through some form of mind–body dualism.

Apart from extending the principle of reflex action to the brain, Laycock also extended the effective stimuli for reflex responses from purely peripheral ones to include central stimuli. The latter could be purely physical, as when the brain reacted to chemical or nervous influences reaching it from within the body, or they could have mental aspects being generated as a result of the brain's own activity. These mental aspects might then appear to be the cause of the reflex response, as in secondary phobic reactions or in voluntarily induced motor hysteria. But after some initial ambiguity on this point Laycock made it clear that his conception was that of an inherently "conative" organization of brain processes, which at times was accompanied by consciousness and at times not. The conscious experience, when it occurred, was not to be thought of as an independent causal force but as a "coincident" property of the brain processes. The importance of this view lay in its denial of the existence of a separate realm of consciousness obeying its own psychological laws, which were different from the laws of biology and physiology. Laycock strongly advocated the study of comparative psychology to throw light on human psychology. Concepts such as reflex and instinct were the common explanatory principles that linked human and animal behavior. Both these principles were expressions of the fundamental biological law of organismic self-preservation.

When we turn to the psycho-physiology of Carpenter, we find some of the same material integrated by a very different framework. Carpenter's father was one of a group of Unitarian ministers who were devoted to the philosophy of Hartley as interpreted by their great mentor, Joseph Priestley.[29] The son was trained in this tradition, using James Mill's *Analysis of the Phenomena of the Human Mind* as his psychological textbook.[30] The only other psychological wisdom that he seems to have absorbed was the emphasis of the Scottish School on the active power of the Will. Carpenter remained faithful to the sensationalist tradition in which he had been raised, but he provided it with a physiological metaphor. Sensations were conveyed from the sensory ganglia of the sensorimotor system to the cerebrum and were there compounded into ideas. Conversely, ideas of movement, formed in the cerebrum, passed down to the sensorimotor system and were there converted into motor impulses going to the muscles. Carpenter's whole account of any action that is not strictly reflex is therefore shot through with mind–body interactionism. He ends up with a dichotomy between a purely automatic level of functioning (reflex and sensorimotor) and a level of intelligent and voluntary action that is not automatic but "self-determined." The reasons for insisting on this dichotomy he states clearly enough:

> To whatever extent, then, we may be ready to admit the dependence of our mental operations upon the organization and functional activity of our Nervous System, we cannot but feel that there is *something beyond and above* all this, to which, in the fully developed and self-regulating mind, that activity is subordinated; whilst, in rudely trampling on the noblest conceptions of our nature as mere delusions, the Materialist hypothesis is so thoroughly repugnant to

the almost intuitive convictions which we draw from the simplest application of our Intelligence to our own Moral Sense, that those who have really experienced these, are made to *feel* its essential fallacies with a certainty that renders logical proof quite unnecessary.[31]

Before 1852, Carpenter had regarded the cerebral hemispheres as the seat of the conscious mind, of intelligence and volition, in accordance with the conventional widsom of the time, and had relegated automatic actions to subcortical levels. He now invented a new category of actions that were automatic, in the sense of being unintentional or involuntary, but that were mediated at the cerebral level. They were cerebral because they were actions produced by ideas, and ideas were only formed at the cerebral level. Below this level there were only simple sensations, and these had already been seen to give rise to automatic sensorimotor actions. But the actions of persons under the influence of suggestion of hypnosis were often directed by quite complex ideas and not merely by elementary sensations. So by an extension of his terminology Carpenter now arrived at the new category of *ideomotor* action.[32]

The theory of ideomotor action was simple. Just as sensations could produce automatic movements, so could ideas. The necessary condition for this effect would be the ineffectiveness of the will. This is what happened in hypnosis or in cases of powerful suggestion. The operative idea would be that of some effect that was expected to occur, for instance, the twitching of the divining rod or the movement of the table on which one's hand was placed. Given this state of expectant attention and a relaxation of volition, due to distraction, somnolence, or whatever, the dominant idea would then evoke the appropriate movement to produce the expected effect. But the individual concerned would be unconscious of the connection between his idea and the actual effect produced, so that the object held in the hand would appear to be moving of its own accord. Thus the theory of ideomotor action maintained that an idea that came to dominate the mind would automatically produce a motor action appropriate to it, without the person either willing the action or being aware of the ideomotor connection. Ideas could attain such a dominant position either through some external influence (suggestion) or through the person's own mental processes.

Carpenter recognized that the phenomenon of ideomotor action was only one instance of a broader category of events that all involved the automatic activity of the highest level of the brain, without volition and without subjective awareness of the operative connections. Here would be included the association of ideas (especially when there were unconscious mediating associations), the phenomenon of involuntary attention, unconscious problem solving (as when the solution appeared suddenly after the problem had been put aside), the artistic productions of genius (where poems or sonatas might appear to be composing themselves), and also dreams and hallucinations. Carpenter picked up the term *unconscious cerebration* to describe what went on in these cases, and he thought that many of the manifestations of insanity could be accounted for by reference to such automatic, unconscious processes.

It seemed to Carpenter that ideomotor action was an example of what Laycock had had in mind in his earlier reference to the reflex function of the brain, and he tried to acknowledge Laycock's priority in this respect. What continued to annoy Laycock was that Carpenter never seemed fully to grasp the crucial difference in their conception of automatic activity. Carpenter's scheme was based on mind-body interactionism all along the way. Physical movements were produced by ideas or by conscious sensations and were also "guided" by such sensations. The significance of this arrangement lies in the fact that it is *mental* events that are the source of the initiation and direction of most of the physical actions of vertebrates. Laycock, on the other hand, denied that mental events as such could produce effects on physical movements. That meant that the initiation and directedness of movement had to be traced to the biological organization. So he conceived of this organization in terms of teleological design. Carpenter, however, had abstracted virtually all elements of spontaneity and directedness from the action itself and had attributed them to a separate mental world. This meant that he was left with a category of motor activity that was "automatic" also in the sense of mechanical. Where Laycock emphasized the inherent purposefulness of the biological organization, Carpenter was more apt to dwell on the acquired repetitiveness of nervous action, the tendency of the nervous system "to grow to the modes in which it has been habitually exercised." Hence it was Carpenter who provided William James with the basis for the famous chapter in which he described the importance of habit for psychology.[33]

Although Carpenter accounted for a great deal of motor behavior in terms of various kinds of involuntary automatism, he was clearly at pains to preserve an area of action for the will so as to provide a psychological guarantee of the possibility of individual moral action. The reconciliation between the demands of necessitarian naturalism and the demands of a strictly individualistic system of morality was purchased at the cost of making all actions of the will indirect. The naive view, according to which the will directly produced bodily movements, had to go. Such direct interventions of the will would have played havoc with the elaborate machinery of automatic activity that formed the main subject matter of the new "mental physiology." Therefore, the will had to exert its effect by making use of already existing automatisms. It could not move a single muscle except by adding its weight to certain sensorimotor or ideomotor mechanisms. But this meant that the will itself became a kind of mechanism: it would create nothing—it only acted by selectively strengthening or weakening already existing tendencies.

> It may be stated as a fundamental axiom, that the Will can *originate* nothing: its power being limited to the *selection* and *intensification* of what is actually before the consciousness.[34]

The action of the will in Carpenter's scheme is indirect in two ways. Firstly, because it produces its results only by acting on tendencies that exist independently of it. Secondly, because it does not act directly on the motor apparatus but only on mental elements, which, in turn, have the capacity to produce bodily movement. The action of the will is therefore purely subjective, and any objective results are simply a byproduct of this internal psychological activity.[35] Carpenter identified the act of volition with the psychological process of attention—"it is solely by the Volitional *direction of the attention* that the Will exerts its domination," he states at the beginning of the *Mental Physiology*.[36] This was essentially the same position he had arrived at nearly thirty years previously: "The will, by a peculiar effort, represses the vehemence of one class of motives by forcibly withdrawing the attention from them and directing it to another of a higher character."[37] When the attention is concentrated on an idea, it becomes "dominant" and excludes other ideas from consciousness. So voluntary attention may be used to keep certain ideas in the mind and to exclude others (by default, as it were). The dominant ideas are the ones that control actual behavior by the principle of ideomotor action. Thus the will controls behavior indirectly by mobilizing attention, which strengthens certain ideas, which then produce the behavior attached to them.[38]

On the basis of these principles, Carpenter elaborated a psychology of conduct that was eminently practical in its intent. He was no ivory tower philosopher seeking answers to the fundamental questions of life but a respected medical authority who gave advice on childhood education, the reform of criminals, and the avoidance of social deviance. His theories about the determinants of human action were closely related to his interpretation of typical social situations in his Victorian environment. Like so many of his contemporaries, his way of dealing with problem situations was through the encouragement of individual moral conduct by means of the manipulation of consciousness. This was of course exactly what his generalized theory of human action demanded. Here is an example of his practical approach:

> Thus it is proved by ample experience that many a man who has not enough strength of Will to keep him from yielding to Alcoholic seduction has enough to make him "keep the pledge" he has taken against it: the mere repetition to himself of a determination to do so, having the good effect of augmenting the force of that determination, and of helping him to keep out of the way of temptation. As it has been said that "a women who deliberates is lost",—the mere entertainment of the idea of a violation of chastity showing how strong a hold the temptation to it has already gained upon her,—so may it be said of the man who is strongly tempted to "break his pledge", that if he once allows himself to "think" about it, the force of that principle is grievously weakened.[39]

Education plays its role primarily by providing the will with specific morally and socially desirable ideas to fix the attention upon. There is also a secondary effect produced by the repetition of good conduct, because enough of such repetition will make the conduct become habitual or "secondarily automatic," thus making further reliance on an uncertain will unnecessary. So education becomes a mixture of the presentation of noble ideas and repetitive drill. Victorian social and educational practice proceeded along the lines advocated by Carpenter quite independently of his theories, which only had the effect of providing these practices with a pseudoscientific rationale.

In this connection it is illuminating to compare the positions taken by Carpenter and by Laycock. It so happens that they both took an interest in the problem of alcoholism, an issue that had taken on serious social dimensions in the industrial slums of Victorian Britain. The growing authority of the medical profession aroused expectations that it would provide answers for such problems, and both Laycock and Carpenter were among the medical pundits who sought to satisfy these expectations. In their relevant publications there is a very clear difference of emphasis, which runs exactly parallel to their theoretical differences in conceptualizing the determinants of human behavior. For Carpenter, the defender of the autonomy of the individual will, alcoholism always remains an individual problem, to be dealt with by the manipulation of the individual consciousness. He was a life-long supporter of the temperance movement, providing a psychological rationale for what was essentially a moralizing approach to the problem.[40] But Laycock, as we have seen, devalued both will and consciousness, seeing them as determined by an objective system that followed its own laws. Accordingly, we find him emphasizing the relationship of alcoholism to constitutional factors and to depressing conditions of life, as among the workingmen who were the main targets of temperance propaganda. He opposed temperance laws and favored the provision of alternative sources of stimulation and satisfaction. The title of his main work on the subject, "The social and political relations of drunkenness,"[41] indicates the direction of his emphasis.

Laycock and Carpenter had the same starting point, both in terms of the practical and empirical problems that they confronted and in terms of the basic theoretical demand they tried to satisfy. Both of them were aware of the need to integrate the phenomena of hypnotism and suggestion with the physiological science they knew, and both were concerned to contribute something to the solution of certain manifest social problems, such as working-class alcoholism. Theoretically, both aspired to answers that would simultaneously satisfy the demands of science and of a normative order that presented itself to them in religious form. But this common problematic did not preclude divergent solutions. The point was that they interpreted the demands of the normative order differently. For Carpenter, the guarantee of the normative order lay in the autonomy of the individual conscience; for Laycock, that guarantee lay rather in a purposeful, directed system that existed outside individual consciousness.[42] Hence, Carpenter produced a theory of action based on the discontinuity of automatic and volitional processes, while Laycock placed the real source of direction and purpose outside the individual will, a view that entailed the subjection of human action to a nonmechanistically conceived natural order.

THE SECOND PHASE:
NEUROLOGY AND PSYCHIATRY

After about 1865, a new tone becomes increasingly audible in British naturalistic speculations about the determinants of human and animal behavior. The theory of natural selection had dealt a death blow to arguments based on teleological design in living organisms, and a growing confidence in the ubiquity of mechanistic determinism left no room for the operation of an autonomous will. Very soon, the compromises proposed by men like Laycock and Carpenter began not only to look scientifically dubious, but also to offer no credible guarantee for the maintenance of the normative order. A younger generation proceeded to take over those aspects of the older doctrines that were compatible with a consistent scientific determinism and to repudiate other aspects that now appeared to smack of unsavory metaphysics.

The neurologist John Hughlings Jackson (1835–1911) had studied with Laycock for several years and repeatedly acknowledged the usefulness of some of the latter's basic ideas.[43] In the present context we need to note only two aspects of Laycock's influence on Jackson. One involved the position of psycho-physical parallelism, which enabled Jackson to adopt a purely functional point of view when analyzing the operation of the higher nervous centers, and to avoid getting bogged down in questions of mind–brain interaction like his predecessors.[44] Jackson objected to the notion of "mental physiology" propagated by Carpenter and others[45] and tried to develop a view of the nervous system that did not involve mental causes having physiological effects and vice versa. His specific philosophy of parallelism was adopted from Herbert Spencer, but the underlying point of view is the same as Laycock's.

More specifically, Jackson adopted Laycock's central notion of cerebral reflex action and used it to establish the principle that all levels of the nervous system, including the cerebrum, functioned in accordance with the sensorimotor model. This had extremely far-reaching consequences, for it meant a final break with the old view, according to which the cerebral hemispheres were conceived as the seat of mental faculties or as the place where the mind played on the nervous system as though it were a piano.[46] Jackson convincingly demonstrated the applicability of the sensorimotor model in his classical work on neurological disorders and extended it to the analysis of aphasia. The physiological concomitants of words are identified as cerebral motor processes. From this it was only a short step to the claim that "mental symptoms from disease of the hemisphere are fundamentally . . . due to lack, or to disorderly development, of sensori-motor processes."[47] If this view was correct, then sensori-motor action ought to be taken as the paradigm for the explanation of all levels of the behavior of animal organisms. This was a suggestion that received reinforcement from the experimental research of

Ferrier on the production of movements by direct stimulation of specific areas in the cerebral hemispheres. Many of these movements were quite complex and could be considered similar to "voluntary" movements performed by the intact animal. Ferrier concluded:

> It must follow from the experimental data that mental operations in the last analysis must be merely the subjective side of sensory and motor sub-strata. This view has been repeatedly and clearly enunciated by Hughlings-Jackson. . . .[48]

The clear implication of this approach was that the mental accompaniments of overt behavior would have to be decomposed into their appropriate sensorimotor aspects before they became relevant to a functional explanation of such behavior. Not only did the new neurophysiology provide no place for the operation of the will, it dispensed with ideomotor action too, replacing it with a ubiquitous sensorimotor scheme. It was the psychology of Bain and Spencer, and not that of Carpenter, which proved to be most congenial to the new generation of neurophysiologists.

Parallel developments were taking place in British psychiatry. Here a key role was played by Henry Maudsley (1834-1918), an extremely influential figure in his profession over a period of nearly half a century.[49] Maudsley was quite a prolific writer, but an early book, *The Physiology and Pathology of the Mind* (first published 1867),[50] seems to have had the greatest impact, being one of the more radical contributions to the new wave of militant scientific naturalism that was then gathering momentum. The influence of Laycock is detectable in this work as well as in the later *Body and Will* (1883).[51] Maudsley takes reflex action to be the basic paradigm for the functioning of all levels of the nervous system. He applies this principle to the analysis of volition:

> Volitional action is fundamentally a reflex or excito-motor process in which a cerebral mechanism of extreme delicacy and intricate complexity of construction, embodying past experiences in its structure, intervenes between the ingoing stimulus and the outgoing movement.[52]

This position leads Maudsley to deny the doctrine of the freedom of the will and to insist on the predictability, in principle, of human behavior. He considers "the will" in the singular to be an unreal abstraction—there are only specific action tendencies, formed in the course of experience, and these go to make up the individual's character. It is not the will, says Maudsley, which determines character, but, on the contrary, the character which determines the will. One consequence of this inversion is a naturalistic reformulation of various social psychological issues that had previously been considered in essentially moralistic terms. Education, for example, is described, not as a process of moral development but as a value-free process of sensorimotor learning.

Maudsley applied the sensorimotor paradigm with great consistency. Thus he believed that acts of thought or of voluntary attention always involved a motor component, although that component might be only incipient. His analysis inaugurates a long line of similar attempts.

In one sense Maudsley generalized the theory of ideomotor action to the point where not only every thought, every idea, but also every feeling and every act of voluntary attention had its necessary motor component. As this component was often not apparent, he had recourse to hypothetical incipient motor activity. His was probably the first example of what was later to be called the "motor theory of consciousness." But strictly speaking he did not use the theory of ideomotor action in the same way as did Carpenter. Conscious states were not the causes of motor activity but rather a product of stimulus–response relationships. Thus, in the infant there were at first no affective states, only responses (such as sucking) to external stimuli (such as nipple) and also so-called "expressive" responses (such as smile) to certain internal stimuli produced by the activity of internal organs. Affective mental states were later acquisitions arising from this foundation and being unnecessary to it. Throughout life, most of the activity of the brain continued unaccompanied by consciousness. Much of our motor activity is the product of sensorimotor connections of which we are not conscious, and the same is true of the ideas and feelings that fill our minds. "The conscious is but a superficial wave moving over the silent depths of the unconscious."[53] While Maudsley's conception of "the unconscious" was not that of Freud, it did include quite an elaborate instinctual equipment serving the preservation of the individual and the propagation of "the race."

The devaluation of consciousness is undoubtedly a striking feature of Maudsley's most influential work. It is clear that this is essentially a *practical* devaluation. Consciousness may still be important in a quasi-aesthetic context, but it does not play the major role in the determination of behavior. Therefore, Maudsley argues quite forcefully against a psychology based solely or even primarily on introspection—a most unusual position to take in Britain, although less unusual among Continental philosophers.[54] Because what takes place in consciousness is so largely determined by processes outside consciousness, and because so much of mental life goes on without the intervention of consciousness, the latter is simply "incompetent" (Maudsley's often repeated term) to give us much useful information about matters of psychological interest. The point to note here is that Maudsley's arguments against introspection have a different basis than do the well-known arguments of Kant and Comte, which were primarily concerned with the *unreliability* of introspection because it inevitably changed its object in the process of observation. This is not Maudsley's main concern. What impresses him is the known existence of processes and relationships that he considers to be of the greatest psychological relevance, but about which introspection cannot provide any information. These matters include infant and animal behavior, the physiology of sensory impression, the action of latent memory traces, the mutual influence of the brain and internal organs, and so forth. What is involved here is primarily a shift in what is considered psychologically interesting and relevant. The plain fact is that Maudsley no longer cares about a psychology of consciousness. It is clear that even if introspection were a reliable descriptive method, he would still deny it any great importance because it can never answer the questions that really interest him. The change in method is only an expression of a change in the substance of what is defined as psychologically interesting. Introspection is not primarily rejected because it is *unreliable* but because it is *incompetent*.

What may be behind this changed psychological interest? Here we must recall the historical setting of Maudsley's contribution. What he was attempting to do was to provide a systematic psychological foundation for the relatively new form of medical practice that had taken shape in the nineteenth-century hospitals for the insane. In England the haphazard reform of society's methods for handling those considered mad had been legally consolidated in the Lunacy Acts of 1842 and 1845. The social changes that followed the Industrial Revolution had led to the growth of a system of hospitals organized on rational bureaucratic principles. A growing class of medical practitioners was involved in the running of these hospitals, the number of whose inmates trebled in a generation. The Association of Medical Officers of Asylums and Hospitals for the Insane was established in 1841, and in 1855 it began to issue *The Asylum*

Journal of Mental Science, which changed to the *Journal of Mental Science* in 1858. Both this journal and such psychiatric texts as existed had an essentially practical orientation. There was as yet little attempt to develop a systematic psychology that would have a bearing on the interests of asylum psychiatry. When Maudsley became editor of the *Journal of Mental Science* in 1862, its scope began to broaden to include relevant theoretical articles of a psychological or even philosophical nature. Then, with his 1867 book, Maudsley attempted to present a psychology that would make use of the same systematic principles in accounting for the normal and for the abnormal phenomena of mental life.

The asylum psychiatry of the time was, however, based on the assumption that, in the last analysis, mental abnormality was based on organic changes. It was this assumption that justified the entire classification of serious mental abnormality as a medical problem and provided the rationale for the extraordinary power wielded by asylum medical officers. This group of psychiatrists had an interest in contributions that strengthened the basic assumption on which their entire professional role rested. Apart from their own clinical practice, such contributions could take two forms. Firstly, one could extend, by means of actual research, the range of conditions for which a specific organic basis was demonstrably established. But there was also a second way. This involved strengthening the plausibility of the assumption of organic aetiology by treating it as only a special instance of a theorem of the widest general applicability, namely, the theorem of the organic dependence of all mental processes, normal as well as abnormal, voluntary as well as automatic. This second way was the one adopted by Maudsley, and in following it consistently he developed certain innovative suggestions for psychological theory. The interesting psychological questions are now the ones that pertain to the functioning of the organic equipment, while the actual content of consciousness, which had been of such supreme interest to the old mental philosophers, is devalued to a mere product of organic processes, a mere ripple on the surface of the events that really matter. In a certain sense Maudsley used the point of view of the asylum psychiatrist as a basis from which to construct a general psychology of normal as well as abnormal states.

Maudsley is fond of contrasting the approach of what he calls "the psychologist of the study" (see the later "armchair psychologist") with that of the "medical psychologist," much to the disadvantage of the former. The psychologist of the study, says Maudsley, can indulge in theories about the freedom of the will, but he is helpless in the face of mental disorder. The psychiatrist, however, has to adopt a different approach:

> But the medical psychologist who has to deal practically with disorders of will and to bring them back to order, if possible, . . . must do as mankind with consistent inconsistency have always done actually, in spite of their theory of the spiritual separateness of will—treat its derangements through the body exactly as if it were entirely dependent on the body, product not prime mover . . . he must learn to fall back upon the physiological conception of a number of confederated nerve-centres, co-ordinate and sub-ordinate, as the physical substrata of all mental functions.[55]

It may be noted in passing that Maudsley's attempt at providing a normal psychology that would have the same kind of relationship to clinical psychiatry as physiology had to clinical pathology was not a practical success. His approach to psychiatry was essentially based on notions of linked moral and physical degeneration and hereditary taint, which were very popular at the time. A tone of moralistic condemnation prevails in the clinical parts of his work and largely prevents him from performing those detailed clinical studies that might have enabled him to make more use of his more specific psychological theories. But in the present context those theories are nevertheless interesting in that they represent the first systematic attempt to work out a psychology of human behavior that is explicitly guided by the practical interests of a professional management of human problems. In the work of Maudsley it is already possible to discern quite clearly a fundamental contradiction that continues to characterize later attempts devoted to the same goal: Value-laden issues of social policy are treated as though they were issues of scientific fact. Even among his Victorian contemporaries it would not be easy to find many examples of writings that are as fiercely moralistic as are those of Maudsley, and yet his conclusions are always presented as though they were the inevitable outcome of scientific necessity. His point of view is consistently that of the defender of the prevailing order against the threats of degeneration and savagery. But he tries to clothe this deep social commitment in a strangely mythical language, where the issues are no longer those of social authority and deviance, of power and weakness, of the conflict of human qualities, but of nerve centers and their interrelationships, of biological constitutions and their fate. Ironically, Maudsley's "science" is more speculative than the introspective observations he discards so emphatically. In good part, it is not science at all but a scientistic ideology of social control.

THE FAILURE OF BRITISH PSYCHO-PHYSIOLOGY

Nineteenth-century British discussions about the physiological conditions of human actions led to no program of experimental research in physiological psychology such as developed in Germany. Why was this?

An obvious reason lies in the weakness of British physiology at this time. Such men as Laycock and Carpenter did pursue empirical research, but this was anatomical in the case of Carpenter and clinical in the case of Laycock. Experimental physiology was very poorly developed in mid-nineteenth-century Britain, compared with the great strides that were being made in France and Germany.[56] On the Continent, physiology had already broken away from the tutelage of anatomy and been transformed into an experimental science. In Britain, the corresponding development did not gather momentum until the last quarter of the nineteenth century. In the absence of a strong experimental physiology there was no convincing model that might have suggested the extension of experimental methods to psycho-physiological problems.

There were obvious institutional obstacles to the development of experimental physiology in Britain. Science and medicine were completely neglected at the ancient universities of Oxford and Cambridge, which had managed to pretend that the industrial revolution stopped at their gates until reform was finally forced upon them. The universities in London and in the industrial towns were very new and could only establish themselves by adopting priorities governed by short-range utilitarian considerations. Physiological research not justifiable by immediate clinical results or by leaning on a discipline of established utility, such as anatomy, had a hard time therefore in getting started. The Scottish universities provided a more favorable climate but had extremely limited resources. Nor did there exist research institutions of the type that provided the basis for the development of French physiology. In general, British physiologists at this time lacked the social and cultural protection that the existence of a well-established scientific discipline affords to its practitioners. This left them far more exposed to the respective demands of technical utility and of ideological relevance than their continental contemporaries.

As a result we find a strange mixture of scientific and non-scientific issues in the work of psycho-physiologists such as Carpenter and Laycock. In this they were not unusual. At that time, the remnants of the tradition of natural theology were still effective in Britain, and those who studied the natural world frequently interpreted their findings in terms of Divine design. Most of the medical psycho-physiologists had a dual commitment both to science and to religion. In fact, their work was dedicated to the reconciliation of these commitments. The problematic to which men such as Laycock and Carpenter devoted themselves can be formulated somewhat as follows: How to conceive the principles of that automatic action whose existence scientific physiology had demonstrated in such a way as to leave room for the operation of a divinely ordained normative order. They solved the problem in different ways: Carpenter by the interaction of a mechanical natural order with the moral will of the individual; Laycock by a teleological view of the psychophysical natural order that was compatible with Divine design. But ultimately they were motivated by the same intellectual interest. Behind this interest stood the great question mark for their social class, namely, how to promote those rational–technical activities on which the progress of industrial capitalism depended, while at the same time containing the social discontent that that progress produced.

In the last analysis, the thought of the British psycho-physiologists was essentially ideological. It did not transcend the specific preoccupations of the social establishment of which they formed a part. For psychology, any scientific yield was blocked by the lack of a methodology around which a new scientific community might have organized itself. As a result, the psycho-physiologists remained totally exposed to the demands and constraints of the general social context. Their theories were little more than quasi-naturalistic rationalizations of certain social practices and social policy positions of their time; they provided a set of pseudo-physiological concepts that made possible the metamorphical expression of essentially social problems and solutions in quasi-naturalistic terms.

But the failure of British psycho-physiology as science is no reason to strike it out of the history of psychology. This would only be justifiable if one decided to limit the legitimate history of psychology to the history of psychology as science. But, in fact, the history of psychology as ideology is at least as worthy of attention, especially as psychology has played a far bigger role in history through its ideological than through its scientific contributions. The theoretical yield of work that has an essentially ideological basis need not be limited in significance to a particular place and time. Analogous social problems can make this theoretical yield seem relevant to other places and other times. Also, scientific development cannot take off from a theoretical vacuum but must make use of the conceptual equipment bequeathed to it.

Part of the historical significance of British psycho-physiology derives from such considerations. In particular, it has to be noted that psycho-physiological discourse crossed the Atlantic and was continued during the last two decades of the nineteenth century by some of the founding fathers of American psychology, notably James, Ladd, and Baldwin. The essential terms of this American discussion were set by its British and not by its German predecessors.[57] It was the British tradition of psycho-physiological thought, including some later developments not considered here, that provided the point of departure and the conceptual framework for the American contributions. But that is another chapter.

NOTES

1. For exceptions to these statements see Leslie Spencer Hearnshaw, *A Short History of British Psychology 1840-1940* (London: Methuen, 1964); and Robert M. Young, *Mind, Brain and Adaptation in the Nineteenth Century* (Oxford: Clarendon Press, 1970).

2. Useful accounts of the changes in the British medical profession between 1815 and 1858 are to be found in: Charles Newman, *The Evolution of Medical Education in the Nineteenth Century* (London: Oxford University Press, 1957); S. W. F. Holloway, "Medical Education in England, 1830-1858: A Sociological Analysis," *History* 49 (1964): 299-324; William Joseph Reader, *Professional Men: The Rise of the Professional Classes in Nineteenth Century England* (London: Weidenfeld and Nicolson, 1966); Noel Parry and José Parry, *The Rise of the Medical Profession: A Study of Collective Social Mobility* (London: Croom Helm, 1976), Chapter 6.

3. James Cowles Prichard, *A Treatise on Insanity and other Disorders Affecting the Mind* (London: Sherwood, Gilbert & Piper, 1835); Marshall Hall, *Memoirs on the Nervous System* (London: Sherwood, Gilbert & Piper, 1837). During this period phrenology established a much closer connection between mental functions and their physical basis. But while it had considerable support among socially marginal medical men, it never became the official doctrine of the medical establishment. See Roger Cooter, "Deploying 'Pseudoscience': Then and Now," in *Science, Pseudo-Science and Society*, ed. M. P. Hansen, M. J. Osler, and R. G. Weyant (Waterloo, Ontario: Wilfred Laurier University Press, 1980).

4. The so-called M'Naghten rules on criminal responsibility were based on a celebrated trial in 1843. See J. Owen, "A Historical View of the M'Naghten Trial," *Bulletin of the History of Medicine* 42(1968):43-51.

5. Baron Ernst von Feuchtersleben, *The Principles of Medical Psychology*, trans. H. E. Lloyd and B. G. Babington (London: The Sydenham Society, 1847; orig. Vienna, 1845).

6. Daniel Noble, *Elements of Psychological Medicine* (London: Churchill, 1853); John Charles Bucknill and Daniel Hack Tuke, *A Manual of Psychological Medicine* (London: Churchill, 1858).

7. Sir Benjamin Brodie, *Psychological Inquiries* (London: Longman, Green, Longman, Roberts and Green, 1854). The first volume is subtitled "The Mutual Relations of the Physical Organization and the Mental Faculties," and the second volume "Physical and Moral History of Man." This work went through several editions.

8. Sir Henry Holland, *Chapters on Mental Physiology* (London: Longman, Brown, Green and Longman, 1852).

9. William Benjamin Carpenter, *Principles of Human Physiology*, 5th ed. (London: Churchill, 1855); William Benjamin Carpenter, *Principles of Mental Physiology with their Applications to the Training and Discipline of the Mind and the Study of its Morbid Conditions* (London: King, 1874).

10. Among these derivative works the following may be noted: Daniel Noble, *The Human Mind in its Relations with the Brain and Nervous System* (London: Churchill, 1858); Robert Dunn, *An Essay on Physiological Psychology* (London: Churchill, 1858).

11. See the biographical account by J. Estlin Carpenter, *W. B. Carpenter, Nature and Man: Essays Scientific and Philosophical* (London: Kegan Paul, Trench, 1882).

12. William Benjamin Carpenter, "Electrobiology and Mesmerism," *Quarterly Review* 93(1853):501-57.

13. James Braid, *The Power of the Mind over the Body: An Experimental Inquiry into the Nature and Cause of the Phenomena Attributed by Baron Reichenbach and Others to a "New Imponderable"* (London: Churchill, 1846).

14. James Braid, *Observations on Trance: Or, Human Hybernation* (London: Churchill, 1850); James Braid, *Magic, Witchcraft, Animal Magnetism, Hypnotism and Electrobiology* (London: Churchill, 1852).

15. Thomas Laycock, "On the Reflex Functions of the Brain," *British and Foreign Medical Review* 19(1845):298-311.

16. Among other things, Laycock translated 18th century works by Unzer and Prochaska for the Sydenham Society. Thomas Laycock (ed.), *The Principles of Physiology by John Augustus Unzer and a Dissertation on the Functions of the Nervous System by George Prochaska* (London: The Sydenham Society, 1851).

17. John Daniel Morell, *Elements of Psychology* (London: Pickering, 1853).

18. John Daniel Morell, "Modern English Psychology," *British and Foreign Medical-Chirurgical Review* 17(1856):272-85, p. 279.

19. George Henry Lewes, *The Physiology of Common Life* (London: Blackwood, 1859). This was followed by a multivolume work on "The Physical Basis of Mind," which was published nearly twenty years later. There is a relatively extended modern account of Lewes' ideas in Hearnshaw, *British Psychology*, pp. 46-53. For a biography of Lewes see R. E. Ockenden, *Isis* (1940):70-86.

20. Herbert Spencer, *An Autobiography* (London: Williams & Norgate, 1904), vol. 1, p. 351.

21. Phrenology has recently come in for a good deal of attention from social historians of science and pseudoscience. See, for example, Steven Shapin, "Homo Phrenologicus: Anthropological Perspectives on an Historical Problem," in Barry Barnes and Steven Shapin (eds.) *Natural Order: Historical Studies of Scientific Culture* (London and Beverly Hills: Sage, 1979). On Bain's and Spencer's flirtations with phrenology see Robert M. Young, "Mind, Brain and Adaptation."

22. Marshall Hall, "On the Reflex Functions of the Medulla Oblongata and Medulla Spinalis," *Philosophical Transactions* 123(1833):635-65; R. D. Grainger, *Observations on the Structure and Functions of the Spinal Cord* (London: Highley, 1837).

23. Georges Canguilhem, *La Formation du Concept de Réflexe aux 17ᵉ et 18ᵉ siècles* (Paris: Presses Universitaires de France, 1955).

24. Laycock, 1845, "Reflex Functions," p. 298.

25. Loc. cit.

26. Ibid., p. 311.

27. Thomas Laycock, *Mind and Brain*, 2 vols. (Edinburgh: Sutherland and Knox, 1860; Reprinted New York: Arno Press, 1976).

28. Thomas Laycock, "Further Researches into the Functions of the Brain," *British and Foreign Medico-Chirurgical Review* 16(1855):120-44, p. 122.

29. See Elie Halévy, *The Growth of Philosphic Radicalism* (London: Faber and Faber, 1972, 1928):pp. 437-38.

30. J. Estlin Carpenter, "Biographical Account of William Benjamin Carpenter."

31. Carpenter, *Human Physiology*, p. 549.

32. While Carpenter invented the term, he did not originate the notion underlying the concept of ideomotor action. James Mill, from whom Carpenter obtained his first ideas about psychology, considered that both ideas and sensations could produce movements quite apart from the operation of volition. He cited the infectious power of yawning, laughter, sobbing, and so forth as evidence that an idea of an action presented to the mind could automatically produce that action. Johannes Muller put forward the same idea a few years later, that is, almost twenty years before Carpenter. But it was Carpenter who popularized the term and applied it to a broad range of phenomena.

33. William James, *The Principles of Psychology* (New York: Henry Holt, 1890), Ch. 4.

34. Carpenter, *Human Physiology*, p. 590.

35. It appears likely that a commitment to a certain type of subjectivist ethics played an important role in the development of Carpenter's views about the role of the will. At the time he first formulated the essence of his theory of volition (i.e., in 1847) he did so with reference to a doctrine forcefully expressed by a fellow Unitarian, the Rev. James Martineau, namely, that moral qualities do not inhere in actions but only in motives. If this is so, then one must conceive of the moral agency, the will, as exerting its influence, not on actions, but on motives to action. See J. Estlin Carpenter's biographical sketch of his father in *W. B. Carpenter, Nature and Man*, pp. 57-60.

36. Carpenter, *Mental Physiology*, p. 25.

37. Carpenter, *Nature and Man*, p. 59. This basic scheme for the operation

of the will seems to have been introduced by the Scottish School of philosophy. See Dugald Stewart, *Elements of the Philosophy of the Human Mind* (London: Cadell and Davies, 1802), pp. 296-99 (orig. 1792). For the influence of the Scottish philosphers on Carpenter's predecessors, see R. Hoeldtke, "The History of Associationism and British Medical Psychology," *Medical History* 11(1967): 46-65.

38. Carpenter tried to reconcile the extensive influence of mental on bodily events implied by his scheme with the principle of the conservation of energy by suggesting that mental energy was convertible into physical energy much as heat was convertible into mechanical energy. See his "The Phasis of Force," *National Review* 4(1857):359-94.

39. Carpenter, *Mental Physiology*, p. 422.

40. W. B. Carpenter, *Temperance and Teetotalism* (Glasgow, 1849): *On the Use and Abuse of Alcoholic Liquors* (London: Churchill, 1850); *The Physiology of Temperance and Total Abstinence* (London: Bohn, 1853); see also Carpenter, *Nature and Man*, pp. 45-46.

41. Thomas Laycock, *The Social and Political Relations of Drunkenness* (Edinburgh: Myles Macphail, 1857 [2nd ed.]). It is worth noting that the divergent practical implications of Carpenter's and Laycock's psychophysiological philosophies run directly parallel to the contemporary political divergence between moralizing individualism and state paternalism. The nature of the problem and the fact that some possible solutions were literally unthinkable leaves only a very few positions that can be taken up in this historical context. For a brief review of the parts of the relevant literature, see Amy A. Pruitt, "Approaches to Alcoholism in Mid Victorian England," *Clio Medica* 9 (1974):93-101.

42. That Laycock pursued the theme of extraindividual systemic direction on the social as well as the biological level emerges not only from his analysis of the causes and treatment of drunkenness but also from a series of "Letters on Political Medicine," which he published in the Dublin Medical Press in 1841. He there develops the then rather unusual conception of medicine as a social agency and becomes an early advocate of what would later be called public health, social medicine, or similar. The most remarkable thing about these letters is the clear distinction between the traditional "civic medicine," based on the individual doctor-patient relationship, and a new order of medical practice that comprises various forms of social intervention, including "colonial medicine" and systematic medical education.

43. For details see S. H. Greenblatt, "The Major Influences on the Early Life of John Hughlings Jackson," *Bulletin of the History of Medicine* 39(1965): 346-76.

44. John Hughlings Jackson, *Selected Writings of Hughlings Jackson*, ed. James Taylor (London: Staples, 1931), 2 vols. See vol. 2, pp. 400-1.

45. Taylor, *Writings of Hughlings Jackson*, vol. 1, p. 52n.

46. Young, *Mind, Brain and Adaptation*, pp. 204-10.

47. Taylor, Writings of Hughlings Jackson, vol. 1, p. 26.

48. David Ferrier, *The Functions of the Brain* (London: Smith, Elder, 1876), p. 256.

49. See Aubrey Lewis, "Henry Maudsley: His Work and Influence," *Journal of Mental Science* 97(1951):259-77.

50. Henry Maudsley, *The Physiology and Pathology of Mind* (London: Macmillan, 1867).

51. Henry Maudsley, *Body and Will* (London: Kegan Paul, Trench, 1883).

52. Henry Maudsley, *The Physiology of Mind* (New York: Appleton, 1878), p. 441.

53. Ibid., p. 446.

54. Maudsley was in fact rather well read outside the standard authorities of British empiricism. See also Kurt Danziger, "The History of Introspection Reconsidered," *Journal of the History of the Behavioral Sciences* 16(1980): 241-62, (p. 243).

55. Henry Maudsley, *Body and Will: Being an Essay Concerning Will in its Metaphysical, Physiological and Pathological Aspects* (New York: Appleton, 1884), p. 259.

56. This matter has been thoroughly explored in Gerald L. Geison, "Social and Institutional Factors in the Stagnancy of English Physiology, 1840-1870," *Bulletin of the History of Medicine* 46(1972):30-58.

57. The neglect of the British roots of late nineteenth-century American psychology by historians like Boring was first noted in Robert M. Young, "Scholarship and the History of the Behavioral Sciences," *History of Science* 5(1966):1-51.

6

Helmholtz, Sensory Physiology, and the Disciplinary Development of German Psychology

R. Steven Turner

Many scientific fields claim the physicist and physiologist Hermann Helmholtz as one of their pioneers and none more avidly than psychology. Here his influence has been traced into such unlikely quarters as Preyer's developmental conception of the child and Sechenov's concept of the reflex. Helmholtz exerted his greatest influence, however, upon sensory and experimental psychology, which between 1875 and World War I was actively establishing itself in Germany and the United States as an autonomous scientific field. To the considerable extent that the young science presupposed strong physiological models of ear and eye function, it owed that aspect of its existence directly to research done by Helmholtz between 1852 and 1867 or to the later attempts of other researchers to develop or correct his theories. This paper examines the nature of that influence, and with it Helmholtz's personal ties to the young discipline and its practitioners.

Carl Stumpf, professor of psychology in Berlin, undertook the first assessment of Helmholtz's contributions to the new psychology. In an essay of 1895 following Helmholtz's death in 1894, Stumpf hailed as milestones in the development of sensory psychology Helmholtz's three-receptor theory of color vision, the publication of his great synthetic *Handbuch der physiologischen Optik* (1856, 1860, 1867), his theory of timbre, his resonance theory of cochlea function, and the impact of his great work on *Tonempfindungen* (1862). Stumpf did not fail to criticize aspects of Helmholtz's intellectual legacy. By 1894, most psychologists, Stumpf felt, agreed that Ewald Hering had decisively refuted Helmholtz's position that simultaneous contrast phenomena arise from unconscious errors of judgment and, more important, that major concessions must be made to the nativist theory of space perception against which Helmholtz had campaigned so long and hard.

Had Stumpf surveyed contemporary opinion more closely, he would have reported that by Helmholtz's death most psychologists and physiologists had long regarded the Young-Helmholtz theory as inadequate as a comprehensive theory of vision, mainly because it failed to describe correctly our white–grey sensations over varying degrees of luminosity. Most preferred the Hering four-process theory, a combination of it and of the new duplicity theory of von Kries, or a position of theoretical agnosticism. On the other hand, Helmholtz's resonance theory of cochlea function reigned almost unchallenged, even though there remained general uncertainty as to how the cochlea perceived beats, where and how noise was heard, and whether Helmholtz's transformation theory of combination tones really explained the intensities at which these tones are heard. Stumpf duly reported his dissent from the Helmholtz explanation of consonance and dissonance, but it is unclear whether that dissent was also shared by many other psychologists. Stumpf pointedly omitted in 1895 any mention of Helmholtz's general theory of perception, an omission that surely reflects a consensus of the community of psychologists.

Yet, as Stumpf noted, the exact status of particular ideas and theories paled in importance beside the greater significance of Helmholtz's work. It had been Helmholtz, Stumpf acknowledged, who above all others had helped to build "the bridge between physiology and psychology that thousands of workers today go back and forth upon."[1] But about the nature of that bridge, or about its importance to the existence of psychology as a science, Stumpf had nothing to say.

THE INSTITUTIONALIZATION OF GERMAN PSYCHOLOGY

The relationship of German psychology to physiology, and with it the influence of Helmholtz, has to be understood within the context of psychology's institutional status. In the German university system until the last quarter of the nineteenth century psychology did not exist as an independent discipline, but rather as a subfield of general philosophy. The philosophers who offered lectures in the field readily incorporated experimental and physiological results that came to their attention, but they normally developed their psychological views and systems mainly through logical, metaphysical, introspective, or purely experiential considerations.

Beginning in the late 1850s, three developments began to destabilize psychology's traditional status as a subfield of philosophy. One was the infectious example of disciplines such as physiology and organic chemistry and modern history, which were taking advantage of rising enrollments and funding to repudiate their status as subfields, break away from their traditional parent disciplines, and establish themselves as autonomous university disciplines.[2] A second factor was the explosion in physiological understanding of the sense organs, a product of the research of physiologists Purkinje, Müller, E. H. Weber, and A. W. Volkmann, and in the next generation of physiologists Karl Vierordt, F. C. Donders, Hermann Aubert, Ewald Hering, Helmholtz himself, and the other members of the "1847 school." Their physiological results so enriched the domain of sensory psychology that they tempted many to believe that the future of psychology lay in a more intimate connection with physiology and a greater reliance upon the experimental method, which had obviously produced such important results for physiology itself. Wilhelm Wundt became the spokesman for this position during the 1860s and early 1870s, but he merely reflected sentiments already in the process of becoming widespread. A third factor was Gustav Fechner's invention of the techniques of psychophysics in the early 1860s. Despite the later, interminable debates over just what psychophysics meant and measured, it seemed to create almost overnight a body of compelling, practicable, uniquely psychological experimental techniques that promised quantitative results as "hard" and as reproducible as anything biophysics could offer. Perhaps to these three factors tending to destabilize the traditional status of psychology could be added a fourth: an intellectual climate in which philosophical speculation and discussion were losing ground to empiricism, experiment, and sometimes materialism in intellectual and scientific prestige.[3]

As a result of these factors, the older tradition of philosophical psychology began to give place to a new tradition that stressed experimental results and physiological considerations and speculations and studied sensation and perception often to the exclusion of higher mental functions. The new tradition was variously called "physiological psychology," "experimental psychology," or simply "the new psychology." It emerged very gradually, and the distinction between the "new" and the "old" psychology was never sharp, as the example of Lotze and Brentano prove. Nevertheless, by 1910 the term "psychology" had come to mean "the new psychology," both for its opponents and proponents.[4]

The determination of the new psychology to become an empirical, experimental science made its institutional position as a subfield of philosophy increasingly anomalous and led to halting steps toward disciplinary autonomy. Some chairs of philosophy, particularly in larger universities that had several chairs in the field, fell into the hands of academics who regarded themselves exclusively as psychologists, even though in most cases the chair itself continued to be formally denoted as a chair of philosophy. Universities created institutes for experimental psychology, perhaps the most devisive criterion of autonomy, even though many of these remained in the hands of *Ausserordinarien*. Younger practitioners began to announce themselves in lecture catalogues as "psychologists" rather than as "philosophers." These developments came very slowly, however, in part because many philosophers *and* psychologists resisted more radical separation of the two fields.[5] In 1910, for example, German psychology was firmly established as an intellectual discipline, with three specialized journals, well-defined research schools, and a series of authoritative texts. But it still possessed few of the institutional trappings of autonomy. Only four psychologists of the day listed themselves officially as "psychologist" rather than as "philosopher," and only six of 21 universities had institutes or seminars for psychology. But by 1925 there were 25 self-styled "psychologists," including seven full professors, and 14 of 23 universities had institutes. Although the association with philosophy remained close, the new psychology had by this time attained a strong autonomous position.[6]

Of all the historical factors that triggered the emergence of the new psychology, the impact of sensory physiology may have been most important. In 1966 Joseph Ben-David and Randall Collins even characterized the new German psychology as a "hybrid discipline," combining the methodology of sensory physiology with the institutional status and goals of philosophy.[7] This characterization exaggerates physiology's influence and, as various critics have noted, understates the continuing importance of the tradition of philosophical psychology; nevertheless, it correctly emphasizes the symbiotic relationship of the two fields.[8] Wilhelm Wundt, who abandoned a career in physiology to become a founder of experimental psychology, first dubbed the new field "physiological psychology" and taught his vast school that experimentation upon the model laid down by sensory physiology is what differentiates the new psychology from the older philosophical tradition.[9]

Not all psychologists shared this enthusiasm for physiology. Brentano warned in 1874 that "not only does it appear little advisable that psychological investigations should give place to physiological ones, but also inadvisable that the latter should be mixed with the former to any considerable extent." There are at present, he opined, only a few sure facts of physiology that are suited to throw light on psychological phenomena, and speculation about hypothetical physiological mechanisms is as much to be avoided today as metaphysical speculation.[10] Even Brentano acknowledged that the possibility of a scientific psychology has had to await the maturation of physiology as a prerequisite science, and that discovery of the highest causal laws of the "succession of psychic phenomena" must await the further development of sensory and neural physiology.[11]

During the 1870s and 1880s the general enthusiasm for physiological psychology drowned out warnings like that of Brentano. In 1890 Wilhelm Wundt's rivals outside Leipzig banded together to create a new, competing journal to challenge the monopoly of Wundt's *Philosophischen Studien*. The editors, psychologist Hermann Ebbinghaus and physicist–physiologist Arthur König, named it the *Zeitschrift für Psychologie und Physiologie der Sinnesorgano* and initiated the series with the bold claim that these two sciences "have consequently grown together . . . to form one whole; they promote and presuppose one another, and so constitute two co-equal members of one great double science."[12] The founding of the *Zeitschrift* represented the high-water mark of physiological psychology in Germany, at a time when Wundt's own interests were already shifting to other aspects of psychology.

The new psychology borrowed much from sensory physiology during the crucial years of its institutional entrenchment between 1870 and 1895. It borrowed from physiology the experimental methods necessary to support a research program and flesh out the techniques of psychophysics, the body of facts and expertise necessary to sustain its teaching and licensing activities, much of the prestige of that well-established and powerful German science, and the methodological program necessary to differentiate itself and raise itself above its parent discipline of philosophy and the older psychological tradition rooted in it. The relationship of Helmholtz as the most famous physiological theorist of his day to the new psychology must be understood against this background of an ambitious and emerging young field and its intellectual and political needs.

HELMHOLTZ AND THE NEW PSYCHOLOGISTS

Unfortunately we know nothing about Helmholtz's personal views concerning the new psychology and its ambitions, and too little about his personal relationships with the pioneers of the new field. Helmholtz seems never to have met Gustav Fechner, but he clearly admired his work. He accepted and carried on the controversial Fechnerian interpretation of afterimages and the belief that simultaneous contrast arises as an optical illusion, an error of judgement; indeed, Helmholtz's whole theory of perception may have its roots in this Fechnerian idea.[13] Helmholtz also accepted and was fascinated by Fechner's proposed logarithmic relationship between sensation and stimulus, despite the absence of any physiological model to explain it. In the second volume of the *Optics* in 1860, Helmholtz proposed to generalize Fechner's Law, such that in the differential fomula

$$dE = A(dH/H),$$

where E is the intensity of the light sensation and H the physical luminosity of the light stumulus, the usual constant A must be redefined as a function of H. This, Helmholtz believed, could preserve the validity of the law in its notorious deviations from experimental data at high stimulus intensities.

During most of the 1870s and 1880s Helmholtz devoted himself to electrodynamics and mechanics. In the late 1880s, however, two factors drew his attention back to physiological and psychological problems in dramatic fashion. One was the necessity of revising the *Optics* for a second edition; the other was the founding of the *Zeitschrift für Psychologie und Physiologie der Sinnesorgane* by Ebbinghaus and Helmholtz's friend Arthur König. Helmholtz not only agreed to join the editorial board but contributed four major articles over the next three years. His death in 1894 cut short what seems to have been a major turn to psychological questions in Helmholtz's research interests.

These late and little-known papers reflect many of the characteristics of Helmholtz's approach to psychological theorizing. All are highly mathematical and physicalist; and all attempt either to generalize and defend Fechner's Law or, assuming the law's validity, to mobilize it in support of Helmholtz's views. The first paper, for example, attempted to save Fechner's Law from its deviations from experimental data at very low stimulus intensities where brightness is the sensation being studied. Having shown in 1860 that deviations at high luminosities could be predicted by assuming A to be a function of H, Helmholtz argued in 1890 that H must be regarded as the sum of the objective light and the intrinsic retinal light integrated over the surface area of the retina. The mottled nature of the intrinsic light complicates the calculation and necessitates representing H as the sum of two integrals, which at moderate intensities of the objective light approximate Fechner's Law in its usual form.[14] This treatment explicitly assumes that Fechner's Law is a relationship in "inner psychophysics," that is, between neural excitation and sensation. For purposes of biophysical modeling, the physiologist can place the intrinsic light on the same footing as a physical, external stimulus, despite its organic origins.

Helmholtz's second venture into psychophysics attempted to extend Fechner's Law to color vision. To date, Helmholtz noted, Fechner's Law had been applied only to the sensations that follow the change of a single stimulus variable, as when brightness varies with the changing intensity of light of a single wavelength or a fixed mixture of wavelengths. Color hues, however, can be stimulated as a mixture of three properly chosen primary colors, and the perceived hue will vary with the relative amounts of each primary in the mixture. Hue, therefore, is a sensory quality constituting a three-dimensional manifold in Riemann's sense and so susceptible to an analogous mathematical treatment. The question is, does Fechner's Law apply separately to each "dimension" contributing to the fused total sensation, that is, does the size of the J.N.D.s of the total color sensation produced by variations in each primary component depend only on the amount of that primary in the mixture, or on the relative amounts of the other primaries as well?

Helmholtz mobilized the results of his own color wheel experiments and the published results of Arthur König on the dichromatic eye of E. Brodhun to argue that the former is more likely correct. If E is a color sensation that has been stimulated by a mixture of three lights, each of which when presented separately would have produced sensations E_1, E_2, and E_3, then evidence suggests that

$$dE^2 = dE_1^2 + dE_2^2 + dE_3^2,$$

analogous to the Riemannian metric formula. This implies,

since dE_1, dE_2, and dE_3 are the effects of different physiological processes, that these physiological excitations exist undisturbed among themselves, without exercising reciprocal influence on each other before they come to consciousness, and that first in the consciousness do they excite the attention through their interaction.[15]

The result therefore confirmed a central tenet of Helmholtz's physiological theorizing and his central objection to all nativist theories of perception. Nervous impulses excited in peripheral nerve endings in the sense organs are transmitted to the sensorium without interaction or organic fusion in the nerves themselves. This extension of Fechner's Law therefore forbids the nativist to postulate neural interactions among the effects of the primary lights, except at the (presumably cortical) level where, on a psychophysical parallelism, these interactions would correspond to potentially conscious events. Helmholtz then went on to set dE_1 and dE_2 equal to his generalized form of Fechner's Law, and for the dichromatic eye for which dE_3 equals zero, to derive mathematically the quantitative color sensations that would follow from these assumptions and test them against observations.

In his third and last paper on psychophysics, Helmholtz drew the central consequence of his earlier work. dE_1, dE_2, and dE_3 refer to any three color sensations regarded as primary colors from which others may be mixed. But if Fechner's Law is a relationship in inner psychophysics, then they may also refer to the three specific physiological primaries predicted by the Young–Helmholtz theory of color vision. Now since all our color sensations are mixtures of all three physiological primaries, the physiological primaries themselves can never be observed pure; they are at best potential sensations. Nevertheless, Helmholtz noted, the formulas of the generalized Fechner Law permit us to locate mathematically the physiological primary colors in relation to the spectral colors on the Newtonian color triangle and so give rough descriptions of their hues. Helmholtz proceeded to do this, in the process confirming the Young–Helmholtz theory and further vindicating his continuing program to use mathematical analysis and assumptions of simplicity between stimulus and sensation to obtain insights into the nature of perception that are closed even to normal introspection.[16]

The most intriguing of Helmholtz's personal ties to the new psychology and its founders was to Wilhelm Wundt. Wundt worked closely with Helmholtz as assistant in the physiology institute at Heidelberg between 1858 and 1864, and their relationship during those years has been the subject of much rumor and speculation. Despite the similarity of their views at this time, there seems to have been little real intellectual exchange between the placid, aloof *Ordinarius* and his proud, fiercely secretive assistant.[17] In the third volume of the *Optics* (1867) Helmholtz drew heavily on Wundt's research results, citing with approval Wundt's study of stereoscopic fusion, judgments of distance by convergence alone, and his measurements of eye movements in general and cyclorotation in particular. He proudly and repeatedly bracketed Wundt with himself, Wheatstone, Volkmann, H. Mayer, and Classen as empiricists and comrades-in-arms against the rival camp of nativists.

Also in the *Optics* Helmholtz criticised Wundt—gently but repeatedly—for several of his opinions. Wundt had argued in agreement with Lotze that we derive our judgments of distances across the visual globe, and with them the retinal "local signs," from our unconscious kinesthetic knowledge of the muscular exertions required to move the gaze across these distances. Wundt had also maintained that the eye's curious obedience to Donder's Law follows from a so-called "principle of easiest muscular exertion." For every orientation the eye assumes the unique degree of cyclorotation that places least strain on the muscles of the eye.[18]

Helmholtz rejected both these views. Experiment and introspective experience both suggest, he countered, that judgments about exertions of the eye muscles are quite unreliable unless their results are constantly compared to a visual image. Kinesthetic awareness may contribute to our perceptions of distances on the visual globe and even to the local signs, but they cannot be the sole or even a major cause. As for the "principle of easiest muscular exertion," it is methodologically pernicious because it merely postulates hypothetical and untestable characteristics of the eye muscles. We can more plausibly assume, Helmholtz argued, that the eye learns through experience to conform to Donder's Law, that is, to assume a unique degree of cyclorotation for every different orientation. This, after all, is the behavior that minimizes distortion in successive glances at an external object and maximizes our visual knowledge of external reality in the easiest manner. These criticisms by the great Helmholtz certainly rankled the young Wundt and may, in fact, have hurt his contemporary reputation.[19]

One further matter may have helped to sour relationships between the two physiologists. As early as 1858, Wundt had argued that human perception, that is, our ability to integrate the raw data of sensation into an awareness of objects, proceeds on the basis of unconscious inductive reasoning. As Wundt put it, psychology postulates as a fact of experience the existence of "the soul as an entity acting out of itself and developing out of itself on the basis of logical laws."[20] Helmholtz, in a popular lecture at Königsberg in 1855 and again in the third volume of the *Optics* in 1867, also advanced the view that perception is mediated by unconscious inductive reasoning. Wundt, unlike Helmholtz, later abandoned this rather idealistic notion in favor of a chemical analogy of perception. But he continued to claim priority over the concept of unconscious reasoning for several years, and his inability to establish that claim may have fed a sense of aggrievement.[21]

Whatever their differences, Helmholtz and Wundt remained on cordial terms during the Heidelberg period. In 1873, two years after he had left Heidelberg for Berlin and a career in physics, Helmholtz wrote at least two letters supporting Wundt's attempts to secure a chair in philosophy. In each he praised Wundt in warm and sincere, if not enthusiastic, terms, noting his "honest zeal," his diligence, and his proven skill in observation and experiment. In each letter Helmholtz endorsed the view that academic philosophy was in serious decline and could be invigorated only by a return to an exact, critical analysis of sensory perceptions, which he took to be the starting point of all epistemology. Only men like Wundt, Helmholtz opined, who have been trained in the scientific method, can achieve this reinvigoration of philosophy. Clearly in 1873 Helmholtz strongly supported the movement toward experimental, physiological psychology. But he regarded it, as did most of its practitioners at that date, as the key to the reform of philosophy rather than as an autonomous science in its own right.[22]

Helmholtz's opinion of Wundt almost certainly declined in the following years. In 1873/74 Wundt published his famous *Grundzüge der physiologischen Psychologie*, which broke decisively with some of Helmholtz's central epistemological views, views that Wundt had largely shared until the early 1870s. Wundt rejected Müller's Law of Specific Sense Energies as a remnant of nativism; he declared the "modern physiological empiricism" (largely of Helmholtz's making) as insufficient and vulnerable to rigorous criticism; and he announced a program to transcend empiricism and nativism through "a deeper going, psychological theory."[23] Wundt remained extremely critical of Helmholtz's opinions in his voluminous later publications and took pains to distinguish his views from those of Helmholtz, even where the distinctions struck some contemporaries as rather forced.[24] We know knothing of Helmholtz's reaction to this apostasy on the part of his former assistant, but he seems never to have mentioned Wundt and his program to transcend physiological explanation through psychology again. The rumor that Helmholtz later blocked Wundt's appointment to Berlin has as yet no documentary support. Helmholtz's enthusiasm for Ebbinghaus's new *Zeitschrift für Psychologie* 16 years later may have derived in part from its determination to be an anti-Wundtian organ. Helmholtz may have viewed the *Zeitschrift* as the key to restoring the old, promising link between psychology and sensory physiology, a link that Wundt of all people seemed prepared to abandon in favor of a more autonomous conception of psychology.

HELMHOLTZ'S METHODOLOGY AND THE NEEDS OF THE NEW PSYCHOLOGY

The reaction of Wundt and others to Helmholtz's work reflected the new psychology's symbiotic and ambivalent relationship with the powerful and established discipline of sensory physiology. Helmholtz's theories came to the new psychology embodied in a web of methodological and philosophical commitments about the nature of mind and about the proper ways of investigating and explaining sensory function. Psychologists found many of these highly congenial and conducive to the ends of their own science. Most generally, Helmholtz's empiricist insistence that the most fundamental processes of mental life—our concept of self, of extension and spatiality, of external objects localized in space—are the results of learning and learned behavior opened up a broad potential for investigations of development and learning. Among the founders of the new psychology in Germany before 1890 only Stumpf sided with the nativists to deny that our intuition of spatiality is not wholly learned, and even Stumpf was prepared to admit that most of our knowledge of the properties of space, as opposed to the bare dictum of spatiality itself, was derived from experience, as Helmholtz had claimed.[25]

Helmholtz's influence strongly reinforced, although it did not create, the "elementist" tendencies of the new German psychology. Until the rise of the Gestalt school in the twentieth century, German psychology presupposed the existence of primitive sensations and took as its task the role of explaining how these elements are combined or compounded into more complex mental entities like perceptions. To Helmholtz, patterns of physical stimuli in the sense organs generate isomorphic patterns of nervous excitations, which, in turn, generate isomorphic patterns of simple and elemental sensations. These sensations are then operated upon by the processes of "unconscious inductive inference" before they emerge into consciousness as complex perceptions. Helmholtz used this simple model to correlate sensations with patterns of stimuli to deduce the nature of the processes in the sense organ that had produced that particular correlation.[26] The model, and the successes Helmholtz achieved using it, reinforced the elementist tendencies of the new psychology.

Helmholtz's physiological methods also served the new psychology in supporting the effectiveness of introspection as a psychological tool. Helmholtz was widely criticized for his assumptions of unconscious inference and the unconscious sensations they seem to presuppose. Helmholtz, however, never felt the paradox of these notions, in part because he was convinced that while these processes are normally unconscious, some at least can be brought to consciousness through the aid of concentration and experimental technique. Helmholtz's most ingenious experiments, and those that most influenced contemporary psychologists, aimed at bringing to consciousness such phenomena as the upper partials of a complex tone, the double images of objects lying outside the horopter locus, and the role of attention in our awareness of the retinal field. Helmholtz's great faith in the power of introspection reassured psychologists of the capacity of mind to inventory its contents, even in ideal cases down to the primitive elements of sensation.

But Helmholtz also espoused philosophical and methodological commitments that the new psychologists could not reconcile with the ultimate requirements of their science. This lessened the value of Helmholtz's theories for them, but it also forced the psychologists of his generation to think more carefully through the differences of physiological and psychological explanation, to define more fully the methodological bases of their science, and to reject many of Helmholtz's ideas or recast them onto a more psychologically secure foundation. These actions all reflected the larger ambivalence of the new psychology's relationship to physiology.

Helmholtz's approach posed difficulties for psychology first in its reluctance to accept the elemental nature of some of our most fundamental introspective experiences. When a complex periodic wave disturbance impinges on the ear, we hear the resulting tone as having pitch and loudness corresponding to the frequency and intensity of the wave's fundamental component; the higher harmonics normally fuse with the fundamental and contribute to the experience mainly by determining the timbre. Is this tonal sensation elemental? No, claimed Helmholtz. The ear "hears" each vibratory component of the original disturbance separately, as loud as the physical intensity dictates. That most of these preconscious sensations never reach consciousness only proves that the complex tone is really a perception, that is, unconscious reasoning has operated on the elemental sensations so that our conscious attention is directed only at some of them. In defense of this view Helmholtz noted that trained ears like his own, when their attention is especially concentrated, can "hear out" the upper partial tones, proving that they are potentially there always as conscious sensations. These psychological assumptions about tonal perception obviously simplify the development of physiological models of the ear and the auditory nerves, since they eliminate the hypothetical mechanisms that would otherwise be required in order to explain tonal fusion as an organic rather than a psychic event.[27]

This interpretation of tones proved very controversial. G. E. Müller attacked it in his dissertation of 1873, noting that for all observers under normal circumstances the experience of a tone is unified and elemental, and that the fusion of the harmonic components must therefore be wholly organic. When trained observers concentrate to hear out a particular partial tone, they must in some way, not yet understood, be inducing a physiological change in the corresponding tuned receptors of the cochlea, which enhances their sensitivity above that of the surrounding receptors and so allows the observer to hear a tone component that would otherwise be perfectly fused with the others. Carl Stumpf in his *Tonpsychologie* of 1890 rejected this idea as physiological speculation, and he agreed with Helmholtz that the upper partials are potentially in consciousness. Stumpf, however, rejected Helmholtz's theory that the consonance and dissonance of tones arise from our subliminal awareness of the degree of mutual beating among the two sets of upper partial tones. He derived a series of laws to describe the phenomena of fusion, consonance, and dissonance that yielded largely the same results as did Helmholtz's theory, but he insisted that the laws must rest on a strictly phenomenological basis, this being the only prudent course for an empirical psychology.[28]

A similar example occurred in the case of color vision. Helmholtz insisted that when light strikes our retinas, each of the three color sensors given by the Young–Helmholtz theory reacts, each generating in the sensorium the sensation of its own physiological primary color. Each such sensation "comes to consciousness" as a real, potential sensation, independent of all the others and each independently obeying Fechner's Law. In the sensorium the three primaries are fused to yield the mixed color of which we are consciously aware. Introspection, however, assures us that contrary to this suggestion the primary colors do not come to consciousness at all, for mixed colors are always experienced as absolutely simple sensations. Must the psychologist, then, rely upon physical analysis and assumptions of neural simplicity to deduce the true, elemental sensations, or may he rely upon bare, introspective experience in his attempts to understand sensation and perception? Stumpf, in his tribute to Helmholtz's influence upon the new psychology, identified this problem as the central issue dividing the physiology and psychology of the senses.[29]

Helmholtz's running debate with Hering and the nativists over the origins of our perception of space posed a related dilemma for the new psychology. Helmholtz conceived this debate partly as about methodology: conceptual and explanatory economy demand that we explain space perception insofar as possible as an empirical, learned response to sensory experience. He also regarded the dispute as partly physiological: the facts of space perception do not, he believed, compel us to postulate hypothetical neural mechanisms and interactions in order to explain them, as nativists try to do. Psychologists saw the issue differently. For them the question was, can spatiality as a dictum of experience be plausibly represented as created or built up from sensory qualities like kinesthetic awareness that are themselves not spatial? And if so, what must be the nature of those prespatial sensations? Or is it inconceivable that any sort of "mental chemistry" could generate spatial perceptions out of nonspatial sensations? Stumpf, one of the lone early nativists among the new psychologists, declared the former possibility to be a psychological absurdity. Even Helmholtz, he insisted, had never claimed that all spatial perception must be regarded as empirical and learned, only that we must learn through experience how the space we innately conceive corresponds to objective, external space.[30]

However plausible Stumpf's apology for Helmholtz's empiricism may have seemed, by the 1880s the climate in German psychology had changed. Hering and Karl Vierordt were tenaciously defending and rendering respectable the nativist position, and Wundt was lapsing further from his early empiricism into obfuscation of the issue. By the 1890s major texts like those of Ebbinghaus and Külpe were espousing moderately nativistic positions, and during the next decade German psychology would turn its back on the controversy altogether.[31] This important change symbolized a decline in Helmholtz's influence and a move in psychology away from the physiological preoccupations of Helmholtz's day toward a more phenomenological and methodologically autonomous stance.

Psychologists also found it difficult to accept the notions of unconscious sensation and unconscious inference that lay at the heart of Helmholtz's theory of perception, and that he never repudiated. By the 1880s psychologists were firmly rejecting unconscious elements as hypothetical entities wholly beyond experience and investigation.

They preferred other analogies to describe the process through which sensations are processed into perceptions: habitual association of ideas along the lines of English psychology, the mental chemistry or "theory of fusions" of Wundt and his school, or a strict phenomenalism. If "unconscious inference" is used to mean nothing more than an involuntary association of mental elements that is intimately governed by interest and attention, Stumpf conceded, then the term can be tolerated, even though it is still misleading, since that process involves neither inference nor anything unconscious. The more circumspect advocates of the term, including Helmholtz, use "unconscious inference" to mean little more than "association" in the traditional sense. Unfortunately other, weaker minds use the term as license to postulate "a whole world of unconscious knowledge."[32]

Stumpf's apology for Helmholtz's empiricism contained a grain of truth; that for his unconscious inferences did not. Helmholtz meant more by unconscious inference than the mere association of ideas, and its use reflected his commitment to a concept of mind that set him apart from the new psychologists. For all his ostensible repudiation of idealism, Helmholtz adhered to a concept of mind as ego, a concept basic to German idealism. Mind as ego lies under an imperative to construct an image of reality in accordance with the a priori principle of causality, through the use of the will and through reflection on the imperfect data supplied by the senses.[33] Although Helmholtz occasionally lapsed into associationist language, and although his empiricism is today widely interpreted as an associationist theory as Stumpf would have it, at base Helmholtz's conception of mental function was rationalistic, not associationist. As the organ of reason, mind can be bound by no laws of development beyond the processes of learning. Helmholtz never explicitly commented upon or repudiated the psychologist's program to deduce psychic laws of combination to which the mind is subject. This program, however, stood at odds to the concept of mind underlying Helmholtz's writings, a concept emphasizing reason, volition, and construction.

This concept of mind shielded Helmholtz from a philosophical issue the new psychology found central. In all his writings on sensory physiology and epistemology, for example, Helmholtz never touched upon the issue of mind–brain interaction. Far from his being a reductionist, it cannot even be definitely established that Helmholtz fully shared the psychophysical parallelism of his day.[34] He normally confused the issue of mind–brain interaction with the larger metaphysical issue of idealism versus realism, which had loomed so large and pressing to his own postromantic generation. For him, empiricism served on a methodological level as a set of assumptions that defined the problem areas to which biophysical methods could be fruitfully applied in the study of sensation, and that relegated to "mind" or "unconscious inference" those that could not be so attacked. On a philosophical level his empiricism reflected his rationalistic concept of mind, the notion that the problem of psychology is not to explain the nature and functioning of mind but rather to explain the nature of the information that flows to and away from the mind. Obviously the new psychology could not accept such a limited program.

At least once his theory of mind and perception led Helmholtz into embarrassing difficulties. Mind, to Helmholtz, is entirely pragmatic and constructionist in its concerns; the process of unconscious reasoning proceeds wholly on the necessity of obtaining useful information about the external world. For this reason unconscious inference lets us go about oblivious to the retinal blind spot, since "seeing it" would contribute no useful information about the external world. In the first editions of the *Tonempfindungen* Helmholtz employed the same principle to explain why unconscious reasoning suppresses the upper partial tones of a complex tone, except as they contribute to the timbre of the fundamental.[35] A complex tone is simply the "sufficient sensory sign" of the external object on which the tone has been produced. For example, if the pattern of upper partials identifies a tone as having been produced on a particular violin, and when that information has been obtained through timbre, no further information about the external world would be obtained by allowing the partial tones to come individually into consciousness.

G. E. Muller was merely the first in a succession of psychologists to ridicule this view, noting among other objections that the tone of a violin is no less a fused sensation for one who has never seen such an object or learned to recognize its timbre as for a practiced violinist.[36] Helmholtz clung to this inadequate position through three editions of the *Tonempfindungen*, abandoning it only in the fourth edition of 1877. That fact reflects the depth of his commitment to the concept of mind as ego and to the pragmatic, investigatory imperative that determines its activities. By the 1890s that concept of mind must have struck the new psychologists as old-fashioned and naive, and most certainly as no conception of mind on which a scientific psychology could rest.

Even Helmholtz cannot be taken as representing all of German sensory physiology. Nevertheless, his relationship to the new psychology may point to some interesting morals concerning the relationship of the two sciences during the period. For purposes of institutional legitimation, the new psychology did try avidly to associate itself with the more prestigious and established field, to acclaim Helmholtz along with Fechner, Herbart, Lotze, and sometimes Wundt as a creator of the new science. The close association with physiology proved very profitable during the early decades of the 1860s and 1870s. At the level of practice, however, as the analysis of Helmholtz's work suggests, the methods and assumptions that supported a program of sensory physiology did not always serve the ultimate interests of psychology as a science. After 1900, German psychology began to shift away from its earlier programmatic commitments. The Gestalt school began to insist upon the irreducible nature of our perceptions and to reject the elementism and mental chemistry of earlier generations; psychologists turned increasingly to nativist conceptions of space perception; volition and higher mental processes began to challenge sensation and perception as the psychologists' main area of research; and there were criticisms of the reliability of introspection as a method. These changes can be plausibly interpreted in part as movements away from the former association of psychology with sensory physiology and its methods. They reflect the growing maturity of the field, the greater security of its institutional position, and its increased intellectual autonomy with respect to philosophy.

NOTES

1. Carl Stumpf, "Hermann von Helmholtz and the New Psychology," *Psychological Review* 2 (1895):1-12, on 2. For a brief account of Helmholtz's career and scientific achievements see "Helmholtz, Hermann von," *Dictionary of Scientific Biography* 6 (New York: Scribner, 1972):241-53 and the bibliography cited on p. 253.

2. Joseph Ben-David and Abraham Zloczower, "Universities and Academic Systems in Modern Societies," *European Journal of Sociology* 3 (1962): 45-85; Peter Lundgren, "Differentiation in German Higher Education, 1860-1930" (unpubl. ms.); Christian von Ferber, *Untersuchungen zur Lage der deutschen Hochschullehrer* (Göttingen: Vandenhoeck & Ruprecht, 1956), pp. 191-209.

3. See for example Franz Brentano, *Psychologie vom empirischen Standpunkt*, 2 vols., 2nd ed. (Leipzig: Felix Meiner, 1924), p. 69.

4. Wilhelm Wundt, *Die Psychologie im Kampf ums Dasein*, 2nd ed. (Leipzig: Kröner Verlag, 1913), p. 7.

5. See Wundt, *Kampf ums Dasein*, pp. 10-28; Carl Stumpf's comments in Max Lenz, *Geschichte der Königlichen Friedrich-Wilhelms-Universität zu*

Berlin, 4 vols. (Halle: Waisenhaus, 1910-)3:205; and Stumpf, *Tonpsychologie,* 2 vols. (Leipzig: S. Hirzel, 1883, 1890)2:vi.

6. Figures from *Minerva. Jahrbuch der gelehrten Welt,* vols. 20 (1910-11) and 27 (1925). *Minerva* 4 (1894-95) lists one academic officially in *Psychologie* and only Berlin, Breslau, and Leipzig as possessing official institutes or collections. Private institutes, that is, those financed by the professor responsible for psychology, or collections of instruments considered part of other institutes, for example, the philosophy seminar or physiology institute, do not appear in the *Minerva* figures. Compare Wundt, *Kampf ums Dasein,* p. 36, and William O. Krohn, "Facilities in Experimental Psychology at the Various German Universities," *American Journal of Psychology* 4 (1891):585-94. For a detailed study of the institutional emergence of German psychology see Mitchell G. Ash, "Academic Politics in the History of Science: Experimental Psychology in Germany, 1879-1941," forthcoming in *Central European History* 14 (1981).

7. Joseph Ben-David and Randall Collins, "Social Factors in the Origins of a New Science: The Case of Psychology," *American Sociological Review* 31 (1966):451-65.

8. Dorothy Ross, "On the Origins of Psychology," *American Sociological Review* 32 (1967):466-72; David E. Leary, "The Philosphical Development of the Conception of Psychology in Germany, 1780-1850," *Journal of the History of the Behavioral Sciences* 14 (1978):113-21; David E. Leary, "Wundt and After: Psychology's Shifting Relations with the Natural Sciences, Social Sciences, and Philosophy," *Journal of the History of the Behavioral Sciences* 15 (1979):231-41, on 236.

9. Wilhelm Wundt, Beiträge zur Theorie der Sinneswahrnehmung (1862) in *The Origins of Psychology. A Collection of Early Writings,* ed. Wolfgang G. Bringmann, mul. vols. (New York: Alan R. Liss, 1976)4:109-206 and vol. 5; Wundt, *Gründzuge der physiologischen Psychologie,* 3 vols., 6th rev. ed. (Leipzig: Wilhelm Engelmann, 1908)1:1-4; and the excellent account by Theodore Mischel, "Wundt and the Conceptual Foundations of Psychology," *Philosphy and Phenomenological Research* 31 (1970/71):1-26. Wundt's programmatic writings reflect an ever-decreasing emphasis on physiology and a growing concern for the unity and uniqueness of psychological knowledge.

10. Brentano, *Psychologie vom empirischen Standpunkt,* 1:93.

11. Ibid., 1:33-35, 66-67.

12. *Zeitschrift für Psychologie und Physiologie der Sinnesorgane* 1 (Berlin, 1890):2-3.

13. Irwin Curtis Baker, "Interactions between the Ideas of Gustav Fechner and Hermann Helmholtz in the Period 1838-1873," unpubl. ms., Ottawa, 1981.

14. Helmholtz, "Die Störung der Wahrnehmung kleinster Helligkeitsunterschiede durch das Eigenlicht der Netzhaut," *Zeitschrift für Psychologie und Physiologie der Sinnesorgane* 1 (1890):5-17.

15. Helmholtz, "Versuch einer erweiterten Anwendung des Fechnerschen Gesetzes im Farbensystem," *Zeitschrift für Psychologie und Physiologie der Sinnesorgane* 2 (1891):1-31, on p. 19.

16. Helmholtz, "Versuch, das psychophysische Gesetz auf die Farbenunterschiede trichromatischer Augen anzuwenden," in ibid. 3 (1891):1-20. Helmholtz also published the more philosophical and speculative article recapitulating his empiricist theory of perception, "Ueber den Ursprung der richtigen Deutung unserer Sinneseindrücke" in ibid. 7 (1894):81-96.

17. See Solomon Diamond, "Wundt before Leipzig," in *Wilhelm Wundt*

and the *Making of a Scientific Psychology*, ed. R. W. Rieber (New York: Plenum Press, 1980), pp. 1-70, especially pp. 28-31 and 51-56.

18. Wundt, *Sinneswahrnehmung*, in *Origins of Psychology* 4:135-45. See also William R. Woodward, "From Association to Gestalt: The Fate of Hermann Lotze's Theory of Spatial Perception, 1846-1920," *Isis* 69 (1978):572-82.

19. Helmholtz, *Helmholtz's Treatise on Physiological Optics*, 3 vols., trans from the 3rd German ed., ed. James P. Southall (New York: Dover Press, 1962) 3:229-30, 558, 70, 121.

20. Wundt, *Sinneswahrnehmung*, in *Origins of Psychology* 5:397.

21. See Diamond, "Wundt before Leipzig," pp. 50-51.

22. Wolfgang G. Bringmann, Gottfried Bringmann, and David Cottrell, "Helmholtz und Wundt an der Heidelberger Universität 1858-1871," *Heidelberger Jahrbücher* 20 (1976):79-88; Felix Schlotte, "Beiträge zum Lebensbild Wilhelm Wundts aus seinem Briefwechsel," *Wissenschaftliche Zeitschrift der Karl-Marx-Universität Leipzig. 5. Jahrgang. 1955/56. Gesellschafts-und Sprachwissenschaftliche Reihe*, No. 4, pp. 333-49, especially 335-37.

23. Wundt, *Grundzuge* 1:iv-vi "Preface to the First Edition."

24. Stumpf, *Tonpsychologie* 2:119-23.

25. Carl Stumpf, *Ueber den psychologischen Ursprung der Raumvorstellung* (Leipzig: S. Hirzel, 1873), pp. 97-103 and compare Edwin G. Boring, *Sensation and Perception in the History of Experimental Psychology* (New York: D. Appleton-Century Company, 1942), pp. 28-34.

26. R. Steven Turner, "Hermann von Helmholtz and the Empiricist Vision," *Journal of the History of the Behavioral Sciences* 13 (1977): 48-58.

27. R. Steven Turner, "The Ohm-Seebeck Dispute, Herman von Helmholtz, and the Origins of Physiological Acoustics," *British Journal for the History of Science* 10 (1977):1-24, on 20.

28. G. E. Müller, *Zur Theorie der sinnlichen Aufmerksamkeit. Inauguraldissertation zur Erlangung der philosophischen Doktorwürde an der Georg-Augusts-Universität zu Göttingen* (Leipzig: A. Adelmann, n.d.), pp. 23-39, and Stumpf, *Tonpsychologie* 2:5, 214, and passim. Compare Boring, *Sensation and Perception*, pp. 357-63 and Wundt, *Physiologischen Psychologie* 3:501-2.

29. Stumpf, "Hermann von Helmholtz," p. 6.

30. Stumpf, *Raumvorstellung*, p. 100.

31. Hermann Ebbinghaus, *Grundzuge der Psychologie*, 4th ed. (Leipzig: Veit & Comp., 1919), pp. 490-4; Oswald Külpe, *Grundriss der Psychologie* (Leipzig: Wilhelm Engelmann, 1893), pp. 385-87; Wundt, *Physiologischen Psychologie* 2:702-5; and Woodward, "From Association to Gestalt," pp. 578-82.

32. Stumpf, *Raumvorstellung*, pp. 313-14; Stumpf, *Tonpsychologie* 1: 90. Ebbinghaus, *Grundzüge*, pp. 56-61; Kulpe, *Grundriss*, p. 300; Brentano, *Psychologie vom empirischen Standpunkt* 1:144-45.

33. Turner, "Empiricist Vision," pp. 55-58, especially for the influence of Fichte on Helmholz. Kurt Danziger points out that Wundt, like Helmholtz, was misinterpreted as an associationist. See his "Wundt and the Two Traditions of Psychology," in *Wilhelm Wundt*, ed. Rieber, pp. 73-88.

34. Nicholas Pastore, in fact, concludes Helmholtz was not a psychophysical parallelist; see his interesting note in his "Helmholtz on the Projection or Transfer of Sensation," in *Studies in Perception*, ed. Peter Machamer and Robert Turnbull (Columbus: Ohio State University Press, 1978), pp. 355-76, on 371.

35. Hermann von Helmholtz, *Die Lehre von den Tonempfindungen*

(Braunschweig: Vieweg) 1st ed., 1856; 2nd ed., 1863; 3rd ed., 1870; 4th ed., 1877.

36. Muller, *Sinnlichen Aufmerksamkeit,* pp. 28–39; Wundt, *Physiologischen Psychologie* 3:501–2; Stumpf mercifully refused to discuss the notion in his *Tonpsychologie.* For Helmholtz's final position on the question see his *On The Sensations of Tone as a Physiological Basis for the Theory of Music,* trans. A. J. Ellis (London: Longmans, Green & Co., 1875), pp. 62–65.

7

Wundt's Program for the New Psychology: Vicissitudes of Experiment, Theory, and System

William R. Woodward

The mania for a plausible smoothness, the shrinking from an appearance of fallibility, seem in fact in Wundt's later writings to be driven so far as seriously to neutralize the clearness and value of the work. A thinker so learned and intelligent, before whose encyclopedic capacity an entire generation bows down with cordial admiration, ought to be above such foibles. Not in such ways were the best parts of the reputation of a Fechner, a Mill, a Darwin, made.[1]

For patient readings and provocative comments on earlier drafts, I am very grateful to Steven Turner, Lothar Sprung, Daniel Robinson, Robert J. Richards, David E. Leary, Deborah Johnson, Arthur L. Blumenthal, and Mitchell G. Ash. I also wish to recognize here the invaluable interdisciplinary efforts of colleagues at the Karl-Marx-Universität Leipzig, DDR 701 Leipzig; their chapters in the Wundt commemoration volume cited here may be obtained (if the volume is out of print) by writing to them directly in the Sektion Rechtswissenschaft (Orschekowski, Rindert), Sektion Psychologie (Metge, Meischner, Lander, Fritsche, Finster), Sektion Marxistisch-Leninistische Philosophie/Wissenschaftlicher Kommunismus (Terton, Metzler, Kreiser). Sektion Kulturwissenssenschaften und Germanistik (Porsch), and the Karl-Sudhoff-Institut fur Geschichte der Medizin und der Naturwissenschaften (Schreier). The preparation of this chapter was supported in part by NIG Grant LM 03492 from the National Library of Medicine and in part by the Alexander von Humboldt-Stiftung. I especially wish to thank my Humboldt sponsors, Carl Friedrich Grauman (Psychologisches Institut, Heidelberg) and Gundolf Keil (Institut für Geschichte der Medizin, Würzburg).

When William James here expressed exasperation at Wilhelm Wundt's inability to acknowledge a serious modification of his theoretical position under the weight of James's and others' criticism, he was actually criticizing an ideal of scholarship that was already in 1894 fast becoming obsolete. The nineteenth-century scholar in the German cultural region had had a unique academic role. This role was defined by breadth and depth of knowledge, as exemplified in encyclopedic systematization and thorough empirical research. Transmission of this knowledge took place in regular lectures and comprehensive publications. The book, rather than the journal article, was still the principal mode of scholarly communication. It served to establish property rights, not only to newly researched facts, but also to an academician's system and to the school or institute in which that system was propagated.

In trying to assess the problematic contribution of Wilhelm Wundt (1832-1920) to the scientific and professional establishment of psychology, we must be careful to give due regard to the traditional role of the scholar, which he assumed. Wundt's psychology is situated in an extensive physiological and philosophical system. The Leipzig chair awarded to him in 1875 was in philosophy; the hope, subsequently fulfilled, was for a person who could extend the limits of philosophy as traditionally conceived to include the advances of the natural and cultural sciences.[2] Ironically, he succeeded almost too well, for his students—and for that matter the entire course of higher education after him—moved rapidly toward a high degree of disciplinary differentiation in experimental psychology, cultural anthropology, sociology, and psychiatry.

That Wundt did not advocate psychology as an autonomous discipline is telling. It should caution us against evaluating him exclusively by the criteria applied to the experimental scientists, as did his younger rival Carl Stumpf:

> I am too little inclined to polemics, or I would collect the whole list of Wundt's sins and try to identify the worthwhile in all that research in which Wundt has deceived the younger generation. . . . How often has psychology already been made 'exact' in this way, to return later to its old paths in *philosophical psychology*![3]

Stumpf was objecting to the subordination of research to a hypothetico-deductive theory, in contrast to his preference for experimental phenomenology. He overlooked the fact that Wundt possessed the theoretician's skill of posing causal explanations and specific experiments for testing them.

This chapter will therefore evaluate Wundt with respect to the criteria of academic professionalization as well as of scientific knowledge.[4] Wundt's profession belongs to a bygone era; for him, psychology was the foundation for an interdisciplinary concern, the unity of knowledge.[5] The problem areas he explored—evolutionary psychobiology, psychophysics, perception, cognition, logic, language, ethics, and culture—will be treated sequentially from lowest to highest, since the trajectory of his books parallelled the trajectory of his theory of emergent evolution (see Table 7-1). His career shift from medicine to philosophy, his founding of the journal *Philosophische Studien* (not psychological studies), his support of the German cause in World War I, and his opposition to a petition for the separation of chairs of psychology from philosophy were all parts of the elite role of one German mandarin, who rose to influence and fell again for the same reason—the will to system.[6]

METHOD AND THEORY ON THE LOSING SIDE IN EVOLUTIONARY PSYCHOBIOLOGY

Wundt's career was shaped by his medical education, which in the 1850s included a heavy dose of anatomy and physiology, overlaid with embryology. His first seven psychobiological books reviewed the literature in these fields and sequentially treated the stages of nervous development. Their governing assumption was the biogenetic law that ontogeny recapitulates phylogeny in the evolution of higher centers from lower ones, from lowest organism to the most developed human brain.[7] Concurrently with the elaboration of this evolutionary brain model, Wundt was developing a philosophical vocabulary for an emergent evolutionary explanation, albeit largely non-Darwinian, of the mind.

The research methods Wundt learned were somewhat at odds with this grandiose theoretical orientation. Because they derived from an earlier era of mechanistic physiology, they were well suited to serve as prototypes for a rudimentary experimental psychology; but they were poorly suited for testing a theory of mental and social evolution. For example, Wundt's first project under Emil Du Bois-Reymond in Berlin, after taking his medical degree at Heidelberg, was to try to resolve a controversy about whether muscle would stretch in direct proportion to the weight of a stimulus hung on it.

TABLE 7-1. Wundt's Program: Subject Classification of Books (first editions)

Year	Psychobiology & Behavior	Sensation & Psychophysics	Perception & Cognition	Feeling & Language	Epistemology & Logic	Ethics, Art, & Society	History of Philosophy & Law
1856	*Untersuchungen über das Verhalten der Nerven* (Researches on the Behavior of Nerves)						
1857							
1858	*Die Lehre von der Muskelbewegung* (Theory of Muscular Movement)						
1859							
1860							
1861							
1862		*Beiträge zur Theorie der Sinneswahrnehmung* (Contributions toward a Theory of Sense Perception)					
1863		*Vorlesungen über die Menschen- und Thierseele* (Lectures on the Human and Animal Mind)					
1864							
1865	*Lehrbuch der Physiologie des Menschen* (Textbook of Human Physiology)						
1866					*Die physikalische Axiome und ihre Beziehung zum Kausalprinzip* (Physical Axioms and their Relation to the Principle of Causality)		
1867	*Handbuch der medizinischen Physik* (Handbook of Medical Physics)						
1868							
1869							
1870							

1871	
1872	
1873	*Grundzüge der physiologischen Psychologie*
1874	(Principles of Physiological Psychology)
1875	
1876	
1877	
1878	*Logik: Erkenntnislehre*
1879	(Logic: Epistemology)
1880	
1881	
1882	*Logik: Methodenlehre*
1883	(Logic: Theory of Scientific Methods)
1884	*Essays*
1885	(Essays)
1886	*Ethik* (Ethics)
1887	*Zur Moral der literarischen Kritik* (On the Morality of Literary Criticism)
1888	
1889	*System der Philosophie*
1890	(System of Philosophy)

(continued)

171

TABLE 7-1 *(continued)*

Year	Sensation & Psychophysics	Perception & Cognition	Feeling & Language	Epistemology & Logic	Ethics, Art, & Society	History of Philosophy & Law
1891			*Hypnotismus und Suggestion*			
1892						
1893			(Hypnotism and Suggestion)			
1894						
1895						
1896		*Grundriss der Psychologie*				
1897		(Outline of Psychology)				
1898						
1899			*Völkerpsychologie: Die Sprache*			
1900			(Cultural Psychology: Language)			
1901				*Sprachgeschichte und Sprachpsychologie*		*Einleitung in die Philosophie*
1902				(Linguistic History and Psycholinguistics)		(Introduction to Philosophy)
1903						
1904					*Völkerpsychologie: Mythus und Religion* (2 vols.)	
1905					(Cultural Psychology: Myth and Religion)	

1906		
1907		*Völkerpsychologie: Die Kunst* (Cultural Psychology: Art)
1908		
1909		
1910	*Kleine Schriften* (Collected Papers)	*Die Prinzipien der mechanischen Naturlehre* (Principles of a Mechanical Theory of Nature)
1911	*Kleine Schriften* (Collected Papers)	*Probleme der Völkerpsychologie* (Problems of Cultural Psychology)
1912		*Elemente der Völkerpsychologie* (Elements of Cultural Psychology)
1913	*Reden und Aufsätze* (Speeches and Essays)	*Die Psychologie im Kampf ums Dasein* (Psychology in the Struggle for Existence)
1914	*Sinnliche und übersinnliche Welt* (Sensory and Suprasensory World)	
1915		*Die Nationen und ihre Philosophie* (The Nations and Their Philosophy)
1916		
1917		*Völkerpsychologie: Die Gesellschaft* (2 vols.) (Cultural Psychology: Society)
1918		
1919		*Völkerpsychologie: Das Recht* (Cultural Psychology: Law)
1920		*Völkerpsychologie: Kultur und Geschichte* (Cultural Psychology: Culture and History)
1921	*Kleine Schriften* (Collected Papers)	

Recognizing that the use of excised tissue was creating a problem, he devised an apparatus to hang weights on the leg of a live frog, and to record the stretching of the tissue directly on a revolving drum.[8] This experimental design, including the single independent variable—physical stimulus—and the single dependent variable—muscular response—would remain the trademark of his experimental career.

This muscle project led naturally to a second on the "mechanism" of the nerves and nerve centers. Wundt was hardly alone in recognizing that the properties of muscle tissue depend on nervous conditions, but he had the merit at least of trying to reconcile the more physicalist approach of his mentor, Du Bois-Reymond, with the more organicist approaches of a younger generation of physiologists. Du Bois's *Untersuchungen über die thierische Elektricität* (Investigation of Animal Electricity) in 1848–49 posited that nerves respond only to changes in voltage, a physicalist assumption that ignored the inhibitory properties of the nervous system. Wundt sought to introduce and to iron out the theoretical differences of Ivan Sechenov and Alexander Herzen, who emphasized central and peripheral inhibitory factors, respectively. He was not very successful, and after two decades he could offer only a descriptive "interference theory" illustrated with the recordings of movements of live limbs under various conditions of temporal delay between two electrical stimuli. The difference in these neuromuscular responses to short and long delays was supposed to reveal the inhibitory influence of "higher centers."[9]

More promising from the viewpoint of the theory of integrative action he was seeking to formulate, as he soon came to recognize, was the contemporary research on cerebral localization and substitution of function among brain areas by means of extirpation and brain stimulation methods. Following the discovery of the Bell-Magendie law governing the spinal arrangement of the sensory and motor nerves, investigators attempted to locate more precisely the sources of these nerves in the brain. The acceptance of the biogenetic law implied that not only do higher centers evolve from lower ones, but that they excite and inhibit them too. Thus the biogenetic law served as an heuristic principle from which to explore brain function by exciting (electrically), inhibiting (by the use of curare), or removing the brain parts at various levels (by animal experiments or human pathologies).[10]

In his epoch-making *Grundzüge der physiologischen Psychologie*

(Principles of Physiological Psychology) in 1874, Wundt combined a mechanistic physiology with an evolutionary psychobiology. Its two most original sections were those on evolutionary features of the brain, and on cognition as studied by expeirmental methods. The theoretical centerpiece for each was the theory of apperception (see Figure 7-1). This theory simply extended, in psychological terms, the biogenetic law described above. In addition, apperception was the mental parallel of interference theory. In keeping with the embryological evidence for a hierarchy of functions in the nervous system, Wundt described the inhibitory and excitatory control of sensation and perception, cognition and volition, by successively higher centers for voluntary "apperceptive" activity. Just as the interference theory guided physiological experimentation, so the theory of apperception would guide psychological experimentation on the levels of function from reflex to voluntary. Underlying both was the biogenetic law that the development of the individual recapitulates the development of the race.

One can now begin to appreciate what Stumpf and James objected to in Wundt's systematization of contemporary research and theory. He did not always indicate who originated his principles or what evidence supported or contradicted them. For instance, he enunciated five laws of conduction, so-called, of which the first two made opposite claims for brain localization and substitution of function; the third simply asserted that brain connections are reflexive; and the fifth argued that brain function depends on both use and specific reflex connections.[11] The fourth law was the crucial one, for here he asserted the Lamarckian principle of inherited habit, the use–disuse principle. This fit his overall conception of excitation and inhibition, since an organ excited was used and an organ inhibited was not used. Wundt came to realize by the mid-1880s that natural selection, which he had earlier grafted onto his system, was a passive principle of the action of the environment on chance variations of the organism.[12] Since this Darwinian mechanism went against his emphasis on the activity of apperception, he allowed it to fade from his system, though he continued to hold that adaptations could occur through the inheritance of acquired characteristics. By 1890, however, thinkers like August Weismann and William James had come to believe, correctly, that minute profitable variations in the germ plasm accumulate over evolutionary time. Wundt, in other words, was on the losing side in evolutionary psychobiology.

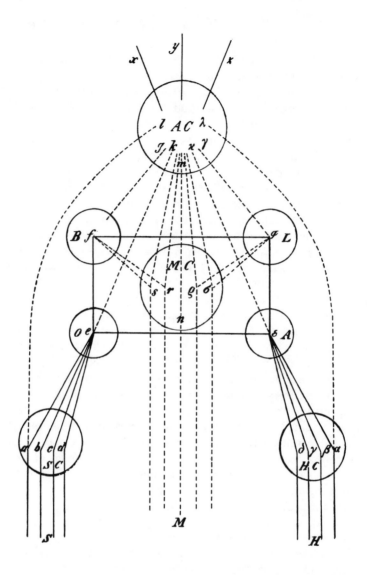

Figure 7-1. Schematic diagram of the brain, showing the close hierarchical connection between higher and lower centers: apperception center (AC), motor
center (MC), centripetal pathways entering the brain (xyz), and centrifugal
pathways leaving it (l, j, k, x, γ, λ). The square indicates that lower centers can
take on automatic functions through the pathways, (fs, fr, ρg, σg) to motor
writing (B) and speech (L) centers. The visual (SC) and auditory (HC) centers
lead via the sensory centers for writing (O) and speech (A) to the apperception
center. The most conspicuous feature is the prominence given to language functions, which Wundt considered intermediate between physiological and cultural
psychology. (From Wundt, *Grundzüge*, 1880, vol. 1, p. 219; 1887, vol. 1, p.
236.)

FROM PSYCHOPHYSICS TO PSYCHOLOGISM

After an initial series of investigations of the muscles and nerves during 1855 to 1860, Wundt let this research lie fallow until the 1870s, perhaps because of the legitimate criticism of Hermann Munk in Berlin.[13] In the intervening period he became preoccupied with sensory psychology. Prior to his apprenticeship in Berlin, he had interned in a Heidelberg clinic and observed the difficulties of hysterical patients in locating sensations. This led to his critique of Ernst Heinrich Weber's anatomical explanation of localization on the skin. In keeping with the popular doctrine of specific sense energies, Weber had assumed that the feelings of touch, pressure, temperature, and common feelings come from separate end organs. Wundt challenged this view, arguing that the functioning of specific sense organs is modified by attention and practice.[14]

This was the beginning of a psychological reinterpretation of existing research on the senses. E. H. Weber had also demonstrated that the proportionate increase of stimulus (*Reiz*) intensity, $\Delta R/R$, is a constant, k. Later, Gustav Theodor Fechner assumed that each of these constant proportions, or "Weber fractions," was a unit of sensation, $S = k\Delta R/R$.[15] By integration Fechner derived his logarithmic law of psychophysics, $S = k \log R$. Wundt shifted the significance of these psychophysical laws to the psychological realm. First, he argued that Weber's law stood for "a special case of a more general law of the relation (*Beziehung*) or relativity (*Relativität*) or our inner states."[16] By relativity, he meant that when a subject makes a judgment or comparison between two physical stimuli, it is not the stimuli but the relative intensity of sensation that is actually being compared. Second, he coined the term "degree of discriminability" (*Merklichkeitsgrad*) and thereby attempted further to relativize Fechner's assumption that sensations are elementary units that can be summed to form a scale. J. Plateau and J. L. R. Delbouef carried this methodological reform further when they produced psychological scales by having the subject halve or double a given stumulus, or find the middle value between two ends of a scale. E. B. Titchener eventually parlayed this law and method into the "reconstruction of psychophysics"; their legacy is felt today in the so-called power law and direct scaling methods of psychophysics enunciated by J. Guilford in the 1930s and S. S. Stevens in the 1950s.[17]

Similar to Wundt's psychological relativizing of sensory intensity was his treatment of sensory quality—for example, pitch and color contrast. He argued that we sense relations of frequencies as pitch directly, "not abstrated from the determination of threshold values of sensation or just-noticeable-differences."[18] Here was his opening for the theory of apperception. For example, complementary colors sensed as the result of the simultaneous or successive presentation of a stimulus color "proceed from that reciprocal interaction of the organ of apperception with the sensory center, as the law of relativity indicates by virtue of its psychological significance."[19] Thus apperception, along with relativity and discriminability, was a third psychological factor in sensation.

Such a "psychologization" of results from anatomy, physiology, and psychophysics was in keeping with efforts of others to carve out an independent subject matter, as well as an autonomous discipline, for psychology. Here we may mention a perfect instance of the manner in which Wundt exerted a pervasive influence yet came under severe criticism. Wundt's discussion of contrast colors had pitted Helmholtz's logical theory of unconscious inference against Hering's physiological opponent processes before defending the psychological theory above. This account was recapitulated by E. B. Dalabarre, the laboratory assistant of William James, in his contribution to James's chapter on "Sensation" in the *Principles*. Only at the end of this Wundtian critique did James interject that

> The full inanity of the law of relativity is best to be seen in Wundt's treatment, where the great *"allgemeiner* [sic] *Gesetz der Beiziehung"* invoked to account for Weber's law, as well as for the phenomena of contrast and so many other matters, can only be defined as a tendency *to feel all things in relation to each other.* Bless its little soul! But why does it change the things so, when it thus feels them in relation?[20]

For James, the psychological relating activity belonged to the "pulse of consciousness" and not to an organ of apperception. Oddly enough, James also followed Wundt's account of Fechner's psychophysics so literally that he quoted over three pages of it before launching a criticism surprisingly akin to Wundt's: "it is these RELATIONS, these DISTANCES, which we are measuring and not the composition of the qualities themselves, as Fechner thinks."[21] Fortunately for psychology, the importance of this debate was not lost in words.

The larger significance of measuring "relations" of sensation, instead of sensations in terms of stimuli, was that psychology thereby achieved liberation from the natural sciences. The immediate issue dividing Wundt and James was the proper application of theory to observation. Wundt preferred theory construction based on hypothetical entities, which he thought were necessary for causal explanation. James allowed only such psychological processes as were immediately confirmable by introspection. This led to different styles of research, Wundt emphasizing parametric studies in which "we change the sensory stimuli in various ways and thereby continually study the mental phenomena," and James doing phenomenological surveys of "the feeling of effort" and "the sense of dizziness."[22] But the main point expressed by both was that consciousness is a datum in its own right, with lawful relations inherent in it. This is what Wundt meant by "psychical causality," and James by his critique of the "psychologists' fallacy" of importing nonpsychological causes.[23] Because mental connections cannot be reduced to physical causes and effects, psychology as a separate domain of explanation was justified in principle. But Wundt and James stopped short of the demand that psychology be made into an autonomous natural science. This was left to the next generation.

SPATIAL PERCEPTION AND THE STATUS OF PSYCHOLOGICAL LAWS

If Wundt was not primarily concerned with establishing psychology as a natural science, the question may arise why he emphasized psychobiology and issues having to do with the central nervous system. His views on spatial perception, for example, were couched in terms of "central innervation" as well as apperception. The answer comes from an appreciation of the place of mind in nature in the German cultural tradition. From this standpoint, the study of psychology belonged to *Wissenschaft*, or the knowledge of the natural and mental realms brought into one coordinated systematic unity.[24]

For Wundt, the limitation of nativistic and empiristic theories of spatial perception was that each contained a measure of truth elevated to dogma. We do have inborn mechanisms of perception, and we do improve in their use through practice. The developmental question remained a joint physiological and psychological one: how do objects come to be localized in perceptual space, given the notorious difficulty of infants and the precision of adults in this regard? Wundt's solution, and the attacks it generated, are revealing of a fundamental difference in the status of psychological laws in the Continental and the Anglo-American traditions.

In the Continental rationalist tradition the problem of perception was to analyze the world of experience into elements and relations; in the British empiricist tradition the problem was conversely to explain the synthesis of the phenomenal world from limited sensory elements and relations. The fact that Wundt worked primarily within the former tradition makes it necessary to understand him in this context, particularly since some of his expositors coming from the latter tradition have incorrectly ascribed "empiricism" and "associationism" to him. Thus, according to a theory formulated by the philosopher J. F. Herbart in the early nineteenth century, our perceptual world is analyzed into mechanical series of qualitative and quantitative sensations. Hermann Lotze, a physician as well as philosopher, anchored this abstract theory in reflex terms in 1852: our sense organs provide the qualitative spatial "coloring" and the limb and eye movements measure these sensations in extent.[25]

Wundt took Lotze's theory one step further. In addition to peripheral "muscular" feelings such as eye movements during fixation of an object, we also make use of central "feelings of innervation" known popularly as effort. Two kinds of visual evidence supported Wundt's interference theory here. Patients with paralysis of the oculomotor muscle consistently overestimate motion in visual space, for, as Wundt explained, "the weakened muscle requires a stronger innervation to execute a certain movement than actually occurred."[26] This phenomenon suggested to Wundt as well as to Helmholtz that central feelings of innervation were involved. A second line of evidence came from Wundt's studies of binocular vision. In estimating the distance of a black thread against a white background, convergence turned out to be more important than accommodation as a clue, and convergence involved peripheral muscular feelings of movement.[27] Thus both central and peripheral feelings combined to yield an index of location in space.

In 1876 Wundt made the strategic mistake of publishing an essay in English emphasizing only one side of his theory, central innervation.[28] For several decades, this imperfect rendition of the views of Helmholtz and Wundt generated confusion and debate. The British experimentalists, Charles Bastian and David Ferrier, contended that there is no such thing as a feeling of outgoing movement, for motor nerves convey no sensory feelings.[29] At best, as William James argued in his essay on "The Feeling of Effort" in 1880, we have incoming sensory feedback from a completed movement.[30] For a time, it seemed that the discovery of kinesthetic receptors would reduce this debate to a mere matter of physiology.[31]

In fact, what James and the others did was to insist upon the primacy of sensorimotor mechanisms in spatial perception; but this much was already taken for granted by Wundt. At the same time,

James separated the apperceptive function into a "still small voice," which in times of severe crisis or irresolution tips the scales of action. In other words, he transferred the problem of the role of conscious mental action from spatial perception to volition. Following William Carpenter and others who drew a sharp line between involuntary and voluntary action, he allocated teleology to the realm of the individual mind, apart from nature.[32]

By comparison, Wundt's psychology was based on a continuum of action from involuntary to voluntary, and the purposive activity of mind in nature. From the point of view of spatial perception, his "law of the correspondence of apperception and fixation" referred to the psychobiological process whereby the eyes make a reflexive adjustment based on their principal axis of rotation, and the mind brings the object to attention. That he did not see this coordination of physiological and psychological laws as a matter of individual choice is indicated by this remark:

> Incidentally, this connection of the laws of eye movements with their function also furnishes one of the most illuminating examples of that immanent teleology of all organic functions . . . because it clearly indicates that the purposive is purposive just because it is also mechanically necessary.[33]

Apperception was no arbitrary subjective act, but the mirror of a lawful reflex process, albeit obeying laws of purpose instead of mechanism.

Evidently the psychological laws of James and Wundt were tied to different ontological and explanatory commitments. For James the possibility of freedom of will was preserved by a conviction of the place of Mind outside Nature; for Wundt this possibility was foreclosed by his "speculative" heritage in *Naturphilosophie*, in which the oneness of Mind and Nature excluded freedom.[34] As Wundt wrote to his student Emil Kraepelin:

> I adhere likewise to determinism; I would not like to call the thought of freedom of will a 'self-deception' however. The question of determinism or indeterminism cannot be empirically decided. . . . The decisive grounds are only of a speculative kind.[35]

Empirically though, the situation was reversed; James allowed will only a "still small voice," while Wundt's voluntarism operated throughout the scale of living things. At either level, the retention of natural scientific categories in the description of consciousness brought inescapable tensions.[36]

A HYPOTHETICO-DEDUCTIVE PROGRAM
OF RESEARCH IN COGNITION

The formulation and testing of the laws of association and apperception and the institutionalization of psychology as an experimental discipline followed in large part the model Wundt provided at Leipzig in the 1880s and 1890s. Because Leipzig served as an international model, the details have more than local interest. When Wundt was called to Leipzig in 1875, he requested and received a storage facility for his own equipment. In 1879 he petitioned the Saxon Ministry of Education for a regular budget, and though the petition was denied he began to offer a laboratory practicum. By 1881 he had founded a journal, *Philosophische Studien*, for the experimental and theoretical work of his school. In 1882 a second petition for the recognition of an "Institute of Experimental Psychology" was refused, but 900 marks was granted for the current year. Finally, when Wundt declined a call to Breslau in 1883, he received official recognition, a regular budget for his laboratory, and a 40-percent raise in his salary. Yet not until 1897 did the Saxon government award him a sizeable institute with a significant budget, apparently the outcome of plans made during his year as rector in 1890–91.[37]

The distinctive feature of Wundt's fiefdom was perceived differently by German and foreign students. For Germans on their way to becoming secondary-school teachers, Wundt offered a place to write a dissertation on almost any philosophical topic in relation to the new psychology of consciousness and behavior, as broadly defined in Table 7-2.[38] To foreigners, who already had degrees, wanting to apprentice in laboratory science, it was an opportunity to combine lectures in the philosophy of mind and the logic of scientific methods with language study and hands-on research. The spectrum of possible topics for both kinds of student was well advertised in Wundt's frequently revised books (see Table 1). Wundt prescribed these topics in professorial fashion, but in a way that tapped his students' interests.[39] Among the most popular topics were perception, cognition, and memory; here Wundt offered a testing ground for his hypothetico-deductive theory of apperception.

The lure of apperception theory stemmed from the weight of the psychobiological evidence supporting the intuitive claim that behavior becomes less instinctual and more voluntary as one ascends the phylogenetic ladder. But the actual principle tested in Wundt's experimental paradigm was a deduction from this biogenetic law applied to thought and action. Wundt hypothesized that consciousness is governed by lower and higher principles of association and apperception. He described these principles by analogy to the physiological principles of excitation and inhibition. In his earlier physiological experiments he had defined excitation as movement following one stimulus, and inhibition as the difference in the movements following two stimuli sequentially presented. In the later psychological analogue, Wundt defined association as the principle underlying the reaction to one stimulus, and apperception as the principle underlying the reaction to two or more stimuli, simultaneously or successively presented.

To make these operational definitions into a platform for systematic experimental research, Wundt needed an experimental design to measure human apperception instead of frog inhibition. An elegant instrument called a chronoscope (see Figure 7-2) replaced the cumbersome chymograph, recording reaction times instead of extent of movement. Dutch physiologists had measured reaction times to tactile, auditory, and visual stimuli, using an astronomers' instrument for recording stellar transits.[40] Wundt noted that these times exemplified mere associative connections; to measure the apperceptive act one had to subtract the associative time from the time for various complex acts.[41] His "subtraction procedure" required the subject to press a telegraph key in response to a visual or auditory stimulus; this was the simple, or associative, reaction time. Then a compound stimulus was presented, with instructions to press the key if it included a white circle but not if it included a black one. Subtracting the simple from the compound reaction time yielded a "discrimination time." Finally, the subject was required to touch the key with the left hand if the circle was white and with the right hand if black. This yielded a "choice time," the volitional component of apperception.[42]

Wundt's results held more promise than substance, for the reaction times proved to be extremely variable and of dubious validity in tapping significant thought processes. Their promise was methodological; the laboratory setting was used to keep the time interval between observation and reaction as short as possible and to produce nearly identical reactions by repetition of the same physical stimuli. Practiced observers were often the researcher or Wundt himself. But practice was not "trained introspection," as in the subsequent program of Edwin B. Titchener in the United States to test the British empiricist doctrine that complex experience is comprised of elementary sensations. Wundt's behavioral emphasis in experimenting on sensation, perception, and cognition did not deserve the reputation Titchener gave it for "introspection" on the "structure" of consciousness. In fact, his restraints on experiment

TABLE 7-2. Wundt's Program: Subject Classification of Doctoral Dissertations

Year	Psychobiology & Behavior	Sensation & Psychophysics	Perception & Cognition	Feeling & Language	Epistemology & Logic	Ethics, Art, & Society	History of Philosophy & Law	Metaphysics & Theology
1876								
1877						X		
1878					X		XXX	
1879	X						X	
1880	X						X	
1881			X		X	X		XX
1882		XX	X					
1883	XX		X		X			
1884							X	
1885	X	XX	XX	X	XX	X	X	
1886		XX	XX				X	
1887			X		X			
1888		X		X	X	X		
1889		X			XX	X		
1890		XX			XX	X	X	
1891	X	X	X			X	XX	
1892	X		X			X		
1893	X	XXX	X		XXX	X	X	X
1894		X	X			XX		X
1895	X		X	X				

Year	Recorded theses (X = one thesis)
1896	X XXX
1897	X X X
1898	X X XX
1899	X XX X
1900	X XXX X X
1901	X X
1902	XX X X XX X XX
1903	X X XX X
1904	XX X X XX
1905	X XXXXX XX X
1906	XXX X X XXX X
1907	XXX X X X
1908	X X X X
1909	X X
1910	XXXX XX XX X XX
1911	X XXX
1912	X XXXX X X
1913	XXXXXX X
1914	X X X
1915	XXXX
1916	
1917	
1918	
1919	X X X
1920	

185

From Miles A. Tinker, "Wundt's Doctorate Students and their Theses 1875–1920," in *Wundt Studies*, pp. 269–79. Cf. Anneros Metge, "Doktoranden Wilhelm Wundt," *Wissenschaftliche Zeitschrift* 2 (1980): 161–66.

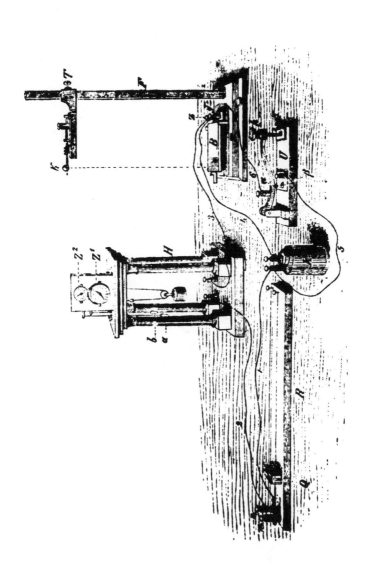

Figure 7-2. Mental chronometry apparatus for the measurement of apperception time by subtracting the simple reaction time to one stimulus from the complex reaction time to two or more stimuli. Pictured here are the Hipp chronoscope (H), the sounder with ball (K) and plate (B), reaction key (K), and rheostat (R). The sounder could be replaced with a visual stimulus device, as described in the text. (From Wundt, *Grundzüge*, 1874, p. 770; 1880, vol. 2, p. 231; 1887, vol. 2, p. 275.)

were rather too strict, for they excluded the study of social behaviors that could not be replicated at will.[43]

The reception of this research program by the medical community was sceptical at first. "I considered it an unfortunate misunderstanding," complained Wundt in retrospect, "that physiologists regarded these things initially as a kind of foreign body which ought to have nothing to do with their subject matter."[44] By comparison, a younger generation of students from the liberal arts rather than medicine saw promise in this "brass instrument psychology." Initially they were occupied in refining his measurements and determining constants; Max Friedrich measured the effect of practice on reaction time, and James McKeen Cattell determined a constant error in the time taken by the electromagnets that activated the chronoscope.[45] A major new orientation was initiated by Oswald Külpe, and carried forth by his later students at Würzburg, when he demonstrated that the subject's performance is strongly influenced by the task (*Aufgabe*) or set (*Einstellung*). The motivational aspect of this "imageless thought" research was actually condoned by Wundt, who wrote that "it deserves further application and development in the same direction."[46] But Wundt censured two extremes of "systematic introspection" for violating his clear division between empirical data collection and theory construction. The "positivist" followers of Ernst Mach and Richard Avenarius trained subjects to report only the content of consciousness devoid of meaning, such as blue patch. The "phenomenological" protegées of Franz Brentano and Edmund Husserl tried to capture this meaning in acts or judgments replete with meaning. But Wundt took an entirely different approach to meaning.

LOGIC, LANGUAGE, AND A
THEORY OF COMMUNICATIVE ACTION

Wundt believed that the higher mental processes are different in principle from the lower ones. In the first place, they are conditioned by society, such that the individual elements of ideas, feelings, and will took on the cultural form of language, myth, and custom.[47] In the second place, the higher processes involve the empirical capacity for choice among various possibilities, namely, value judgments. Wundt accordingly divided his task methodologically. The normative task of his *Logik* was to show how thought ought to proceed in the ideal case. The empirical task of his *Völkerpsychologie*

(Cultural Psychology) in its first two volumes on language, was to explore how thought does in fact proceed in the language and behavior of different animals and societies.

In 1875 Wundt delivered one of his first public lectures at Leipzig on the subject of "language and thought." In it he explained why the Leipzig *Junggrammatiker* (Young Grammarians) could not succeed in their goal to place language on a natural scientific foundation. Language could never be explained by reflexes, for even in its most rudimentary form as emotional expression and gesture, language betrayed meaning. This meaning was constituted by one individual seeking to communicate with another. The methods of studying language would have to do justice to this characteristic. "We do not need to set up the experiment for nature has long since done this for us."[48] He referred to the deaf and dumb, who lack hearing and cannot learn phonetic language without great effort, but who do learn to communicate through the language of gesture.

Wundt nevertheless brought experimentation to language through two avenues, of which the first was his theory of behavior and volition. Previous theories of Johannis Müller, Alexander Bain, and Hermann Lotze had assumed a gap between voluntary and involuntary movements. Wundt filled this gap with his theory of "drives," which can become both more automatic through use and more differentiated through choices.[49] He tested this theory by manipulating the sensory and motor direction of apperception experimentally. Instructions to concentrate on response led to shorter, to concentrate on sensory stimulus to longer reaction times. Practice shortened and discrimination lengthened reactions. By extension, of course, language was based on voluntary and automatic movements of gesture and phonetic speech production.

The other avenue to experiment on language was Wundt's theory of emotion and emotional expression. Darwin's principle of "serviceable associated habits" emphasized the effect of past experience in determining facial expression; but Wundt argued that it did not do justice to the affective side in two respects. He proposed that apperception governs the mimetic movements, as when the hand involuntarily points to the person to whom we speak. This proto-linguistic sign shows that we anticipate future effects of our action, not only past successes. Accompanying the choice of future effects is emotion, which could be measured in duration, intensity, and quality by recording the pulse with a plethysmograph.[50]

In his logic Wundt approached language from the normative and theoretical side. His first volume on "theory of knowledge" argued that the psychological "stream of thought" was primary and that both logical structures and natural language developed from it.

Apperception was the volitional process of selecting one dominant meaning, dA, from the whole idea, A_1, A_2, A_3, . . .—for example, the concept of dog from many particular ideas of dogs. The connection of two such ideas into a single meaning was a proposition, $A = B$, and the connection of propositions into a syllogism or inference another meaning: $A = B$, $B = C$, therefore $A = C$. Whereas logic connected concepts in a linear fashion, language was more fluid. For example, the first words of a child expressed the meaning, if not the form, of a judgement; "my gift" may mean "I give" or "I have given," all expressed as

$$\overset{\frown}{A \quad B}.$$

To the sentence "he teaches music" Wundt gave the syntactic form

$$\overset{\frown}{A \quad \overset{\frown}{B \quad C}},$$

and the sentence "he teaches the child music" became

$$\overset{\frown}{A \quad \overset{\frown}{B \quad \overset{\frown}{C \quad D}}}.^{51}$$

In two respects, Wundt shared the tenets of symbolic logic developed by Gottlob Frege. Both rejected Aristotle's justification of linguistic categories (such as subject and predicate) by appeal to logical forms (such as proposition), which were in turn assumed to express metaphysical relations (such as object and attribute). Instead, they each developed a functional analysis of meaning, whereby languages with different grammars, or different grammatical structures within the same language, may convey the same logical content. They parted company most dramatically in their respective "logicism" and "psychologism"; Frege endorsed a conception of logic as syntax independent of psychology and language, and Wundt was firmly committed to their reciprocal development.[52]

Wundt's linguistic turn in logic had special importance for the justification and methods of cultural psychology. In his logic as "theory of method" he showed that Aristotelian logic was based on deduction as subsumption and induction as enumeration. The new logic of science, first exhibited by Galileo, dissolved this sharp distinction into a joint method of discovering empirical laws by induction and then assuming them as hypotheses from which to deduce testable consequences.[53] The *Natur-* and *Geisteswissenschaften* were alike in their scientific languages for deriving causal laws; their basic difference was in the complexity of their problems. The complexity of *Völkerpsychologie*, for example, was twofold: its historical character, which could not be captured in atemporal sociological laws of "societies"; and its communal products, which cannot be reduced to the work of definite individuals. In the methods of cultural psychology, consequently, there was overlap and difference; the scientific methods of statistics and experiment took on secondary importance to the linguistic methods of criticism, interpretation, and comparison.[54]

In 1900 Wundt finally published the first two volumes of his *Völkerpsychologie* on language. Here he brought together his entire armamentarium of theories and methods of behavior and volition, emotion, and logic in a theory of communicative action. The first volume demonstrated that movements of articulation in vocalization are subservient to culturally conditioned meanings. Supported by the Darwinian argument that language and gesture developed together, Wundt opposed the prevailing theory of the evolution of language through imitation and the association of word meanings and sounds in volume two.[55] He showed with sentence diagrams how language is a psychological product of the analysis of meaning into syntactic structures.

Despite a piecemeal reception, this enormous structural theory of language rooted in physiology, logic, and psychology did leave its mark in psychology. The Leipzig Ganzheit School carried on Wundt's concept of structure, which was shared with Wilhelm Dilthey's cultural forms, Eduard Spranger's "life forms," the Gestalt qualities of the Graz School, and the Gestalt psychology of the Berlin School.[56] The Prague School begun by Anton Marty, a follower of Franz Brentano's "empirical psychology" of acts instead of contents, construed Wundt's sentence diagrams as "psychic functions."[57] This school set the stage for later American functional and behavioral theories of language. In addition to these derivatives, two theoretical developments deserve to be called critical extensions of Wundt's psycholinguistics.

Karl Bühler eventually became the spokesman for the Prague School of functional linguistics. Through his study of animal psychology, he came to criticize the strong emphasis Wundt gave to humans and, in particular, to the speaker. He conceived language as an utterance in a "performance field" consisting of the speaker, the hearer, and the meanings that they share.[58] This "communication act" was a social process in a way in which Wundt's individualistic psychology of sentence production was not. The Chicago School of social behaviorism under George Herbert Mead gave Wundt a similar critique. Mead suggested that in a dog fight, for example, the bared fangs mean one emotion and the tail tucked in flight means another. Wundt's theory expressed such a conversation of gestures, in which the response of each dog became a stimulus for the other. But it did not adequately convey that the gesture becomes a "significant symbol" or linguistic utterance when it conveys a meaning to the listener independent of the speaker's emotion. Moreover, instead of assuming an individual self antecedent to the communication, social behaviorism regards it as the outcome of a functional interaction of two or more persons—a "social act."[59]

ETHICS, CULTURAL PSYCHOLOGY, AND THE LAST CAMPAIGN

The logic and psycholinguistics met a lively reception in comparison to Wundt's ethics and cultural psychology. Among professionals, at least, the call for an interdisciplinary field to subsume sociology and anthropology, ethics and religion, art history and law, was out of step with the countertrend to differentiate these very subjects as autonomous disciplines. Wundt's *Völkerpsychologie*, in its volumes from 1905 on, was largely greeted with silence. Our historical interest in this phase of his career will consist chiefly in setting out the architectonic of a neglected side of his system, locating it in the historical context of NeoKantianism, and revealing some of its political aspirations and liabilities.

The integrity of Wundt's system, and the relation of the cultural to the natural sciences within it, needs to be highlighted here. Wundt reiterated in his *Ethik* in 1886, in his second edition of the *Vorlesungen über die Menschen und Thierseele* (Lectures on the Human and Animal Mind) in 1892, and in his *Völkerpsychologie* between 1900 and 1920 that his goal was "an investigation of the developmental laws of language, myth, and culture."[60] The way to this project was prepared by an extensive study of the empirical norms that regulate the family, community, state, and nation. The methods of discovering these norms were largely comparative and historical; in this respect, Wundt built on the foundations of comparative linguistics and historical sociology. Having constructed a bridge from psychology to social ethics, Wundt walked back across it to a cultural psychology based on the primacy of the social over the individual mind.[61]

The underlying philosophy of science was throughout in tune with contemporary NeoKantianism. The Southwest German Schools at Marburg and Heidelberg were allied in preserving Kant's distinction between the causal and the purposive realms.[62] Natural science provided explanations in terms of cause and effect, while cultural science offered means and purposes.[63] Wundt's account of the origin of art, religion, and law showed that the more complex the action, the more unintended consequences occur; this principle of the "heterogeny of ends" was illustrated in the phantasy life and the moral law as discovered within each individual, where the development of cultural norms was bound to a particular historical circumstance that could not be inferred from the "social psychology" of the present day.[64] Yet the quest for developmental laws set Wundt's enterprise apart from history.

Beneath this rhetoric of coexistence between science and values lay a deepfelt defence of the status quo in university organization, wherein psychology belonged to institutes of philosophy, and students were required to demonstrate wide cultural *Bildung* (Education) as well as technical proficiency in natural scientific methods. Wundt believed, in company with Wilhelm Dilthey and Wilhelm Windelband, that the "causality of character" is illuminated through the historical review of great men and their ideas.[65] To the contention of a younger generation that psychology was in crisis because it lacked autonomous institutes for research and teaching, Wundt replied that the real crisis was in university reforms adequate to the needs of a newly industrialized society.[66] A critic of capitalist "utilitarianism" and the Marxist "principle of surplus value," he held a mandarin belief in the good will of the state to carry out social reforms such as career-oriented education and the extension of educational opportunities to the working classes and to women.[67]

CONCLUSION

One of the perils of an interdisciplinary program is that it may be read, or misread, piecemeal. That this fragmentation occurred in Wundt's case is clear from the divergent development of each of his major problem areas reviewed here. Nevertheless his major impact was programmatic. In North America, his *Grundzüge der physiologischen Psychologie* helped to legitimize an autonomous "New Psychology," while in Europe his *Völkerpsychologie* served to preserve a disciplinary bifurcation between natural scientific and cultural scientific psychology.[68] While Wundt did not condone completely either impact, he did at least partly help to bring both about. His skill in the politics of higher education and scientific institutionalization emerges as the key to his career, an attribute to which he pointed himself in his memoirs.[69] This ability to catalyze two such different professional identities for the discipline stands out above Wundt's vicissitudes of experiment, theory, and system.

NOTES

1. William James, "Professor Wundt and Feelings of Innvervation," *Pyschological Review* 1 (1894):73.
2. See Stephen Toulmin and David E. Leary, "The Cult of Empiricism in Psychology, & Beyond," in Sigmund Koch and David E. Leary (eds.), *A Century of Psychology as Science: Retrospections and Assessments* (New York: McGraw-Hill, in press). Cf. Alfred Arnold, *Wilhelm Wundt. Sein philosophisches System* (Berlin: Akademie, 1980).
3. Carl Stumpf to William James, 8 Sept. 1886, Houghton Library, Harvard (bMS Am 1092.9).
4. Cf. Jerome R. Ravetz, *Scientific Knowledge and its Social Problems* (New York: Oxford University Press, 1971), and Henrika Kuklick, "Boundary Maintenance in American Sociology: Limitations to Academic 'Professionalization'," *Journal of the History of the Behavioral Sciences* 16 (1980):201-19.
5. Arthur L. Blumenthal, "Wilhelm Wundt: Psychology as the Propadeutic Science," in *Points of View on the History of Modern Psychology*, ed. C. Buxton (New York: Academic Press, 1981).
6. Cf. Fritz K. Ringer, *The Decline of the German Mandarins: The German Academic Community, 1890-1933* (Cambridge, Mass.: Harvard University Press, 1969). On Wundt's politics, see Arnold, pp. 21-26; on his opposition to the petition, see Mitchell G. Ash, "Wilhelm Wundt and Oswald Külpe on the Institutional Status of Psychology: An Academic Controversy in Historical Context," *Wundt Studies*, ed. W. G. Bringman and R. D. Tweney (Toronto: C. J. Hogrefe, Inc., 1980). Access to the social and political context of Wundt's career is now available through the catalogue of 618 (unpublished) letters from 1854 to 1919: "Wilhelm Wundt (1832-1920). Verzeichnis der Briefe aus dem Nachlass von Max Wundt." ed. and annotated by Gustav A. Ungerer (Heidelberg: 1979), ca. 60 pp. The catalogue is held by Universitäts-archiv Tübingen, Wilhelmstr. 32, 74 Tübingen, W. Germany, as are photocopies of the letters in typed form. Original letters are in the Leipzig Wundt Archiv administered by Wolfram Meisschner and Anneros Metge.
7. In the stage explanations of embryology and the functional explanations of comparative anatomy, "the same law of development is found, in that the earlier stages of the higher vertebrates are similar to the continuing levels of organization of the lower ones." Wilhelm Wundt, *Grundzüge der physiologischen Psychologie* (Leipzig: W. Engelmann, 1874 [1880, 1887, 1893, 1902-1903, 1908-10-11]), p. 43.
8. Wilhelm Wundt, *Die Lehre von der Muskelbewegung* (Braunschweig: F. Vieweg, 1858). He adapted this apparatus, the chymograph, from the physiologist Carl Ludwig. Cf. Wilhelm Wundt, *Erlebtes und Erkanntes* (Stuttgart: Kröner, 1920), pp. 109-10.
9. Wilhelm Wundt, *Untersuchungen zur Mechanik der Nerven und Nervencentren*, 2 vols. (Stuttgart: F. Enke, 1871, 1876); cf. Judith P. Swazey, *Reflexes and Motor Integration: Sherrington's Concept of Integrative Action* (Cambridge: Harvard University Press, 1969).
10. Valuable secondary literature, although it overlooks Wundt, includes: Robert M. Young, *Mind, Brain and Adaptation in the Nineteenth Century* (Oxford: Clarendon, 1970); Stephen J. Gould, *Ontogeny and Phylogeny* (Cambridge, Mass.: Harvard University Press, 1978); and Paul Cranefield, *The Way in and the Way Out* (Mt. Kisco, N.Y.: Futura, 1974).

11. Wundt, *Grundzüge*, 1874, p. 231; ibid., 1887, vol. 1, p. 241. Cf. Judith P. Swazey, "Action propre and Action commune: the Localization of Cerebral Function," *Journal of the History of Biology* 3 (1970):213-34.

12. Robert J. Richards, "Wundt's Early Theories of Unconscious Inference and Cognitive Evolution in their Relation to Darwinian Biopsychology," in *Wundt Studies*, pp. 42-70.

13. Solomon Diamond, "Wundt Before Leipzig," in *Wilhelm Wundt and the Making of a Scientific Psychology*, ed. Robert Rieber (New York: Plenum, 1980), pp. 1-80.

14. Wilhelm Wundt, *Beiträge zur Theorie der Sinneswahrnehmung* (Leipzig/Heidelberg: C. F. Winter, 1862), p. 55. Cf. W. R. Woodward, "Hermann Lotze's Critique of Johannes Müller's Doctrine of Specific Sense Energies," *Medical History* 19 (1975):147-57.

15. Lothar Sprung and Helga Sprung, "Gustav Theodor Fechner," *Urania*, Radio lecture, 23 July, 1980, 24 pp. Cf. Wolfgang Schreier, "Fechners experimentelle Methoden in der Psychophysik," *Beiträge zur Wundt-Forschung II* (Leipzig: Karl-Marx-Universität, 1977), pp. 22-29.

16. Wundt, *Grundzüge*, 1880, vol. 1, p. 351.

17. For an exhaustive historical–theoretical overview up to 1905, see Edwin B. Titchener, *Experimental Psychology*, 4 vols. (New York: Macmillan, 1901, 1905), vol. 2, pt. 2, p. xci and passim. Cf. W. R. Woodward, "Kuhn, Popper, Lakatos and Psychophysics: A Case Study in Scientific Revolutions," paper presented at American Psychological Association Convention, Toronto, 1979.

18. Wundt, *Grundzüge*, 1880, vol. 1, p. 396.

19. Ibid., p. 460.

20. William James, *Principles of Psychology*, 2 vols. (New York: Holt, 1890), vol. 2, p. 28.

21. Ibid., vol. 1, p. 546.

22. Wundt, *Beiträge*, p. xxix. Cf. Kurt Danziger, "The History of Introspection Reconsidered," *Journal of the History of the Behavioral Sciences* 16 (1980):241-62; Anneros Metge, "Wilhelm Wundts Position zur psychophysischen Methodik," *Beiträge zur Wundt-Forschung* (Leipzig: Karl-Marx-Universität 1975), pp. 52-62. See also William R. Woodward, "Introduction," *Essays in Psychology*, in *The Works of William James* (Cambridge: Harvard University Press, in preparation).

23. Cf. Theodor Mischel, "Wundt and the Conceptual Foundations of Psychology," *Philosophy and Phenomenological Research* 31 (1970):1-26. Cf. Woodward, "Introduction," *James*, note 22.

24. Cf. Hans V. Rappard, *Psychology as Self-Knowledge*, trans. L. Faili (Aasen, The Netherlands: Van Gorcum, 1979), pp. 84-110.

25. William R. Woodward, "From Association to Gestalt: The Fate of Hermann Lotze's Theory of Spatial Perception, 1846-1920," *Isis* 69 (1968): 572-82.

26. Wundt, *Beiträge*, p. 413; cf. Wundt, *Grundzüge*, 1880, vol. 2, p. 91.

27. Wundt, *Beiträge*, pp. 194, 415; Wundt, *Grundzüge* 1880, vol. 2, p. 95.

28. Wilhelm Wundt, "Central Innervation and Consciousness," *Mind* 1 (1876):161-78. Cf. *Grundzüge*, 1874, pp. 316-17.

29. Charles Bastian, *The Brain as an Organ of the Mind* (New York: Appleton, 1880), p. 543; David Ferrier, *The Functions of the Brain*, 2nd ed. (New York: G. P. Putnam's Sons, 1886 [1876]), pp. 382f., 461.

30. William James, "The Feeling of Effort," *Anniversary Memoirs of the Boston Society of Natural History* 8(1880):1-34.

31. Cf. Helen E. Ross, "Sensations in Innervation—A Review from Wundt to the Present Day," in *Wilhelm Wundt: Progressives Erbe, Wissenschaftsentwicklung und Gegenwart*, ed. W. Meischner and A. Metge (Leipzig: Karl-Marx-Universität, 1980), pp. 129-40.

32. Kurt Danziger, "Mid-Nineteenth-Century British Psycho-Physiology," this volume, chapter 5.

33. Wundt, *Grundzüge*, 6th ed. (1910), vol. 2, p. 563.

34. Kurt Danziger, "The Two Traditions of Wilhelm Wundt and William James," in *Wilhelm Wundt*, ed. Rieber.

35. W. Wundt to Emil Kraepelin, April 2, 1880, in Wundt, *Nachlass*, Tübingen University. Robert J. Richards provided this quotation and valuable assistance with the argument.

36. Edmund Husserl, *The Crisis of European Sciences and Transcendental Phenomenology*, trans. D. Carr (Evanston, Ill.: Northwestern University Press, 1970 [1954]), pp. 230-32. Cf. Richard P. High, "Perceptual Realism in William James's Theory of Spatial Perception," *Journal of the History of the Behavioral Sciences* 17 (1981), in press.

37. Wolfgang G. Bringmann, Norma J. Bringmann, and Gustav A. Ungerer, "The Establishment of Wundt's Laboratory: An Archival and Documentary Study," in *Wundt Studies*. Cf. Wolfgang G. Bringmann and Gustav A. Ungerer, "The Establishment of Wilhelm Wundt's Leipzig Laboratory," *Storia e Critica della Psicologia* 1 (1980):11-28. Wolfgang G. Bringmann and Gustav A. Ungerer, "The Foundation of the Institute for Experimental Psychology at Leipzig University," *Psychological Research* 42 (1980):5-18.

38. Samuel Fernberger, "Wundt's Doctorate Students," *Psychological Bulletin* 30 (1933): 80-83. Mitchell G. Ash provided this reference and the point it supports.

39. Michael M. Sokal, "Graduate Study with Wundt: Two Eyewitness Accounts," in *Wundt Studies*, pp. 210-25.

40. Josef Brozek and Martin Sibinga, *Origins of Psychometry: Johann Jacob de Jaager, Reaction Time, and Mental Processes* (Nieukoop: B. de Graaf, 1970 [1865]).

41. Wilhelm Wundt, "Neuere Leistungen auf dem Gebiete der physiologischen Psychologie," *Vierteljahrreschrift für Psychiatrie* 1 (1867): 23-56.

42. Wundt, *Grundzüge*, vol. 2, pp. 225-54. Cf. Horst Gundlach, "Inventarium der älteren Experimentalapparata im psychologischen Institut Heidelberg sowie einige historische Bemerkungen," *Bericht aus dem Psychologischen Institut der Universität Heidelberg*, 1978.

43. Danziger, "The History of Introspection Reconsidered," pp. 248-50.

44. Wundt, *Erlebtes*, p. 195.

45. Peter J. Behrens, "The First Dissertation in Experimental Psychology: Max Friedrich's Study of Apperception," in *Wundt Studies*, pp. 193-209; Sokal, "Graduate Study," *ibid*.

46. Wundt, *Grundzüge*, 1911, vol. 3, p. 449. Cf. David Lindenfeld, "Oswald Külpe and the Würzburg School," *Journal of the History of the Behavioral Sciences* 14 (1978): 132-41.

47. The continuity of Wundt's concern with the higher mental processes and methods appropriate to them is disputed by Carl F. Graumann, "Experiment, Statistik, Geschichte. Wundts erstes Heidelberger Programm einer Psychologie," *Psychologische Rundschau* 31(1980):73-83. Cf. Holzkamp, note 68.

48. Wilhelm Wundt, *Essays* (Leipzig: W. Engelmann, 1885), p. 258.

49. Kurt Danziger, "Wundt's Theory of Behavior and Volition," in *Wilhelm Wundt*, ed. Rieber, pp. 89-115. The following figure illustrates this

drive theory in both the *Grundzüge* and *Völkerpsychologie*, vols. 1-2, *Die Sprache* (2nd ed., Leipzig: W. Engelmann, 1904 [1900]), vol. 1, p. 40:

Drive movements

Automatic movements   ⟵   Voluntary movements

50. Wundt, *Die Sprache*, vol. 1, pp. 43-50; the data on emotion is borrowed from Alfred Lehmann, *Die körperlichen Äusserungen psychischer Zustände* (Leipzig: O. R. Reisland, 1899).

51. Adapted from Wilhelm Wundt, *Logik*. vol. 1. Wundt, *Erkenntnisslehre* (Stuttgart: Enke, 1893 [1880]), pp. 1-93 on "the development of thought," examples adapted from pp. 55, 60. Cf. Gerhard Terton, "Bemerkungen zu sprachlogischen Ansätzen bei Wilhelm Wundt," in *Progressive Erbe*, pp. 386-92.

52. See Lothar Kreiser, "Wilhelm Wundts System der Logik," in *Progressive Erbe*, pp. 323-32. Cf. Hans Sluga, *Gottlob Frege* (London: Routledge & Kegan Paul, 1980), pp. 65-95.

53. Wilhelm Wundt, *Logik*, vol. 2. *Methodenlehre*. pt. 1. *Allgemeine Methodenlehre. Logik der Mathematik und der Naturwissenschaften*, 2nd ed. (Stuttgart: Enke, 1894 [1883]), pp. 25-39, 288-90, 345. Cf. Gerhard Terton, "Die Stellung Wilhelm Wundts in der Methodologiediskussion der traditionellen Logik," *Wissenschaftliche Zeitschrift der Karl-Marx-Universität* 2 (1979): 207-13; Helmut Metzler, "Zur Einordnung des Wundtschen Logikconcepts in die Logikentwicklung—Diskussionsbemerkungen," in *Progressive Erbe*, pp. 393-99.

54. Wilhelm Wundt, *Logik*, vol. 2; Wundt, *Methodenlehre*, pt. 2; *Logik der Geisteswissenschaften* (2nd ed.; Stuttgart: Enke, 1895 [1883]), pp. 51-150. Cf. Wundt, *Völkerpsychologie*, vol. 1; Wundt, *Die Sprache*, pp. 1-33.

55. Wundt, *Völkerpsychologie*. vol. 2. Wundt, *Die Sprache*, pp. 614-39. Cf. Peter Porsch, "Bemerkungen zur Kontroverse von Wilhelm Wundt und Hermann Paul. Zur Kritik ihrer Satzkonzeptionen," *Wissenschaftliche Zeitschrift der Karl-Marx-Universität* 2 (1979): 227-33.

56. Theo Herrmann, "Ganzheitspsychologie und Gestalttheorie," *Die Psychologie des 20. Jahrhunderts*, ed. Heinrich Balmer, vol. 1 (Zürich: Kindler, 1979), pp. 573-658. Cf. Hans-Jürgen Lander, "Hauptentwicklungslinien in der Entwicklungsgeschichte der wissenschaftlichen Psychologie und deren psychologiehistorische Bedeutung," in *Progressive Erbe*, pp. 21-47.

57. Josef Vachek, *The Linguistic School of Prague* (Bloomington: Indiana University Press, 1966).

58. Arthur L. Blumenthal, *Language and Psychology* (New York: John Wiley, 1970), pp. 50-63. Cf. Karl Bühler, *Sprachtheorie: Die Darstellungsfunktion der Sprache* (Jena: Fischer, 1934).

59. *George Herbert Mead on Social Psychology*, ed. Anselm Strauss (Chicago: University of Chicago Press, 1954), pp. 154-61.

60. The subtitle of the multivolume *Völkerpsychologie* was "*eine Untersuchung der Entwicklungsgesetze von Sprache, Mythus and Sitte.*"

61. The metaphor is Wundt's, in *Völkerpsychologie*, vol. 1, p. 23. Cf. Wilhelm Wundt, *Ethik. Eine Untersuchung der Tatsachen und Gesetze des sittlichen Lebens*, 4th ed. (Stuttgart: Enke, 1912 [1886, 1892, 1903]); the book is divided into the facts, the development, the principles, and the chief "life regions" of morality, including the person, society, nation, and humanity.

The point of departure is myth, which contains the moral world order of a people, followed by a review of ethical theories from antiquity to modern times. Fact and theory are joined in the principles of morality, which are then applied to a practical ethic of the "life regions."

62. Werner Flach and Helmut Holzhey, eds. *Erkenntnistheorie und Logik im Neukantianismus. Eine Textauswahl* (Hildesheim: Gerstenberg, 1979).

63. The division was not merely methodological, but society conditioned by the objective of the ruling classes to use natural science for their own technological and ideological purposes, argues Georg Eckhardt, "Wilhelm Wundts Völkerpsychologie, ihre Vorläufer und Folgen," in *Progressives Erbe*, pp. 90-99. Cf. Gustav A. Ungerer, "Wilhelm Wundt als Psychologe und Politiker," Psychologische Rundschau 31 (1980):99-110. Ungerer uses biographical sources to show unequivocally the politically oriented ethics which connects Wundt's institutional efforts for scientific psychology with his active interest in liberal social reforms.

64. An example is the cultural concept of demon, which is a god in the making, accompanying man, yet endowed with superhuman powers. Cf. Wundt, *Volkerpsychologie*, vol. 4; Wundt, *Mythus und Religion* (Leipzig: Engelmann, 1906), p. 368. See Gunter Lehmann, "Die kunstlerische Kultur im konzeptionellen Verstandnis der Volkerpsychologie," in *Progressives Erbe*, pp. 344-49.

65. Wundt, *Ethik*, vol. 3, p. 12. Cf. Thomas E. Willey, *Back to Kant: The Revival of Kantianism in German Historical Thought, 1860-1914* (Detroit: Wayne State University Press, 1978).

66. Mitchell G. Ash, "Academic Politics in the History of Science: Experimental Psychology in Germany," *Central European History* 14 (1981), in press; Christina Fritsche, "Zur Rolle Wundt's in der Krisendiskussion der Psychologie," in *Progressives Erbe*, pp. 273-81. Cf. Wilhelm Wundt, "Die Leipziger Hochschule im Wandel der Jahrhunderte," in *Reden und Aufsätze* (Leipzig: Engelmann, 1913), 1909, pp. 371-73.

67. Wilhelm Wundt, *Völkerpsychologie*, vol. 10; W. Wundt, *Kultur und Geschichte* (Leipzig: A. Kröner, 1920), pp. 315, 334. Cf. Ruth Finster, "Zu einigen Aspekten der Bildungspolitik W. Wundts," in *Progressives Erbe*, pp. 374-85; Walter Orschekowski and Rolf Rindert, "Der Einfluss von Kant, Fichte, und Hegel auf die rechtsphilosophischen Positionen Wilhelm Wundts," in *Progressives Erbe*, pp. 333-43.

68. For a Marxist interpretation of the "repression" of cultural psychological methods, see Klaus Holzkamp, "Zu Wundts Kritik an der experimentellen Erforschung des Denkens," in *Progressives Erbe*, pp. 141-53. Cf. Graumann, note 47.

69. Wundt, *Erlebtes*, preface. Three phases of this political skill are very sensitively described by Gustav A. Ungerer in "Wilhelm Wundt und Heidelberg," *Badische Heimat* 1 (1978):31-43; "Heidelberg vor der Reichsgründung 1871. Der Freundeskreis Wilhelm Wundts," *Badische Heimat* 3 (1979):423-438; and with Wolfgang G. Bringmann, "Experimental vs. Educational Psychology: Wilhelm Wundt's Letters to Ernst Meumann," *Psychological Research* 42 (1980):57-73.

8

Freud and Biology:
The Hidden Legacy

Frank J. Sulloway

In 1924 Karl Abraham acquired a copy of one of Sigmund Freud's earliest scientific publications, which had appeared in 1878 and had dealt with the neuroanatomy of *Petromyzon planeri*, a primitive form of fish.[1] Upon hearing this, Freud responded with the following comment: "It is making severe demands on the unity of the personality to try and make me identify myself with the author of the paper on the spinal ganglia of the petromyzon. Nevertheless I must be he, and I think I was happier about that discovery than about others since."[2] What exactly does the neuroanatomy of petromyzon have to do with psychoanalysis? Much more than one might think, especially if we focus on the author of that paper rather than on the paper itself.

It is my contention that Freud, through the years, has become a crypto-, or covert, biologist, and that psychoanalysis has become,

Previous versions of this paper were delivered at the Convengo su Psicoanalisi e Storia delle Scienze, Gabinetto Scientifico Letterario G. P. Vieusseux, Florence, June 29, 1980; the History of Science Society Annual Meeting, Toronto, October 17, 1980; and the Meet-the-Author Session of the American Psychoanalytic Association Annual Meeting, San Juan, Puerto Rico, May 8, 1981. I am especially grateful to Nathan G. Hale, Jr. and Robert R. Holt for their critical comments on this paper.

accordingly, a crypto-biology.[3] This contention, which builds upon a minority voice in Freud scholarship, really involves two main arguments. The first is that Freud, who began his scientific career as a biologist, always remained committed to biological reductionism, and, indeed, that his most creative inspirations derived in significant part from biology.[4] In saying this, I do not mean to imply that psychoanalysis is nothing but biology masquerading as psychology. Rather, it is a sophisticated psychobiology, the biological sources of which have never been adequately appreciated.[5]

This interpretation of Freud and psychoanalysis runs directly counter to a complex myth that both Freud and his followers have sought to propagate—a mythology that pictures Freud as the lonely "psychoanalytic hero" who, all by himself and against a universally hostile outside world, "invented" a totally original psychology through analysis of his patients and (heroically) of himself. This brings me to my second main contention, namely, that psychoanalysis has cultivated a highly functional collection of myths about its own origins. The purpose of these myths has been to legitimate psychoanalysis as a "pure psychology" (Ernest Jones's phrase)—a psychology supposedly developed by Freud's remarkable intellect in a manner that is, above all, neatly in accordance with psychoanalytic theory itself.[6] The entire history of psychoanalysis has therefore been constructed by folding psychoanalytic theory back upon itself and upon the mind of the intellectual hero who originated it. In other words, traditional psychoanalytic history has become a circular history par excellence.

In making these claims, it is not my intention to judge or condemn the fascinating process by which the Freud legend arose. I seek merely to understand this process of mythification, to document it, and to clarify its role in the rise of the psychoanalytic movement.

FREUD'S SCIENTIFIC RELATIONSHIP WITH WILHELM FLIESS

No figure has been victimized by as many myths and misconceptions in the service of the psychoanalytic cause as has Wilhelm Fliess (1858–1928), the Berlin physician and biologist, whose friendship with Freud spanned the fifteen crucial years from 1887 to 1902 in which psychoanalysis took form (Figure 8-1). Moreover, in many important respects Freud's much-misunderstood relationship with

Figure 8-1. Sigmund Freud and Wilhelm Fliess (*right*) in the summer of 1890. (Courtesy of Sigmund Freud Copyrights, Ltd.)

Fliess illustrates, in microcosm, the crypto-biological character of Freud's thought system as a whole.

According to Ernest Jones, Ernst Kris, and other psychoanalyst-historians, Fliess was a baneful pseudoscientist whom Freud tolerated as a "listener" owing to his scientific isolation and rejection during the 1890s. "Whatever help . . . Fliess gave to Freud," Jones has commented, "it must have been essentially that of psychological encouragement; the purely intellectual assistance could only have been minimal. . . . So the talks were duologues rather than dialogues."[7] In particular, Fliess is said to have functioned as a crucial transference figure during Freud's heroic self-analysis in the fall of 1897. The self-analysis, in turn, is said to have led to Freud's revolutionary discovery of infantile sexuality, an insight that finally invalidated his previous "seduction" theory of neurosis and simultaneously freed him of his need for biology and Fliess.[8]

What Freud's biographers, including Jones, do not seem to have known, however, is that Fliess was a pioneer in the field of infantile sexuality. His own ideas on this subject appeared in an 1897 monograph nine months before Freud began a systematic self-analysis. Fliess was led to this subject through his interest in three ideas—ideas that seem bizarre and misguided in historical hindsight, but that nevertheless enjoyed considerable scientific respect in Fliess's day. The first of these notions, which he published at the urging of Freud, posited an intimate connection between the nose and the female genitalia, a connection that Fleiss documented in the 1890s by pointing to such clinical phenomena as vicarious nosebleeding during pregnancy and swelling of the turbinate bone during menstruation.[9] Fliess's second principal idea was that all human beings are bisexual —possessing chemical substances (what today would be called hormones) common to the opposite sex as well as their own. This second idea was in turn linked to Fliess's third scientific preoccupation, namely, his belief that all life is regulated by two rhythms, a 23-day male cycle and a 28-day female cycle.

Although all three of Fliess's theories were subject to considerable debate around the turn of the century, these theories were also considered scientifically plausible by many of Fliess's colleagues— Freud included. To appreciate the acceptance these ideas enjoyed, one must understand the implicit evolutionary context in which they seemed to make intuitive sense to those of Freud's generation.

The relations between the nose and the female genital organs had a long prehistory of medical research prior to Fliess's interest in this subject. In America, John Noland Mackenzie anticipated many of Fliess's ideas in an 1884 paper in which he cited most of the same clinical phenomena as did Fliess a decade later. Mackenzie attributed these pathogenic phenomena to "the [phylogenetic] connecting link between the sense of smell and erethism of the reproductive organs exhibited in the lower animals."[10] Indeed, the genitalia, the nipples, and the nose are the only parts of the body to possess erectile tissue; and all three parts, as Mackenzie pointed out, become simultaneously erect during sexual arousal. This is why some people suffer from chronic nasal disturbance such as sneezing during sexual intercourse.

In the 1890s, Mackenzie's and Fliess's views enjoyed increasing recognition and were endorsed, for example, by Freud's eminent

Viennese colleague Richard von Krafft-Ebing in his famous *Psycho-pathia Sexualis.*[11] A few years later, Berlin sexologist Iwan Bloch also subscribed to Fliess's views, citing in this connection Ernst Haeckel's related theory that "erotic chemotropisms" (smell in the wider sense) were the "primal source" of all sexual attraction in nature.[12] Freud was personally familiar with this evolutionary logic, and he even scored Iwan Bloch's discussion of Haeckel's primal-smell theory in his own copy of Bloch's book.[13] As one pro-Fliessian summed it all up in 1914, "All this petty quibbling [about Fliess's findings] can change nothing. The relationship between the nose and the genitalia is one that is founded deep in the history of evolutionary development."[14]

The subject of vital periodicity also had an evolutionary rationale that has gone unmentioned by Freud's biographers. In 1871 Charles Darwin had discussed the whole subject at some length in *The Descent of Man.* He personally attributed the weekly and monthly periodicities in many temporal aspects of vertebrate growth and reproduction to the descent of all higher vertebrates from a tidal-dependent marine organism similar to the present-day ascidians. The ascidian, or sea-squirt, is a potato-sized organism that was once thought to be a plant. But in 1866 the Russian embryologist Aleksandr Kovalevsky made the remarkable discovery that the embryonic stages of the ascidian possess a primitive notochord.[15] The ascidian was therefore hailed by Darwin and Haeckel as the missing link between vertebrates and invertebrates, a highly important piece of propaganda for evolutionary theory.

The ascidian, which lives in tidal zones, has its vital cycles regulated fortnightly by changes in the tides. Its food supply consequently undergoes changes week by week. On the basis of such facts, Darwin had inferred that some animal closely allied to the present-day ascidians must have been the original source of man's own periodic functions in gestation, growth, and disease; and these cycles, he argued, continue to betray man's "primordial birthplace" in the sea.[16]

Finally, the ascidian, like our remote vertebrate ancestors, is *bisexual*, Darwin emphasized. This line of reasoning subsequently gave rise to the dominant theory of homosexuality in the late 1890s, namely, that this condition was a simple reversion, or developmental arrest, approximating an ancestral state.[17] The relationship between bisexuality, homosexuality, and arrested libidinal development was in turn crucial to Sigmund Freud's whole theory of psychosexual development, and it was Fliess who first brought this line of thought to Freud's attention in the 1890s.[18]

In short, the Darwinian and evolutionary context of Fleiss's ideas on nose and sex, vital periodicity, and human bisexuality made them seem far more plausible to Freud and his contemporaries than psychoanalytic historians have led us to believe. Man, said Charles Darwin in *The Descent of Man* (1871), was descended from a bisexual, lunar-cycle-dependent, tidal organism whose libido, said Ernst Haeckel in his *Anthropogenie* (1874), was originally triggered by chemotropisms (or smell in the wider sense). Seen in this evolutionary context, Fliess's ideas appeared to many to occupy the visionary forefront, not the lunatic fringe, of "hard" science. By 1913, when the Medical Society for Sexual Science was founded in Berlin, partly to help gain recognition for Fliess, there were some individuals, like Albert Eulenburg, the eminent neurologist, ardent Fliessian, and first president of that society, who thought that Freudian psychoanalysis, not Fliessian sexual biology, was the real pseudoscience of the two great medical "systems" of the day.[19]

What concerns me here, however, is not the popularity Fliess's theories enjoyed around the turn of the century, but rather the influence they exerted on Freud. Although all three of Fliess's scientific preoccupations had a lasting impact upon the fundamental conceptions of Freudian theory, Fliess's theory of vital periodicity was perhaps the most fruitful because it implied the necessary existence of spontaneous infantile sexuality—one of Freud's two most famous discoveries, the other being the meaning of dreams. According to Fliess, the mother's two periods (the 23- and 28-day cycles) were transmitted to the child in earliest embryonic life and were supposed to determine the sex of the offspring and to regulate its further maturation and vital activities until its death. It was to show that his two periodic rhythms were biochemically *sexual* in nature that Fliess was drawn to the problem of infantile sexuality. Fliess's periodicity theory, in contrast to prevailing scientific belief, posited that sexuality begins with conception and intrauterine life, not with puberty. Birth itself was supposed to be triggered by the tenth menstrual cycle (hence the average gestation period in man, Fliess argued, of 270-80 days).[20] And so it was that Fliess seized eagerly upon the little-recognized evidence for spontaneous infantile sexuality, and particularly for the periodicity of its manifestations, as major corroboration of his overall system of ideas.

In his monograph of 1897 he boldly asserted his case and backed it up with considerable observational evidence. He claimed, for example, that little boys regularly experience erections on their periodic days "as early as the first months of life."[21] Fliess also insisted that the impulse to sensual sucking occurs on such days and is merely a substitute for masturbation. He made similar claims about the sexual nature of the excretory functions. In fact, Fliess largely anticipated Freud's later views about infantile erotogenic zones and the polymorphously perverse nature of infantile sexuality. Remember, moreover, that Fliess's average infant was not just sexual; it was doubly so—bisexual (itself a potentially "perverse" condition). Finally, Fliess preceded Freud in believing that infantile sexual activity could lead to a childhood actual neurosis, as his monograph plainly shows in the case history of little Fritz, aged $3\frac{3}{4}$.[22]

Thus, when Sigmund Freud later claimed to have discovered infantile sexuality, listing that as one of "the most unexpected" findings of his psychoanalytic researches, he was in fact reiterating one of Wilhelm Fliess's equally pioneering insights.[23] What Freud discovered during his famous self-analysis, a year after Fliess's monograph had appeared, was not infantile sexuality per se, but rather a largely personal—that is, autobiographical—confirmation of Fliess's prior findings.

Freud did not just adopt infantile sexuality from Fliess, however. He adopted much more, in particular the *biological* framework of that discovery, including the periodic and chemical aspects of the process. Not only did Freud accept the periodic, Fliessian nature of childhood sexual development, as can be seen in several passages of the *Three Essays on the Theory of Sexuality* (1905), but he also endorsed Fliess's biomedical extension of this conception to include the periodic nature of childhood anxiety neurosis. In *The Interpretation of Dreams* (1900), for example, Freud wrote about attacks of anxiety in childhood: "Investigation would probably show a periodicity in the occurrence of the attacks since an increase in sexual libido can be brought about not only by accidental exciting impressions but also by successive waves [*schubweise*] of spontaneous developmental processes."[24]

Schub ("push," "shove," or "thrust") and *schubweise* ("by thrusts") were the terms used by Wilhelm Fliess to describe the periodic ebb and flow of all developmental processes. Freud, who adopted these terms from Fliess, meant them to be understood in the Fliessian sense of *thrust*, the technical meaning they have in physics. These terms, used throughout Freud's own writings on infantile sexuality, have been consistently mistranslated into English (for example, *Entwicklungsschübe* as "progressive steps of development"—Freud actually meant "thrusts of development"—and *Schübe* as "steps," when Freud actually meant Fliessian "thrusts").[25] Freud also had Fliess's laws in mind when he spoke of *Verdrängungsschübe*

—"thrusts of repression." Freud made this particularly clear in 1913 when he suggested that the key to childhood fixations might lie in Fliess's laws of *"Entwicklungsschübe."*[26]

This *thrust*like aspect of human development was one that Freud and Fliess had jointly sought to corroborate in the mid-1890s by collecting relevant data from their various patients, relatives, spouses, and children. In fact, Fliess even got Freud into the act of testing his periodic laws on the intrauterine phase of human development. Fliess's first child (Robert), who served as the guinea pig in many of Fliess's observations on infantile sexuality, and Freud's sixth and last child (Anna) were born in the same month (December 1895). Just how far Freud's scientific cooperation with Fliess's researches proceeded may be gathered from the following anonymous, but surely Freudian, observation subsequently attributed to "a friendly colleague" by Fliess, who cited his anonymous friend "word for word":

> My wife (VI para [delivery]) felt the first movements of the child on July 10th [1895]. On the 3rd of December came the beginning of labor and birth. On the 29th day of February her period resumed again. My wife has always been regular since puberty. Her period runs somewhat over 29 days. Now, from the 3rd of December to the 29th February exactly $88 = 3 \times 29\frac{1}{3}$ days elapsed and from the 10th of July to the 3rd of December $146 = 5 \times 29\frac{1}{5}$ days passed. For a period of somewhat over 29 days the birth therefore ensued right on time and the first movements of the child fall on the 5th menstrual date.[27]

That these observations were made by Sigmund Freud and dealt with his wife and youngest child Anna is corroborated by the date of birth—Anna Freud was indeed born on 3 December 1895—and by the birth order of the child—Anna was indeed Frau Freud's sixth delivery. Moreover, Fliess later used birth information on all the Freud children, as well as those of Freud's sister, in his larger book *Der Ablauf des Lebens* (Figure 8-2).[28] Such, then, was the nature of the Fliessian periodicity that, according to Ernst Kris, contributed nothing to the creation of psycho-analysis and supposedly lay at the very "periphery" of Freud's scientific interests.[29]

Fliess's ideas about infantile sexuality influenced Freud not only in the general manner I have just reviewed, but also in a series of other specific ways that encompassed the Freudian notions of sexual latency, sublimation, reaction formation, critical stages in childhood sexual development, and even Freud's theory of repres-

Zwölftes Beispiel.

Frau Marie Freuds Kinder

Grete	4. August	1887
Lili	22. November	1888
Martha	17. November	1892

$$476 = \text{I}$$
$$1456 = \text{II}.$$

$$\text{I} = \quad 476 = 17 \cdot 28$$
$$\underline{\text{II} = 1456 = 52 \cdot 28}$$
$$\text{I} + \text{II} = 1932 = 69 \cdot 28 = 3 \cdot 23 \cdot 28.$$

Figure 8-2. Fliess's biorhythmic calculations concerning the temporal intervals separating the birth dates of the three children of Marie Freud (Freud's sister). The second child was born 17·28 days after the first, and the third child was born 52·28 days after the second. Finally, the interval between the first and the third child (I + II) is an even multiple of 23·28. (From Fliess, *Der Ablauf*, p. 51.)

sion. In saying this, I do not mean to impugn Freud's originality, for he extended and transformed all of these Fliessian notions in creative and fruitful ways. But Freud's creativity does not diminish Fliess's importance in this transformation of ideas. I have documented these various influences and intellectual transformations elsewhere,[30] and I shall explore only one aspect of them here, namely, those associated with Freud's general theory of oral, anal, and genital stages in childhood sexual development.

THE BIOGENETIC CONTEXT OF FREUD'S THEORIES

Fliess's theories commanded Freud's respect not only in an evolutionary context but also in a *biogenetic* one. According to the "fundamental biogenetic law" advanced by Ernst Haeckel and other late-nineteenth-century thinkers, "ontogeny recapitulates phylogeny": that is to say, in man, the development from fetus to adulthood (ontogeny) is a brief recapitulation of the entire history of the race (phylogeny).[31] (See Figure 8-3.) Freud's endorsement of this law constitutes perhaps the least appreciated source of a priori biological influence in all of psychoanalytic theory. For if the developing

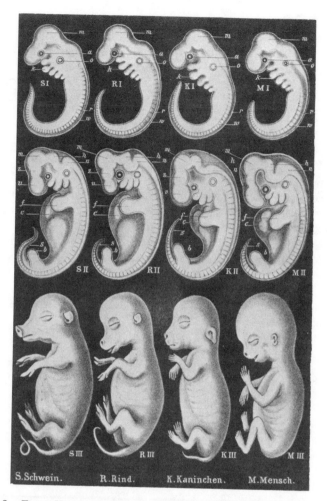

Figure 8-3. Ernst Haeckel's famous illustration of the biogenetic law. *Left to right*: embryos of the pig, cow, rabbit, and human as they supposedly recapitulate their common ancestry. (From *Anthropogenie*, Plate 7.) Haeckel, in accordance with an erroneous acceptance of the theory of the inheritance of acquired characteristics, believed that adult stages become modified by experience and that these modifications are then inherited and recapitulated at increasingly earlier stages in the descendants. In other words, ontogeny was thought to be a sort of memory for phylogeny, the experiences of which become condensed and abbreviated by ontogenetic repetition. In currently accepted Darwinian theory, there is no such recapitulation in the Haeckelian sense. Embryos are not miniature versions of ancestral *adults* but merely embryos. They resemble one another more closely than adults simply because natural selection has acted far more intensely upon the adult stages during the course of evolution, causing these later stages, but not the embryos, to diverge.

207

child recapitulates the history of the race, it must likewise recapitulate the *sexual* history of the race. This was one reason why Freud was so enthusiastic about applying Fliess's periodic laws to childhood sexual development, since sexuality in our remote ancestors was presumably far more periodic than it is today.[32] The child is therefore destined to repeat these periodic processes.

The biogenetic law was also the primary reason why oral and anal zones were such basic sources of infantile sexual excitation in Freudian theory. Viewed in terms of this law, the prepubertal human being must have the innate potential to reexperience all of the archaic forms of sexual pleasure that once characterized the mature life stages of our remote ancestors. According to Ernst Haeckel and his popularizer Wilhelm Bölsche, sexuality evolved from a primeval saclike organism, the gastraea, which was the original form of all multicellular life.[33] The first stage of sexuality was oral—eating, the incorporation of one gastraea by another. Gradually, as the gastraea evolved a gastrointestinal tract, the sexual organs became associated with the cloaca, as in the crocodiles. Finally, true genitalia emerged —the genital phase.

Not only did this phylogenetic logic underlie Freud's earliest (December 6, 1896) insights into the "extended" and "polymorphously perverse" nature of infantile sexual activity,[34] but it also gave him, in later years, his most irrefutable justification for these views. Here is what he had to say on this key point in his *Introductory Lectures on Psycho-Analysis*:

> In forming our judgement of the two courses of [instinctual] development—both of the ego and of the libido—we must lay emphasis on a consideration which has not often hitherto been taken into account. For both of them are at bottom heritages, abbreviated recapitulations, of the development which all mankind has passed through from its primaeval days over long periods of time. In the case of the development of the libido, this *phylogenetic* origin is, I venture to think, immediately obvious. Consider how in one class of animals the genital apparatus is brought into the closest relation to the mouth, while in another it cannot be distinguished from the excretory apparatus, and in yet others it is linked to the motor organs—all of which you will find attractively set out in W. Bölsche's valuable book.[35] Among animals one can find, so to speak in petrified form, every species of perversion of the [human] sexual organization.[36]

Freud elaborated upon this recapitulatory logic when he repeatedly maintained in other writings that each major substage in the child's "pregenital" phase of sexual development has preserved a specific legacy of this phylogenetic influence.[37]

It is likewise no accident that Karl Abraham, the disciple who contributed the most to the psychoanalytic theory of libidinal stages, was himself a former embryologist.[38] Quick to endorse Freud's general biogenetic statements, Abraham referred to the ontogenetic half of this doctrine when he emphasized that the human anus is developed from the primitive blastopore mouth.[39] His astute propaganda for the theory of infantile sexuality did not go unnoticed by Freud, who cited Abraham's observation in the next edition of the *Three Essays on the Theory of Sexuality*.[40]

Thus, what many critics of psychoanalytic theory have considered an arbitrary equation of *sensual* with *sexual* in early childhood experience was not so at all to Freud. Biogenetically, Freud, as well as many of his contemporaries, perceived no other choice in the matter. How far from the truth, then, is the myth that Freud's biogenetic speculations were merely "late" and "peripheral" adjuncts to his serious psychoanalytic researches.[41] These biogenetic assumptions were absolutely crucial to his whole theory of psychosexual development and were also responsible for many of its most serious defects. It was the biogenetic law, for example, that gave Freud's developmental theories their supposedly universal character and allowed him to argue that a child need not be breast-fed to pass through the oral stage, or threatened with castration to experience a castration complex. In his writings on this subject he repeatedly stressed that "the phylogenetic foundation has . . . the upper hand," providing these phases with their regularity, their independence from culture, and their frequently terrifying and traumatic force.[42] Thus when Fritz Wittels, in his 1924 biography of Freud, ridiculed the idea that every child is threatened with castration, Freud confidently replied in the margin of his copy *"und die Phylogenese?"* ("and what of phylogeny?")[43]

FIXATION, REGRESSION, AND ORGANIC REPRESSION

Freud's biogenetic conception of sexual development lent itself to three additional notions that are also derived in significant part from Darwinian theory. I am referring to Freud's theories of fixation, regression, and organic repression, all developed in the late 1890s.

According to the theory of fixation, the various component instincts of the libido can become arrested at any stage of development prior to reaching their final goal—that is, genital satisfaction with a member of the opposite sex. Such preliminary stages are necessarily perverse and phylogenetically archaic, since they involve modes of sexual functioning other than genital pleasure.

The earliest mention of the idea of fixations (or developmental arrests) is not in Freud's psychoanalytic writings but rather in his neuroanatomical ones. In his researches on petromyzon, published in the late 1870s, Freud showed that certain large ganglion cells had apparently been arrested in their evolutionary migration from the spinal chord to the periphery (Figure 8-4). Freud concluded that "it is not surprising if, in an animal that in many respects represents a permanent embryo, there are cells that have remained behind and that indicate the path the spinal ganglion cells once traveled."[44] To use Freud's later psychoanalytic terminology, such laggard cells were "fixated" in the midst of their evolutionary course.

Years later, Freud cited the case of petromyzon in his *Introductory Lectures on Psycho-Analysis* as a biological analogy to the theory of libidinal fixations.[45] But the doctrine of developmental arrests was no mere "analogy." Freud had continued to use it in his work on cerebral paralyses in the 1880s and 1890s,[46] and he subsequently transferred it from that neurological application to the domain of human sexual development.

Regression, the notion that disease involves a reversal of normal developmental processes, is closely allied to the concept of fixation in Freud's theory. Neurotics become ill, according to Freud, either through a complete fixation of the libido or through a partial fixation followed by a subsequent regression to the point of libidinal fixation. Freud adopted the theory of regression (dissolution) from John Hughlings Jackson, who in turn borrowed it from the evolutionary philosophy of Herbert Spencer. The theory of regression enjoyed widespread use in the late nineteenth century among those psychologists influenced by evolutionary theory.[47]

As Freud began to make his biogenetic beliefs more explicit in his published writings after 1910, the notion of a regressive tendency became even more crucial to his psychoanalytic system of thought. If the biogenetic law, as Freud thought, relentlessly compels the child to recapitulate the forward progress of the race, it becomes difficult to account for neurosis (which is the outcome of regressions to prior points of fixation) without positing a counterbalancing *force* of regression. For without such a counterbalancing

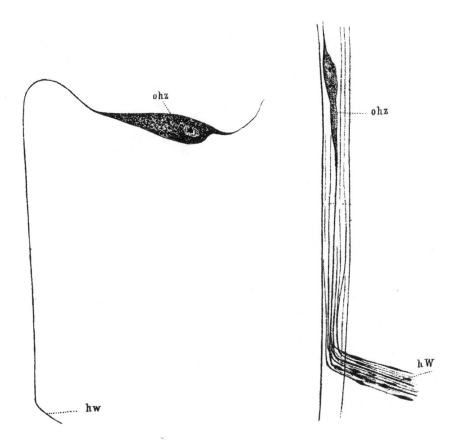

Figure 8-4. A transitional cellular element (*ohz*) between the central canal and the posterior nerve root (*hW*) of petromyzon. *Left*: the cell in isolation. *Right*: the cell *in situ*. Intermediate in form between large unipolar cells near the central canal and the bipolar ganglia of the periphery, this cell appears to mark the evolutionary path of ganglion cell migration toward the periphery. (From Freud, "Über Spinalganglien des Petromyzon," Plate 3, Figures 3 and 4.)

force, everyone would eventually reach psychological normality, and neurosis would be only a passing phase of development. In *Beyond the Pleasure Principle* (1920), Freud indeed concluded that just such a regressive force must exist. Following out the inexorable logic of this idea, he termed this regressive tendency a "death" instinct, since its ultimate outcome, if allowed to operate unrestrained, would be a condition of nonlife, the stage prior to life. Freud contrasted this death instinct with the biogenetically progressive force inherent in the "life" instincts, and he reasoned that their joint operation governs both normal mental life and regression to neurosis. Freud's enigmatic notion of a death instinct is therefore the logical culmination of his biogenetic conception of human psycho sexual development.

Freud's notion of organic repression, which encompasses his later theory of primal repression, dates from Freud's speculations in the Fliess correspondence about man's adoption of upright posture. Freud believed that the sense of smell, so important in mammalian sexuality, had given way to the visual sense in human sexual evolution when man become bipedal. As a result, smells formerly pleasurable to man (such as excremental and sexual odors) were repudiated and became a victim of reaction formation and organic repression.[48] The child, Freud believed, is forced to recapitulate this attitude toward excremental odors. The anal stage and its repression are accordingly innate.[49] In later years, Freud expanded this theory to encompass the whole subject of primal repressions, which determine the course of normal and abnormal development. "Man's archaic heritage," he explained in 1919, "forms the nucleus of the unconscious mind; and whatever part of that heritage has to be left behind in the advance to later phases of development . . . falls a victim to the process of [organic] repression."[50] Susceptibility to neurosis, Freud concluded, is the price man must pay for this phylogenetic advancement.

It is possible, in short, to trace many of the most basic psychoanalytic concepts to Freud's prior thinking along biological lines. Included among these psychobiological aspects of Freudian theory are the notion of infantile sexuality, particularly its polymorphously perverse and periodic (*schubweise*) nature; the theory of erotogenic zones; sexual latency; sublimation; reaction formation; critical stages in psychosexual development; and the theories of fixation, regression, the death instinct, and organic repression. It is possible to document, moreover, many other such ties to biology, including those that led Freud to his theories of dreaming, religion, and the origins of civilization.[51] But why, if this is so, did Freud tend to deny these ties to biological theory in his later years? True, he never ceased believing that biology was "a land of unlimited possibilities."[52] But why did he also state, to cite a characteristic remark, that "We have found it necessary to hold aloof from biological considerations during our psychoanalytic work and to refrain from using them for heuristic purposes. . . ."?[53] In historical retrospect, this and other similar disclaimers about possible biological influences in psychoanalysis reveal a considerable ambivalence on Freud's part.

RIVALRY, REDUCTIONISM, AND THE EMERGENCE OF AN INDEPENDENT SCIENCE

The gradual emergence of Freud's ambivalence toward biology was the product of several mutually reinforcing influences. First, Freud tended to equate biological reductionism with neurophysiological reductionism, something that he had indeed largely abandoned as a premature quest in the 1890s, just as he had earlier rejected the even more crude attempts of his contemporaries to localize certain brain functions and nervous disorders within specific areas of the brain. In this connection, there can be little doubt that Freud was personally quite sincere in his belief that a general *psychological* theory, freed from the uncertain trappings of a poorly understood neurophysiology, was the goal to which psychoanalysis should aspire in his own lifetime. Similarly, Freud's findings increasingly led him to reject the prevailing medical doctrine of hereditary degeneration. He therefore saw psychoanalysis, in contrast to the contemporary neurophysiological doctrines he had spurned, as a distinctly psychological and environmentalist science of the mind. Additionally, his new therapeutic methods tended to give special visibility to these psychological aspects of his theories, and it was through this largely psychological level of discourse that psychoanalysis achieved much of its subsequent popularity. But Freud's theories, in contrast to his methods of therapy, were hardly any less biological after 1900 than before, since he had increasingly replaced one form of biological reductionism (neurophysiology) with another more promising one (evolutionary theory) during the late 1890s. Freud was apparently unaware, however, of just how biological his thinking had really remained. In this connection, the influence of Darwinism in late-nineteenth-century medical psychology was so widespread as to be almost invisible to many of those, including Freud, who incorporated evolutionary ideas into their thinking. But Freud's deemphasis of the biological roots of psychoanalysis encompassed more than just his own incomplete awareness of Darwinian and other biological influences. It is Freud's *ambivalence* toward biology that requires explaining, and one must look still further for the full reasons behind this growing ambivalence.

Freud's estrangement from Fliess provides an especially important key to understanding Freud's dramatic reversal in attitude toward biology after 1900. According to the traditional psychoanalytic account of the estrangement, Freud's self-analysis finally freed him of his neurotic need for Fliess and thereby allowed him to recognize his friend for the pseudoscientist he really was.[54] This traditional explanation is patently absurd, since Freud continued to believe in Fliess's theories long after the estrangement was complete.[55] Indeed, Freud never abandoned his belief that human development is regulated by a biological periodicity or that Wilhelm Fliess had documented two such vital periods. Freud objected only to Fliess's later use of complicated multiplications, additions, and subtractions in order to account for irregular temporal sums and hence to Fliess's disregard for environmental influences as a source of exceptions to his periodicity theory. The real explanation for their estrangement lies in the increasing rivalry that marked their cooperative attempts at biological reductionism.

In the 1890s, Freud had looked to Fliess to provide him with the biological underpinnings of his psychoanalytic findings, a task that Fliess more than amply fulfilled. By 1899, however, Fliess felt entitled to claim a certain share in Freud's theoretical formulations and to be given credit where credit was due. He also had been extending his own work in psychoanalytic directions, and he felt that Freud should reciprocate by formally acknowledging a place in psychoanalysis for the theories of bisexuality and periodicity. The issue therefore arose as to whose scientific domain was really the more important in their collaborative work; and Freud, anxious to preserve the independence of psychoanalysis, increasingly shied away from Fliess's attempts to unify the two approaches. Fliess naturally felt slighted by this attitude. The estrangement came to a head at their Achensee "congress' in 1900 when Freud flatly refused to acknowledge the applicability of Fliess's periodic laws to the course of recovery achieved during psychoanalytic therapy.[56] Simultaneously, Freud suffered a severe case of amnesia about Fliess's priority in applying bisexuality to the psyche when he suddenly claimed this insight at Achensee as his own discovery.[57] Fliess, convinced that Freud was trying to steal his ideas, decided to withdraw from their relationship. Freud, however, had no desire to end such a valuable association, and he desperately tried to win Fliess back with the announcement that he was going to write a book called "Bisexuality in Man," for which he would need Fliess's considerable help! Freud even offered to let Fliess coauthor the book, which was later published in 1905 as the *Three Essays on the Theory of Sexuality*. Fliess flatly refused this offer, and so the relationship finally came to an end in 1902.

Or almost to an end; for subsequently there was an unfortunate priority dispute involving Freud, Fliess, and the philosopher Otto Weininger. In 1900 Freud had unwittingly been the instrument by which Fliess's theory of bisexuality had found its way to Weininger through one of Freud's students, Hermann Swoboda. Weininger had actually come to Freud in 1902 with a manuscript, in which Fliess's purloined theory of psychical bisexuality played a prominent role. The manuscript, entitled *Geschlecht und Charackter*, immediately became a bestseller when it was published in 1903.[58] In it, Weininger had foolishly claimed the notion of bisexuality in the psyche as his own discovery; and Freud, knowing Weininger's true source for the idea, had failed to correct the situation. Fliess, who was naturally anxious to establish his priority over Weininger, subsequently published portions of his correspondence with Freud in which Freud had admitted to an unconscious desire to rob Fliess of his originality.[59] Freud was outraged; and, in partial retaliation, he deleted one of his three acknowledgments of Fliess's scientific influence from the later editions of the *Three Essays on the Theory of Sexuality*.

The emotional scar left by the estrangement was a deep one. Above all, the estrangement was what prompted Freud to begin reevaluating the proper relationship between biology and psychoanalysis. Biological theory, as he had painfully learned from the Fliess episode, was a double-edged sword. In the 1890s, Freud had used it with great success to provide the foundations for a complex and highly sophisticated psychobiology of mind. But there was no guarantee that his followers, in the future, would choose to emphasize the same biological assumptions and therefore the same psychobiological consequences. Indeed, the rise of the psychoanalytic movement was punctuated by the same sorts of reductionistic and biological disagreements that had characterized Freud's estrangement from Fliess. Various followers began to stress different biological suppositions, and they were soon developing rival theories that proved incompatible with Freud's own. Stekel, Adler, and Sadger, for example, all sought to apply Wilhelm Fliess's theories of bisexuality and periodicity to various psychological problems. Freud strenuously opposed these efforts. To Karl Abraham he wrote in 1914: "The subjection of our psycho-analysis to a Fliessian sexual biology would be no less a disaster than its subjection to any system of ethics, metaphysics, or anything of the sort. . . . We must at all costs remain independent and maintain our equal rights. Ultimately we shall be able to come together with all the parallel sciences."[60]

When Alfred Adler, drawing upon the theory of bisexuality, developed his novel ideas about inferiority feelings and the masculine protest, Freud responded bluntly at the Vienna Psychoanalytic Society:

> . . . one faces his [Adler's] expositions with a certain feeling of alienation, because Adler subjects the psychological material too soon to biological points of view, thus arriving at conclusions that are not yet warranted by the psychological material.
> . . . The example of Fliess, who offers a biological characterization [of the neuroses], has misled many.[61]

"Adler is a little Fliess come to life again," Freud declared to Ferenczi in 1910. "And his appendage Stekel is at least called Wilhelm."[62]

In the case of Carl Jung, the principal source of disagreement with Freud was Jung's variant interpretation of libidinal evolution. Jung believed that portions of the libido had become desexualized in the course of phylogeny and were now the basis for many nonsexual aspects of neurotic symptomology. Jung also rejected Freud's doctrines of infantile sexuality and sexual latency on biological grounds. "Such a process of development," Jung argued, "would be biologically unique. In conformity with this theory we would have to assume, for instance, that when a plant forms a bud from which a blossom begins to unfold, the blossom is taken back again before it is fully developed, and is again hidden within the bud, to reappear later on in a similar form."[63] Jung flatly dismissed this biological scheme as an "impossible supposition."

It is in the context of these defections over the biological assumptions of his own and other's theories that Freud increasingly came to see himself as a pure psychologist. It was his rivals, Freud claimed, not himself, whose theories were unfortunately tainted by excessive and unwarranted biological points of view.[64] Knowing that his innovative and far-reaching paradigm of mind needed considerable time to be tested, Freud actively sought to limit his remaining followers to the safer domain of pure psychology. Once, when prompted to define his attitude toward the organic approach to mental illness that Adler and Stekel had termed *organ language*, Freud unhesitatingly replied: "I had to restrain the analysts from investigations of this kind for educational reasons. Innervations, enlargements of blood vessels, and nervous paths would have been too dangerous a temptation for them. They had to learn to limit themselves to psychological ways of thought."[65] "It was they," John Burnham similarly comments about Freud's followers, "who particularly . . . saw in his [Freud's] writings the 'purely psychological' level of discourse. Those born later than Freud were more at ease than he with [psychological] 'fictions' . . . , that is, hypothetical models. . . ."[66] Moreover, a strictly psychological conception of the origins of psychoanalysis allowed Freud's followers to envision his outmoded Lamarckian and biogenetic assumptions as "late" and "peripheral" additions to his theoretical repertoire. Freud was generally seen as having been spurred on in this respect by the more speculative tendencies of Ferenczi and Jung, who became convenient scapegoats for explaining Freud's own endorsement of these biological principles.[67]

In addition, a strictly psychological account of the origins of psychoanalysis constituted a strictly empirical account, one emphasizing the clinical basis of Freud's discoveries at the expense of the theoretical preconceptions that gave these clinical findings much of their meaning. An empiricist conception of Freud's discoveries was also highly consonant with Freud's own positivist leanings. Further enhancing this positivist conception of history was the Baconian self-image revolutionary movements in science typically seek to cultivate in the face of vehement opposition.[68]

Greatly reinforcing this psychological perspective on psychoanalytic history was the whole process of psychoanalytic education that Freud and his movement soon developed. To the average psychoanalyst, who was increasingly taught his discipline through a training analysis involving an enormous commitment of time and expense, it became difficult to imagine that Freud might have learned much of his own science somewhat differently, that is, in the physiological laboratory and from books and ideas that were to a large extent psychobiological. Compared with later psychoanalysts, Freud's intellectual development was unique, and much of that uniqueness has remained little appreciated by psychoanalysts. Who, for example, among psychoanalysts today ever reads Freud's still-untranslated works in neuroanatomy and neurophysiology or studies in detail his pre-1900 publications? Indeed, the whole tenor of traditional psychoanalytic history has been to write about the past in such a manner that it appears to lead up to, and to confirm, the *present* conception of the "psychoanalytic experience." This tendency, termed "Whiggish history" by Herbert Butterfield, has greatly enhanced the psychological and clinical perspectives that psychoanalysts have developed about their own history. But it has also provided a powerful obstacle to reconstructing the history of psychoanalysis as it really happened.[69]

BIOLOGY AND THE FREUD LEGEND

It is hardly surprising, then, that Freud's *own* biological assumptions eventually became crypto-biological ones, obscured by the increasingly elaborate psychoanalytic accounts that he and his biographers provided for the emergence of his ideas. Freud, for example, never once mentioned his personal debt to Wilhelm Fliess's pioneering researches on infantile sexuality. In fact, he repeatedly claimed that he himself had been the first to discover the sexual life of the child and that only *his* researches—particularly his invention of the psychoanalytic method—had made this discovery possible. "None, however, but physicians who practise psycho-analysis," he wrote in his *Three Essays on the Theory of Sexuality*, "can have any access whatever to this sphere of knowledge. If mankind had been able to learn from a direct observation of children, these three essays could have remained unwritten."[70]

Freud also failed to mention Fliess, even once, in his *Autobiography*. Until the Fliess correspondence was finally published in 1950, few analysts had any idea how close these two men had once been. Moreover, Fliess's theories had been thoroughly refuted in the meantime, so the discovery of his intimate personal association with Freud during the latter's years of great discovery was about as welcome as if a Velikovsky had turned out to be Albert Einstein's closest confidant during the development of relativity theory. This embarrassing situation was partly neutralized when the editors of the Fliess correspondence (Ernst Kris, Marie Bonaparte, and Anna Freud) omitted from publication most of those portions of Freud's letters in which he sought to relate his emerging theories to the scientific work of his friend Fliess.[71] After 1950, innumerable myths and misconceptions about Fliess were fostered by psychoanalyst-historians, especially Ernst Kris and Ernest Jones, in order to minimize Fliess's intellectual role in Freud's life. These misconceptions eventually allowed psychoanalytic history to be stood on its head, as with the following assertion by Marthe Robert: "It can be assumed . . .

that when Freud came to think that the links between his psychology and physiology and physics were looser than he had first believed —for instance, when he discovered infantile sexuality—Fliess had some difficulty in following him along a path so far removed from his own."[72] So Fliess—the incorrigible pseudoscientist—was apparently incapable of understanding infantile sexuality, the very subject he had been so instrumental in bringing to Freud's attention in the 1890s!

Elsewhere I have documented this process of mythification more extensively than I can do here.[73] But I would like briefly to delineate the way in which Freud's increasingly crypto-biological status as a thinker has nurtured the Freud legend. The more Freud and his psychoanalyst–biographers lost sight of Freud's manifold intellectual ties to Fliess, biology, Darwinism, and many other contemporary sources of inspiration, the more they required a convincing substitute history to explain how Freud had actually made his discoveries. The myth of the isolated hero, with its dramatic emphasis on Freud's self-analytic path to discovery, effectively supplied that substitute history.

Fritz Wittels first suggested in his 1924 biography of Freud that Freud's self-analysis must have been the source for his pioneering discovery of infantile sexuality.[74] Freud, despite his formal objections to many aspects of Wittel's book, acquiesced to this particular suggestion, although he never made such a claim himself. Over the succeeding years, the story of Freud's mysterious self-analysis became invested with many other aspects of intellectual discovery, until it seemed almost limitless in its powers of historical explanation. To the self-analysis were attributed Freud's abandonment of the seduction theory, his formulation of the Oedipus complex, the free association technique, the concepts of transference and resistance, and even Freud's discovery of the unconscious.[75] "Psychoanalysis proper," concludes one such spokesman for this traditional position, "is essentially a product of Freud's self-analysis."[76] Anything with no other apparent historical explanation was attributed to this "catch-all" event in Freud's life. Take, for example, Freud's puzzling abandonment of biological reductionism and the *Project for a Scientific Psychology* (1895) in favor of a pure psychology. No problem. The self-analysis, says Reuben Fine, precipitated "the decisive change in . . . [Freud's] interests from neurology to psychology, and created a whole new science, psychoanalysis."[77] In short, what may be characterized as "the myth of the hero" became a highly convincing alternative to Freud as a nineteenth-century psychobiologist.

FREUD'S ACHIEVEMENTS IN RETROSPECT

Where does this revisionist historical analysis leave Sigmund Freud? Acceptance of Freud's historical debt to biology requires a rather uncongenial conclusion for many psychoanalytic practitioners, namely, that Freud's theories reflect certain outmoded nineteenth-century biological assumptions, particularly those of a psychophysicalist, Lamarckian, and biogenetic nature. There can be little question that these faulty assumptions bolstered the heart of his developmental theories, inspired many of his most controversial psychoanalytic claims, and prevented Freud from accepting negative findings and alternative explanations for his views. So plausible were these assumptions in Freud's day that he was not always aware, even himself, of how much faith he placed in them or of how much his seemingly "empirical" observations were influenced by them. But plausible or not, such assumptions are nevertheless wrong; and much that is wrong with psychoanalytic theory, as Freud conceived it, may be traced directly back to them. To cite a prime example, dozens of systematic research studies have been unable to provide convincing corroboration for the theory that oral and anal stages of development are the *direct* sources of the various personality traits that Freud himself ascribed to these stages.[78] But if one is not wedded to Freud's biogenetic views, which dictated the close conceptual ties between abandoned erotogenic zones, reaction formation, organic repression, and character traits, it is possible to see why Freud's particular developmental explanation might prove problematical. Similar examples of psychoanalytic ideas having an unsound biological base might be cited from the theory of dreaming, Freud's binary conception of life and death instincts, and his views on culture and civilization.

Still what remains today of Freud's insights and influence is remarkable indeed and provided ample testimony to his greatness. What is more, a historical understanding of Freud's achievements in no way diminishes the man's genius, which has hitherto been shrouded in psychoanalytic legend.[79] Above all, Freud's writings may be said to contain a richness of thought and observation about human behavior that will continue to outlive the particular theoretical constructs he championed.[80] In Freud's own lifetime, amidst the storm of controversy over his psychoanalytic claims, Havelock Ellis summed up this timeless quality to Freud's insights: "But if . . . Freud sometimes selects a very thin thread [in tying together his theoretical arguments], he seldom fails to string pearls on it, and these have their value whether the thread snaps or not."[81]

As for the Freud legend, we must not be too harsh on those who created it. For psychoanalytic history is really no different from history in general, which customarily has its origins in myth. If myth has nevertheless continued to rule psychoanalytic history, this circumstance reflects not only the highly functional role myth has played in the psychoanalytic movement but also the indisputably heroic life Freud actually led. The Freud legend, then, is a natural outgrowth of Freud's intellectual greatness or, more precisely, of the countless intellectual battles and elaborate protective mechanisms that such greatness inevitably inspires.

NOTES

1. Sigmund Freud, "Über Spinalganglien und Rückenmark des Petromyzon," *Sitzungsberichte der kaiserlichen Akademie der Wissenschaften [Wien]*, Mathematisch-Naturwissenschaftliche Classe 78, III. Abtheilung (1878): 81–167.

2. Sigmund Freud and Karl Abraham, *A Psycho-Analytic Dialogue: The Letters of Sigmund Freud and Karl Abraham 1907–1926* (New York: Basic Books; London: Hogarth Press and The Institute of Psycho-Analysis, 1965), p. 369.

3. Frank J. Sulloway, *Freud, Biologist of the Mind: Beyond the Psychoanalytic Legend* (New York: Basic Books; London: Burnett Books/André Deutsch, 1979).

4. The crucial issue of historiographical debate in Freud scholarship is not whether psychoanalysis partakes of biological points of view; that is undeniable and has never been contested. What is in dispute are the precise origins and implications of these biological points of view. In particular, the issue is whether Freud's theories were primarily derived *inductively* from clinical research and also led him, incidentally, to certain fundamental biological insights; or, instead, whether Freud made certain biological principles the original foundations of a psychology that was then largely and *deductively* derived from them. As early as 1930 Ernest Jones steadfastly insisted that psychoanalysis "does not . . . [involve] any deductive application of biological principles"—"Psychoanalysis and Biology," in *Proceedings of the Second International Congress for Sex Research, London 1930*, ed. A. W. Greenwood (Edinburgh and London: Oliver and Boyd, 1930), p. 604. Similarly, Jones later claimed that although Freud's researches contributed in important ways *to* biology (and not vice versa), these contributions were largely "incidental" to his main work in psychology. "Freud had thus in his purely psychological studies lighted on biological laws of the widest validity"—Jones, *The Life and Work of Sigmund Freud*, 3 vols. (New York: Basic Books, 1953–57), vol. 3, p. 305.—See also Freud's similar statement in his 1915 Preface to *Three Essays on the Theory of Sexuality* (1905), in *The Standard Edition of the Complete Psychological Works of Sigmund Freud*, 24 vols., ed. and trans. James Strachey (London: Hogarth Press

and The Institute of Psycho-Analysis, 1953–74), vol. 7, p. 131. This position has received widespread support from traditional Freud scholarship and has become the basis for various psychoanalytic reconstructions of Freud's discoveries (see notes 6, 7, 8, 43, 54, and 71). The alternative claim that Freud's thinking was influenced deductively, and often adversely, by biological assumptions was broached by various Neo-Freudians (for example, Karen Horney, Harry Stack Sullivan, and others), beginning in the late 1930s. More recently, this position has been given a historical foundation by the researches of a number of Freud scholars. The most important of these are Robert Holt, "A Review of Some of Freud's Biological Assumptions and Their Influence on His Theories," in *Psychoanalysis and Current Biological Thought*, ed. Norman S. Greenfield and William C. Lewis (Madison and Milwaukee: University of Wisconsin Press, 1965), pp. 93–124; "Beyond Vitalism and Mechanism: Freud's Concept of Psychic Energy," in *Historical Roots of Contemporary Psychology*, ed. Benjamin B. Wolman (New York: Harper & Row, 1968), pp. 196–226; Peter Amacher, *Freud's Neurological Education and Its Influence on Psychoanalytic Theory*, *Psychological Issues* 4, no. 4 (Monograph 16) (1965); and Karl H. Pribram and Merton M. Gill, *Freud's 'Project' Re-assessed: Preface to Contemporary Cognitive Theory and Neuropsychology* (New York: Basic Books; London: Hutchinson Publishing Group, 1976). This recent literature has emphasized Freud's continued commitment to neurophysiological reductionism. Although I agree in most respects with this position, I do not believe that it has focused on the most essential features of Freud's psychobiological synthesis. It is my contention, developed here and more fully in *Freud, Biologist of the Mind* (see note 3), that psychoanalysis arose when Freud, strongly influenced by the Darwinian biology of his times, substituted an evolutionary for a physiological model of the mind. For additional references to the extant literature on this subject, see *Freud, Biologist of the Mind*, pp. 13–17, 20, 119–20, 238 n., 439, 442, 495. On the historiographical inadequacies inherent in an *inductivist* versus a *deductivist* dichotomization of Freud's relationship to biology, see note 68.

5. I use the word *psychobiology* here to denote Freud's revolutionary synthesis of biology and psychology, together with his lifelong goal of uniting psychology with biology. The word is not used to denote a conception of the psyche as an essentially biological entity. Nor does it mean the study of psychology in its biological aspects alone (a more limited denotation of this term common in current scientific research). I have employed the word *cryptobiology* to denote a portion of Freud's thinking that has become obscured from historical view, not as a description of his motives in this process or as a description of psychoanalysis as a whole.

6. Jones, *Life and Work*, vol. 1, p. 395.

7. Ibid., p. 303; and Ernst Kris, Introduction to *The Origins of Psycho-Analysis, Letters to Wilhelm Fliess, Drafts and Notes: 1887–1902*, by Sigmund Freud (New York: Basic Books; London: Imago, 1954), p. 43.

8. Jones, *Life and Work*, vol. 1, p. 307; Kris, Introduction to *Origins*, pp. 33–35, 43–46; Reuben Fine, *The Development of Freud's Thought: From the Beginnings (1886–1900) through Id Psychology (1900–1914) to Ego Psychology (1914–1939)* (New York: Jason Aronson, 1973), pp. 218, 242; David Shakow and David Rapaport, *The Influence of Freud on American Psychology*, *Psychological Issues* 4, no. 1 (Monograph 13) (1964):44; and Giovanni Costigan, *Sigmund Freud: A Short Biography* (New York: Macmillan, 1965; London: Robert Hale, 1967), pp. 53–54, 60–61.

9. Wilhelm Fliess, *Neue Beiträge zur Klinik und Therapie der nasalen Reflexneurose* (Leipzig and Vienna: Franz Deuticke, 1893); "Magenschmerz und Dysmenorrhoe in einem neuen Zusammenhang," *Wiener klinische Rundschau* 9 (1895):4-6, 20-22, 37-39, 65-67, 115-17, 131-33, 150-52; and *Die Beziehungen zwischen Nase und weiblichen Geschlechtsorganen: In ihrer biologischen Bedeutung dargestellt* (Leipzig and Vienna: Franz Deuticke, 1897).

10. John Noland Mackenzie, "Irritation of the Sexual Apparatus as an Etiological Factor in the Production of Nasal Disease," *The American Journal of the Medical Sciences* n.s. 88 (1884):360-65; "The Physiological and Pathological Relations between the Nose and the Sexual Apparatus of Man," *The Journal of Laryngology, Rhinology, and Otology* 13 (1898):109-23.

11. Richard von Krafft-Ebing, *Psychopathia Sexualis, with Especial Reference to Antipathic Sexual Instinct: A Medico-Forensic Study*, 10th ed., trans. F. J. Rebman (London: Rebman, 1899), p. 34.

12. Iwan Bloch, *Beiträge zur Aetiologie der Psychopathia sexualis*, 2 vols. (Dresden: H. R. Dohrn, 1902-3), vol. 2, p. 201; Ernst Haeckel, *Anthropogenie oder Entwickelungsgeschichte des Menschen: Keimes- und Stammes-Geschichte* (Leipzig: Wilhelm Engelmann, 1874), pp. 656-57; see also Ernst Haeckel, *Anthropogenie oder Entwickelungsgeschichte des Menschen: Gemeinverständliche wissenschaftliche Vorträge*, 2 vols. 4th ed. (Leipzig: Wilhelm Engelmann, 1891), vol. 1, p. 147; vol. 2, p. 886, n. 195.

13. Freud Library, London. I am grateful to Anna Freud for permission to examine that portion of her father's personal library retained by him when he immigrated to London in 1938.

14. A. Siegmund, 20 March discussion of "Die Nase in ihren Beziehungen zu den Sexualorganen," a lecture delivered by Max Senator before the Ärzliche Gesellschaft für Sexualwissenschaft und Eugenik in Berlin on February 20, 1914, *Zeitschrift für Sexualwissenschaft* 1 (1914):77.

15. Aleksandr Kovalevsky, "Entwickelungsgeschichte der einfachen Ascidien," *Mémoires de l'Académie Impériale des Sciences de St.-Petersbourg*, 7th series 10, no. 15 (1866).

16. Charles Darwin, *The Descent of Man, and Selection in Relation to Sex*, 2 vols. (London: John Murray, 1871), vol. 1, p. 212 n.

17. Krafft-Ebing, *Psychopathia Sexualis*, pp. 332-33.

18. Freud, *Origins*, pp. 178, 220; *Three Essays*, p. 166.

19. Iwan Bloch, "Worte der Erinnerung an Albert Eulenburg," *Zeitschrift für Sexualwissenschaft* 4 (1917):243.

20. Fliess, *Beziehungen*, p. 47.

21. Ibid., p. 198.

22. Ibid., pp. 192-94.

23. Sigmund Freud, *An Outline of Psycho-Analysis* (1940), in *Standard Edition*, vol. 23, p. 153.

24. Sigmund Freud, *The Interpretation of Dreams* (1900), in *Standard Edition*, vol. 5, p. 585.

25. See, for example, Freud, *Origins*, p. 233.

26. Sigmund' Freud, "The Disposition to Obsessional Neurosis: A Contribution to the Problem of the Choice of Neurosis" (1913), in *Standard Edition*, vol. 12, p. 318, n. 1.

27. Fliess, *Beziehungen*, p. 128.

28. Wilhelm Fliess, *Der Ablauf des Lebens: Grundlegung zur exakten Biologie* (Leipzig and Vienna: Franz Deuticke, 1906), pp. 51, 60.

29. Kris, Introduction to *Origins*, p. 43.

30. Sulloway, *Freud, Biologist of the Mind*, pp. 188-213, 235-37.

31. Ernst Haeckel, *Generelle Morphologie der Organismen: Allgemeine Grundzüge der organischen Formen-Wissenschaft, mechanisch begründet durch die von Charles Darwin reformirte Descendenztheorie*, 2 vols. (Berlin: Georg Reimer, 1866), vol. 2, p. 300; see also *Natürliche Schöpfungsgeschichte* (Berlin: Georg Reimer, 1868); and *Anthropogenie*. For a critical analysis, both historical and scientific, of the biogenetic law, see Stephen Jay Gould, *Ontogeny and Phylogeny* (Cambridge and London: Harvard University Press, Belknap Press, 1977).

32. Sigmund Freud, *Civilization and Its Discontents* (1930), in *Standard Edition*, vol. 21, p. 99.

33. Ernst Haeckel, "Die Gastrula und die Eifurchung der Thiere," *Jenische Zeitschrift für Naturwissenschaft* 9 (1875):402-508; Wilhelm Bölsche, *Das Liebesleben in der Natur: Eine Entwickelungsgeschichte der Liebe*, 3 vols. (Berling and Leipzig: Eugen Diederichs, 1898-1903).

34. Freud, *Origins*, pp. 180, 186-87, 231-32.

35. Freud is referring here to Bölsche's *Das Leibesleben* (see note 33).

36. Sigmund Freud, *Introductory Lectures on Psycho-Analysis* (1916-17), in *Standard Edition*, vols. 15-16, vol. 16, p. 354.

37. Sigmund Freud, *Three Essays*, p. 198; "From the History of an Infantile Neurosis" (1918), in *Standard Edition*, vol. 17, p. 108.

38. Karl Abraham, *Selected Papers*, with an Introductory Memoir by Ernest Jones, vol. 1: *Selected Papers on Psychoanalysis*, trans. Douglas Bryan and Alix Strachey (New York: Basic Books, 1953; London: Hogarth Press, 1954), pp. 10, 503.

39. Karl Abraham, *Versuch einer Entwicklungsgeschichte der Libido auf Grund der Psychoanalyse seelischer Störungen* (Leipzig, Vienna, Zurich: Internationaler Psychoanalytischer Verlag, 1924).

40. Freud, *Three Essays*, p. 199.

41. Jones, *Life and Work*, vol. 3, pp. 324, 329; Shakow and Rapaport, *The Influence of Freud*, p. 32, n. 37; Lucille B. Ritvo, "The Impact of Darwin on Freud," *The Psychoanalytic Quarterly* 43 (1974):187-89.

42. Freud, *An Outline*, pp. 188-89.

43. Fritz Wittels, *Sigmund Freud: Der Mann, die Lehre, die Schule* (Leipzig: E. P. Tal, 1924), p. 145; *Sigmund Freud: His Personality, His Teaching, and His School* (London: G. Allen & Unwin, 1924), p. 161.

44. Freud, "Über Spinalganglien des Petromyzon," p. 139; see also "Über den Ursprung der hinteren Nervenwurzeln im Rückenmark von Ammocoetes (Petromyzon Planeri)," *Sitzungsberichte der kaiserlichen Akademie der Wissenschaften [Wien]*, Mathematisch-Naturwissenschaftliche Classe 75, III. Abtheilung (1877):15-27.

45. Freud, *Introductory Lectures*, vol. 16, p. 340.

46. See, for example, Sigmund Freud, *Die infantile Cerebrallähmung*, in *Specielle Pathologie und Therapie* 9, II. Theil, II. Abt., ed. Hermann Nothnagel (Vienna: Alfred Hölder, 1897), Chap. 4, §2-4; chap. 5, §B(a).

47. Between 1880 and 1900 the concept of regression was used in an evolutionary sense by James Sully and Thomas Smith Clouston in England; by Théodule Ribot, Pierre Janet, and Paul Sollier in France; by Jules Dallemagne in Belgium; and by Adolf Meyer in America. I have discussed the history of the concept more extensively in Sulloway, *Freud, Biologist of the Mind*, pp. 272-73.

48. Freud, *Origins*, pp. 186, 231-32.

49. Sigmund Freud, "Preface to Bourke's *Scatalogic Rites of All Nations*" (1913), in *Standard Edition*, vol. 12, p. 336.

50. Sigmund Freud, " 'A Child is Being Beaten': A Contribution to the Study of the Origin of Sexual Perversions" (1919), in *Standard Edition*, vol. 17, pp. 203-4.

51. See further Sulloway, *Freud, Biologist of the Mind*, especially pp. 117-18, 327-46, 358-59, 361-415.

52. Sigmund Freud, *Beyond the Pleasure Principle* (1920), in *Standard Edition*, vol. 18, p. 60.

53. Sigmund Freud, "The Claims of Psycho-Analysis to Scientific Interest" (1913), in *Standard Edition*, vol. 13, pp. 181-82; see also *Three Essays*, p. 131; and *Introductory Lectures*, vol. 15, p. 21.

54. Jones, *Life and Work*, vol. 1, p. 307; Kris, Introduction to *Origins*, p. 43; Costigan, *Sigmund Freud*, pp. 60-61; and Max Schur, *Freud: Living and Dying* (New York: International Universities Press, 1972), p. 72.

55. Freud and Abraham, *A Psycho-Analytic Dialogue*, pp. 100, 209; Jones, *Life and Work*, vol. 1, p. 291; Freud, *Beyond the Pleasure Principle*, p. 45.

56. Freud, *Origins*, p. 324 n.

57. Sigmund Freud, *The Psychopathology of Everyday Life* (1901), in *Standard Edition*, vol. 6, pp. 143-44.

58. Otto Weininger, *Geschlecht und Charakter: Eine prinzipielle Untersuchung* (Vienna: Wilhelm Braumüller, 1903).

59. Wilhelm Fliess, *In eigener Sache: Gegen Otto Weininger und Hermann Swoboda* (Berlin: Emil Goldschmidt, 1906), pp. 22-23.

60. Freud and Abraham, *A Psycho-Analytic Dialogue*, p. 171.

61. Herman Nunberg and Ernst Federn (eds.), *Minutes of the Vienna Psychoanalytic Society*, 4 vols., trans. M. Nunberg in collaboration with Harold Collins (New York: International Universities Press, 1962-75), vol. 2, p. 432.

62. Quoted in Jones, *Life and Work*, vol. 2, p. 130.

63. Carl Gustav Jung, *The Theory of Psychoanalysis* (1913) in *The Collected Works of C. G. Jung*, 18 vols., ed. Gerhard Adler, Michael Fordham, Herbert Read, and William McGuire (Executive Editor), trans. R. F. C. Hull, Bollingen Series XX (New York: Pantheon Books, 1953-66; Princeton: Princeton University Press, 1967-76; London: Routledge & Kegan Paul), vol. 4, p. 164.

64. Freud, *Three Essays*, pp. 131, 133.

65. Sigmund Freud to Viktor von Weizsaecker, October 16, 1932, cited by Viktor von Weizsaecker, "Reminiscences of Freud and Jung," in *Freud and the 20th Century*, ed. Benjamin Nelson (New York: Meridian Books, 1957), p. 68.

66. John Chynoweth Burnham, "The Medical Origins and Cultural Use of Freud's Instinctual Drive Theory," *The Psychoanalytic Quarterly* 43 (1974): 197, n. 16.

67. Wittels, *Sigmund Freud* (English translation), p. 168; see also note 41.

68. In his *Autobiography* Charles Darwin claimed that when he opened his series of notebooks on the transmutation of species in the late 1830s, he proceeded to work "on true Baconian principles, and without any theory collected facts on a wholesale scale. . . ." In fact, Darwin assumed the truth of evolutionary theory from the beginning of his notebook series; and he practiced the hypothetico-deductive, not the inductive, method throughout his inquiries on this subject. As with Freud, Darwin's overly empiricist descriptions of his working methods as a scientist were influenced by the highly controversial nature of his theories. Privately, Darwin greatly approved of, and admitted to practicing, the hypothetico-

deductive method in all his researches. See Charles Darwin, *The Autobiography of Charles Darwin: With Original Omissions Restored*, ed. Nora Barlow (London: Collins, 1958 [1876]), pp. 119, 158–64; and Michael Ghiselin, *The Triumph of the Darwinian Method* (Berkeley and Los Angeles: University of California Press, 1969), p. 4.

A failure to distinguish properly between the inductive, deductive, and hypothetico-deductive methods in scientific research has unfortunately led Ernest Jones and other traditional Freud scholars to formulate an unnecessarily black-and-white dichotomy between *induction* and *deduction* in reconstructing the development of Freud's ideas. Given the choice between these two methodological extremes, psychoanalyst–historians have naturally sought to account for Freud's achievements in terms of a strictly inductivist (that is, a purely clinical and psychological) scientific methodology. (See note 4.) In this same connection, Stephen Brush's article "Should the History of Science Be Rated X?" (*Science* 183 [1974]:1164–72) should be required reading for those psychoanalysts who believe, like most scientists in general, that science progresses in the same empiricist manner by which it is taught.

69. See Herbert Butterfield, *The Whig Interpretation of History* (London: G. Bell and Sons, 1931). On the unique difficulties that the training analysis creates for an objective understanding of Freud, see Heinz Kohut, "Creativeness, Charisma, Group Psychology: Reflections on the Self-Analysis of Freud," in *Freud: The Fusion of Science and Humanism. The Intellectual History of Psychoanalysis*, ed. John E. Gedo and George H. Pollock, *Psychological Issues* 9, nos. 2/3 (Monographs 34/35) (1976):379–425.

70. Freud, *Three Essays*, p. 133.

71. For evidence of these omissions, see Sulloway, *Freud, Biologist of the Mind*, pp. 137, 144, 188, 198; Jones, *Life and Work*, vol. 1, pp. 288, 300, 302, 304; Freud, *Origins*, pp. 179, n. 1, 181, n. 2; and Schur, *Freud*, pp. 96, 106–7, 111, 116, 133, 143–44, 147. Although Ernest Jones, James Strachey, Max Schur, and several other psychoanalyst–historians have been permitted to see the unpublished portions of the Fliess correspondence, I was denied access to this material by Anna Freud on the grounds that the correspondence will eventually be published in full.

72. Marthe Robert, *The Psychoanalytic Revolution: Sigmund Freud's Life and Achievement* (New York: Harcourt, Brace & World, 1966), p. 98.

73. Sulloway, *Freud, Biologist of the Mind*, pp. 419–95.

74. Wittels, *Freud* (English translation), p. 107.

75. Fine, *Development of Freud's Thought*, p. 29.

76. Harry K. Wells, *Pavlov and Freud*, vol. 2: *Sigmund Freud: A Pavlovian Critique* (New York: International Publishers, 1960), p. 189.

77. Fine, *Development of Freud's Thought*, p. 31.

78. Many researches have confirmed Freud's clinical observation that certain character traits cluster in identifiable patterns that Freud termed "oral" and "anal". What has not been confirmed, however, is that these character traits definitely have their origins during the various developmental stages, and in association with the specific erotogenic zones, claimed by Freud. See further Paul Kline, *Fact and Fantasy in Freudian Theory* (London: Methuen, 1973), pp. 45–94, 346–47; and Seymour Fisher and Roger P. Greenberg, *The Scientific Credibility of Freud's Theories and Therapy* (New York: Basic Books; Hassocks, Sussex: Harvester Press, 1977), pp. 80–169, 399–402.

79. Freud's genius lay less in the discovery of totally original facts and theories, as legend would have us believe, than in his synthesis and brilliant intellectual transformation of numerous preexisting lines of research. I have expanded upon this concept of intellectual transformations as it applies to Freud's creative achievements in Sulloway, *Freud, Biologist of the Mind,* pp. 193-94, 203-4, 205, 213, 215, 218, 231, 235, 236, 318-19, 358, 373, 475, 497, 499-500. See also I. Bernard Cohen, *The Newtonian Revolution in Science, with Illustrations of the Transformation of Scientific Ideas* (Cambridge and New York: Cambridge University Press, 1980).

80. For informative assessments of the present status of Freudian theory, including critical reviews of the numerous attempts to test psychoanalysis experimentally, see the literature cited in note 77.

81. Havelock Ellis, Review of *A Psycho-analytic Study of Leonardo da Vinci [Eine Kindheitserinnerung des Leonardo da Vinci]*, by Sigmund Freud, *The Journal of Mental Science* 56 (1910):523.

III

INTELLECTUAL INTERESTS
AND SOCIAL CONDITIONS

9

The Logic of Scientific Development and the Scientific School: The Example of Ivan Mikhailovich Sechenov

Mikhail Grigorevitch Yaroschevskii

INTRODUCTION

Science is a complicated organism that develops in a highly uneven fashion. The term "organism" is used metaphorically here and certainly does not mean that the construction and progress of science can only be interpreted with biological concepts. Nonetheless, we would like to make use of this analogy and remember the well-known words of Sechenov, who emphasized that the environment

Editors' note: This chapter is a translation of portions of an essay by Prof. Yaroschevskii, "Die Logik der Wissenschaftsentwicklung und die wissenschaftliche Schule," in Semen R. Mikulinskii, et al., eds., *Wissenschaftliche Schulen*, vol. 1 (Berlin: Akademie-Verlag, 1977). The translation is by Mitchell G. Ash and is published by permission. Thanks are due to Prof. Dr. Günter Kröber, Director of the Institute for the Theory, History and Organization of Science of the Academy of Sciences of the German Democratic Republic and one of the coeditors of the above-named volume, for his assistance in making initial contact with Prof. Yaroschevskii, to Dozent Dr. Lothar Sprung of the Psychological Section of the Humboldt University, Berlin, G.D.R., for checking the translation, and to Dr. Sprung and Dr. Helga Sprung for translating the Russian references given in these notes. The bibliographic information in the original references has been supplemented by the translator where possible.

that influences the organism must also be included in its scientific definition.[1] The development of the system of science outside the social–historical environment is just as unthinkable as the independence of a living body from external conditions. It does not follow from this that the relative independence of the system is denied. In that case it would suffice to know the physical and chemical characteristics of the atmosphere, the earth, and so on, to understand the behavior of biological entities, or to know the social and economic conditions of the existence of science to understand its specific structure and dynamics.

The specific character of science has been one of the epistemological sources for idealistic conceptions, according to which the growth of science is expressed in the spontaneous unfolding of intellectual structures. From this point of view, individual structures are thought to succeed one another according to a preprogrammed "drama of ideas," for which social–historical events are only the external decoration. Marxism denies this "internalistic" approach and views science as a form of human activity derived from society as a whole. Science is a partial system within the total system of social relations. The former is determined by the characteristics and development of the latter and becomes an ever more influential factor in development with increasing social progress. Bourgeois ideology accuses Marxism of ignoring the specific character of scientific knowledge and reducing intellectual life to the material life of society. If the methodological orientation of Marxism really were what its enemies imagine it to be, the analysis of the laws of scientific development would cease to have any real meaning from a Marxist point of view, since these laws could not be distinguished from those of other social phenomena. It would then be impossible to make science a special object of social knowledge different from any other. Yet despite all distortions, the methodological principles of Marxism in no way remove the question of the specific character of science from the agenda, but open up instead new perspectives for its elaboration.

A THREE-ASPECT MODEL
OF SCIENCE AS HUMAN ACTIVITY

As the "science of science" has developed, the traditional, logical–mathematical analysis of thought has given way to a new approach, the focus of which is the logic of scientific development. When we speak of logic here, we mean that not only the content but also the forms and structures of scientific thought change in determinate ways. The classes of knowledge that have the highest degree of generality are customarily called categories. Philosophical categories, for example, quantity and quality, form and content, organize the activity of human thought in all its forms of appearance. Alongside these exist general concepts in every science, which reflect the constant, invariant aspects of the reality investigated. The categories are structurally connected to one another; they form not a mere totality but a network, the categorical structure of the science in question. It is a task for detailed historical and comparative research to discover which categories are the basis of a given science and how the different components of a science relate to one another. The formation of a categorical network and the replacement of one network by another take place according to an objective logic that is independent of the conscious intentions of individuals or of groups.

In order to describe and understand the logic of scientific development, special methods as well as a special language that are different from those of logic as a philosophical and scientific (that is, mathematical) discipline are required. Science, however, is not an autonomous but a socially determined system. The fact that the content of scientific ideas is retained even when the social conditions of their creation change does not in any way justify the conclusion that social factors are indifferent or merely external to the development of science. Social factors influence the development of science directly by way of ideological and philosophical disputes, which for their part reflect the polarity of social classes and groups. The social determination of the logic of scientific development is not restricted to this alone, however. The products of scientific knowledge are always collective. The activity of an individual scientist, even that of a genius, is not an expression of the requirements of the logic of scientific development in themselves, but rather of these requirements as reflected in the prism of the specific characteristics of the scientific community in a concrete period of time.

Every step of an individual belonging to one of these communities is illuminated by an invisible apparatus of evaluation and criticism, under the influence of which a specific research strategy is created and the membership of the individual in this or that group of scientists is indicated. This, in turn, influences the real position of the scientist, as does the fact that he and others are aware of that position. The positions and programs of the collective to which a particular researcher belongs, the structure and dynamics of the development of formal and informal collectives, the manner of communication among the members of a collective, the strategy, tactics, and style of its leadership as well as other aspects of the communications and informal activity of the scientific community also require specific concepts for their explanation, which do not coincide with the categories of the logic of scientific development.

The logic of scientific development is thus realized by way of the mutual interaction of individual scientists and among scientists in a scientific community; but this interaction is itself mediated by the objective-logical movement of knowledge. The most important driving force of this movement is the concrete individual; a new idea cannot be born except as part of the "psychological environment" of such an individual. The scientific study of creativity cannot ignore this environment as something mystical, but must find ways and means for its objective, causal analysis. The usefulness for this task of traditional psychological research on productive thinking and the creative personality is extremely limited, because both the conceptual schemata involved and the empirical methods on which they are based are ahistorical. Only when the scientific personality is taken as a historical figure and understood from both an intellectual-operational and a motivational point of view can we explain why psychological characteristics are an indispensible factor in scientific progress. Objective-logical and social-psychological concepts can only reflect the scientific process in two dimensions. In order to obtain a "spatial" picture, a third dimension, that of personality, must be added.

The concepts with which each of these dimensions can be described are presently being developed in science studies. For the time being, however, only a very modest stock of terms is available. One of these is that of the school. According to Thomas Kuhn, schools play no essential role in "normal science" but arise either during the period before that of "normal science" or in periods of crisis. At times during which the paradigm exerts its undivided power, the schools are silent.[2] From the viewpoint of the concept of categorical structure, however, the conflict of schools is not a deviation from "normal science," but rather a factor of immeasurable importance in its progress. The idea of a homogeneous paradigm as described by Kuhn cannot provide a logical-objective basis for the specific character of individual schools, because all members of the scientific community are supposed to be committed to the same paradigm. The categorical viewpoint makes such a basis possible and thus permits the determination of the function of schools in the development of science. It is important to recognize here that the different components of a categorical structure do not develop in the same way and thus may receive a different theoretical projection in opposing schools.

This justifies us in speaking of the categorical profile of a school, the specific way in which the categorical network common to all scientists in a given field of research is presented in the unique research program of a concrete school. Since a categorical profile is a necessary feature of a scientific school, this aspect may mark the primary dividing line between national schools. For example, we may say as a first approximation that in the physiology of the nervous system in the nineteenth century three national schools existed, which differed from one another along methodological lines. In Germany the physical–chemical approach dominated (Helmholtz, Ludwig, Brücke, and so forth). In France the orientation was toward research on the functions of the various parts of the spinal chord and the brain (Magendie, Flourens, and others), and in Russia the organism as a whole in its interaction with the environment was grasped on the basis of the principle of evolution.

The term "school," however, describes scientific and social phenomena of different kinds. The etymology of the term shows that schools originally had a pedagogical function. They served as channels of communication between teachers and students, who affiliated themselves with a certain scientific tradition by means of such channels. In this sense schools remain an important social-psychological factor in scientific progress. The term "school" is thus many-layered. It describes different forms and levels of communication, interaction, and association among scientists. The specific character of each of these levels is determined by the correlation between logical, social, and psychological factors, each of which requires differentiated analysis. In the following section we wish to determine the heuristic value of this three-aspect model of science as a human activity in the case of the physiological school of Ivan Mikhailovitch Sechenov.

THE SCHOOL OF SECHENOV
AS AN EDUCATIONAL INSTITUTION

The 1860s marked a fundamental turning point in Russian history; during these years the country began to take the road to capitalist development. The natural sciences received a strong impetus from this new social situation. Among the natural sciences, physiology had a special place, not only because physiological science was closely bound up with social, especially with medical, practice, but also because of the significance of this science for philosophical world-views. The younger generation sought in physiology answers to fundamental questions of human existence supported by the experience of natural science. The issue of the essence of psychical processes aroused special attention. Scientific psychology did not yet exist; psychology was understood to be a part of idealistic philosophy, which in Russia was closely connected to theology. Physiology, however, in which objects were considered that had been viewed until that time as properties of a bodiless "soul," revealed the dependence of these objects upon material causes and nervous mechanisms. The successes of physiology demonstrated the power and superiority of natural scientific thinking; they supported the belief in the scientific method and in the possibility of its application to human behavior. Without taking these circumstances into account, the great popularity that physiology enjoyed in Russia, far beyond a small circle of specialists, cannot be understood.

The leading Russian physiologist during this period was Ivan Mikhailovitch Sechenov, who had returned to Russia from Germany in 1860. He had studied in Germany for a number of years and had worked in the laboratories of the young but nonetheless dominant representatives of the new physical–chemical orientation in physiology—Ludwig, Helmholtz, Brücke, Du Bois-Reymond and others, who had shaken vitalism and supported the strictly causal view of biological phenomena. Sechenov advocated the new ideas as Professor at the Medical-Surgical Academy in St. Petersburg. "The primary contribution of I. M. Sechenov, however, is not so much that he made known to his hearers in glowing terms the current state of physiology in the west, but that he had the ability to stimulate younger scientists to the independent elaboration of scientific issues and thus laid the foundations of the Russian physiological school."[3] Of interest in this estimate of Sechenov's teaching by one of his closest pupils is the primary emphasis upon the motivation to do independent work on physiological problems. This is an important— although, as we shall see, certainly not the only—function that a scientific school is called upon to fulfill. To accomplish this it was necessary to orient the teaching program solely to the training of researchers, not of physicians with technical knowledge and skills. In an empirical science such as physiology, however, this meant carrying out laboratory work. Sechenov's laboratory became during these years a center of research not only in physiology, but also in toxicology, pharmacology, and clinical medicine.

This, in turn, presupposed Sechenov's own concern with problems of scientific methodology, a concern demonstrated already in his first publication, which he sent to the *Moscow Medical Journal* while he was studying in Germany. Under the title "Electricity and Physiology," the article presented in substance a historical outline of the development of electrophysiology from Galvani to Du Bois-Reymond. Here the historical viewpoint was designed to support a methodological position. "The destiny of an applied science," he wrote, "is closely connected to the development of the theories upon which it is based. As soon as a new thought arises or a discovery is made, a mind is always found who endeavors to bring this discovery and these thoughts into applied science."[4]

Thus, in a journal intended for physicians, Sechenov pointed out with great emphasis that the successes of practical medicine are dependent in the highest degree upon progress in theory. Physiological theory, at first glance far removed from the practical needs of physicians, was seen as a condition for the progress of medicine and for its liberation from mere empiricism. On the other hand, for Sechenov, the stricter the relationship of the researcher to the facts, the more reliable his theoretical knowledge would be. He spoke out energetically against the substitution of a ready phrase for an empirical solution. Sechenov saw in the introduction of experimental physiology a means of reshaping the entire way of thinking of Russian physicians. "The absence of physiological instruments in Russian universities deprives the Russian doctor of the opportunity to become directly acquainted with experimental physiology. He is familiar only with the results of this science, but the ways in which they were obtained remain generally unknown to him. It is thus fully impossible for him to appear in scientific circles with independent criticism."[5]

Theoretical breadth, critical thinking in connection with concrete analysis, boldness in the statement of hypotheses and their examination in experiments—these principles, which were characteristic of Sechenov's teaching and research activity, produced traditions that extended beyond Sechenov's students to other physiologists and, as we have seen, not only to them. Along with intellectual qualities, Sechenov also cultivated moral virtues that characterized him, his work, and his behavior, and above all the courage of his convictions. His entire biography bears witness to this, especially critical episodes such as his departure from his honored Medical-Surgical

Academy when I. I. Mechnikov was unjustly attacked by the reactionary portion of the faculty, or his unshakeable insistence upon the ideas of his principal work, *Reflexes of the Brain*, although highly-placed officials had informed him that his appointment to a professorship at the University of Novorossiisk was delayed precisely because of this treatise.[6] Sechenov's personality thus made him a teacher not only from a scientific but also from a moral point of view.

Our characterization of Sechenov as the founder of the Russian physiological school would be completely insufficient, however, if we were merely to point out that his attitude to university teaching implied the ability to transmit to his students certain motivational, intellectual, and personal qualities along with methodological principles; for such qualities and principles were characteristic of many scientists who represented different schools during other historical periods. In order to discover the specific character of a scientific school, we must turn to the logic of scientific development as a necessary condition of a school's origin, rise, and decline. The more important the categorical progress achieved by a school, the more clearly it differentiates itself from other schools, and the more significant is its leader. Sechenov stood at the summit of the Russian physiological school not only because he developed in young scientists the motivation to work out scientific problems independently, but also because he founded a new kind of scientific orientation that embodied the transition from one categorical network to another.

After his return from Berlin to Petersburg, Sechenov presented his dissertation, "Materials for a Future Physiology of Alcoholic Drunkenness."[7] It was introduced with "theses," about which N. E. Vvedenskii later stated that they "clearly outline both the situation of struggle at that time between the two dominant orientations in physiology and the passionate character of the young scientist and student of Du Bois-Reymond and Helmholtz."[8] The dominance of physics and chemistry was expressed not only in relation to methods of biological research, but also in Sechenov's understanding of the nature and determination of biological phenomena. He later advocated the physical–chemical nature of life as well. All progressive physiologists of the period proceeded from this conviction. A new principle of explanation was thus introduced into the different branches of physiological science, including the theory of the nervous system, in which Sechenov had become interested during his student days in connection with his passionate enthusiasm for psychological problems.

In the theory of the nervous system the so-called "anatomical principle" had previously been dominant. This was understood to be the explanation of nervous function on the basis of the structure and arrangement of nerve endings and connecting pathways. One achievement of the "anatomical principle" was the first experimentally reliable model of the reflex arc, a linkage of two partial arcs, the afferent and the efferent, located in the spinal chord and the lower regions of the brain (Bell–Magendie law). A shift had thus resulted in the categorical structure of physiological thought. The category of the reflex, which had already been recognized long before the discovery of the reflex arc, received a new, natural-scientific content. As later events would show, however, this change was only of limited character and provided no support for the future successes of neurophysiology.

To the extent to which the physical–chemical line of thought was successful, the "anatomical" orientation in the theory of the nervous system was replaced by the "molecular" or mechanistic view. This orientation was also adopted by the Swiss physiologist Moritz Schiff, whose best-known student was Alexander A. Herzen, son of the liberal political publicist Alexander I. Herzen. The categorical profile of this school was formulated in the constants of mechanics and not those of anatomy, namely stimulus strength, excitation strength, stimulus or excitation extensity, and so forth. For the advocates of the "anatomical principle," the organism was a closed system with a preformed structure, in which the pathways along which a reaction to a stimulus occurred were as unalterable as the structure itself. The advocates of the "mechanical principle" viewed the organism as an open system that maintained only relative stability in the cycle of matter and energy. However, they interpreted the interaction between organism and environment in terms that inhibited explanation at the qualitatively different level of biological phenomena.

Again a new categorical network arose; the problems and categories were transformed. Principles gained increasingly in theoretical and practical importance, which permitted the explanation of biological phenomena from the evolutionary point of view. This process took place in the thinking of many scientists, but in the physiology of the nervous system the transition from a molecular-energetic to a biological explanation of nervous activity is connected above all with the name of Sechenov.

Proceeding from the standpoint of anthropological materialism under the influence of the intellectual and philosophical climate of Russian society at that time, Sechenov comprehended man as a complex totality and avoided both epiphenomenalism, which denied the independent significance of psychical phenomena, and dualism, which presented the physical and the mental as two independent principles. He developed the view that the nervous system is a unity and not a conglomerate of organs; however, he did not view it only as an energetic unity, as did the physical–chemical school, but revealed the levels of its construction, showing that each level, acting in obedience to the reflex principle but in more and more complicated ways, makes its own contribution to the regulation of the behavior of the organism as a whole. These regulations seemed to him to be self-regulations subordinated to the task of active adaptation to the external environment.

Sechenov stimulated his students to discover facts independently and to take a critical attitude toward them. Had he cultivated these qualities within the categorical framework of the physical–chemical school, in whose laboratories he had worked for three and a half years at the side of its most gifted representatives, then the school whose foundations he then laid would have been merely an off-shoot, a branch, and not an independent orientation with a face of its own. The securing and deepening of the new biological approach formed the tradition in which succeeding generations were educated. Precisely for this reason, biologists from the most varied fields saw him as their teacher, even those who had never studied with him directly.

Interesting from this point of view are the memories of I. I. Mechnikov of his first visit to Sechenov with A. O. Kovalevski, another biologist. Both young scientists were concerned with zoology, not with physiology; but they nonetheless viewed Sechenov immediately as their teacher. Mechnikov relates the reason for this: "The physiologists were convinced that the solution of the problems of life could be achieved in only one way, by reducing them to simpler phenomena of physics and chemistry." Sechenov, on the other hand, "was in no respect such a narrow defender of the new orientation in physiology as most of his colleagues."[9]

When we look at Sechenov's contribution, at his influence on his students and at their successes in the subsequent development of science, it becomes necessary in our opinion to speak of the Sechenov school in the sense in which we have used the term until now—as a large cohort of researchers in various fields of biological and medical science, trained under the direct influence of the "father of Russian physiology." Different from this is the school of Sechenov in the narrower sense, as a group of younger physiologists who worked out the concrete research program he had developed together with their teacher and under his leadership. In our opinion, this distinction is of essential significance. In the absence of other terms, we designate the scientific school in this narrower sense "the school as research collective." The following exposition will be concerned exclusively with this form of school.

THE SCHOOL OF SECHENOV AS RESEARCH COLLECTIVE

A scientist can pursue several research programs either successively or parallel. Sechenov, too, had several such programs, but only one of these was carried out by his school as a research collective, while he mastered the others alone. This program was directly connected with his discovery of central inhibition and is presented in his *Reflexes of the Brain* as the schema of the "brain machine."

Even before central inhibition was discovered and the corresponding theory developed, a phenomenon was observed that appeared strange in light of then-dominant concepts of nervous activity. The brothers Ernst Heinrich and Wilhelm Weber, and later also Eduard Pflüger, discovered that a physical stimulus could not only bring an organ into an active state but could also effect a delay in the motor reaction. The delay of muscular activity by the stimulation of a nerve had been found in the internal organs. However, it occurred to Sechenov that skeletal muscles could also be inactivated in a similar manner. Such a supposition was at first glance highly speculative. Among the "theses" attached to Sechenov's dissertation was the following: "There are no nerves which delay movement."[10] In fact, at that time nerves that could delay movement had been found for the muscles of the heart and the small intestine, but not for the muscle systems that regulate behavior in the external environment.

But why did Sechenov even raise the issue of the mechanism of inhibition? This did not result from the logic of his physiological work. The reasons lay elsewhere, in the field of psychology, for which he had already sought physiological bases during the period of his enthusiasm for the physical–chemical orientation. For this there is direct evidence from his countryman Boris N. Chicherin, later a famous jurist and idealist intellectual, whom Sechenov had met in Heidelberg. As Chicherin remembered it, "We had vehement arguments about free will. . . . He attempted to derive psychology from physiology with superficial leaps, which were of course not at all scientifically founded and only led to the introduction of logical fantasies into exact research methods."[11]

What seemed to Chicherin to be "fantasies" led to experimental investigations that opened up one of the most important chapters in the history of neurophysiology and contributed to the reshaping of the categorical network of thought about nervous phenomena. The willed activity of human beings is clearly expressed in the ability to resist external influences and put up barriers against unwanted impulses. But precisely this important feature could not be explained by the dominant ideas on the function of the brain. For physiologists it was at that time practically an axiom that the nervous system works according to the reflex principle; they knew of no other that could be made consistent with science. The reflex principle implied, however, that an external stimulus immediately releases an answering reaction of the muscle—a re-*action* and not the delay of one.

Where is the substrate of this ability to resist intruding stimuli? According to the idealistic conception it was the soul (Chicherin did not think that such an explanation was fantastical); according to Sechenov it was the brain centers. So long as their "delaying function" was not yet proven, however, there was no reason to prefer Sechenov's answer to Chicherin's. The discovery of peripheral inhibition indicated that during excitation an inhibiting influence can in principle proceed from a nerve to the muscles. Yet—we quote again from the "theses" —"There are no nerves which delay movement." Since Sechenov nonetheless remained convinced that inhibition, like excitation, takes place in a material organ and not in the immaterial soul, he gave a new direction to research: if the nerve centers cannot inhibit the work of the muscles, then they "delay" it. This supposition directed his attention to the various regions of the cerebral cortex. His research led to the discovery of the centers he was seeking. As Charles Scott Sherrington stated, "The thesis of the inhibiting influence of one part of the nervous system on the others had already been stated by Hippocrates; as a working hypothesis in physiology, however, it became generally recognized doctrine only after Sechenov in 1863."[12]

The concept of inhibition that was thus introduced into physiological thought resulted in a reshaping of its categorical structure, the importance of which was fully recognized only later. At first, however, it encountered the resistance of physiologists who described nervous activity with mechanical concepts. These physiologists, especially the school of Schiff, explained the process of excitation as the result of an energy conversion from an external stimulus to a movement impulse in the nerve cells. They saw no need to introduce a concept foreign to their categorical network such as inhibition, or to ascribe an independent biological significance to this phenomenon. However, they did not polemicize against the concept itself, but against the experimental facts presented by Sechenov in support of his discovery. One of these facts was that in lower vertebrates the reflexes are strengthened after removal of the head. There was only one explanation for this fact in the physiological literature, and it came from Schiff.[13] He proceeded on the assumption that the spinal chord transferred excitation impulses in all directions: part of the excitation proceeds to the brain and releases sensations there; another is transferred to the motor nerves. In the case of a frog whose head has been removed, the entire excitation is transferred to the motor nerves. The sensory impulse is spread over a lesser area of nerve, and the reflexes are strengthened for this reason. For Sechenov, on the other hand, the strengthening of the reflexes is a result of the fact that the centers that delay the reflex in a normal animal have been removed.

His arguments for the existence of "inhibiting centers," however, were indirect; direct proofs were required. At the end of 1862 he could present these as well, when he was able to effect a delay in a motor reaction by stimulating sections of the thalamus. This discovery became the primary support for his schema of the "brain machine," which he described in his *Reflexes of the Brain.*[14] He supposed that the brain is a sort of machine that functions according to the reflex principle: the stimulus is reflected by the higher nerve centers to the muscles. This machine, however, as opposed to a watch or other mechanisms, has special parts that permit it to strengthen or delay the reaction.

This hypothetical schema was now made the basis of a research program that brought together into a scientific school all those who worked with Sechenov. When Sechenov began to teach, he did not yet possess this program. Although many scientists worked in his laboratory (which was then called the "cabinet") during the first years of his professorship, they did not form a school in this sense. Sechenov himself worked until 1863 on problems of "animal electricity" and the physiology of the gases in the blood, and there is no evidence that he carried out these researches with anyone else. The situation changed after the publication of *Reflexes of the Brain.* Now young people grouped themselves around Sechenov and worked out the new schema of the "brain machine" with him and under his direction. This was cooperative work in the truest sense of the word, characterized by a common theoretical goal, common hypotheses, common methods, and direct communication among teacher and students. The young researchers around Sechenov did not limit themselves to working out different pieces of the common program, but made contributions of their own to it. They not only enriched the conception with new results, but also presented Sechenov with questions that stimulated him to develop the concept further.

This is already clear from the data of the first young researcher who undertook the experimental development of Sechenov's schema, the talented physician I. G. Berezin. His results were presented in the second edition of *Reflexes of the Brain* to confirm that mechanisms are at work in the higher nervous centers, which strengthen the reflexive reaction to a stimulus.[15] Although the hypothesis of "delaying" centers already had an experimental basis, the idea that "strengthening" centers also exist had not yet been supported by experiment. Berezin investigated sensitivity to temperature in frogs. A normal animal quickly removes its extremities from ice water. If the hemispheres are removed, however, the animal remains completely quiet when the extremities are dipped in the water. As Sechenov interpreted these experiments, "It is somewhat different when the area of skin subject to cooling is enlarged and the entire rear half of the rump is dipped in the ice water—then the frog moves its legs. Is it not obvious that in the case of the production of movement by cooling the skin the hemispheres react in the same way when the cooled surface is enlarged? Everyone knows that this last condition strengthens the cooling effect as such (the feeling of cold becomes unbearable), thus the hemispheres also have a strengthening influence upon the effect cooling-movement."[16]

Berezin's experiments seemed to support Sechenov's conclusion that the brain plays a strengthening role. This was only true at first glance, however; for although Sechenov cited the results of his student in support of this view, their true scientific significance was quite different. Sechenov saw the cause of the strengthening of the reflex in affective states (in his terminology the "passions"), or in the growth of an organic need, while Berezin ascribed it to sensitivity. The terms "sensitivity" and "feeling" are etymologically related; but they must be kept separate, because they designate different physiological realities.[17] Sensitivity means the ability to sense, the capability of discriminating among external stimuli independent of the perceiver. Sensitivity to temperature and the feeling of hunger are in completely different relation to the sensing organism. Originally Sechenov did not make this distinction and placed "fear sensations" and the feeling of cold on the same plane. Objectively, Berezin's experiments laid the foundation for the distinction of these phenomena from one another which Sechenov carried out in his subsequent work. The results of his student were for him evidence that in the absence of the hemispheres the strength of the stimulus and its danger for the organism must be significantly larger if analogous reactions are to occur. The hemispheres therefore perceive stimuli that have not yet led to serious disturbances of the life process but could do so. This characteristic of the brain significantly increases the ability of the organism to resist and avoid harmful influences. Thus emerged the concept of the "warning" role of sensitivity. We see, then, that Sechenov's original idea of the "brain machine" began to change and become more differentiated under the influence of his student's results. We thus have reason to suppose that such "feedback" between teacher and students (as researchers) is a constituting feature of a productive scientific school.

However, Sechenov's school as research collective concentrated its efforts upon the problem of inhibition and not upon the strengthening of reflexes. The reason for this was that the concept of inhibition most clearly expressed the emergence of a new categorical network in physiological thinking, which began to replace the earlier, mechanistic one. Of course, the idea of the "warning" function of sensitivity was an innovation that also reflected the rise of a new categorical network, such as the category "signal," which corresponded to the category "stimulus" in the earlier network. But the issue of sensation as "warning" was not yet on the agenda of physiology at that time.

Although the fact of central inhibition was experimentally confirmed again and again, much still remained unclear. Another student of Sechenov's, F. Matkevitch, characterized the situation very well: "Of the centers which delay reflex movements it is proven only that they exist. Where these centers and their conductors are localized, how these mechanisms are set in motion, and finally, which of their parts control which regions of the central nervous system—all this remains unexplained, as before."[18] Matkevitch therefore did not limit himself to confirming the fact of the inhibiting influence of the brain upon motor activity. In order to examine the thesis experimentally, he posed a series of questions. Some of these questions seemed to his teacher to have been solved, but the student indicated the necessity of further investigation without doubting the basic fact. At the same time he posed questions of importance for the entire schema, for example "how—in what way—these mechanisms are set in motion." For Sechenov there was no other answer to this question than: "by means of the reflex." Matkevitch, however, held that this view was not empirically supported and thus stimulated Sechenov's school to new researches, which were only completed five years later.

While searching for new methods, Sechenov suggested that Matkevitch investigate the influence of alcohol, strychnine, and opium on the inhibition centers. Sechenov himself took part in these experiments. The results were that opium removes or cancels out central inhibition, while strychnine does not. Sechenov's papers on inhibition and an essay by Matkevitch were published in foreign journals. The experimental material and the theoretical conclusions in these papers attracted the attention of physiologists in western Europe and were immediately incorporated into their textbooks. This initiated the polemic that then broke out between the school of Schiff and that of Sechenov.

The categorical bases for the differences between the two schools have already been discussed; we can therefore limit ourselves here to a sketch of the role that this polemic played in the development of the research of Sechenov's school. After studying the work of Sechenov and Matkevich, Schiff's student Alexander A. Herzen performed a series of experiments in Italy during the summer of 1864.[19] He interpreted the fact, which he also accepted, that stimulation of the "Sechenov centers" results in a weakening of the reflexes, in the manner of the Schiff school, according to which this weakening is a result not of the influence of the inhibiting mechanisms that actively delay the reflexes, but of the exhaustion of the grey matter. Herzen's work stimulated Sechenov to undertake a new series of experiments, which he carried out in his Petersburg laboratory with his students V. V. Pashutin, M. A. Spiro, and others. Pashutin obtained the most interesting results. From him came the idea of using an induction current variable in strength and duration to stimulate the supposed inhibiting centers. In the course of his work he discovered one of the fundamental phenomena of nervous activity—its phasic character—and in this context he brought facts to light that were incompatible with the explanations of Schiff and Herzen. Sechenov did not help Pashutin with this work, but varied the form of the experiments he had done before and rechecked both Herzen's and his own results. These investigations were published in 1865 in a work coauthored by Sechenov and Pashutin, *New Experiments on the Brain and Spinal Chord of the Frog.*[20] This is the only piece of work that Sechenov published with another author. At that time it was a unique event when a world-renowned professor published a monograph with a student.

Of course Sechenov's students were influenced by his ideas and plans, but he continually encouraged the attitude in them of following the truth and not the teacher. As Pashutin emphasized in his first publication, "I approached the investigation of the question in a fully unprejudiced manner, and must thank Professor Sechenov for his constant advice not to distort the facts in the service of an idea."[21] In the course of Pashutin's work, too, some of Sechenov's earlier ideas were altered.

For three and a half years Sechenov and his students were taken up with the study of intercentral relations in the nervous system. The tension did not leave Sechenov's health unaffected. He took a one-year leave for foreign travel, not only to recover but also to fill in the gaps in his histological knowledge. From Karlsbad he traveled to Graz, where the histologist Rollett worked. At this time his former student Nadeshda P. Suslova also came to Graz; she had completed her medical studies in Switzerland and was preparing to defend her dissertation. Sechenov gave Suslova a topic that was directly connected with his research interests, the delaying influence of the brain on a vegetative organ—the lymphatic system of the frog's heart. When Sechenov directed the research of his students, he took part in the experiments directly; this he did here, also. Suslova's arrival altered his original program of study. He left histology alone and returned to his favorite topic, central inhibition. As we read in a letter of his, "now I understand why destiny first led me abroad and then brought Suslova to Graz. It had to do with the solution of the very problem to which I constantly felt more attracted than to all the other issues in physiology."[22]

After five years of strenuous work, during which he had re-examined his discovery, he still did not think that the problem of central inhibition had finally been solved. During the work with Suslova on the frog's brain he achieved a suppression of the activity of both the lymphatic heart and the reflexes of the spinal chord by stimulating a cross-section in the region of the thalamus. "I could hardly express my joy, because the entire question of the existence of delaying mechanisms in the frog's brain was answered by this experiment."[23] Sechenov did not publish the results of these experiments, which he valued so highly, but gave them to Suslova for her dissertation, the single conclusion of which was: "The experiments show directly that in the brain of the frog, in the places where Professor Sechenov localizes his delaying mechanisms for the reflexes of the spinal chord, such delaying entities exist for the lymphatic and the blood heart."[24]

Sechenov's work that ends this period was his book *On the Electrical and Chemical Stimulation of the Sensitive Nerves in the Spinal Chord of the Frog*, which appeared in Russian in 1865 and in German in 1868.[25] Basically this was the last publication of Sechenov's school as a research collective. The program was exhausted, and Sechenov did not have a new program for research into neurophysiological mechanisms. His school, the research collective, fell apart. Some of the students who had earlier worked on the nervous system transferred to other topics. V. V. Pashutin, whom Sechenov thought to be the best of his students, turned to problems of digestion. K. V. Voroshilov, another student, investigated the nutritional value of meat and beans.[26] In his report on the work of the physiological laboratory for the academic year 1869-70, his last at the Medical-Surgical Academy, we read that Sechenov himself "is concerned at present with the state of carbon dioxide in the blood."[27]

Sechenov carried out his new research program alone, without coworkers or students. At Petersburg University the servant Osip Kucharenko was his only assistant. "Ivan Mikhailovich appeared mornings in the laboratory and called in a quiet monotone as he walked by, 'Osip!'. Osip immediately left whatever he was doing, followed Sechenov, and they locked themselves in. Ivan Mikhailovich let no one enter."[28] As head of the chair of physiology he now devoted his time and energy as researcher primarily to the chemical dynamics of solutions. In his lectures and practical exercises a second generation of students formed, from which came such outstanding contributors to Russian biology and medicine as N. E. Vvedenskii, N. G. Usinskii, B. F. Verigo, N. P. Kravkov, G. V. Tschlopin, and others.[29] But a school as research collective, which had existed from 1863 to 1868, existed no longer.

CONCLUSION

From this overview of Sechenov's activity as leader of a scientific school we may now draw the following general conclusions.

First of all, it has become clear that at least three forms of scientific school must be distinguished: (1) the scientific school as an educational institution; (2) the school as a research collective; (3) the school as a general scientific orientation, which takes on national and perhaps also international character under certain social-historical conditions. Among the problems of exactly distinguishing these forms from one another are, first, that the same scientist, such as Sechenov, can be the leader of each of the three types of school, and. second, that, as in every other typology, "pure" forms occur seldom, mixed forms most frequently. Nonetheless we will attempt to order schematically the manifold phenomena designated by the term "school."

In this process the conception of science as human activity, in the three aspects outlined above, reveals its heuristic value. One may not define a school by its leader alone, although it often bears his name. Of course the biography of the leader also reflects these three aspects, since no phenomenon of scientific activity can be understood in its historical completeness outside them. However, the relationship between the objective–social and individual–psychological aspects appears in a completely different light in the analysis of the behavior and personality of the leader of a school and in the analysis of the school as a whole.

The school as an educational institution is an essential component of science as human activity, since this activity presupposes the production not only of ideas but also of trained scientists, without whom traditions cannot be maintained, the "staff of knowledge" cannot be passed on, and thus science as a social–historical system cannot exist. The issue of the teacher–student relationship requires special analysis, since within this relationship the personality of the researcher who takes on the role of the leader (teacher, master) directly and inevitably influences those who go through the school. We have seen in the case of Sechenov that he played not only the role of the transmitter of science who synthesized the newest achievements of physiology, but also that of the "motivator" who produced specific attitudes in his students, educated them in intellectual and moral qualities, and cultivated progressive methodological principles.

The basis for the consolidation of the school as research collective, on the other hand, is a research program that expresses more-or-less adequately the "needs of the age"—we mean irreversible historical time in which the movement of knowledge occurs. The author of a research program is a "programer." The program is his exclusive creation, for an essential condition of a scientific product is its uniqueness and unrepeatability. Accordingly, not only the objective–logical aspect is reflected in every program, but also the individual–psychological aspect, the level of aspiration of the person who proposes it. The level of aspiration always has a reference point, which the individual can find only in the scientific community, in the circle of personified bearers of science, with whose programs he unconsciously or consciously compares his own.

In certain situations, one of which we have examined here, the program becomes a point of attraction for others, generally younger scientists. The leading scientist then appears not only as an educator in the context of an institution for scientific training, and not only as a programer who can carry out the project he has invented by himself, but also as the organizer of a school as research collective. He then takes on the assignment of research problems and the comparison and generalization of results. Like every other activity, this organizational work must constantly be motivated. If we view the program from the outside, it seems as though it were realized by a series of steps independent of the subject (namely, the scientist). As we have already emphasized, however, both objective–logical and intimate–personal aspects are contained in a research program, embodied in the scientist's claim to have achieved a unique contribution to knowledge. In order to share this claim with others, the need to do so must also exist. At the same time, all those who align themselves with the new program must also be motivated in a certain way. All of them hope not only to solve the problems assigned to them as part of a program presented by others, but also to succeed in making a unique contribution to the general progress of knowledge, as the code of science requires, and thus to confirm themselves as personality and scientist.

It follows from this that one of the most important functions of the leader of a school is the development in students of "inner" or "intrinsic" motivation. The distinction between extrinsic and intrinsic motivation occurs often in the psychological literature and in science studies. Our use of these terms is somewhat different from that which is generally customary, however. Pelz and Andrews, for example, directly relate the productivity of a scientist to the kind of motivation involved. "When we turned our attention to the *source* of motivation, we clearly found that those who relied on inner sources (their own ideas) were highly effective, whereas those who relied on supervisors for stimulation were below par."[30] From this standpoint the relationship between the creative activity of the leader and that of the students becomes a formal one, with no connection to the content or the program of that activity. Motivation that is rooted in the researcher is called "intrinsic," that which comes from the leader "extrinsic."

We are of the opinion, however, that alongside this two-dimensional view a three-dimensional approach is also possible, in which the logic of scientific development is taken into account. The leader of a scientific school thus appears as the person who includes others in the realization of a program, which, in turn, reflects the requirements of the logic of science and thus arouses intrinsic motivation in them. They do not follow the leader because he is the leader but because he expresses the logic of scientific development. If the program upon which a school is based is exhausted, and the school nonetheless attempts to maintain itself because of external circumstances, such as the status claims of the leader, then it will inevitably become an obstacle in the way of scientific progress, since its members will lack intrinsic motivation.[31] Conversely, its collapse then becomes a condition of further progress. A scientific school can prosper only so long as collective intrinsic motivation exists in it, rooted in a common, developing research program.[32]

The case of Ivan M. Sechenov also poses the issue of the national scientific school as a general orientation in a given field of knowledge. Sechenov expressed most clearly and typically a tradition that allows us to speak of a Russian physiological school in the nineteenth century, in contrast to the German and French schools. This issue still needs careful historical investigation; with respect to neurophysiology, however, we may say that the Russian school is defined by the investigation of neuropsychical functions as regulators of the activity of the organism as a whole in its indivisible connection with the environment. This tradition was later carried on by the schools of Ivan P. Pavlov and A. A. Uchtomskii. The development of national traditions does not mean the separation of a unified, historically objective logic of scientific development into national components. The role of any social grouping among scientists is evaluated according to the progress it makes within this unified logic. These groupings sometimes take on international character as well; such groups then become training-grounds for researchers from various countries. Such a school was that of the German physiologist and philosopher Wilhelm Wundt in experimental psychology.

Three categories of researchers could be distinguished. Some scientists have no scientific school and carry out research programs basically alone. Others always need to have other researchers around them and become points of attraction especially for younger scientists, for example Pavlov, Ludwig, Hall and others. Finally, there is a third group, around whom a scientific school as research collective forms only during a certain period of achievement, when a corresponding research program exists, while other programs are pursued alone. Sechenov and Wundt belong to this group. The analysis of their activity is especially interesting, because it shows how the rise of a school depends upon the requirements of the logic of scientific development. Under its pressure scientists temporarily become organizers and leaders of a school, then go their own ways when the program has been worked out.

A school requires above all devotion to science, the acquisition of its conceptual and methodological apparatus, its value orientation, and its categorical structure. However, science and its logic, under the influence of which the creative personality is developed, exist neither in the form of a Popperian, subjectless "world three," nor in the form of an all-encompassing Kuhnian paradigm comparable to the paradigms of declination or conjugation in grammar. Science is always personified in concrete individuals and groups. Communication with these results in the socialization of the future researcher; for by means of this communication he acquires social–historical experience and is stimulated to achieve a reputation with his own contribution to scientific progress. The communication of young scientists with established members of their discipline can occur by way of publications as well as directly. Yet even the most passionless, most exact text is not a collection of "protocol sentences," as the positivists would have it, but implicitly contains the personality and the system of interpersonal relations in which the author is involved.

Viewed in this light, a school is a form of individual participation in the production and consumption of knowledge in the context of specific interpersonal relations. The researcher often proceeds through several schools, and has several teachers. Taken together, all this forms the scientist's manner of thinking and creates the richness of "personal knowledge," without which creativity is impossible.[33] In this sense every school is unique. Its "biography" is as unrepeatable as those of the individuals who make it up. Thus arises the question of the extent to which the activity of scientific schools can be made an object of scientific knowledge at all. Our analysis serves to support the idea that the "building material" we need to solve this problem, which is made available to us by logic, sociology, and psychology, must be worked on and "sculpted" in such a way that it becomes usable for an interdisciplinary synthesis. Then we will have the means to reconstruct the life of a scientific school in its complete uniqueness and to determine the sources of its strengths and weaknesses, the mechanism of its development, and its role in the progress of science.

NOTES

1. Ivan Mikhailovich Sechenov, "Dve zakliuchitel'nye snachenii tak nazyvaemych rastitel'nych aktov v zhivotnoi zhizny" [Two Concluding Remarks Concerning So-Called Acts of Development in Animal Life], *Medicinskii Vestnik* (1861), no. 28.

2. Thomas Kuhn, *The Structure of Scientific Revolutions*, 2nd ed. (Chicago: University of Chicago Press, 1970).

3. M. N. Saternikow, "Biograficeskii ocherk I. M. Sechenova" (Biographical Sketch of I. M. Sechenov), in *I. M. Sechenov: Izbrannye trudy* (Leningrad & Moscow: 1935), p. xv. Trans. in I. M. Sechenov, *Biographical Sketch and Essays* (New York: Arno Press, 1973).

4. I. M. Sechenov, "Elektichestvo v fiziologii" [Electricity and Physiology], *Moskovskaya medicinskaya gazeta* (1858):109.

5. I. M. Sechenov, *Nauchnoe nasledstov* [Scientific Papers/Posthumous Works], vol. 3, S. I. Vasilov, V. L. Komarov, et al., eds. (Moscow, 1956), p. 20.

6. Mikhail G. Yaroschevskii, *Ivan Mikhailovich Sechenov* (Leningrad, 1968), p. 219.

7. I. M. Sechenov, *Materialy dlia buduscei fiziologii akogol'nogo op' ianeniia* [Materials for a Future Physiology of Alcoholic Drunkenness], St. Petersburg, 1860).

8. Nicolai Evgenovich Vvdedenskii, "Pamiati I. M. Sechenova" [In Memoriam I. M. Sechenov], in *Polnoe sobranie socinenii* vol. 7 (Leningrad, 1963), p. 28.

9. Illia Illich Mechnikov, *Stranicy vospominanii* [Memoirs] (Moscow & Leningrad, 1946), p. 47.

10. I. M. Sechenov, *Materialy*, p. 1.

11. Boris Nicolaevich Chicherin, *Vospominaniia Puteshestvie za granicu* [Memoirs on the Way to the Border] (Moscow, 1932), p. 89.

12. Charles Scott Sherrington, "The Spinal Chord," in *Schaffer's Textbook of Physiology*, vol. 3 (Edinburgh, 1900), p. 838.

13. Cf. J. Moritz Schiff, *Lehrbuch der Physiologie des Menschen. 1. Band. Muskel- und Nervenphysiologie* (Lahr: C. H. Shauenburg, 1859).

14. I. M. Sechenov, *Refleksy golovnogo mozga*, in *Izbrannye filoskie i psichologicheskie proizvedeniia* [Selected Philosophical and Psychological Works] (Moscow, 1947); English: *Reflexes of the Brain*, trans. S. Belsky (Cambridge, Mass.: M. I. T. Press, 1965).

15. Sechenov, *Refreksy*.

16. Ibid., p. 89.

17. Editors' note: the Russian words for these terms are "cuvstvitel'nost" and "cuvstvo"; thus the etymological relationship exists in Russian as well as in English.

18. F. Matkevich, "O deistvii alkogolia, strichnina i opiia na centry, zaderzhivaiushchie otrazhennye dvizheniia v mozgu liagushki" [The Influence of Alcohol, Strychnine and Opium on the Inhibitive Activity of the Frog's Brain], *Medicinskii Vestnik*, No. 1 (1864):2.

19. Cf. Alexander Alexandreivich Herzen, *Expériences sur les centres modérateurs du l'action reflexe* (Florence: Bettini, 1864).

20. I. M. Sechenov & V. V. Pashutin, *Neue Versuche am Hirn und Rückenmark des Frosches* (Berling: A. Hirschwald, 1865).

21. Viktor Vasilevich Pashutin, "Effekty razdrazheniia ekeltichestvom

zaderzhiva iushchich mechanizmov golovnogo mozga u liagushki" [Effects of Electrical Stimulation on the Inhibitive Mechanism of the Cerebrum in the Frog], *Medicinskii Vestnik*, Nrs. 34–40 (1865):311.

22. Sechenov, *Nauchnoe nasledstvo*, p. 240.

23. Ibid.

24. Nadeshda Suslova, *Beiträge zur Physiologie der Lymphherun* (Zurich, 1867).

25. I. M. Sechenov, *Über die elektrische und chemische Reizung der sensiblen Rückenmarksnerven des Frosches* (Graz: Leuschner & Lubensky), 1868.

26. Sechenov, *Nauchnoe nasledstvo*, p. 50.

27. Ibid.

28. A. A. Uchtomskii, *Sobranie sochinenii* [Complete Works], vol. 6 (Leningrad, 1962), p. 143.

29. Cf. Khachatur Sedrakovich Koshtoianc, *Ocherki po istorii fiziologii v Rosii* [Sketch of the History of Russian Physiology] (Moscow: Akademii nauk, 1946).

30. Donald C. Pelz and Frank M. Andrews, *Scientists in Organizations: Prorductive Climates for Research and Development* (New York: John Wiley, 1966), p. 109.

31. Mikhail G. Yaroschevskii, "Vnutrenniaia motivaciia kak faktor nauchnogo tvorchestva" [Intrinsic Motivation as a Factor in Scientific Achievement], in *Materialy k pol'sko-sovetskomu simpoziumu po kompleksnomu razvitiiu nauki* (Moscow: Akademii nauk, 1967), pp. 95-98.

32. Cf. B. A. Frolov, "Kollektiv und Motivation des Schopfertums," in *Wissenschaftliches Schöpfertum*, ed. Günter Kröber & M. Lorf (Berlin: Akademie-Verlag, 1972), pp. 257-67.

33. Michael Polanyi, *Personal Knowledge* (Chicago: University of Chicago Press, 1958).

10

The Introduction
of Scientific Psychology in Spain
1875-1900

Helio Carpintero

INTRODUCTION

The introduction of scientific psychology in Spain was part of a broad
process of incorporating modern science into the realm of Spanish
culture and social institutions.

During the eighteenth century, the Enlightenment produced
a movement toward modernization and toward European ideas in
general.[1] However, the work of small but promising groups, closely
linked to others in both England and France, was destroyed by the
French invasion in 1808, which produced a massive popular reaction
uniting an intolerant Catholic stance against modern "errors" and
the natural desire for political independence. At the very beginning
of the nineteenth century, Spain was set apart from the rest of
Europe, and Spanish society itself suffered an internal division
between those who favored freedom, the new ideas, and the constitutional monarchy, and those who continued to favor the Old
Regime, political order, religious tradition, and, in general, a mentality

The author wishes to thank his colleagues José M. Peiro and José L.
Miralles of the University of Barcelona for their critical reading of this paper,
and Mitchell Ash for his help with the translation.

subject to the traditional powers of Church and Monarchy. This division, which has often been called "the two Spains,"[2] has affected the life, culture, society, and science of the country. The appearance of modern psychology in Spain must therefore be studied within this context.

SPAIN IN THE NINETEENTH CENTURY

In every respect, the nineteenth century in Spain was an age of profound conflicts.[3] Following the War of Independence against Napoleon (1808-14), Ferdinand VII (1814-33) imposed an absolute government within the country. Revolts and uprisings led by liberal groups brought about a constitutional reign for three years (1820-23), which, though brief, encouraged them in the desire for freedom and political change. Spanish universities were closed for years during the reign of Ferdinand VII, and a great number of liberals emigrated either to England or to France until the reign of Isabella II (1833-68). When they returned, they brought with them the new way of life called romanticism.

Conflicts between liberals and traditionalists caused three civil conflicts known as the "Carlist Wars," which, along with strife and struggles between different liberal groups, finally brought about the Revolution of 1868 and the end of the reign of Isabella II. Several different forms of government were then tried: another monarchy with Amadeo de Saboya (1870-73); a Republic (1873); a military government (1874); and, finally, the restoration of the Bourbon monarchy with Isabella's son, Alfonso XII (1875-85) on the throne. The period known in Spain as the "Restoration" (1875-1925) was an age of progress and of political, social, intellectual, scientific, and technical incorporation with the rest of the continent. It was during this period that the incorporation of scientific psychology first took place.

The political conflicts of the nineteenth century deeply troubled the world of Spanish thought and philosophy. French sensualism marked the first years of the century, when Condillac, Destutt de Tracy, and Pinel were translated by "enlightened" Spaniards. However, their influence was stunted by an attitude of purely passive reception and the lack of freedom of thought and speech.[4] The death of Ferdinand VII in 1833 marked the beginning of a transformation. New ideas appeared along with the writings of Spanish phrenologists, who had been unsuccessful in making their works known during previous attempts in 1806 and 1822. Antisensualist ideas and tendencies taken from the Scottish school of "common sense" philosophy made an entrance in Spain, as did a movement similar to the French spiritualism of Victor Cousin. These three movements were efforts undertaken to modernize and "europeanize" the Spanish mind.

Mariano Cubí (1801–75) was an interesting representative of the phrenological movement. He had read the works of Gall, Spurzheim, and Combe and had traveled to the United States, Cuba, and Mexico before beginning to disseminate phrenological ideas in Spain in 1843. Although he was put on trial by the Church in 1847, he conducted debates, published books, carried out demonstrations of phrenological diagnosis in cities and towns, and was able to maintain his fervor and transmit it to a group of disciples in Catalonia—particularly to Magín Pers y Ramona (1803–88), founder of the *Revista Frenológica* ("Phrenological Review"; 1852–54). As in other countries, phrenology was an innovative study of the mind's faculties, underscoring the organic conditions of mental life.[5]

The second intellectual movement that had repercussions for psychology consisted of the group of authors influenced by the Scottish school of common sense. They appeared between 1840 and 1850 and attempted to offer an analysis of the human mind in agreement with the reflections of conscience, the acceptance of the laws of association, the assumption of mental faculties, and the acknowledgment of the reality of the world on the basis of a psychic tendency that leads us to believe in its extramental existence. José Joaquín de Mora (1783–1864) was influenced by the works of Thomas Reid, Dugald Stewart, and Adam Smith. The ideas of Ramón Martí de Eixalá (1808–57) and especially Javier Llorens y Barba (1820–77) approached those of the later thinkers Sir William Hamilton and Victor Cousin. The analysis of knowledge or "ideas" required a basis supplied by psychology, which studied nonspatial and conscious "internal acts"; psychology thus provided a helpful path toward a philosophy of common sense.[6]

Another Spaniard, the priest Jaime Balmes (1810–48), sought to combine rationalist philosophy both with Scholasticism and with the Scottish school of thought. Balmes confronted the phrenologists in order to preserve the spiritual and free nature of the human soul. He maintained that the soul's unity is the foundation for the diversity of its faculties, and that its activity appears in the form of sensations, ideas, feelings, volitions, empirical thoughts, and needs and ideals. He reached and influenced a large public, especially through the publication of a book called *El Criterio* ("The Criterion," 1845), in which he expounded a practical logic for human affairs in popular form.[7] Tomás García Luna (c. 1810–80) and others followed closely the French spiritualism of Victor Cousin and Pierre Maine de Biran and helped to propagate their ideas among the middle classes to such an extent that from 1845 on a course called "Principles of psychology, logic, and ethics" was taught to students in secondary education (Pidal's Plan of studies).

Pedro Mata y Fontanet (1811–77), a Catalan doctor, soon became a fierce opponent of the spiritualist school. He began his attack by reviewing every psychological and psychiatric topic from a medical point of view. Interested in the problems of legal medicine, Mata wanted to determine the limits between a normal mind and an abnormal one, as well as the specific characteristics of the intermediate phenomena between normality and abnormality, such as dreams, hallucinations, and sleepwalking. Convinced that all life is a mere combination of purely physical and chemical forces (antivitalism), he maintained that psychology is a part of physiology and that the soul is a synthesis of organic forces acting through the brain and directing its impulses by way of reflection, when it is in the state of rational control; this state can be diminished or lost by alterations. Mata opposed the introspective analyses of spiritualism in psychology, just as he opposed hippocratic theories in medicine. A controversial figure, he brought a sense of topicality and novelty to the field of psychological analysis; this prepared the way for later ideological change.[8]

In the meantime, a series of circumstances marked the advance of even more radical and opposite forms of thought. On the one hand, the Church established a pact or Concordat with the monarchy in 1851, which stated that only Catholicism would be officially taught in Spain. A group of writers and thinkers began to lean toward foreign scholastic authors who were proposing a return to the works of St. Thomas Aquinas. Among these "neoscholastic" thinkers, Fr. Zeferino Gonzalez (1831–94) reconstructed the psychology of the human soul in agreement with thomistic philosophy and in clear opposition to the French spiritualist tradition, which had until then been predominant within psychology.[9]

On the other hand, a new nucleus of men organized around the figure of Julián Sanz del Río (1814–69) drew inspiration from German culture, proposed a new strictness in social and political ethics, and aspired toward a reconstruction of Spanish society, an authentic regeneration, through the creation of a new legislation, a new pedagogy, and the cultivation of the sciences. This general idea of reform defined the aims and essence of the "Krausist group," as they were called, and it was precisely through this group that scientific psychology was introduced into Spain.

THE KRAUSISTS AND PSYCHOLOGY

Julián Sanz del Río, the founder of the krausist movement in Spain, was a philosophy professor at the University of Madrid. Having met Victor Cousin in Paris, he later went to Germany, where he worked in Heidelberg with some of the disciples of K. F. C. Krause (1781–1832), an idealist philosopher who sought to give a metaphysical foundation to scientific thought. For Krause, the world is founded upon absolute Being (pan-en-theism), which embraces both Nature and Spirit; man is precisely the vortex of the natural and the spiritual. The knowledge of things and of man produces a clearer concept of the Divinity. All science, therefore, and especially anthropology, in which psychology is to be found, is of the utmost philosophical importance. Among Krause's disciples, some applied his ideas to the field of law, others to the field of history. In psychology, both Guillaume Tiberghien (1819-1901) and Heinrich Ahrens (1808-74) published studies that were to influence Krausism in Spain.

Sanz del Río and his followers began to defend a new "humanism" within the realm of Spanish culture inspired by a deep, though noncatholic, religiosity and by an individual and social ethical sense far removed from that which had prevailed during the final years of the reign of Isabella II. These Krausist professors and intellectuals, staunch defenders of freedom of thought and teaching, became the target of persecution led by "neo-Catholic" thinkers, who eventually brought about their expulsion from the universities in 1868, after the so-called "controversy of living tests" in which they were presented as sources of erroneous ideas influencing young students. Nicolás Salmerón (1838-1908), Fernando de Castro (1814-74), and Francisco Giner de los Ríos abandoned the University along with Sanz del Río. Their expulsion caused the professors of the University of Heidelberg and the philosophy congress of Prague to protest and to send a message of solidarity to these Spanish thinkers. It was a small but important sign of Spain's new "European" dimension.

Sanz del Río was convinced that the analysis of thought and the study of human subjectivity would lead to something more than pure phenomena. He sought a force or an inner cause that is able by use of reason to discover the laws and the real foundations of experience. From the child's psyche, in which a natural, spontaneous spirit is directly related to objective reality, to the reflective individuality of the rational subject, an evolution occurs in which language plays an essential part, because it expresses the spirit to the self, to the body, and to other individuals. Proof of the integration of the natural and the spiritual in human reality is the person who develops knowledge and subjects himself to the morality of a rational and free being embodied in a physical world.

This Krausism, similar in many aspects to the movement of *Naturphilosophie* in Germany, proposed new ideals for intellectual and social life. The Revolution of 1868, which ended the monarchy, seemed to offer the opportunity to put these ideas into social practice; the absence of political stability ended these attempts, however, and when the monarchy was restored in 1875 a new age of order began.[10]

PSYCHOLOGY IN THE RESTORATION PERIOD

A long-drawn-out series of conflicts was brought to an end during the Restoration Period. Political order was imposed from Madrid, and economic, industrial, intellectual, and scientific development took place. But this brought about opposition movements that would later increase in strength: regionalism, especially in Catalonia and the Basque country, objected to the centralism of Madrid; the labor movement was a consequence of industrialization; intellectuals adopted a highly critical attitude toward the new state of affairs. After Spain's defeat in the war with the United States, which resulted in the loss of her last colonies in 1898, many called for a profound and regenerating change in the country and gathered in a broad movement inspired by the "generation of 1898."

The Krausist group met new difficulties during the first years of the Restoration. One of its members, Nicolás Salmerón, became president of the first Republic; but several university professors, Giner de los Ríos among them, were separated from their teaching posts in 1875 as a result of their refusal to teach according to Catholic dogma. The following year Giner, together with some friends, set up an "Institución Libre de Enseñanza" [Free Institution of Education] as a private center of education. The "Free Institution of Education" became a fundamental nucleus for the intellectual and scientific development of the country.

Some important figures of the Krausist movement were directly related to the New Psychology. Of these Francisco Giner de los Ríos

(1839-1915) was undoubtedly the most outstanding personality.[11] Giner was not a psychologist but a law professor and above all an intellectual. He was nevertheless deeply interested in psychology, because it could offer radical knowledge of man as an incarnate spirit. Giner, as a Krausist, sought to place his thought on a scientific basis. Science is verified and systematic knowledge that aims at a reconstruction of the real world as a whole in order to establish the firm foundations of a philosophy that raises itself to the fundamental reality. In this manner Giner attempted, by studying man, to synthesize philosophy and positive science.

He published *Lecciones sumarias de psicología* [Summary Lessons in Psychology] in 1874; these were reissued with slight changes in 1877. He had shown interest in "El alma de los animales" [The Animal Soul] some years before, in 1869, and later paid attention to the social dimension of man and to society conceived as a "social person" (1899). The ideas on psychology outlined in these works are based on the philosophy of Krause and Sanz del Río, Ahrens and Tiberghien, as well as "the anthropology, psychological physiology and the newest psychophysics of Wundt, Fechner, Lotze, Helmholtz, Spencer and many others. . . ."[12] He mentioned the names of Darwin, Carus, Büchner, or Bain when talking about the animal soul; and he cited Spencer, Fouillée, Schäffe, or Wundt in relation to the "social organisms." Giner, in short, made an enormous effort to modernize the information then available in Spain. A brief summary of his psychological theories follows.

Giner starts from the act of knowing, which reveals a conscious ego, substantial and responsible for its acts, set against a body. That body is part of nature and thus subject to physical and chemical laws; it is not a result or consequence of the ego and presents its modifications to conscience only to a minimal extent. Man is "a spirit with a body."[13] Because the spirit is organized in accordance with the body, both factors intermingle and result in a "psychophysical cycle"[14] of interaction between them, in which reciprocally body and spirit appear as dynamic realities.

The spirit within the body has three ways of acting: thinking, feeling, and willing. These three "faculties" make complementary activities possible. By thinking, a certain amount of knowledge can be achieved about objects present in the mind. Our feeling capacity tends to fuse subject and object; and will, for its part, makes an object the end of the subject's activity. All these components are combined into a whole that we would now call personality. They originate different "animical combinations" that integrate every person's individuality, which is thus made singular through sex, animical qualities (character), greater or lesser energy (temperament), and aptitudes and vocation.

Giner, in his "Lessons," follows the teachings of Tiberghien very closely.[15] But when examining the "psychophysical cycle," he makes use of data coming from the New Psychology on the study of the mind–body interactions. He points out two functions between both factors: first, the soul receives physiological states and modifications and reacts to them with a certain "echo and resonance" (sensation), regulated by laws such as Weber–Fechner, adapted in each receptor to a single type of stimulus and later making possible perceptive structuration processes. The spirit, on the other hand, acts upon the body in the form of movements, among them expressive movements, one of which is language. To separate both functions does not exclude, according to Giner, their cooperation, since even the sensation implies muscular actions of an attentional type, and movements generate new sensorial messages.[16] Giner's early work *Summary Lessons* thus added some new points from experimental psychology to the traditional Krausist psychology.

Giner, as a jurist, also showed interest in law and society.[17] The romantic idea of the "folk spirit" [*Volksgeist*] appears here in the form of Spencer's social organicism. Every individual possesses mind and reason that is not only reflective but transcendent knowledge as well, open to absolute values and ideals. Society, Giner thought, can thus also be seen as an organism with a certain collective mind, a differentiated structure, and a certain common end—in short, as a social person, who exerts influence upon people and opens up a series of possibilities and limitations to them. Here we see that ideas that exceeded the range of early experimental psychology had to be applied in Giner's theory of society.

These notes are sufficient to understand the significance of the New Psychology in the intellectual horizon of the Institution's founder. His data were fit for the construction of a wide philosophical vision. Psychology was not excluded from, but integrated into, an existing system. Psychology, moreover, when it was brought into the world of the Free Institution of Education, was adapted to its central preoccupations. The Institution's founders were interested in the reform of Spanish society, but it was soon realized that such a reform had to occur through a spiritual renewal, which could only take place through education. Psychology, therefore, was soon working for the pedagogical interests of the Institution.[18]

A second Krausist figure interested in psychology was Professor Urbano González Serrano (1848-1904), author of numerous essays.[19]

He explained his idea of the soul in his psychological works as an energy or teleological entelechy different from the body and capable of an activity of its own between excitation and response, having both receptivity and spontaneity. González Serrano, like many other Krausists, thought that the new psychophysics implied a monist position that he considered poorly grounded. He thought the soul "exists and lives longer and better the more it opens itself to the legitimate influences of the body and the outer world."[20] The soul, being energy, can have different types of activity: some of these are unconscious, such as reflex actions; others are rational; and some of them are both reflective and rational. The basis of activity lies not in intelligence but in sensibility, and sensibility can be educated by taking into account its motives or interests, which derive to a great extent from a social influence.

In a study of Goethe's personality, González Serrano tried to show the convergence of vital incentives and impulses, with powerful reflections capable of achieving an aesthetic and rational reconstruction of what the poet had experienced in his spontaneous life. Body and soul converge in phantasy or in imagination, and these constitute the object of a "physiological psychology," which does not limit itself to the introspection of mental states. In the study of psychophysical interactions, even the world in which the subject is situated must also be taken into account.

González Serrano, a well-read man, was acquainted with the theories of Taine, Lotze, Ribot, Spencer, Fouillée, Wundt, Bain, and Delboeuf. Psychology, in his work, had connections with both philosophy and natural science; it was oriented to a study of man which integrated the originality of the individual and the culture received from the social milieu.[21] In his last works an interest in psychology was added to his interest in sociology, and a truly personal and critical sense was evident in all of them.

The third name from the Krausist group to be taken into account is that of the psychiatrist Luis Simarro (1851–1921), who became the first professor of experimental psychology in the Faculty of Sciences at the University of Madrid in 1902.[22] Simarro wrote few scientific works, and his thought therefore has to be reconstructed from the pieces of information his disciples have given. Some of them, such as Gonzalo Rodríguez Lafora or Juan Vicente Viqueira, became important figures in the constitution of Spanish psychology in the twentieth century. Simarro, a Mason and a member of the Monist League founded by Haeckel, was a progressive spirit. His training as a psychiatrist under Charcot (1880–84) and other French professors and his good background in neurology made him one of the leading medical figures of his day.

For a number of years Simarro gave courses on the physiology of the nervous system and on physiological psychology at the Free Institution of Education and other educational centers in Madrid. In his conception of psychology as a natural science he tried to avoid a return to spiritualist substantialism by making use of Wundtian ideas. But he thought it necessary to incorporate ideas not only from German experimentalism but from the associationist system of the English psychologists as well. Historically, associationism had had an important predecessor in Spain: Luis Vives, in the sixteenth century. Simarro, taking an explanatory point of view, thought that associations are based upon a basic process called "iteration," the formation of organized pathways in the nervous centers.[23] This process could be of help in the understanding of instinct (hereditary association), habit, memory, and even the formation of ideas.

Simarro seems to have been influenced by Theodor Ziehen, the German psychophysiologist, whose *Leitfaden der physiologischen Psychologie* (Themes of Physiological Psychology) was translated on his initiative, with a prologue by him.[24] His interest in integrating philosophy and psychophysiology led him to consider the process of thought as something that "we know how it takes place, but not what it is";[25] he nevertheless admitted that mind, like reflex action, was "an instrument for life."[26] He thus paved the way for the incorporation of functionalism into the psychological interests of the Free Institution of Education. Some of Simarro's works refer to the problem of the psychophysiology of mental fatigue. We also know that he tried to work out some tests of perception, which were later used by the first Spanish psycho-technicians.[27] However, his interest in the use of psychological knowledge in other fields, such as psychopathology and education, did not produce a great amount of research. He was involved in political controversies and discussions, he spent much energy on the Mason cause, and all this had a negative effect upon what could have been his scientific production.

When the Free Institution of Education was established in Madrid in 1876, a magazine, or *Boletín de la Institución Libre de Enseñanza* [Bulletin of the Free Institution of Education], was started, which helped to spread their attitude of respect for science and interest in the formation of a modern and European mentality.[28] Other journals spreading the European presence in the Spanish cultural world were founded at the same time. José del Perojo (1852–1908) started the *Revista Contemporánea* [Contemporary Review], where new ideas from Neokantism and positivism found their place; the *Revista Europea* [European Review] and *Revista de España* [Spanish Review] also contributed to the change in the intellectual atmosphere.[29]

The transformation brought polemics and quarrels as well. In 1876 a public debate began on the importance to be assigned to Spanish contributions to scientific progress. The "polemic of Spanish science" set figures from the Krausist group such as Gumersindo de Azcárate (1840-1917) against a group of intellectuals of Catholic orientation. Among them was Marcelino Menéndez Pelayo (1856-1912), a man learned in Spanish literature and culture, who first became prominent in this polemic. The first group was convinced that Spanish scientific failure had been due to the intransigence of Catholic orthodoxy, which prevented free and creative thought from developing by means of inquisitorial proceedings. Menéndez Pelayo put forward the thesis that a previously existing Spanish science had recently been forgotten and laid aside, and he urged its revival.[30]

The first Spanish translation of a work by Charles Darwin was also made in 1876—precisely the work devoted to *The Descent of Man*.[31] Books and articles referring to evolutionism had appeared before, but the polemic on this theme grew stronger in the years following the publication of this work. Scientists, prelates, doctors, and literary men took part in the discussion. It was an opportunity to incorporate new ideas about man's reality and his psyche. Works by authors distant from religious orthodoxy, such as Ludwig Büchner or David Friedrich Strauss, had already been published in the years of political unrest before the Restoration. Texts by Kant, Spencer, Alexander Bain, Henry Maudsley, Wilhelm Wundt, and Théodule Ribot were incorporated now.[32]

An important change in Catholic attitude toward positive science was brought about by Pope Leo XIII's publication of the encyclical *Aeterni Patris* in 1879. This promoted a spirit receptive to discoveries and new ideas within an orthodoxy determined by the philosophy of St. Thomas Aquinas. Spanish Neoscholasticism proved to be uncreative, borrowing the necessary materials for its inspiration from Italian and German authors. Some Spanish neoscholastics, however, had been working on Aquinas before Rome gave the new orientation. The previously mentioned Dominican friar Zeferino González had an open mind and was especially prominent. Others, however, among them Juan Manual Orti y Lara (1826-1904), resumed their polemic against the new ideas, uniting in a confused mixture evolutionism, ideas about faith and morals, intelligence and instinct, the scientific method, theology, and law.[33]

The polemic did not limit itself to the cultivated circle of literary magazines, but also reached the great public. In 1876 Benito Pérez Galdós (1843-1920), leading writer of the realistic movement in Spain, published *Doña Perfecta*, a dramatic story in which a lady with traditional ideas clashes with an engineer, symbol of scientific and reforming European mentality. This work, together with others by Pérez Galdós and by Leopoldo Alas, "Clarín" (1852-1901), portrayed in a literary form of high quality the tensions existing in Spanish society. The Democratic Socialist Workers' Party of Spain [Partido Democrático Socialista Obrero Español] was set up by Pablo Iglesias (1850-1925) in 1879, and among its members are to be found progressive intellectuals interested in psychological questions, such as the psychiatrist Jaime Vera (1858-1918), a leading Spanish marxist theoretician, and the university professor Julián Besteiro (1870-1940) to whose ideas we will turn in the following pages. In these ways different points of view about social and political problems were offering new possibilities to the Spanish people.

TOWARD A POSITIVE MENTALITY

Steps were slowly taken toward the new science. The generations of Spanish scientists born between 1800 and 1830 worked during the Restoration years to make possible a recovery of the habits of scientific work and "the creation of institutions."[34] But following them arose a generation of "experts" in various specialties. A number of persons born around 1856 belong to this generation: Luis Simarro (1851-1921), already discussed above, Santiago Ramón y Cajal (1852-1934), and Ramón Turró y Darder (1854-1926). Others of importance are Jaime Ferrán (1850-1929), discoverer of the vaccine against cholera, the historians Eduardo de Hinojosa and Marcelino Menéndez Pelayo, the engineer Leonardo Torres Quevedo, and the chemist José Rodriguez Carracido. This is the generation that carried out truly scientific investigation.[35]

From our point of view Ramón y Cajal has special interest.[36] His histological investigations led to the establishment of the neuron theory of the nervous system, according to which discrete entities, the neurons, come into contact with one another by contiguity and are accompanied by the glia cells. These results encouraged Cajal to propose an interpretation of the psychological phenomena that seem to be in close relationship with neurological structures. Cajal defended an associationist interpretation of the psyche in which functions are linked to specific cerebral localizations, whose connections make possible more complex physical processes. The establishment of "objective psychology or physical histology" would enable the scientist to "subordinate the series of psychical acts reflected in the mind to a parallel series of physico-psychical phenomena performed in the cells."[37]

After making a distinction between the peripheral and the central or "cerebral" nervous system, Cajal admitted that the process of evolution and improvement of the nervous system were closely connected with quantitative and qualitative changes in the brain, where associative neurons prevail. Associations between neurons have a hereditary basis, but they can be modified through education and habit, that is, by learning, which produces stronger and more direct routes of connection. When these associations react to phenomena that are also connected in the external world, the work of the brain is adequate and perfect; when there are no strong associations, each "cerebral province" becomes a sort of "autonomous canton," an independent fragment similar to Spanish cities that declared themselves autonomous, following the cantonal model of Switzerland, in 1873. "Images" in the cerebral regions would sometimes come together, and other times remain isolated, making talent possible by multiplying the connections and explaining the traditional mind by means of "subtle bonds of the nervous fibres."[38] Together with perceptive bilateralism, there would be a monolateralism for primary and secondary memory and thus a diversified and hierarchical conception of cerebral dynamics.[39]

Associations, Cajal thought, give form to psychical processes; also necessary is energy, will, a soul, an active principle that activates the voluntary mechanisms of motility and thought. This energy should have a localization as well, and Cajal sometimes imagined it could be in the neurons of the short axon (or Golgi 2), which could be "condensers of energy" and "commuters of intercommemorative current."[40]

Cajal was interested in phenomena such as suggestion and hypnotism. He interpreted perception as a process with increasing centripetal energy, and he saw in the glia cells an element of resistance and isolation of neurons. Evidently, a systematic psychological theory is difficult to build on all this. But Cajal opened the way to investigations that were to place his histological school in the van of his speciality.

Another nucleus of investigators was located in Barcelona, where a medical and intellectual tradition existed that benefited from the political and social renaissance of Catalonia and has maintained a personality of its own in philosophy and psychology since the Restoration period. The investigator Ramón Turró y Darder (1854-1926) was an outstanding figure in this Barcelona school.[41] Starting from the study of biological immunization processes, Turró developed a homeostatic conception of the organism, which stemmed from Claude Bernard's physiology. Equilibrium always results from the fulfillment of needs and lacks that have originated in the organism's activity. Needs are specific; they require therefore specific substances to satisfy them and to provoke concrete actions directed toward the acquisition and appropriation of these substances. There exist, therefore, a "trophic" sensibility for food, "trophic" reflex actions that fulfill needs, and a whole learning process for the relation of object signs to their effects on the organism. For Turró there is a motivational basis that underlies knowledge and also intelligence and forms the basis of the whole behavior, and that is hunger, the primary need.[42] Psychical life, which is characterized by its teleological dimension, is essentially related to physiological life. There exists a "functional unity," which José de Letamendi (1828-97), a Catalon author, had already defined and which Augusto Pi y Sunyer (1879-1965), a disciple of Turró, continued to explore: a nonrepresentable, incomprehensible, but at the same time indubitable, unity, which makes physiology and psychology possible. Turró combined in his work ideas from Spencer's evolutionism with others from Helmholtz's theory of perception. He later proved receptive to Pavlov's theories of reflex action. To a certain extent, Helmholtz's theory of unconscious inference served as a generic model for the "trophic inference" that Turró proposed. But his psychological work was occasional; his disciples Pi y Sunyer and later Emilio Mira were the ones responsible for having stressed this aspect of Turró's achievement.

A favorable influence was exerted by some outstanding men of letters in Spain who showed a lively interest in psychological themes. While Spanish society was slowly becoming aware of the activity performed by the investigators already mentioned, the new naturalistic novel, following Emile Zola's literary model at a certain distance, paid attention to the psychological construction of characters and their accommodation to their social background.

Toward the end of the century, Spain's defeat in its confrontation with the United States (1898) and the subsequent loss of its colonial empire (the Philippines, Puerto Rico, and Cuba) proved decisive for the country. It seemed to engender a discovery of Spain's own dramatic reality, its historic truth. One new movement responded to the recommendation of a book by Joaquín Costa (1844-1911), *Reconstitución y europeización de España* ("The

Reconstitution and Europeanization of Spain") published in 1900. Costa, whose thought is close to that of Giner de los Ríos, sharply criticized the social, historical, and political situation in Spain, and at the same time urged a renewal in the collective mentality by means of a "Europeanization" of the administrative and political structure as well as of education and thought.

A second equally important phenomenon resulted from Spain's defeat: a group of men born around 1871, who came to be known as "Generation of 1898,"[43] tried to create a new sensibility to their own country, landscape, and history by means of their literary and artistic production. They made an effort to bring about a national reflection, almost a national "introspection." Angel Ganivet, following St. Augustine, wrote: *"Noli foras ire: in interiore Hispaniae habitat veritas."* [Do not go abroad: truth resides in the heart of Spain].[44] Some of the greatest participants in this national reflection show the influence of psychology. Jose Martinez Ruiz "Azorin," like Ganivet, finds that the root of all of Spain's ills is "abulia," the lack of the will, investigated by Théodule Ribot. Pío Baroja presents in several of his novels a kind of "social Darwinism," a struggle for life within society, and he admires the life of the "man of action" in a sordid and poor world.[45]

Miguel de Unamuno (1864-1936) was the thinker at this time who offered the most profound reflections on human life. Unamuno, a widely read man who was most strongly influenced by Spencer, later by Kierkegaard and James, made personality the center of his concerns. The personality of every person is the result of that person's actions; but what people look for while making themselves is their own immortality and survival after death. William James' *will to believe* has been transformed into a *will to survive* in Unamuno. To attain this end, both feeling and thought, deeply rooted in life and serving neither abstract logic nor morality nor pure science, must cooperate. Unamuno's literary production—novels, dramas and poetry—is intended to illustrate his existential reflection on humanity and human personality.[46]

STEPS TOWARD THE TWENTIETH CENTURY

Steps were gradually taken toward the establishment of centers and institutions whose function was to support the new psychology outside the universities. The Free Institution of Education published in its "Bulletin" works in pedagogical psychology by Alfred Binet,

James Sully, Herbert Spencer, and others by Spanish authors. In addition, the school's teaching used a psychology adapted to child-comprehension. Lessons prepared and published by José de Caso provide interesting testimony of this. These lessons, which attracted critical comment from Gabriel Compayré among others, offered a functional interpretation of psychical phenomena far beyond primitive Krausism. Their goal was the consideration of human activity as a whole. With the help of simple and immediate examples, interpretations were offered of sensation, knowledge, memory, the role of sensibility, or of action motivated by will. It became an outstanding psychology for children uniquely combining psychological and pedagogical values.[47]

Other centers, such as the Athenaeum of Madrid, a nucleus of progressive culture in the nineteenth century, supported psychological investigation by means of lectures and competitions. In 1895 a committee that included figures such as Santiago Ramón y Cajal and Luis Simarro awarded a prize to an essay on psychophysics by a young professor, Julián Besteiro (1870–1940), who would become one of the most outstanding socialist intellectuals in Spain. Besteiro, closely following Wundt, Delboeuf, and G. E. Müller, explained psychophysics as an area of the new experimental psychology that studies psychical states in relation to the physical phenomena of the surrounding world. The explanation of these states must be given by physiological psychology, which looks for their sources in organic processes.[48]

Interest in psychology, however, grew slowly. Pedagogy was aided by the creation of a research center in Madrid, the "Museo Pedagógico Nacional" [National Pedagogic Museum] in 1882, in which a laboratory for experimental anthropology as applied to education was established. Simarro took charge of it and carried out investigations.[49] Some years later, in 1907, a Committee of Scientific Investigation for further studies abroad [Junta de Investigaciones Científicas para la ampliación de estudios en al extrajero] was established under the presidency of Santiago Ramón y Cajal.[50] This group supported the Europeanizing effort of the progressive minorities in Spain. Two events of interest took place between these two dates: in 1902, Simarro took the first and only chair of experimental psychology in the Faculty of Sciences at the University of Madrid; in 1906, Santiago Ramón y Cajal, together with the Italian Camilo Golgi, was awarded the Nobel Prize. All these were steps toward the scientific and intellectual recovery that would take place in Spain during the twentieth century, led by such outstanding figures as José Ortega y Gasset, Gregorio Marañón, Gonzalo Rodriguez

Lafora, Nicolás Achúcarro, Pío del Río Hortega, and José Miguel Sacristán, to name but a few.

The process of incorporating scientific psychology into Spanish thought and society proved to be slow and complex. The political and social situation of the country allowed a radical division between Europeanist and conservative groups to occur. Within this scheme of "Two Spains," psychology was supported by the progressive Krausist group, which was later affiliated with the Free Institution of Education. Psychology was, therefore, incorporated together with a metaphysically directed philosophy, but was soon applied to educational and pedagogical problems.[51] Still later, the development of a medical approach to psychological problems under the influence of Ramón y Cajal led many young investigators to an orientation that was close to, but nonetheless very different from, that of the New Psychology.

On the other hand, the lack of an institutional location in the Universities, which inhibited the work of men of science such as Turró, and Simmaro's inability to gather a strong group of disciples around him in Madrid, were considerable drawbacks to the development of scientific psychology in Spain. The new attitude that was necessary would be brought back to Spain from their travels and studies abroad by the new spirits who then shaped twentieth-century Spanish culture. At the beginning of the century, however, scientific psychology in Spain was still largely a hope.

NOTES

1. For a short presentation of Spanish history, see "Spain, History of," *The New Encyclopaedia Britannica* (London: H. H. Benton, 1974). See also Salvador de Madariago, *Espana* (Madrid: Espasa Calpe, 1979), Richard Herr, *The Eighteenth Century Revolution in Spain* (Princeton, N.J.: Princeton Univ. Press, 1958).

2. Fidelino de Figueiredo, *Las dos Españas* (Santiago: Universidad de Santiago de Compostela, 1933); Ramón Menéndez Pidal, *Los españoles en la historia*, 2nd ed. (Madrid: Espasa Calpe, 1971).

3. Raymond Carr, *Spain: 1808-1939* (Oxford: Oxford Univ. Press, 1966); Manuel Tuñon de Cara, *La España del siglio XIX* (Barcelona: Laia, 1974).

4. See R. Herr, *The Eighteenth Century Revolution in Spain*, part I, ch. iii; see also Alain Guy, "Ramon Campos, disciple de Condillac," in *Pensée hispanique et philosophie française des lumières* (Toulouse: Univ. de Toulouse-le Mirail, 1980).

5. Edelmira Domenech, *La frenologia* (Barcelona: Univ. de Barcelona, 1977); Tomás Čarreras y Artau, *Estudios sobre Médicos-filosofos Españoles del siglo XIX* (Barcelona: C.S.I.C., 1952); Ramón Čarnicer, *Entre la ciencia y la magia. Mariano Cubi* (Barcelona: Seix y Barral, 1969).

6. F. Javier Llorens y Barba, *Lecciones de filosofia* (Barcelona: Univ. de Barcelona, 1956); see also Joaquin Carreras y Artau, "Un maestro barcelonés de Menéndez y Pelayo: Javier Llorens y Barba," *Revista de filosofia*, 15 (1956): 445-63.

7. Alain Guy, *Los filosofos españoles de ayer y de hoy* (Buenos Aires: Losada, 1966).

8. Pedro Mata, *Tratado de la razón humana* (Madrid: Bailly-Bailliere, 1858); *Tratado de la razón humana en sus estados intermedios* (Madrid: Bailly-Bailliere, 1864); *Tratado de la razon humana en estado de enfermedad* (Madrid: Bailly-Bailliere, 1878).

9. Ramón Cenal, "La filosofia española en la segunda mitad del siglo XIX," *Revista de filosofia*, 15 (1956):403-44; Juan Vicente Viqueira, "La filosofia española en el siglo XIX y comienzos del siglo XX," in Karl Vorlander, *Historia de la filosofia* (Madrid: Beltran, 1924), II:441-66. See also G. Fraile, "El P. Ceferino Gonzalez y Dioz Tunon (1831-1894)," *Revista de Filosofia*, 15(1956):465-88.

10. Pierre Jobit, *Les éducateurs de l'Espagne contemporaine: les krausistes*, 2 vols. (Paris: Bibl. Ecole des Hautes Etudes Hispaniques, 1936); Juan Lopez Morillas, *El krausismo español. Perfil de una eventura intelectual* (Madrid: Fondo de Cultura Económica, 1980); Elias Diaz, *La filosofia social del krausismo español* (Madrid: Cuadernos para el Dialogo, 1973); Julian Marias, "El pensador de Illescas," in *Obras IV* (Madrid: Revista de Occidente, 1960).

11. Francisco Giner de los Rios, *Obras completas* (Madrid: La Lectura-Espasa Calpe, 1916 ff.); *Lecciones sumarias de psicologia* (Madrid: Imp. Noguera, 1874; (2nd ed. Madrid: Imp. Alaria, 1877). All citations of the *Lecciones* refer to the 2nd edition.

12. Giner, *Lecciones*, p. vii.

13. Ibid., pp. 13-14.

14. Ibid., p. 63.

15. Giner followed the work of G. Tiberghien, *La science d l'âme dans les limites de l'observation* (Bruxelles: Librairie Polytechnique de Decq, 1868), but he added some psychophysiological data along Wundtian lines.

16. Giner, *Lecciones*, pp. 61-85.

17. Giner, *La persona social. Estudios y fragmentos* (Madrid: Victoriano Suarez, 1899).

18. Enrique Lafuente Niño, *La psicologia española en la época de Wundt; la aportación de Francisco Giner de los Rios*, (Madrid: Ph.D. thesis Univ. Complutense, 1978; mimeo); Enrique Lafuente Niño, "Sobre los origenes de la psicologia cientifica en España. El papel del movimiento krausista," *Estudios de psicologia*, 1 (1980):139-47.

19. Urbano Gonzalez Serrano, *Manual de psicologia, lógica y etica. I. Manual de psicologia* (Madrid: Imp. G. Hernández, 1880); *La psicologia contemporánea* (Madrid: Imp. Hernando, 1880); *La psicologia fisiologica* (Madrid: Fernando Fe, 1886); *La sociologia cientifica* (Madrid: Fernando Fe, 1884); *Estudios psicológicos* (Madrid: Saenz de Jubera, 1892); *Goethe. Ensayos criticos*, 2nd ed. (Madrid: Imp. Carrión, 1892); *Psicologia del amor*, 2nd ed. (Madrid: Fernando Fe, 1897); *Critica y filosofia* (Madrid: Bibl. Economica Filosófica, 1888). On this author, see Concepción Saiz, *Urbano González Serrano (Boceto*

biográfico) (Madrid: Victoriano Suarez, 1914); Adolfo Posada, "Fundamentos psicológicos de la educación segun González Serrano," *Boletin de la Institución Libre de Enseñanza* 16 (1892):1-9, 17-20; Gabriel Talavera, *Urbano Gonzalez Serrano y la psicologia española del siglo XIX* (Valencia: Univ. Valencia, 1975 Grad. thesis, mimeo); Juan Valera, "Psicologia del amor," in *Obras completas II* (Madrid: Aguilar, 1961), 1573-86.

20. U. Gonzalez Serrano, *Manual de psicologia*, pp. 17-18.

21. U. Gonzalez Serrano, *La sociologia cientifica*, p. 140.

22. Luis Simarro published all his scientific work as short articles in the *Boletin de la Institución Libre de Enseñanza;* among them are "El curso de M. Ranvier" (1880-1881), "El exceso de trabajo mental en la enseñanza" (1889), "La teoria del alma, segun Rehmke" (1897), "Sobre el concepto de la locura moral" (1900), "La iteración" (1902); on Simarro, see Juan Vicente Viqueira, *La psicologia contemporánea* (Madrid: Labor, 1930), and Temma Kaplan, "Luis Simarro, Spanish histologist" and "Luis Simarro's psychological theories" in *Actas III Congreso Nacional de historia de la Medicina* (Valencia, 1969), II: 523-33, 545-55.

23. Juan Vicente Viqueira, *La psicologia contemporánea*, p. 58.

24. Th. Ziehen, *Compendio de psicologia fisiologica*, trans. G. Rodriguez Lafora, foreword by L. Simarro (Madrid: Bailly-Bailliere, 1910).

25. L. Simarro, "La teoria del alma, segun Rehmke," *Boletin de la Institución Libre de Enseñanza*, 21 (1897), p. 384.

26. Juan Vicente Viqueira, *La psicologia contemporánea*, p. 58.

27. T. Kaplan, "Luis Simarro's psychological theories," p. 554.

28. León Esteban Mateo, *Boletin de la Institución Libre de Enseñanza. Nómina bibliográfica (1877-1936)* (Valencia: Univ. Valencia, 1978); Belén Carrión Navarro, *Temas psicológicos en el B.I.L.E. (Siglo XIX)* (Valencia: Univ. Valencia, 1975; Grad. thesis, mimeo).

29. Diego Nuñez Ruiz, *La mentalidad positiva en España: Desarrollo y crisis* (Madrid: Tucar, 1975).

30. Pedro Lain Entralgo, *España como problema*, 3rd ed. (Madrid: Aguilar, 1962); Pedro Lain Entralgo, *Ciencia y vida* (Madrid: Seminarios y Ediciones, 1970).

31. Diego Nuñez Ruiz, *El darwinismo en Espana* (Madrid: Castalia, 1969).

32. Among the translations were: Immanuel Kant, *Principios metafisicos del Derecho* (Madrid: Victoriano Suarez, 1873), I. Kant, *Critica de la razon practica* (Madrid: Iravedra, 1876), and I. Kant, *Critica del juicio,* (Madrid: Iravedra, 1876); Herbert Spencer, *Los primeros principios* (Madrid: Perojo, 1879); Alexander Bain, *La ciencia de la educación* (Valencia: Bibl. Profesional de Educacion, 1882); Theodule Ribot, *La psicologia inglesa contemporanea*, 2 vols. (Salamanca: Imp. Cerezo, 1877), *Psicologia alemana contemporanea* (Salamanca, 1878); Henry Maudsley, *La patologia de la inteligencia* (Madrid: Calleja, 1880), *Fisiologia del espiritu* (Madrid: Calleja, 1880), *El crimen y la locura* (Madrid: Calleja, 1880); Wilhelm Wundt, *Elementos de fisiologia humana* (Madrid: Libr. Menendez, 1882).
the new ideas can be seen in Juan Manuel Orti y Lara, *El catecismo de los textos vivos* (Madrid: Bibl. de "La ciencia cristiana," 1884).

34. Jose M. Lopez-Piñero, "Introductión histórica," in P. Gonzalez Blasco, J. Jiménez Blanco, and Jose M. López-Pinero, *Historia y sociologia de la ciencia en España* (Madrid: Alianza, 1979), p. 77.

35. On the generation of 1856, see Julian Marias, "La generación de

1856," in *Obras* (Madrid: Revista de Occidente, 1961) VI, 522-27. On the idea of "generation" as seen in the recent Spanish philosophical tradition of J. Ortega y Gasset and Julian Marias, see Julian Marias, *Generations: A historical method* (Tuscaloosa: Alabama Univ. Press, 1970); Julian Marias, "Generations" in *International encyclopaedia of the social sciences*, ed. D. L. Sills (New York: Macmillan & Free Press, 1968); Nerina Jansen, *Generation Theory*, (Pretoria: Univ. of South Africa, 1975).

36. See Dorothy F. Cannon, *Explorer of the human brain. The life of Santiago Ramón y Cajal (1852-1934)* (New York: Schuman, 1949); Pedro Lain Entralgo, *Espana como problema;* Pedro Lain Entralgo y Agustin Albarracin, *Nuestro Cajal* (Madrid: Rivadeneira, 1967).

37. Santiago Ramón y Cajal, "Foreword" to Tomás Maestre, *Introducción al estudio de la psicologia positiva* (Madrid: Bailly-Bailliere, 1905), p. xvi.

38. Ramón y Cajal, "Foreword," p. xiii.

39. On this point, see Tomás Maestre, *Introducción al estudio de la psicologia positiva*, p. 197-205, which offers a brief account of Ramón y Cajal's views.

40. Ramón y Cajal, "Foreword," p. xv; a popular account of his ideas on volition and genius is to be found in his well-known book *Reglas y consejos sobre investigacion cientifica (Los tónicos de la voluntad)*, 8th ed. (Madrid: Beltran, 1940).

41. Ramón Turró, *Origenes del conocimiento. El hambre* (Barcelona: Minerva, 1914); *La base trófica de la inteligencia* (Madrid: Residencia de Estudiantes, 1918); *Filosofia critica* (Barcelona: Editorial Catalana, 1918). On Turró's ideas, see Alain Guy, *Los filosofos españoles de ayer y de hoy*, p. 113-17; P. Domingo San Juan, *Turró, hombre de ciencia mediterráneo* (Barcelona: Pòrtic, 1970); José L. Miralles, "Antecedentes de la obra de E. Mira y Lòpez en la fisiologia catalana del siglo XIX," *Revista de Historia de la Psicologia*, 1 (1980): 89-119; Juan Riera, "Positivismo cientifico en la obra de Ramón Turró," *Medicina e Historia*, 32 (1974):i-xvi.

42. Turró, *La base trófica de la inteligencia*, p. 65-68.

43. On the "Generation of 1898" see: Pedro Lain Entralgo, "La generación del 98," in *Espana como problema;* Luis S. Granjel, *Panorama de la generación del 98* (Madrid: Guadarrama, 1959).

44. Angel Ganivet, *Idearium español*, 7th ed. (Madrid: Victoriano Suarez, 1944).

45. See, "Azorin," *La voluntad* (1902); from Pio Baroja, the trilogy dedicated to "La lucha por la vida" (*La busca, Mala hierba, Aurora roja*) and the series "Memorias de un hombre de acción"; see also D. King de Arjona, "La voluntad and Abulia in Contemporary Spanish Ideology," *Révue Hispanique* (1928).

46. Miguel de Unamuno, *Vida de Don Quijote y Sancho* (1905) and *Del sentimiento trágico de la vida en los hombres y en los pueblos* (1913); on this topic see Julián Marias, *Miguel de Unamuno* (1943) in *Obras* (Madrid: Revista de Occidente, 1961) vol. IV; José Ferrater Mora, *Unamuno. Bosquejo de una filosofia* (Buenos Aires: Editorial Sudamericana, 1957).

47. José de Caso, "La enseñanza de la Antropologia en la escuela," *Boletin de la Institucion Libre de Enseñanza* 7 (1883) 152-56, 187-90, 235-38, 285-87; 8(1884), 266-68; 9(1885), 125-27, 134-37; the critical remark is found in Gabriel Compayré, *Psicologia teórica y práctica aplicada a la educación* (Paris: Bouret, 1898), p. 10.

48. Julián Besteiro, *La psicofísica* (Madrid: Imp. Rojas, 1897); on Besteiro's life and political importance, Andrés Saborit, *Julian Besteiro* (Buenos Aires: Losada, 1967).

49. Leon Esteban Mateo, "Cossio, el Museo P(edagogico) N(acional) y su actitud comparativista europea," in *Homenaje al Dr. D. Juan Regla Campistol* (Valencia: Univ. Valencia, 1975), II, 391–403.

50. Germán Gómez Orfanel, "La Junta para Ampliacion de Estudios y su politica de pensiones en el extranjero," *Revista de Educacion*, 243 (1976):28–47.

51. Some brief introductions to the evolution of psychology in Spain are to be found in Helio Carpintero, "La psicologia española: pasado, presente, futuro," *Revista de Historia de la Psicologia* 1(1980):33–58; Helio Carpintero, *Historia de la Psicologia* (Madrid: Univ. Nacional Educacion a Distancia, 1976) ch. xxxv; Mariano Yela, "La psicologia española: ayer, hoy y mañana," *Revista de psicologia general y aplicada*, 141–42 (1976):585–90; Miguel Siguan, "La psicologia en Espana," *Anuario de Psicologia* 16(1977):7–21; Ramón León and Josef Brozek, "Historiography of Psychology in Spain: Bibliography with Comment," in Josef Brozek and Ludwig J. Pongratz, eds., *Historiography of Modern Psychology* (Toronto: C. J. Hogrefe, Inc., 1980):141–51.

11

French Crowd Psychology: Between Theory and Ideology

Alexandre Métraux

INTRODUCTION

The study of mass behavior and mass communications has until now received little sustained attention from historians of science. This may be due in part to the fact that since its beginnings in approximately 1880, the field has been the joint venture of a host of different disciplines, including psychiatry, criminology, anthropometrics, ethnology, sociology, psychology, and communications research. Moreover, "mass psychology," "collective psychology," "crowd psychology," or whatever kindred name we may use, refers not only to a joint venture of different disciplines, but also to a field that constitutes for the historian of science a fuzzy subject matter in itself.

Research on mass behavior and mass communications did not follow the pattern of a linear and more or less continuous evolution, but rather that of a jumpwise emergence and disappearance of

I would like to warmly thank William Woodward and Mitchell Ash for their help with the preparation and writing of this chapter. I would also like to acknowledge the benefits I have had from conversations with Serge Moscovici (Paris) and Michael Sommer (Heidelberg).

paradigms unrelated to one another. The subject area was never successfully defined as either basic or applied research, not did it free itself from ideological overtones and political commitments, mostly both to economic liberalism and to political conservatism. Finally, research on mass behavior and mass communications did not offer any intersubjectively agreed upon and testable solution for the many problems it raised, but adapted itself quite uncritically to the changing social problems with which it was confronted from outside.

However, the fuzziness of this field of research should not repel us. On the contrary, it allows us to explore certain aspects of a relatively young and still emerging discipline, which are likely to remain invisible in established sciences.[1] This holds in particular for the French version of mass psychology, the *psychologie des foules*, despite its many ambiguities and the controversial status of both its scientific and its practical claims.

What follows is an attempt to grasp one specific aspect of the emergence of crowd psychology, the transformation of a more-or-less coherent system of beliefs and prejudices concerning the nature of crowds into a set of interrelated and seemingly well-tested theories of crowd behavior.[2] I shall first briefly outline the historical situation of French crowd psychology between 1880 and 1920. Then I shall try to specify the ideological context hidden behind the seemingly neutral rhetoric of crowd-psychological discourse, focusing on a single key topic, social manipulation by means of suggestion and hypnosis.[3] In the final part, I shall discuss the results of the investigation from a historiographical viewpoint and indicate how studies on the history of this discipline may challenge traditional views on social psychology in general.

THE HISTORICAL SITUATION OF FRENCH CROWD PSYCHOLOGY (1880–1920)

Serge Moscovici has recently argued that crowd psychology developed in reaction to the power the lower classes acquired in France after 1850.[4] He also points out that crowd psychology was set up in order to lay the foundations of a systematic and scientific analysis of the multifarious phenomena of crowd behavior. The aim of French crowd psychologists was thus twofold. On the one hand, they sought to understand the contemporary transformation of French society; on the other, they were searching for scientifically validated remedies against a severe social illness: the slow disruption of society or the nation caused by the uncontrollable revolt of the crowd or the mob against traditional order.[5]

Although crowds had already been a historical factor long before 1870,[6] their impact on social and political life grew rapidly in the last third of the nineteenth century. Crowds became influential through the organization of mass movements, such as labor unions, as well as through anarchistic groups, various types of Labor Exchange, and so forth.[7] In 1881, the Parliament voted the first law concerning the freedom of the press, and in 1884 the first labor union law.[8] Both laws provided a legal frame for the propagation of liberal social and economic ideas, but exacerbated the conservatives, among them the crowd psychologists, who began to polemicize in their scientific writings against socialist, anarchist, and communist creeds and programs.

For some psychologists, the new phenomenon of the crowd as a driving societal force was only a result of industrialization and accelerated urbanization. As Joseph Maxwell wrote in his *Psychologie sociale contemporaine* in 1911, the industrial revolution drove a great number of people into already overcrowded cities that did not offer decent or even sufficient housing conditions; at the same time, the mechanization of labor (*machinisme*) contributed to the lowering of practical and intellectual skills. In particular, the industrial revolution led to the formation of "homogeneous crowds" conceived of as groups of "approximately the same social elements having the same origin, the same education, the same spirit, the same needs and the same drives."[9]

However, such a characterization of the crowd is an exception in French literature; for psychologists and sociologists usually resorted to a value-loaded vocabulary when they characterized the object of their investigation. Thus, crowds were said to be instinct-driven,[10] criminal,[11] credulous,[12] primitive,[13] simplistic,[14] irascible,[15] brutal,[16] incoherent,[17] violent,[18] feminine,[19] and so forth. This seems to indicate that the attitude of crowd psychologists toward the groups they were studying was not dictated by scientific impartiality only.

Any reconstruction of crowd psychology should therefore neatly distinguish between two quite different historical processes that took place in French society during the first decades of the Third Republic. On the one hand, there are the objective transformations occurring as a consequence of industrialization, urbanization, and other socioeconomic events; on the other, there is the perception or subjective interpretation of these transformations by scientists who, though they were trained in different disciplines and worked under different conditions, shared at least a common evaluative frame of reference. Of course, both the objective transformations of French society and their subjective interpretation were determinants of the emergence of crowd psychology. Its outlook, content, and rhetoric, however, were probably much more determined by the common evaluative frame of reference shared by crowd psychologists than by any other factor.

Thus, when Jean Bourdeau loudly proclaimed in 1905 that "We are entering the era of crowds,"[20] we cannot infer from such a statement that the phenomenon of the crowd was adequately interpreted by French social scientists, but only that their research was motivated by what appeared to them to be a profound societal transformation. As Nye correctly emphasized with regard to crowd psychology in general, "we must, however, reluctantly, accept 'false' conceptions as historically valid if they were believed to be so."[21]

French crowd psychologists enjoyed a great public reputation until approximately 1920. Their works were sympathetically received by conservative intellectuals, politicians, writers, and academics and very strongly criticized by progressive, leftist groups. Here, as elsewhere in French society and culture, the Dreyfus affair was a focal point of bitter antagonism. Such political divisions probably account for the fact that crowd psychologists remained at the margin of the university system, from which they were excluded by Émile Durkheim and his colleagues and friends in the university administration.[22] This antagonism between Durkheim and his followers on the one hand, and the more or less coherent group of crowd psychologists on the other, sheds light on the social and institutional situation of psychology in general, and of crowd psychology in particular, until the outbreak of World War I.

Durkheim's model for the institutionalization of the social sciences had been the psychological laboratory founded by Wilhelm Wundt at the University of Leipzig.[23] With the support of high-ranking officials of the Ministry of Public Education, Durkheim had pleaded for an institutional reform of the social sciences, including collective psychology. He had already achieved some progress in this direction when crowd psychologists began to demand positions and privileges in the university, which they believed they deserved because of their reputation. However, their demands, repeated year after year, were not met.

The foundation of the psychological laboratory at the *École pratique des Hautes Études* in Paris on January 28, 1889, did not even slightly lessen the tension between the social scientists led by

Durkheim and the crowd psychologists.[24] Henri Beaunis and Alfred Binet, the first directors of the laboratory, had both undertaken research in the field of suggestion, hypnotism, unconscious automatism, and the like—that is, in a field closely akin to the domain to which crowd psychologists paid special attention. However, the goals of the laboratory were analogous to those of the Leipzig laboratory, to make observations of sensory and motor dependent variables under various experimental conditions. The chasm between these two divergent trends of socio-psychological and sociological research remained unaltered over time. Le Bon's resentment against his and his followers' exclusion from the university is reflected in his many attacks against the French university system and its educational principles.[25]

However, in terms solely of social visibility and influence, the marginal group of crowd psychologists won out against both the Durkheim group and the laboratory psychologists. Gustave Le Bon (1841–1931), undoubtedly the most outspoken, dogmatic, and colorful representative of crowd psychology, succeeded at building up an effective network of communication outside that of the official social sciences. His books alone sold approximately half-a-million copies and reached an audience much larger than that of many well-known writers of that time.[26] His literary output was certainly greater than that of the average scientist, so much so that he could easily live from it. As the editor of a series of outstanding scientific works, the *Bibliothèque de Philosophie scientifique* published by Flammarion in Paris, he even gained some ideological control over the contributors; he did not refrain from imposing changes of content on the authors he edited when the latter diverged too much from his own political opinion.

Thanks to his famous *salon* at the *rue Vignon*, which met every week, and to his informal relationships with politicians—Poincaré and Clémenceau, to mention only two of them, regarded him as an expert in political psychology and as a grey eminence in matters of leadership, national renascence, and political strategy—Le Bon could exert some direct influence upon decision-making processes in the power centers of the Third Republic.

As a prolific vulgarizer of many scientific doctrines of the day,[27] he constantly gave proof of his competence and expertise, and occasionally accepted contracts to carry out experimental research for others in his private laboratory.[28] Yet even his busyness did not stop his enemies from charging him with stubbornly sticking to theories that had proven to be false, and of unduly claiming priorities of discovery; his debate with Einstein over the priority of discovery of the theory of relativity was a complete disaster.[29] But such mishaps did not—or could not—deter his prestige. On the contrary, they even helped to strengthen it among his followers, who pitied the unjust victimization of a great man.

Finally, Le Bon was instrumental in introducing the systematic study of the behavior of crowds into the field of military psychology. Indeed, the antidemocratically-minded military establishment not only recognized in Le Bon a political ally, but also a scientist whose theories could be made a part of the curriculum at the *École de Guerre Supérieure* and at *Saint-Cyr*, the leading military schools in France. The congeniality between Le Bon and other crowd psychologists and the military establishment was the result of two originally independent historical processes that merged at a certain point of time.

On the one hand, crowd psychologists had developed their theories in order to account for the power that crowds acquired under specific circumstances. The detailed analysis of these specific circumstances and of the mechanisms that were responsible for the manipulation of crowds would, so they thought, enable them to deduce practical rules from theoretical insights. These rules, if properly applied by social agencies—the government, the police, the court, the army, and so forth—would, in turn, permit them to take control over crowds.

On the other hand, the French Army faced serious difficulties after its defeat in the war of 1870/71. Industrialization did not progress as rapidly in France as in the German Empire;[30] one result was the inferiority of French military equipment compared with the more sophisticated and powerful weapons in Germany. Furthermore, the decrease in the birth rate in France in the last third of the nineteenth century created long-term economic and strategic problems—hence the government's strong moves against all moral liberalism,[31] and the concern of military staffs about the insufficient number of soldiers. The basic inferiority of the French Army in terms of technical and human resources had to be compensated for somehow by psychological and moral superiority. Crowd psychology was regarded as the adequate means to achieve this—its application would not cost much, it was easily learned, and it seemed to fit the crowd-like aggregate of a large number of soldiers, who could be manipulated by expert leaders and thus reach a level of heroism unusual for regularly trained soldiers.[32] The military elite of the Third Republic doubtless shared with nearly all crowd psychologists a conservative and even antidemocratic attitude. However, these practical considerations certainly outweighed political allegiances and greatly contributed to the social success of crowd psychology.

French crowd psychology thus serves as a convenient and compelling example for challenging historians' views on the early development of modern psychology. Crowd psychology was, at least in France, socially more influential than its contemporary counterpart, experimental psychology, which is still regarded as the historical prototype of the science of psychology as such. It achieved its reputation despite the fact that, unlike experimental psychology of the Wundtian type, it did not have an institutional infrastructure in the university, and was constantly marginalized by official science. Around the turn of the century, experimental psychology of the Wundtian type was rapidly expanding on an international scale. Crowd psychology, however, remained a phenomenon geographically limited to France and, to a lesser degree, to Italy. After World War I, it had some followers in Egypt, Turkey, Rumania, and Japan, a fact that demonstrates once again its marginality.[33] Paradoxically, when after 1920 the reputation of crowd psychology began to decline in France, some of its major themes were either taken up by mainstream psychologists or rediscovered independently of the French psychologists. The continuity of crowd-psychological themes over time has not been recognized by historians of psychology, probably because it has been obfuscated by the cleavage between the different idioms used by psychologists. A common denominator hardly exists between the terminological peculiarities of Le Bon and his friends, the stimulus–response vocabulary adapted by Floyd Allport, Freud's and Martin's psychoanalytic way of speaking about crowds, and today's more familiar language employed by students of mass communications.

The continuity of crowd-psychological themes is in itself an interesting issue for historians and theorists of social psychology. Indeed, the fact that highly differing schools and trends of social psychology vary significantly with respect to conceptual apparatus and methods of investigation, but not with respect to some basic ideas about the nature of crowds, the role of the leaders of crowds, the suggestibility of such a social aggregate, and so forth, may be indicative of an overall bias dominating the last hundred years of research in this area. I shall return to this point after analyzing the central theoretical component of French crowd psychology: the theory of hypnotic suggestion.

THE PARADIGM OF SUGGESTION

French crowd psychologists were concerned simultaneously with several problems of more-or-less equal theoretical and empirical importance. Their main textbooks contain not only chapters dealing with differential psychology, national characters and the differences between them, and the evolution of the races, but also chapters on topics such as suggestion, the structure of social aggregates, the role of the leader, the theory of emotion, the theory of collective egoism and individual altruism, and so on. Crowd psychology as such thus consists of a number of components or subtheories imported in part from other sciences, and in part elaborated by the crowd psychologists themselves. A careful reading of the texts, however, leads sooner or later to the conclusion that the subtheory concerning the manipulation of crowds through social influence, persuasion, or some other means represents the essential part of crowd psychology, and that theoretical considerations of the problems dealt with in other crowd-psychological subtheories are ultimately of secondary importance.

Yet crowd psychologists did not reach final agreement on any of these subtheories. One example may suffice to illustrate this absence of agreement. Gabriel Tarde distinguished between the public and the crowd in order to solve a problem pertaining to the subtheory of the structure of social aggregates. His conception of the public was of a "purely spiritual community" or a "dissemination of physically separated individuals among whom there exists only mental cohesion."[34] The crowd, however, is an aggregate of individuals acting in close physical contact with one another within a given limited space.[35] But Tarde did not admit that the processes of social influence could vary between structurally different social aggregates. According to him, beliefs, opinions, and attitudes are transmitted from one individual to another according to the law of imitation. In imitation, the *brain* of one individual produces through some action at a distance the replica of his or her ideas in the *brain* of some other individual; the latter, in turn, is said to trigger the imitative behavior of the second individual.[36]

Another, quite different view of mental influence was held by Maurice Milloud. In an article published in 1910, Milloud conjectured that a previous affective or emotional similarity between the influencing individual or group and the influenced one was a necessary, though not a sufficient, condition for the propagation of ideas.[37]

Emotional similarity thus functions in Milloud's frame as an *explanans* for the receptivity of some groups to a given social influence and, conversely, for the resistance of some other groups. In short, Milloud's thesis was that influence as such takes place only within structurally homogeneous groups, whereas the thesis of Tarde amounted to saying that individuals influence each other irrespective of their social status, role, or similar.

Yet, despite such more-or-less serious divergences concerning the various subtheoretical components of the theory of crowd behavior, French psychologists agreed with one another on the following two principles. First, social aggregates, in particular crowds, rest on suggestion—that is to say, on some sort of physical or non-physical power by which an individual exerts influence on some other individual.[38] Second, as a result of suggestion or some other sort of influence, collective behavior, especially the behavior of crowds, displays traits that are symptomatic of an earlier, inferior stage of social evolution. Differently put, suggestion leads to moral and intellectual regression.

The generic term "suggestion" was used by French psychiatrists, psychologists, and sociologists in various contexts. It was meant to denote an event or process in which three distinct parts are involved. Abstracting from the specificities of the medical, psychological, and sociological discourse in which the term occurs, one could say that it refers to (1) an agent, (2) a patient, and (3) a medium, force, or power by which or through which the agent acts upon the patient. The task of scientific investigation was to describe, specify, and explain the medium, force, or power and thus to add to the prescientific understanding of the process of suggestion something that either did not mention such a medium, force, or power at all, or erroneously attributed suggestive power to some demon or devil or malevolent spirit.

French medical and social-psychological writings contain innumerable descriptions of the phenomenon called "suggestion." Clinical observations of *folie à deux*, accounts of mass and mob demonstrations, histories of collective hysteria, or the spread of fashions and rumors, and so forth have all been connected with the topic. However, as to the *valid scientific explanation* of suggestion, it seems that even decades of research did not dispose of a certain embarrassment on the part of the experts. In a mood of helplessness, Georges Dumas remarked in 1911 that the mechanism by which motor, effective, or representational states are propagated had not yet been determined.[39] After some thirty consecutive years of work, Le Bon himself admitted that he had reached the limits of "positive science" and that suggestion was still a "mysterious mechanism."[40] No wonder, then, that competing explanations of suggestion were proposed and discussed.

These competing explanations were developed in three approaches that may be distinguished from one another as follows:

1. the *epidomiological approach*, which was heavily influenced by the science of bacteriology;
2. the *sociological approach*, which drew in part from psychology and in part from ethnology and general sociology;
3. the *psychiatric approach*, which drew from psychiatric nosology, the mental sciences, and a bit of chemistry and magnetism.

The epidemiological approach

According to the proponents of this approach, suggestion of ideas, attitudes, behavioral patterns, whether normal or pathological is just another instance of contagion. The medical literature thus mentions not only a *contagium vivum*, but also a *contagium psychicum*, analogous to organic agents of contagion such as microbes, which cause a person's mind to be contaminated with the ideas, habits, attitudes of another person.[41]

It should be noted that this approach was construed in such a way as to exactly parallel the model of bacteriological epidemiology. In the latter, it was common to separate the process by which an illness is spread from the (hygenic, meteriological, and so on) conditions that facilitate contagions. Similarly, educational conditions, alcoholism, religious creeds, and similar were said to be factors that could facilitate the contagion of ideas. But such conditions were rigorously distinguished from the causal agent of contagion itself, and the latter was defined as taking place between two individuals only.[42]

The epidemiological approach is historically interesting because it sheds light upon the role and the limitations of metaphors in an emergent discipline such as crowd psychology. Indeed, the sciences of bacteriology and epidemiology served as a model for crowd psychology. The former had found a coherent and testable description for the contagion of illnesses. It now became the lens through which a new *explanandum* (mental contagion) was seen. But the putative referent of the expression "mental contagion" remained, so to speak, unfulfilled, since the *contagium psychicum* had not been discovered. In other words, the place of the causal agent of mental contagion in the network of laws with which the epidemiological approach operated is only formally, but not materially, defined.[43]

The sociological approach

The proponents of this approach held that suggestion is, in Crocq's words, any "idea introduced into the human brain, whether this idea stems from a human being or results from external impression."[44] Without doing violence to the texts, suggestion may be equated with the receptivity of the human organism to any physical or social impression. But a word of caution must be added. Tarde seems to have been aware that such a broad conception did not make the process of suggestion any clearer, and that it may have resulted from the incorporation of overgeneralized psychiatric hypotheses that were applied to social psychology and sociology. A passage from his famous book *Les lois de l'imitation* of 1890 corroborates such an interpretation:

> Do we know the essence of this suggestion from person to person that constitutes social life? No! For if we consider suggestion in itself, in its state of purity and higher intensity, it turns out to be one of the most mysterious phenomena—a phenomenon that our psychiatrist–philosophers investigate these days with passionate curiosity, but without succeeding in understanding it completely: somnambulism.[45]

The reference to psychiatry shows that we are, in fact, confronted with a *rapprochement* of a special kind. Indeed, the psychiatric theory of hypnosis and hypnotic somnambulism served as a model with the help of which *any social relation whatsover*—including that between members of a crowd—was defined.

The psychiatric approach

From the viewpoint of theoretical elaboration, at least, the psychiatric approach seems to have been the fundamental one. It dealt with problems that obviously had not been solved in the epidemiological approach, and it was the basis from which the sociological approach was derived. Its central place in the search of a coherent theory of suggestion must therefore be emphasized here. In fact, however, it was not crowd psychology proper that laid the basis for understanding the dynamics of social aggregates, but general psychology. Tarde, for example, emphasized that sociology and social psychology rest ultimately on individual-psychological principles.[46] Individual-psychological principles were also used by Le Bon and his followers when they addressed genuinely crowd-psychological problems. One could consequently say that crowd psychology, as far as the issues of the formation and locomotion of crowds are concerned, is *derivative* from general and differential psychology; this is particularly true for its use of the theory of suggestion. Alfred Binet's analysis of the mechanism of perception with hypnotized subjects is, as far as I can see, the best example for the use of the psychiatric paradigm as a link between general psychology and the theory of suggestion in crowd psychology.[47]

Around 1885, associationism was the *idée fixe*, the guiding principle of French psychologists such as Théodule Ribot, Pierre Janet, Binet, and others.[48] The works of Hyppolite Taine and John Stuart Mill were their primary source of inspiration. A peculiarity of the evolution of psychology in France, however, was that psychologists took a vivid interest in, and occasionally worked with, psychiatrists. Thus, medical thinking came to imprint a specific style upon the theory of associationism. The studies of perception in hysterics and neurotics under hypnosis written by Binet between 1884 and 1887 in collaboration with Charles Féré, a follower of Charcot at the Salpêtrière, are significant in this regard because they contain the outline of a cerebral (or neurophysiological) theory of association.[49]

According to Binet, whenever a sensation reaches the brain through the afferent nervous system, it is associated with an image, defined as a trace of an earlier sensation that is now stored in the central nervous system. The brain itself is conceived as a kind of reservoir or box where all the earlier elementary data (images) are deposited and wait to be activated and processed, that is, combined with the elements of the sensory afflux (sensations). This box, reservoir, or container presents itself as an anatomically and physiologically structured set of distinguishable regions or centers, each of which corresponds to a mental or organic function.[50] Now, depending upon the circumstances, an accoustic sensation, for example, may call out in the center corresponding to the auditory function an image and produce there the percept of a sound. In other words, the associative synthesis of sensations and images constitutes what Binet calls the "percept" of which the person becomes aware.[51] But the same sensation may, in addition, activate the visual center, evoke there some image of a color, and produce in combination with the auditory image a phenomenon of synesthesis.

There is little doubt that Binet regarded the brain as a system of functionally distinct chambers or vessels communicating with one another. But the association of sensations and images is conceived differently from the association of different cerebral centers. What was seen psychologically as a *synthesis* of mental elements (sensations and images) by Binet is now treated as an *addition* of simultaneously functioning, but topographically distinguishable, brain centers.

Without such an additive interpretation of the cerebral association, it would make no sense to speak of the functioning of individual centers. Furthermore, the design used by Binet in several quasi-experiments to test the cerebrosensory doctrine of association would have been theoretically unsound. The quasi-experimental idea was to interrupt the afflux of sensations of one kind in order to inhibit some brain activities locally and to activate some other brain centers locally by means of sensations of some other kind in such a way that the images thus produced would be the analogue of a full-fledged percept. The method employed in order to attain this theoretically defined goal was hypnosis.

A brief report of one of Binet's quasi-experiments on visual perception will make this point clear. A white sheet of paper is presented to a hypnotized subject. The experimenter suggests that a red cross is to be seen at the center of the sheet. The subject is then requested to fixate upon the center of the cross. After a while, the sheet of paper is exchanged for another, equally white sheet. The subject is then asked what color he or she sees. According to Binet' subjects, the answer—invariably the same—is that the cross is green.

The proposed explanation of the phenomenon is this: due to the effect of hypnosis, the afflux of visual sensations is inhibited and therefore no longer affects the center of vision; but the message of the experimenter triggers, through the mediation of the speech center and then the visual center the image of a color habitually associated with the color word. The subject's brain then produces the afterimage with the name of the complementary color used in the subject's answer to the experimenter.[52]

In a second quasi-experiment, Binet and Féré took one further step. They investigated a process caused by a purely physical force but phenomenally analogous to the process just described. Some hysterical patients, we are told, are sensitive to magnetic forces and display what was then called "mental polarization." This polarization manifests itself in many ways, for it concerns "the inversion of any functional state whatsoever."[53] To a hypnotized hysterical subject the generalized hallucination of yellow is suggested. The subject sees the surroundings—persons and things—as though he or she were looking through yellow glasses. A magnet is then applied to the head of the subject who, after a while, sees the yellow disappear, while the surroundings become dark, as if daylight had faded away. This phenomenon is explained by mental polarization, which causes the complementary hallucination to arise, that is, the replacement of the yellow color by its complementary color, violet.[54]

Both quasi-experiments (as well as several similar ones) are concerned above all with the inhibition of the actual visual sensations through hypnosis, the activation of images in the visual center through verbal messages, and the natural or artificial causation of the complementary after-image. Yet, since magnetic forces may polarize any function, that is, cause the disappearance of a memory-item remembered before the application of the magnet, or cause the inhibition of a motor act in the course of its performance, they have (or may have) exactly the same effect as the experimenter's verbal messages on a hypnotized subject. For all these phenomena, particularly the classical case of a loss of memory or of the resurgence of an inhibited memory-item, may also be due to hypnosis as such. Binet thus performed a kind of "physicalization" or "materialization" of social influence (that is, of the impact of the hypnotizer upon the hypnotized subject). Of course, such a "physicalization" suited the crowd psychologists well, because it allowed them to attribute the extraordinary impact of a person and of his or her messages upon social aggregates to some physical force.

On the basis of what has been said until now, the psychiatric approach to suggestion may be more fully formulated. "Suggestion" as a technical term refers to a process in which, by means of verbal or other messages, the conditions of the modification in the functioning of the individual's brain are created; the efficient causal agent, however, is either a physical force, such as that of a magnet or of a chemical substance, or said to be still unknown.

As to the validity of Binet's conception of hypnotic suggestion, two aspects should be carefully distinguished from one another. On the one hand, we may critically reconstruct Binet's theory from today's scientific standpoint and conclude that, according to the now accepted standards, both associationism in general and the neurophysiological doctrine of strict cerebral localization must be rejected. But such a presentistic view is ultimately of little help, because it does not permit one to grasp the relevance certain conceptions, paradigms, or theories had in the past. On the other hand, one may look for critiques of the psychiatric approach contemporary with Binet's own writings, which indicate that the sociophysiological theory of suggestion is nothing but the result of spurious speculations motivated by empirical data, which turn out to be artefacts upon closer scrutiny.

Joseph Delbouef, who was not only a leading specialist on psychophysics in the French-speaking countries, but also an expert in magnetism, showed that he could easily obtain under controlled conditions exactly the same results as Binet and Féré on a non-neurotic subject whom he had trained in only four hours to perform the same tasks. In addition, he showed that the phenomena of polarization observed by Binet could also be obtained when a piece of wood was applied instead of a magnet. Finally, he argued that the psychiatric approach to suggestion had made a mistake in category by physicalizing the causal agent of the mental processes concomitant to the organic processes that took place in a subject under hypnotic conditions.[55] Although the psychiatric approach to suggestion was the most elaborate and structured one, so much so that it can be regarded as a kind of paradigm, it was proven by approximately 1890 that it was not supported by empirical evidence, and that it was conceptually unsatisfactory. In other words, the theory of suggestion that Binet had painfully elaborated turned out to be a nontheory even to his contemporaries.

THE IDEOLOGICAL USE
OF THE PARADIGM OF SUGGESTION
IN CROWD PSYCHOLOGY

Why, then, did crowd psychologists still make such generous use of the psychiatric approach? For what reasons did they base their attempts at explaining the behavior of crowds primarily on this approach, even though they admitted more-or-less reluctantly that it may have been faulty, or incomplete, or even misleading?

A first proof of the theoretical relevance of the psychiatric approach lies in the innumerable references to it in the crowd-psychological literature. Le Bon relates his studies to the "contemporary researchers"[56] who worked in the field of the subliminal causes of human action, and he explicitly refers in another passage to the studies made on unconscious automatism.[57] A second proof is the actual use of the theory of hypnotism. In his *Psychologie des foules*, Le Bon states: "Careful observations seem to prove that the individual who is immersed for a long while in an active crowd, and due to the odors emanating from the latter or for any yet unknown cause, falls into a peculiar state, closely resembling the state of fascination of a hypnotized person under the influence of the hypnotizer."[58] Moreover, Le Bon and other psychologists attribute to the leader of a crowd the ability to act upon the latter through hypnotic suggestion.[59]

Yet, this second proof is not very conclusive, for it could also relate to some other approach to suggestion. A third proof is needed; in order to establish it, a brief digression to a key topic connected with the theory of hypnotic suggestion has to be made. A subject under the influence of a hypnotizer loses, so to speak, the unmediated contact with the physical world, because the inhibition of the sensory afflux predisposes the mental life to be dominated by mere images. One could as well say that the subject's mind is restricted to images of pseudo-representational content, since these images are evoked by the verbal messages of the hypnotizer. But there is more to it than this. The hypnotized subject also produces these images in a totally automatic manner. The subject's mind is thus not only limited in its activities to acts of imagining, but also shut off from every possible self-monitoring control. Thus, pseudo-representational imagination and unconscious automatism go hand in hand. Of course, the same holds true by extension for acts: the hypnotized subject performs exactly those acts that stand under the external command of the hypnotizer.

This essential link between words, images, and acts—which is a characteristic of the psychiatric approach—was made an indispensable component of crowd-psychological theory. It served to make two points. First, members of crowds are, above all, impressed by images evoked by some hypnotizing leader, and, as a result of the predominance of images, rational or even scientific checking against reality is no longer possible. Second, members of crowds regress to a prior level of evolution where instinctive, automatic, unconscious patterns of behavior and thinking dominate. Hence, a phylo-ontogenetic parallelism obtains between the behavior of crowds, of children, and of so-called primitive tribes.[60]

Furthermore, since the individual members of a crowd are all recipients of the messages of a hypnotizing leader, each individual in a crowd has the same images, is behaviorally oriented toward the same goal, and remains so as long as he or she is subjected to the influence of the leader. Thus, the crowd as such may be seen as a single entity and be treated as though it were just one person. This clearly amounts to reducing the complexity of social aggregates such as crowds to theoretically simpler structures that can be dealt with in terms of individual and differential psychology.

The main crowd-psychological claim, that crowds are single entities easily manipulable by a leader, was now specified on the basis of the psychiatric approach and couched in scientific terms. As far as only this claim is concerned, one may conclude that it was minimally justified by empirical evidence, or even that it was erroneous, but not that it formally contradicts the main theoretical propositions of the psychiatric approach.

However, this crowd-psychological claim was, in addition, made the object of crude ideological interpretation. Put differently: the gap between the main theoretical component of crowd psychology—the empirically dubious theory of hypnotic suggestion—and the whole of crowd psychology was filled with views that owe everything to ideology and nothing to science. The discrepancy becomes manifest in several contradictions that are to be found in Le Bon's and his followers' works.

Le Bon once remarked that leaders of crowds are mostly neurotic persons who, through self-suggestion, are hypnotized by the idea they propagate. Since the state of being hypnotized is equivalent to a mental state dominated by unconscious automatism, the leader and the crowd are said to behave irrationally. But Le Bon also maintained that crowds, though generally destructive and morally perverted, might also behave heroically under the leadership of an expert with hypnotizing abilities. The military application of crowd psychology was justified by this very possibility, for it was assumed that the leader would be an expert with scientific training who would rationally and purposefully manipulate the soldiers. Now, which alternative must be accepted? If hypnotic suggestion has to be regarded as a process of nonreciprocal, interpersonal causality, then crowds are neither better nor worse than the ideas they believe in, and as such they can no longer be considered as bad or good, destructive or heroic, intellectually and morally enlightened or primitive, and so on. In other words, it is solely with respect to the content of the leader's messages that qualities such as "aggressive," "violent," or "cruel" can be attributed to crowds. A contradiction thus exists between propositions about the regressive character of crowds in general, and propositions about certain psychological properties of crowds that act under the leadership of a rational, well-trained, self-conscious expert in hypnotism.

Another quite patent contradiction is also symptomatic of the speculative and ideological outlook of French crowd-psychological reasoning. Le Bon and his followers often emphasized the instinctive, irrational sources of utopian projects such as the socialist and communist programs. Such programs, they maintained, appeal to uncritical minds because they evoke images referring to some future paradise or ideal society. And this is particularly true of that programmatic idea of socialism and communism which aims, against all scientific evidence as well as against any realistic attitude toward the world, at transforming a differentiated society into a homogeneous and egalitarian one where interindividual differences will be abolished. Socialism, then, is said to lead to the formaticn of a kind of macro-crowd where there is no longer a place for critical questioning, innovation, independence, or some form or other of dissent.

Crowd psychologists directed their theory of elitism against such collectivist programs. But they also postulated that the elite achieves its leading social position thanks to superior intelligence and moral integrity. In this social position, it would have the duty to educate the people. However, education was defined by Le Bon as "the art of making the conscious pass into the domain of the unconscious."[61] Once again, so-called primitive and regressive socialist or communist movements are not different from well-educated groups, since in both cases a leader has succeeded in making unconscious mental processes the dominant cause of behavior. The manipulation of a crowd by a socialist or communist proselytizer thus rests exactly on the same principles of suggestion and external control by a leader as the education of the elite.

This second contradition, to which several others could be added, makes clear that crowd psychologists drew conclusions much too hastily from specific hypotheses about hypnotic suggestion. By applying these conclusions to broad issues of the nature of crowds and similar social aggregates, they created a speculative and ideologically biased discipline. Moreover, by attributing regressive and primitive traits to crowds because of the irrational effects of hypnotic suggestion and the predominance of unrealistic imagery, and by underlining their own realistic, scientific, and critical knowledge based on individual efforts and higher intelligence in the service of progress, they also offered a pretense of well-founded arguments against the socialists and communists of the day.

Neither the lack of evidence nor the obvious contradictions inherent in French crowd psychology actually bothered Le Bon, his followers, or his admirers too much. It was ultimately more important to give the appearance of a psychological theory with a scientific outlook, a transparent structure, and plentiful corroboration by hundreds of observations. Such a theory could be used as a tool for analysis as well as a weapon for the protection of individual values, economic efficiency, and the superiority of the elite against the threat of egalitarian socialism. Instead of burdening themselves with a thorough investigation of the sociohistorical causes of the phenomena they feared,[63] the French crowd theorists superficially psychologized complex social problems.

CONCLUSION

Historical analyses of crowd psychology may also be relevant for the reconstruction of research on mass behavior and mass communications in general, for two reasons:

First, a retrospective survey on research done in the field of mass behavior reveals that a number of themes and ideas have recurred quite frequently since 1880; among these are the role and impact of leaders in more-or-less structured groups, the irrationality of the crowd, the potential threat of rebellious minorities to society, the receptivity to suggestion, the hidden persuaders, the sleeper effect, the loss of the individual's self-control in crowds, and the preponderance of emotions in collective behavior. This thematic continuity strikingly contrasts with the discontinuity and diversity of the theoretical approaches offered in this area of research. Such a contrast confronts the critical historian of psychology with several questions. Is the recurrence of themes and ideas due primarily to some ideological or other bias, which supersedes the incomplete interpretation of observations and experimental data within different, partly incompatible theoretical approaches or paradigms? Does empirical research on mass behavior provide any sufficient basis for a clearcut distinction between common-sense beliefs and theoretically sound hypotheses about the nature of the mass or of the crowd? Or did the evolution of research in this field gradually impose a change in the technical vocabulary, without leading to a modification of our understanding of the phenomena of collective behavior, so that we may think we know something about these phenomena when we shift from the vernacular to the vocabulary of the behavioral sciences? An analytical frame such as that developed in this chapter at least opens up some perspective within which these and similar questions may reasonably be handled.

Second, despite the promising sound of labels such as "social psychology," "collective psychology," and "mass psychology," some leading researchers since 1880 have, for various reasons, retained an individualistic viewpoint. An implicit consequence of this is that mass behavior may adequately be explained in terms of individual behavior. Put another way, one could say that there is nothing essentially different in the behavior of masses or crowds as compared to the behavior of single individuals put together. Yet, we may ask whether the reduction of a complex subject matter to its elements and thus the negation of properties that are characteristic only of the complex subject matter—the social aggregate, the crowd, the mass —are adequate to the task of a scientific analysis as such. The reconstruction of French crowd psychology, the first mass-psychological doctrine, provides a schema within which problems such as the individualistic orientation, the methodological bias and the psychologization of social problems in research on mass behavior and mass communications since 1880 might be addressed.

NOTES

1. On the importance of such comparative analyses for the history and theory of psychology, see Kurt Lewin, *Wissenschaftstheorie I*, ed. A. Métraux (Bern/Stuttgart: Huber & Klett-Cotta, 1981).

2. The suspicion that French crowd psychology is mere ideology couched in a scientific discourse was expressed in strong terms by Theodore Zeldin, who maintains that Gustave Le Bon "in fact offered methodological guidelines more than conclusions based on a thorough investigation of anything like all the loyalties that were influential in the society of . . . his day." See *France 1884-1945*, vol. II: *Intellect, Taste and Anxiety* (Oxford: Clarendon, 1977), p. 28. However, Zeldin gives minimal evidence to support his suspicion, though I take it to be legitimate in principle. His thesis that Le Bon developed his view on crowds on the basis of the observation of horses, on the other hand, is a gross simplification that cannot stand even a weak test.

For a similar suspicion about crowd psychology, see B. F. Porshnev, "Kontrsuggestiya i istoriya" [Counter-suggestion and History] in B. F. Porshnev & L. I. Antsiferova (eds.), *Istoriya i psikhologiya* [History and Psychology] (Moscow: Izdatel'stva "Nauka," 1971), pp. 7-35. In this article, Porshnev maintains that the history of mankind runs between two poles: suggestion and countersuggestion. Le Bon and other French crowd psychologists are said to reflect the aspect of suggestion only and to discard uncritically the counter-aspect of the progress from suggestion to scientific rationality.

3. The only historical monography published on crowd psychology is Robert A. Nye, *The Origins of Crowd Psychology: Gustave Le Bon and the Crisis of Mass Democracy in the Third Republic* (London/Beverly Hills, Cal.: Sage, 1975). Nye's book, which focuses mainly on Le Bon's life and work as well as on the sociohistorical situation during Le Bon's lifetime, contains valuable information from unpublished materials. However, theories of crowd psychology are dealt with only incidentally, and the discussion of what I consider to be central to crowd psychology—the theory of suggestion—is rather superficial. This is why I will pay special attention to the topic of suggestion.

4. Cf. Serge Moscovici, "Bewusste und unbewusste Einflüsse in der Kommunikation," *Zeitschrift für Sozialpsychologie* 12 (1981):94. Moscovici is one of the rate authors who combine the study of the history of science and ideology with empirical research in social psychology and sociology. Among his writings on the history of science, *L'expérience du mouvement: Jean-Baptiste Baliani disciple et critique de Galilée* (Paris: Herrmann, 1967); "Notes sur le 'De Motu Tractatus' de Michel Varro," *Revue d'Histoire des Sciences et de leurs Applications* II (1958): 108-29; "L'histoire des science et la science des historiens," *Archive Européen de la Sociologie* 7 (1966):116-26; and his monograph *La psychanalyse, son image et son public*, 2nd, rev. ed. (Paris: Presses Universitaires de France, 1976) should be mentioned here. His latest work deals with mass psychology in general; see *L'âge des Foules. Un traité historique de psychologie des masses* (Paris: Fayard, 1981).

5. Despite the plentiful medical terms used in crowd psychology, the concept 'social organism' is alien to this discipline. See, for example, Gabriel Tarde, *Etudes de psychologie sociale* (Paris: V. Giard & E. Briere, 1898), p. 135.

6. See George F. Rudé, *The Crowd in History: A Study of Popular Disturbances in France and England* (New York: John Wiley and Sons, 1964).

7. On the unsuccessful anarchist insurrection led by Kropotkine at Lyon on March 18, 1870, and the anarchist troubles at Montceau-les-Mines in 1879 as topics of crowd-psychological research, see, for example, Jean Bourdeau, *Socialistes et sociologues* (Paris: Felix Alcan, 1905), pp. 173-174.

8. On the historical importance of the press as a means of communication in the French working class, see the challenging study by Jacques Rancière, *La nuit des proletaires* (Paris: Fayard, 1981).

The labor union law made possible the later foundation of the *Confederation General du Travail*, the first well-organized French labor union. On labor unions as themes of crowd psychology, see, for example, Gustave Le Bon, *La Psychologie politique et la défense sociale* (Paris: Flammarion, 1912), pp. 202-25. The first edition of this book was published in 1910.

9. Joseph Maxwell, *La Psychologie sociale contemporaine* (Paris: Félix Alcan, 1905), p. 110.

10. Paul Pottier, "La Psychologie des manifestations parisiennes," *La Revue des Revues* (15 June 1899): 580.

11. Gabriel Tarde, *L'opinion et la foule* (Paris: Félix Alcan, 1901), pp. 159-226.

12. Pottier, "La Psychologie des manifestations," p. 571; see also Le Bon, *Psychologie politique*, p. 131.

13. Ibid., p. 131.

14. Ibid., p. 126.

15. Gustave Le Bon, *Psychologie des foules*, (Paris: Félix Alcan, 1916), p. 25. The first edition of this book was published in 1895.

16. Ibid., p. 36; see also Maxwell, *Psychologie sociale*, p. 62.

17. Gabriel Tarde, *La Philosophie penale* (Lyon: A. Storck, 1890), p. 310.

18. George Dumas, "La contagion mentale, I," *Revue philosophique* 70 (1910):226.

19. Le Bon, *Psychologie des foules*, p. 26.

20. Bourdeau, *Socialistes*, p. 127.

21. Nye, *Le Bon*, p. 2.

22. The exception is Gabriel Tarde, whose work has been extensively analyzed by Jean Millet, in *Gabriel Tarde et la philosophie de l'histoire* (Paris: Librairie philosophique J. Vrin, 1970).

23. See Alexandre Métraux, "Die zeitgenössische Würdigung des Wundtschen Instituts durch den französischen Soziologen Durkheim," in Wolfram Meischner & Anneros Metge (eds.), *Wilhelm Wundt—progressives Erbe, Wissenschaftsentwicklung und Gegenwart,* (Leipzig: Karl-Marx-Universität, 1980), pp. 244-56; see also A. Métraux, "Wilhelm Wundt und die Institutionalisierung der Psychologie," *Psychologische Rundschau* 31 (1980):84-98.

24. See Alfred Binet *et al.*, *Introduction à la psychologie expérimentale* (Paris: Félix Alcan, 1894), pp. 1-16.

25. See, for example, Le Bon, *Psychologie politique*, pp. 102-17.

26. See Nye, *Le Bon*, p. 3.

27. Among Le Bon's books that clearly aimed at vulgarization, the following titles should be mentioned: *L'évolution de la matière* (Paris: Flammarion, 1905) and *L'évolution des forces* (Paris: Flammarion, 1907).

28. Photographs of instruments used by Le Bon in his laboratory are included in the books mentioned in note. 27.

29. See Nye, *Le Bon*, pp. 256-57.

30. A comparison between the steel production in Germany and France illustrates the strength of the German industry, which produced 1,262,000 tons of steel in 1870, whereas France produced 1,178,000 tons in the same year. The percent increase rate of production per decade until 1900 was for Germany 95.95%, 66.13%, and 84.15%, and for France 46.43%, 13.74%, and 39.75%. The treaty between France and Germany after the war of 1870/71 obliged the French government to pay 4.0 billion gold marks to Germany, although Germany's actual war costs were only about 2.2 billion gold marks. The difference was used for industrial investment. Thus France indirectly contributed at its own expense to the industrialization of Germany. See also Wilhelm Treue, *Gesellschaft, Wirtschaft und Technik Deutschlands im 19. Jahrhundert* (Munich: Deutscher Taschenbuch Verlag, 1975), pp. 229-37.

31. On the neo-Malthusian movement in France, see Francis Ronsin, *La grève des ventres. Propagande neo-malthusienne et baissé de la natalité en France (XIXe-XXe siecles)* (Paris: Aubier-Montaigne, 1980).

32. The main sources of crowd-psychologically oriented military writings are François de Négrier, "Le moral des troupes," *Revue des Deux Mondes* 25 (1905):481-505; commandant de Grandmaison, *Dressage de l'infanterie en vue du combat offensif* (Paris: Berger-Levrault, 1906); and brevete Gaucher, *Etude sur la psychologie de la troupe et du commandement* (Paris: Lavauzelle, 1909). On the topic of psychological and moral superiority, see in particular Volker Wieland, *Zur Problematik der französischen Militärpolitik und Militärdoktrin in der Zeit zwischen den Weltkriegen* (Boppard am Rhein: Harald Boldt Verlag, 1973), pp. 35-45.

33. See Nye, *Le Bon*, pp. 164-66.

34. Tarde, *L'opinion*, p. 2.

35. See ibid., p. 13.

36. See Tarde, *Etudes*, p. 49.

37. See Maurice Milloud, "La propagation des idées," *Revue philosphique* 69(1910):580–600 and 70(1910):168–91.

38. For a general discussion of the concept of suggestion in the psychology of the time, see R. Brugeilles, "L'essence du phénomène social: la suggestion," *Revue philosophique* 75(1913):593–602.

39. See Dumas, "La contagion mentale, II," *Revue philosophique* 71 (1911):384.

40. Le Bon, *Psychologie politique*, p. 139.

41. For further details concerning the medico-psychological discussion of contagion, see Vladimir M. Bekhterev, *La suggestion et son rôle dans la vie sociale* (Paris: Boulangé, 1910), chap. I. This is the French translation by P. Keraval of *Vnushenie i ego rol' v obshchestvennoi zhisni*, to which French authors occasionally referred.

42. See Dumas, "La contagion mentale, II," p. 406.

43. On the topic of metaphors and models in the theory and history of science, see Mary Hesse, *Revolutions and Reconstructions in the Philosophy of Science* (Brighton: Harvester Press, 1980), pp. 111–24.

44. Jean Crocq, *L'Hypnotisme scientifique* (Paris: Société d'éditions scientifiques, 1896), p. 205.

45. Gabriel Tarde, *Les lois de l'imitation* (Paris: Félix Alcan, 1890), p. 82.

46. Tarde, *Etudes*, p. 47.

47. On the work of Alfred Binet, see Theta M. Wolf, *Alfred Binet* (Chicago/ London: The University of Chicago Press, 1973). Unfortunately, Binet's early works on suggestion, hypnotism and so forth, are not treated adequately by Wolff.

48. For Binet's interpretation of associationism, see his *La psychologie du raisonnement* (Paris: Félix Alcan, 1896), chap. I. The first edition of this book was published in 1886 and contains mostly materials relevant to studies made during Binet's stay at Charcot's clinic.

49. See also Alfred Binet & Charles Féré, *Le magnetisme animal* (Paris: Felix Alcan, 1887).

50. The reader should be reminded that cerebral physiology of that time was dominated by the theory of strict localization, a theory strongly supported by Broca's and Wernicke's discoveries concerning the neurophysiology of speech.

51. See Binet, *La psychologie du raisonnement*, pp. 64–68.

52. Ibid., p. 35.

53. See Alfred Binet & Charles Féré, "La polarization psychique," *Revue philosophique* 10(1885):369–402.

54. Ibid., p. 390.

55. See Joseph Delboeuf, *Le magnétisme animal. A propos d'une visite à l'école de Nancy* (Paris: Félix Alcan, 1889), pp. 5–24.

56. Le Bon, *Psychologie politique*, p. 139.

57. See ibid., p. 141.

58. Le Bon, *Psychologie des foules*, p. 18.

59. See ibid., p. 103.

60. Of course, evolutionary theories were also a part of French crowd-psychological thinking, but their exact impact has not yet been analyzed. For the introduction of evolutionary theory into French philosophy and science, see the excellent study by Yvette Conry, *L'introduction du darwinisme en France au XIXe siècle* (Paris: Librairie philosophique J. Vrin, 1974).

61. Gustave Le Bon, *La Psychologie de l'education* (Paris: Flammarion, 1902), p. 4.

62. As far as I can see, the only author who made a timid attempt at analyzing the socioeconomic causes of the phenomenon of the crowd was the psychologist G.-L. Duprat in his textbook *La psychologie sociale, sa nature et ses principales lois* (Paris: Librairie Octave Doin, 1920).

63. See also Erika Apfelbaum, "Origines de la psychologie sociale en France," *Revue française de sociologie* 22 (1981): 397–407; Ian Lubek, "Histoire de psychologies sociales perdues: le cas de Gabriel Tarde," *Revue française de sociologie* 22 (1981): 361–395.

12

Origins of Child Psychology:
William Preyer

Siegfried Jaeger

The hope expressed by Ellen Key in 1900 that this century would be "the century of the child" was based in part on the fact that a scientifically based child psychology began to emerge in the last half of the nineteenth century. Suspended by observation and experimentation and based in part on Darwin's theory of evolution, child psychology promised to give education a rational foundation; attempts were also made to create an independent science of the child extending beyond psychology.[1] The outward manifestations of these developments included a rapid increase in publications in child psychology, teaching and research programs in the universities, and the founding of organizations, specialized journals and research stations in Great Britain, France, Germany, the United States, and other industrial countries.[2]

In this chapter I will show, in an analysis of the works and times of William Thierry Preyer, how social developments, deflected and mediated in many ways, influence the construction of scientific theories, and how these, in turn, are used to solve sociohistorical problems. I also hope to make clear that the advancement of science

For finishing the manuscript I am heavily indebted to the editors, especially Mitchell Ash. Only their friendly support and critique allowed me to bring the article into the framework of this book.

does not necessarily mean the progress of knowledge. By trying to identify barriers to knowledge, I would like to contribute to the possibility of a theory that can overcome these barriers by dealing consciously with them. In this sense the history of psychology can be helpful to psychology in general.

My concentration on Preyer, despite all the limitations of his work, is justified primarily by the fact that a pioneering role has been attributed to him. However, given the international character of child research, this selection is somewhat arbitrary. I hope, therefore, that this chapter will stimulate research about parallel developments in other countries.[3]

I will first describe the situation in child psychology before Preyer, in order to gain a baseline for the description of later theoretical and methodological developments. Second, an outline of the social context of scientific theory in Germany after 1850 will clarify Preyer's reception of Darwin and locate his epistemological work. Finally, I will interpret Preyer's work on child psychology as a result of his understanding of nature and society and discuss its practical pedagogical and political implications.

BEGINNINGS OF CHILD PSYCHOLOGY[4]

The need for a psychology of the child is present when the normal educational forms for children appear to be ineffective or socially problematic. What is necessary, however, is by no means always possible. The process of transforming social problems into scientifically workable questions presupposes on the one hand that practical problem situations will be articulated in general categories, and on the other that the various sciences already have problem-solving strategies at their disposal that permit specialized treatment of these problems. Such a constellation was given in a special way at the time of the German Enlightenment.

Efforts toward a psychology of the child reached a high point first in the circles of the so-called "philanthropists," a group of men of letters and theoreticians with practical experience as educators, who hoped to advance the transition to bourgeois society by improving education. During the transitional phase from education by private tutors to general public education, they tried to win respect for bourgeois rationality. Practically, they created model educational institutions (the *philanthropina*);[5] theoretically, they elucidated the prerequisites of pedagogical knowledge of the nature of the child and of society. In this attempt they took economic, social, and political relations in Great Britain and France as models, and followed the educational theories of the French Enlightenment, particularly Rousseau, and the British empiricists, particularly Locke.

The guiding idea was that under existing social conditions no individual could develop to a full potential. It was considered necessary "to learn from the child" which abilities could be developed in what ways through education, in order to realize the specifically human qualities of freedom, reason, and social independence.[6] The philanthropists' conception of education was based on the distinction between human nature and society. Society was understood both as the prerequisite for, and the limit of, individual development. Conversely, the development of individuals through education was seen as a condition of social progress, which, in turn, created the possibility of individual self-reliance and freedom in the broader sense.

To clarify the psychological bases of education, a developmental history of the mind as a part of the history of nature was required. However, such a history is problematic since the only sure means of psychological knowledge, self-observation, is a result of the rational development to be explained. Moreover the observation of others, among its other difficulties, also depends upon self-observation.[7] The philanthropists attempted to solve this problem as the physicians of their day had done, by subjecting individual experiences and observations to public discussion, in order to clarify not only theoretical problems, but also the methodological difficulties that arose in the completion of "educational histories."[8]

It became increasingly clear to the philanthropists that these difficulties could only be overcome by a division of effort. The "pedagogical observer" required special training. In addition to the main goal of improving education, observations must be carried out simply to learn more about the nature of the child. These observations were varied according to the situation and supplemented by other material, such as biographical data and school statistics. Ernst Christian Trapp (1745–1818) described how systematic observations might be conducted, despite the absence of an experimental psychology analogous to experimental physics.[9] Children of the same age should be observed, counted, and timed as to the objects they choose and the ideas, perceptions, expressions, and actions that arise in the process. "One would conduct the experiment in all possible combinations of age, number, constitution, differences of the children and of the objects." This idea was amplified by the thought that "the objects can also be living persons whom one mixes with the other objects."[10]

By comparing single observations and observations in "experimental societies" of up to twenty children, Trapp sought to investigate problems such as the effectiveness of individual and group education and the conditions of the formation of groups. By "eavesdropping on every step children take," observers in the schools should record both the causes and effects of behavior and the expenditure of time and energy required for different teaching subjects, thus placing experiments in school improvement on a mathematical basis. Statistical investigations conducted in France on the economical use of labor in relation to wages were to be transferred to pedagogy. The hope was that a rational application of physical, intellectual, and moral energy "could begin a revolution in our education and thus a revolution in our customs and in our political institutions"[11]

When Joachim Heinrich Campe (1746–1818) called in 1785 for "an exact diary about all noticed bodily and mental changes of the child, which would be continued without interruption from the moment of birth by a 'psychological observer'," the emergence of specialized research in developmental psychology was nearly complete.[12] Campe's work stimulated the publication of many such journals.[13] It was in this context that the philosopher Dietrich Tiedemann (1748–1803) published his "Observations on the Development of the Mental Abilities in Children," a chronologically structured report on the earliest development of his son.[14] He was particularly concerned, however, with the sensory and cognitive functions associated with the development of the body and did not emphasize educational influences.

As a result of the threat posed by the French Revolution to the rulers of the German states, the tradition of the empirical exploration of the child founded by the philanthropists was interrupted. Their "pedagogical materialism" and their "cosmopolitanism" appeared more-and-more suspect, and their "systemless empiricism" was replaced by classical-humanistic and specifically national conceptions of education. Historicist currents in politics and in literature drifted against the Enlightenment ideal. In science, romantic *Naturphilosophie* carried on the idea of development, but the practical aim of an empirically-based change in individuals and society was long delayed. The psychology of Johann Friedrich Herbart (1776–1841) influenced pedagogical theory throughout the nineteenth century, but it did not lead to empirical research in child psychology until the 1870s.[15]

In the 1850s the physicians J. E. Löbisch, Berthold Sigismund, and Adolf Kussmaul took up anthropological, physiological, and animal researches and integrated them with their own observations of children.[16] Sigismund, in particular, supported the popular education movement of democratic teachers during the period before the Revolution of 1848. He sought to stimulate parents to observe their own children, and linked this effort to the hope that a "society of cooperative research" could be founded analogous to existing organizations for naturalists. These men saw their work as preparation for a new, general developmental psychology. Since they did not know of their Enlightenment predecessors, we may call their efforts a second beginning. It is to the context of that beginning that we now turn.

THE SOCIAL CONTEXT
OF THEORETICAL DEVELOPMENTS
IN GERMANY AFTER 1860

The unsuccessful revolution of 1848 left both central demands of the German bourgeoisie, political power and national unity, unfulfilled. The economic prosperity introduced by the Industrial Revolution of the 1830s continued, though interrupted by crises, under feudal-clerical control during the restoration period. It accelerated considerably after the establishment of national unity under Prussian leadership in 1871. The way to becoming an industrial world power with imperial intentions was not without social frictions, however. While the wealthy bourgeoisie complied more and more with these forms of political rule and understood how to use military and colonial endeavors for its own purposes, the rest of the bourgeoisie was divided on ideological and religious issues, on foreign policy, and especially on the so-called "social question."

Both the bourgeoisie and the nobility agreed in their diagnosis of the outward manifestations of the "social question." The growing strength of the organized working-class movement was reflected in the steady increase in parliamentary seats held by the Social Democratic Party, despite a ban on its organizations and publications between 1878 and 1890. The deterioration in living conditions in the expanding working-class districts of industrial cities was increased by rapid population shifts from rural areas. Negative effects on children also resulted from spreading criminality, prostitution, and dissolution of traditional ties to family, church, and state. However, there was little agreement on practical approaches to these problems, since an identification of their real causes in the social relations themselves would have challenged the existing order, and precisely this had to be prevented.

A colorful spectrum of suggestions included calls for political compromises on isolated issues of labor law and social policy, for improvements in the upbringing and education of working-class children, and for the regulation of hygiene and nutrition. A tug-of-war between political compromises, such as Bismarck's social legislation, and police repression was supplemented by a cautious reformism. The manifestations of the social question were broken into questions of detail that could be dealt with by individual scientific disciplines. In this way the hope was kept alive that existing social injustice would become easier to handle. Reformism was institutionalized in organizations such as the *Verein für Socialpolitik* [Association for Social Politics], founded in Berlin in 1872.

Social developments had very different effects in the natural sciences and in the humanities. The traditionally strong humanities lost influence compared with the natural sciences, as the practical importance of the latter in the process of industrialization, particularly in chemistry, electrical engineering, transportation, and communications, became apparent. The status shift away from the humanities, in particular philosophy, had intellectual roots as well. After its zenith in the philosophy of Hegel, idealism lost ground to the materialism of Marx, and some scientists applied their own practical materialism to theories of nature, society, and consciousness.

Many of the democratic scientists who were active in the Revolution of 1848 fell back upon detailed work in their fields during the restoration of the 1850s, or they drifted toward liberal-conservative positions in reaction to the demands of the working-class movement. In general, political abstinence permitted the expression of political positions at best by implication in popular scientific works. Thus, scientific research provoked debates over vitalism, the immortality of the soul, preformation, and teleology. One academic controversy became a public dispute when the Göttingen physiologist Rudolph Wagner used his speech at the thirty-first Convention of German Naturalists and Physicians in 1854 to attack materialism, which, in his opinion, was gaining ground among natural scientists. Such views, he said, "must bring science under suspicion of totally destroying the moral foundations of social order."[17] Only by supporting and maintaining this order would scientists fulfill their duty to the nation.

The opposing position was vigorously presented in numerous works by so-called vulgar materialists (*Vulgärmaterialisten*) including the zoologist Karl Vogt (1817–95), the physiologist Jakob Moleschott (1822–93) and the forensic physician Ludwig Büchner (1824–99), who addressed "the educated of all estates . . . and not only the aristocracy of education." They saw in the spreading of scientific knowledge "the guarantee of a social order that shall be based on the equality of all people, the same degree of freedom for everyone and the creation of the greatest possible temporal happiness."[18] The main points of the materialism dispute were later repeated in the controversy surrounding Darwin's theory of evolution and in the debate about the limits of scientific knowledge stimulated by Emil Du Bois-Reymond's "Ignorabimus" speech of 1872. The dilemma of bourgeois scientists was to find a philosophical formula compatible with existing scientific knowledge, which also permitted the acceptance of prevailing ideological principles and the retention and further development of bourgeois social conditions. Ernst Haeckel observed these efforts without understanding them when he registered a change in the philosophical opinions of his colleagues.[19] In the treatment of Preyer's work which follows, we will show how he reacted to this dilemma.

PREYER'S CONTRIBUTION
TO DEVELOPMENTAL PSYCHOLOGY

In the *Origin of Species* Charles Darwin only implied that his theory would have consequences for mental and social development "in the future."[20] William Thierry Preyer (1842–97) claimed to have made Darwinism fruitful for psychology; we want to show how he fulfilled this claim. Since the life and work of Preyer as a physiologist are little known, the biographical context in which his development-psychological works arose will be presented briefly.

The son of an industrialist, Preyer received a careful education at home in Moss-Side, near Manchester. In 1854 this education was supplemented by his attendance at the Clapham Grammar School near London, and between 1855 and 1859 at Gymnasiums in Duisburg and Bonn. During his medical studies at Bonn, Berlin, Heidelberg, Vienna, and Paris, he heard the lectures of such important scientists as Du Bois-Reymond, Brücke, Helmholtz, Ludwig, and Claude Bernard. These studies were interrupted by his participation in an expedition to Iceland in 1860. On the basis of this and of his reading of Darwin's *Origins* in 1861 he wrote one of the first Darwinian dissertations in Germany on the topic of the extinction of the spectacled garefowl. The influence of Darwin permeated all of Preyer's subsequent work, culminating in his Darwin biography of 1896.

In 1865 Preyer became lecturer for zoological physics and zoological chemistry in Bonn. Here he gave lectures on Darwin which were very well attended. In 1867 he qualified in physiology in Jena under Czermak, who stimulated him to investigate the sensations of color, temperature, and sound. After Czermak's death in 1869, he became the director of the physiological institute. As Jena developed into a center of Darwinism under Haeckel and Gegenbaur, Preyer served as a go-between through his written and personal contacts with Darwin between 1868 and 1881. Preyer gave up his professorship in Jena in 1888 because of ill health, but lectured at the University of Berlin until 1893 on the history of physiology and on hypnotism. In addition, he devoted more and more time to questions of school reform.

Preyer published over 50 scientific works.[21] He tried, for example, to formulate his theory of the relationship between stimulus intensity and muscle contraction in a "myophysical law" analogous to Fechner's psychophysical law; but this was soon considered obsolete. Nonetheless, his writings on developmental physiology and developmental psychology should be seen as efforts to explore systematically the "general conditions of life" on behalf of Darwinian theory. In other work on the tasks and limits of our knowledge of nature, he tried to show the practical consequences of science, especially for politics, health care, and education.

PREYER'S RECEPTION OF DARWIN AND ITS SOCIOTHEORETICAL IMPLICATIONS

The rapid spread of Darwinian theory in Germany was prepared by the work of Carl Ernst Baer and Johannes Müller in the comparative morphology of vertebrates. The need arose for an integration of these findings to replace the speculative natural philosophies of Schelling and Oken. Despite its numerous opponents, Darwin's theory of evolution rapidly gained a following in scientific circles and was elevated to a "natural history of creation" or a "general developmental history of the organisms" by Ernst Haeckel (1834–

1919), whose biogenetic law described ontogenetic development as an abridged, rapid recapitulation of phylogenetic development.

Open questions and uncertainties in Darwin's theory promoted its speculative expansion to fields outside the natural history of organisms and its consequent reduction to a methodological principle. The subsumption of the humanities and social sciences into natural science made it seem possible to resolve the prevailing dualism into a monistic system founded on the unity between nature and the knowledge of nature. Thus all true science would be natural philosophy.[22] The first scientific journal of the Darwinists in Germany had the appropriate title *Kosmos, Zeitschrift für eine einheitliche Weltanschauung auf Grund der Entwicklungslehre* [Kosmos, Journal for a Unified World-view on the Basis of a Theory of Development].[23]

Darwin's ideas penetrated very quickly into psychology. As Wilhelm Wundt wrote in his *Lectures on the Human and Animal Mind* in 1863, a work he later called a sin of his youth: "the law of variation and the law of inheritance of individual characterists can both today be proven . . . for the mind."[24] Haeckel went one step further when he treated anthropology as a part of zoology:

> Of all the branches of anthropology, not one is so affected and altered by the theory of descent as psychology. . . . In order to understand correctly the highly differentiated, delicate mental life of civilized man, we must, therefore, observe not only its gradual awakening in the child, but also its step-by-step development in lower, primitive peoples and in vertebrates.[25]

Haeckel called Wundt's *Lectures* one of the first serious attempts "to base a monistic psychology on the firm ground of comparative zoology."[26] But he was also open to Wundt's criticism that materialism had traced the mental back to the physical without making mental processes the subject of direct experience.

The political consequences of applying Darwinian theory to social development were also quickly recognized. In 1865 Friedrich Albert Lange (1828–75) saw this as the core of the social question: "whether, in fact, that natural law (of differentiation as the result of the struggle for life) shall remain the only way to the perfection of man, or whether with the strengthening of man's reason a new factor enters, and with it a turning point in the struggle for life."[27] Lange did not doubt that development in bourgeois society, with all its devastating consequences for human living conditions, was subject to this "natural law." He hoped, however, that a revolution could be avoided by replacing this law with another "that is able to grow out of the sympathetic cooperation of men, and ideas of equality and common progress."[28] As a means of helping this "law," which was hardly more than an appeal to reason, to become effective, he demanded social reforms, universal suffrage, and self-sufficient, collective organization of the workers.

Attempts were thus already under way in Germany to appropriate Darwin's theory for psychology, to develop it into a general evolutionary history of the organism, and to indicate its social and political consequences when William Preyer began his work. He nonetheless claimed to be the first, or one of the first, to recognize the necessity of applying Darwin's principles in these ways, but the question of priorities is therefore less important than the interpretation of Darwin which made this extensive application possible.

In 1869 Preyer wrote that Darwin uses the category "struggle for existence" in too broad a sense, since the resistance of the organism against external influence is only a form of adaption.[29] The category "struggle" should therefore be replaced by the category "competition" (*Konkurrenz*), which makes clearer that we are dealing with a contest between two organized creatures of the same species, both in nature and in society. Natural competition, Preyer thought, can be traced back to inorganic nature, since physical and mental manifestations of development are nothing more than the attraction of related, and the repulsion of indifferent, particles. The entire struggle for life is, in the end, only a "struggle for space." Preyer's social and political ideals were the guiding thread in his "refinement" of Darwinian theory. The struggle for existence is a competition for space in the broadest sense. Progress results from superiority in the competitive struggle of those who can adapt best to existing conditions resulting from inherited dispositions or acquired characteristics, and who pass these advantages on by heredity. Useful and more perfected characteristics are thus preserved. That which is most important for survival will be achieved all the faster with increasing differentiation or division of labor, built up from that which exists in the present. Perfection will never be reached, however; only temporary conditions of stability, or "compromises," are achievable.

Preyer also described the consequences of the struggle for life in education and ethics. Only the person who is versatile, talented, and educated has success, or, in other words, power and position in society. Talent and labor are not in opposition to one another, for the ability to work is itself innate. This does not contradict the possibility of humane relationships of people to one another, since this struggle is only to the smallest degree personal and conscious. Thus the factory owner or doctor does not try to take the life of a competitor but strives instead to produce better goods or to operate with more dexterity. In short,

> Competition is progress. . . . the society of man will not, for any price, let itself be deprived of the right, like the animals and plants, to eliminate that which is recognized to be imperfect, that which is not useful, and everything that is destructive, i.e. unpleasant, for it, to the best of its ability.[30]

When Preyer formulated these views for the first time, he was in close correspondence with his friend, the economist and later Prussian state secretary, Hugo Thiel. In Thiel's essay of 1868, "Concerning Some Forms of Rural Cooperatives," we find Preyer's theses in their concrete, original form.[31] Thiel used Darwin to show that free competition in the economy is not voluntary, but is a necessity of nature. The temporary need for confederates is the main foundation of humane relationships between people. Therefore, according to Thiel, political and social strivings have success only when they do not remove mutual struggle, but let it emerge more purely and sharply in order that the best can triumph more quickly, with fewer victims and without being suppressed by the coalition of other, worse elements. Cooperatives only appear justified in a certain developmental phase, when they permit the struggle to be more readily taken up and more energetically carried out.

Thiel's arguments were directed against the cooperative movement of the time, which had the goal of dividing the entire society into numerous such groups serving various purposes and linked to one another by bonds of solidarity. F. A. Lange had demanded such self-administered cooperatives in 1865 to strengthen the position of the working-class movement. It is therefore not surprising that Preyer dismissed Lange's work as "onesided" and "not of universal validity."

In 1879 Preyer formulated his political goals explicitly:

> The abolition of free competition with the phantom of equality and equal rights in all necessities of life as dreamt by misleading socialism would cause the immediate transformation of the healthy state organism into a decaying carcass. Competition is not only the soul of industry and trade but also the most powerful lever of scientific and artistic progress, the most important driving power for labor, self-development, the development of the dispositions of character and all talents and virtues, for the perfection of the material and intellectual well-being of the individual and the entire nation.[32]

Fortunately, Preyer's concept of competition among nations extended as much to the building of clinics, poorhouses, and working-class housing as to the production of fortresses and cannons. National welfare and institutions of public benefit became weapons in the contest of the peoples of the world. The interest of the citizens in maintaining the state turns competition into a necessity for them.

Preyer had to admit in 1896, however, that not all "citizens" followed him in this insight. Even Darwin had not fully developed the social consequences of his theory.

> This is one of the causes for the unjustified and contradictory conclusions which have been drawn from Darwinism, especially in the more recent false doctrines of social democracy. . . . Heredity, competition, adaptation, selection and the law connecting these natural facts discovered by Darwin show everyone . . . that the inequality of man is a necessity of nature which must become more pronounced the more culture advances, due to the ever advancing division of labor.[33]

In the animal and plant world individuals are subject to the whole, yet they retain their individuality. In society the problem consists of finding the right form of subordination that considers this individuality. Ignorance is responsible for the fact that so many citizens hate the state.

In Preyer's reconstruction Darwinism became a scientific apology for the existing conditions of domination and social inequality. The practical task of science is to distribute this "knowledge" and to identify the forms in which individuals can contribute to the progress of the state.

THE EPISTEMOLOGICAL FOUNDATIONS OF PREYER'S WORK IN DEVELOPMENTAL PSYCHOLOGY

In 1869 Preyer had interpreted the Darwinian theory of evolution as a mechanics of organic development. The laws of inorganic nature permit the attribution of quantitatively, not qualitatively, different higher forms of development to elementary forms. In 1873 he felt compelled to express his views against both materialism and mechanism, without giving up his claim to a "unified view of the world and life including consciousness."[34] He conceded that life cannot be explained by mechanics alone, but argued that it cannot be explained without mechanics. Particularly in the question of the origins of life and sensation, a mechanistic explanation must fail. By 1880 Preyer had revised the categories of matter and life: "The faculty of sensation adheres to all matter, sensation only to the living body."[35]

By attributing latent subjectivity to atoms and latent life to formed matter, Preyer had reversed the entire theory of evolution.[36] "The living was first. The inorganic is now evidently formed according to the laws of physics and chemistry by life processes and was formed earlier in the same way."[37] Preyer knew that he was conceding a point to idealism here, but every theory has, in his opinion, nonempirical foundations. Similarly, the speculative aspect of the competition principle is for him "the main lever of its achievements."[38] The goal of empirical research under these provisions is to acquire knowledge of all the conditions of life, and the task of psychology is to determine, along with physiology, the conditions of inner life. In this way Preyer wished to prove that Du Bois-Reymond's retreat from mechanical explanation is unnecessary. The phenomena of consciousness thus remain explicable.

Preyer also wished to defend the validity of causal law against Mach, who restricted the goal of natural science to showing the functional dependence of phenomena upon one another. According to Preyer, a satisfactory explanation of nature demands that only one fundamental fact remain, the fact of knowing present in the knowing subject. This itself cannot be explained, because any attempt to do so presupposes that which is to be explained:

> How the world is constituted thus depends upon us, to the extent that our sensations and the unique way in which the intellect objectifies them by ordering them in space and time determine the formation of our world.[39]

Scientific laws thus attribute the observed behavior or reactions of natural phenomena to nonempirical causes. They are arbitrary laws imposed by individuals, questions of opinion and often of belief. With this argumentation Preyer can hold on to mechanism's claim to provide a comprehensive explanation of nature; but the principles of this explanation are themselves unexplainable, arbitrary acts of the human mind. The constitution of the material world becomes, in this way, an ideal construction. How is this compatible with evolutionary theory?

For Preyer psychic development is primarily the unfolding of a potentiality. This requires experience, but the formation of experience is itself determined by the innate ability to draw conclusions. On the question of the origins of the ability to think in terms of cause and effect, he decided against Mill and in favor of Kant.

> The process, by means of which an idea arises when perception occurs, is already a conclusion about a cause. The idea still contains the cause. Causality is thus given simultaneously with the faculty of having ideas, and is therefore a function of the brain.[40]

Thus, for Preyer, the theory of evolution justified postulating a natural genesis for causality, but only if this fell into a time in which the ability to experience did not yet exist.

Preyer's reversal of the theory of evolution and his placing of potentiality before actuality were the results of his attempt to mediate epistemologically between materialism and idealism. In what follows I will show how these ideas took on a defining role in his conception of child psychology.

PREYER'S CHILD PSYCHOLOGY AS THE RESULT OF HIS UNDERSTANDING OF NATURE AND SOCIETY

Preyer had a broad program for treating both mental and physical aspects of early human development. The essay "Psychogenesis" of 1880 represented the preparation for his main work *The Mind of the Child*, published in 1882, while *The Mental Development of the Child* of 1893 offered a summary, practical applications, and suggestions for further research.[41] Of the embryo-physiological and physical part of this program, the *Specielle Physiologie des Embryo* was published in 1885, but no further volume appeared. This was, no doubt, due to the appearance of Karl Vierordt's *Physiologie des Kindesalters* in 1885.[42] "Psychogenesis" was thus for Preyer the development of the human and animal mind, a part of scientific or, more exactly, of physiological psychology; he could grasp psychogenesis as mental development because he did not separate the categories psyche [*Seele*] and mind [*Geist*]. In this way, the ontogenetic psychology of the child, whose goal should be "an empirical history of reason," becomes the most important part of the mental development of humanity in general.

In 1873 Preyer saw in the comparative anatomy and physiology of simple organisms the key to the explanation of the human mind. He sought to supplement this with the observations of the instincts of animals and the intellectual development of school children, using teachers as observers.[43] Later he argued that the human mind cannot be understood from the development of the animal mind alone, despite their kinship. Instead, the main point of methodological access is the mental development of the child during the first years of life. Physicians, naturalists, linguists, and educators "have until now turned up very little material for the construction of a developmental history of the mind based on facts."[44] Independent, physiologically-schooled researchers must carefully observe a large number of newborn babies, critically compare the results received, and control one another reciprocally in order to avoid premature generalizations. A diary beginning at birth is required, based upon daily observations of several hours. Training must be strictly forbidden, and certain questions must be answered by repeated observations and harmless experiments. Statistical investigations are certainly desirable, but they cannot replace continuous observation of healthy, normally developing children.[45]

Because the child is solipsistically considered as an unfolding potentiality, its development is not seen from the viewpoint of confrontation with the natural and social environment, but rather with the aim of identifying its innate dispositions:

> Inheritance is just as important as one's own activity in psychogenesis. Here no one is a simple upstart who could develop his mind alone by means of his own experience. On the contrary, each must develop and revive the hereditary dispositions and the traces of the experiences and activities of his forefathers.[46]

It is essential, however, to find precise criteria to separate hereditary from individually acquired material. At first Preyer went ahead subtractively. If there are no external causes to be found, then one should look for inner causes. If these presuppose experiences and ideas, they are acquired; if not, they are hereditary. He then defined a positive criterion: "hereditary means all characteristics of the organism which repeat themselves periodically. . . . That which persists regularly for a long time in many generations is called hereditary."[47] In the light of such a criterion Preyer's attempt to identify the hereditary determination of human nature had to fail, for it gave free rein to speculation about dispositions.

Preyer then described the development of newborn babies, on the basis of observations of his son in the first three years of life. The child is initially dominated by drives, without will, and steered by reflexes and instincts. Here the presentation followed the genetic relationships of basic psychic functions, first the development of the senses and feelings, then the will, and finally the intellect and language. The motor of development is the unconscious causal drive, which structures sensory material and movements; he called this "the innate disposition to perceive and form ideas, that is the innate intellect."[48] What was called a methodological principle for the exploration of the child's development, the avoidance of all drill, reappeared here as a psychological principle: every training, every artificial instruction is to be avoided, particularly in the first years of life. The hereditary dispositions determine the direction and sequence of the relevant developmental steps, which are realized through competing ideas. In this way the first successful imitative movements arise from the competition of all possible impulsive, reflex, instinctive, and other movements, a sign that finally an idea is victorious, that the will is there. Thus it is time, Preyer said, to "let natural development occur more physiologically."[49]

PRACTICAL IMPLICATIONS FOR PEDAGOGY

Physiological education rests, in the first place, upon the bodily substrate of all intellectual activity, in this case the central nervous system. In order to direct the will, one must control the child's ideas of movement, In order to avoid or eliminate training tricks that obstruct natural development, one must not only watch the child but the employed servants as well.[50]

Preyer's concept of a natural, physiological pedagogy can be formulated as follows: "first nature without training and then culture." Consideration of the bodily substrate requires a "dietetics of the brain" to maintain mental health by staying away from taxing or harmful stimuli. The main content of education is the direction of the will, as long as it can be guided, since "the power of the will is the mightiest weapon in the struggle for life."[51] It is the human will that forms the destiny of mankind, not accidental circumstances, environment, or education. In the formation of the will, as in education in general, it is most important to develop the most useful of the countless hereditary dispositions as completely and harmoniously as possible, first by selecting appropriate sense impressions and then by regulating movements and later actions. On the other hand, dispositions harmful to the child and to society should be obstructed right from the start, nipped in the bud, as it were.[52] The direction of the will is, therefore, primarily a pin-point selection of dispositions, so that knowledge of these becomes the fundamental prerequisite of educational action.

Preyer's physiological pedagogy emphasizes early childhood development, but its consequence is a reformation of the entire school system on an allegedly natural foundation. In a lecture "Naturforschung und Schule," presented to the Sixtieth Convention of German Physicians and Naturalists in 1887, Preyer demanded that the flag of science finally be planted in the traditional school. The anachronistic and unphysiological force exercised there, which obstructs the development of the individual and the nation, should be eliminated. The school should devote more time to the education of character through moral and physical hygiene and less time to rote instruction.

> School teaching on a natural foundation is not as much concerned with the elimination of the requirement to learn dead languages as with replacing superfluous words with necessary facts, the abstract with the clear, the doctrinaire with the inductive, the alien with the German. The main point is and remains the education of the child's good natural dispositions favourable to a good life and to the father-land, and the thwarting of bad natural dispositions detrimental to society and the child itself. Education and instruction must master hereditary defects, and increase hereditary advantages. Learnedness does not do this.[53]

Preyer formulated here the protest of natural scientists against the school system, in particular against the Gymnasium which over-burdened pupils physically and mentally and provided too little room for scientific subjects, modern languages, and physical education. The ineffectiveness of the Gymnasium was shown by the fact that only four percent of the pupils achieved the *Abitur*. Offered only by the old philological–humanistic Gymnasium, this degree was the only way of admission to the university, the civil service, and shortened military service. In the face of the continually growing importance of scientific and medical subjects, expressed in the enormous increase of students and lecturers in these fields at the expense of philosophy and philology, Preyer saw this admissions policy as anachronistic. He therefore demanded the recognition of diplomas from so-called

Realgymnasien, technical academies and polytechnical schools. These institutions could then prove themselves in free competition with the humanistic *Gymnasien*, which until then had been "artificially bred."

Preyer saw very clearly the ideological importance of classical education when he addressed himself to the objection that without it, materialistic neobarbarism, utilitarianism, nihilism, and at best a realism without moral foundations would break out. He opposed this view by saying that the roots of the evil lie for the most part in the schools themselves, where the children of all estates learned too much of the non-German and too little of the German. Instead, better history instruction must make clear the benefits of a monarchical state, which he called the natural result of Darwinian thinking.

Preyer formulated here not only the interests of the naturalists but also one position within the German school reform movement of the time. This position claimed that the existing school system was able neither to satisfy the changed needs of industry for qualified workers, nor to master the class conflicts that reached even into the schools. Advocates of individual, personality, and social pedagogy, and of art and industrial arts education, sought to combat manifestations of loss of individuality and to create the missing feeling of national identity and cultural consciousness. At the same time, they wished to provide the qualified workers required for Germany's survival in international competition through an education oriented to practical life.

Common to all positions was that they assigned a central role to psychology in their reform ideas, but turned against the intellectualism and formalism of Herbartian pedagogy. In a decree of May 5, 1889, Kaiser Wilhelm II demanded that "the school be made useful at every level in order to work against the spread of socialist and communist ideas"; one year later, taking up Bismarck's warning against the rise of a dissatisfied, intellectual proletariat, unable to work and dangerous to the state, he supported a reform of the Gymnasium in Preyer's sense.[54] After this, two school reform associations were founded, one of which brought together the Herbartians while the other, the "Allgemeine Deutsche Verein für Schulreform," elected Preyer and Hugo Göring as chairmen.

The Kaiser had established a model of "national education" in his reform of the cadet corps. Many features of the "New German School," which Preyer's association advocated, was similar to the Kaiser's model; logically he was seen as "the born protector" in the struggle for the reform of the public school system.[55]

PREYER'S HISTORICAL IMPORTANCE

Preyer did not stand alone or even at the beginning of research in child psychology. In his methods and categories he was in no way original in comparison with the level of reflection already achieved by the philanthropists. If he is still considered to be the "father" of child research, this is perhaps because of the scrupulous exactitude with which he made his own observations and coordinated them with other physiological and psychological findings in his systematic works. *The Mind of the Child* went through nine German editions by 1923, and was published in English, French, and Russian translations. The book only became obsolete when experimental research in child psychology led to more highly specialized theories of development, which referred to modern theories of general psychology.

It was not my intention to establish that Preyer observed this or that detail incorrectly, or to point to single theoretical positions that appear ludicrous from a modern point of view. The intention was, instead, to make explicit the theoretical context of Preyer's child psychology, something which he did not do himself. The specific form taken by his psychological theory construction can thus be clarified, though not explained; for a theory cannot be explained by referring to another theory. I also intended to show how one scientist, operating within the confines of exact science as he saw it, reacted to the social problems of the second half of the nineteenth century. By developing theoretical positions on the fundamental social conflicts of the time, he appeared to provide solutions to practical problems that were politically neutral.

Neither Preyer's social Darwinism nor his idealistic theory of knowledge, and certainly not his nationalistic excursions, are of interest for the construction of theories today. The most important problem, rather, is the demarcation line between the physical and the social sciences, or, in specifically psychological terms, their real convergence in the problem of understanding individual development in the field of tension between nature and society. At the level of society, Preyer's teachings on competition and compromise, based as they were on the historical experiences of the last century, can only be a warning example for us of the consequences of a naturalization of the social, of putting faith in a law of nature as the foundation of social progress. At the level of nature, however, Preyer's attempts to grasp phylogenetic development psychologically on the basis of Darwinian theory have by no means exhausted their potential.

The German philanthropists used the concept of human nature in their struggle against existing social conditions, and also to achieve an understanding of individual development in the transition to bourgeois society. Preyer used the concept of nature, including human nature, as a means of defending bourgeois rule and of justifying individual subordination. This does not mean, however, that the concept of human nature may not still be used today to justify social reform.

NOTES

1. See Oscar Chrisman, *Paidologie. Entwurf zu einer Wissenschaft vom Kind* (Jena: Vopelius, 1896).

2. According to my count, the number of publications in child psychology after the boom between 1870 and 1880 doubled between 1880 and 1890 and trebled between 1890 and 1900. While Germany led France, Great Britain, the United States, and Italy until 1890, by 1900 there were twice as many publications in the United States as in Germany.

3. For current research see Günther Reinert, "Grundzüge einer Geschichte der Humanentwicklungspsychologie," in *Psychologie des XX. Jahrhunderts*, vol. I (Zurich: Kindler, 1976), pp. 862-96.

4. I use the category descriptively to identify works concerned with an empirically based construction of theories of child development.

5. The first Philanthropinum was founded in 1774 in Dessau.

6. See Friedrich Engel, *Versuch einer Theorie von den Menschen und dessen Erziehung* (Berlin: Lange, 1753).

7. See anon., "Versuch über die Wichtigkeit der Untersuchungen, die den menschlichen Verstand betreffen," *Berlinisches Magazin* 3(1767):583-99. This was a translation of "The Importance of an Inquiry into the Human Mind," *Universal Magazine* n.d., whose author was very likely Thomas Reid.

8. See Johann Karl Wezel, "Über die Erziehungsgeschichten," *Pädagogische Unterhandlungen* 2(1778):21-43.

9. E. C. Trapp, *Versuch einer Pädagogik* (Berlin: Nicolai, 1780). The book was written on the occasion of Trapp's accession to the first and, for a century, only professorship for pedagogy in Germany, at the University of Halle.

10. Trapp, *Versuch*, p. 67.

11. Ibid., p. 73.

12. J. H. Campe (ed.), *Allgemeine Revision des gesamten Schul- und Erziehungswesens von einer Gesellschaft praktischer Erzieher*, 1(1785), p. XXIV.

13. On the history of the diaries, see Wayne Dennis, "Historical Beginnings of Child Psychology," *Psychological Bulletin*, 46(1949):224-35.

14. D. Tiedemann, "Beobachtungen über die Entwicklung der Seelenfähigkeiten bei Kindern," *Hessische Beiträge zur Gelehrsamkeit und Kunst*, 2(1787):313-33, 486-503.

15. See H. Schwabe and F. Bartolomai, "Über Inhalt und Methode einer Berliner Schulstatistik," *Berliner Städtischer Jahrbuch* 4(1870):1-77. In addition

to being a subtle psychological analysis of educational statistics, this work contains a survey of the "contents of Berlin children's minds on entering school."

16. J. E. Lobisch, *Entwicklungsgeschichte der Seele des Kindes* (Wien: Haas, 1851); Berthold Sigismund, *Kind und Welt* (Braunschweig: Vieweg, 1856); Adolf Kussmaul, *Untersuchungen über das Seelenleben des neugeborenen Menschen* (Heidelberg: Winter, 1856).

17. R. Wagner, *Menschenschöpfung und Seelensubstanz* (Göttingen, 1854), p. 29.

18. K. Vogt, *Köhlerglauben und Wissenschaft* (Gieben, 1855), p. 637. Cf. Frederick Gregory, *Scientific Materialism in Nineteenth Century Germany* (Dordrecht-Holland: D. Reidel, 1977).

19. E. Haeckel, *Die Welträthsel* (Bonn: Straub, 1899), p. 118.

20. Ch. Darwin, *The Origin of Species* (New York: Burt, n.d.), p. 504.

21. For a bibliography, see *Börsenblatt für den Deutschen Buchhandel* 64(1897):5417-19.

22. Haeckel, *Generelle Morphologie der Organismen*, vol. 1 (Berlin: Reimer, 1866), pp. 441-47.

23. The journal was published in 19 volumes from 1877 to 1886.

24. W. Wundt, *Vorlesungen über die Menschen- und Thierseele*, vol. 2 (Leipzig: Voss, 1873), p. 355.

25. Haeckel, *Generelle Morphologie*, vol. 2, p. 434.

26. Wundt, *Vorlesungen*, vol. 1, p. 18.

27. F. A. Lange, *Die Arbeiterfrage* (1865), 13th ed. (Leipzig: Kröner, 1910), p. 38.

28. Ibid., p. 44.

29. W. Preyer, "Der Kampf um das Dasein," in *Aus Natur und Menschenleben* (Berlin: Allgemeiner Verien für Deutsche Literatur, 1885 [1869]), pp. 1-38.

30. Preyer, *Natur- und Menschenleben*, p. 93.

31. See ibid., p. 321.

32. "Die Konkurrenz in der Natur" (1879), in *Naturwissenschaftliche Tatsachen und Probleme* (Berlin: Paetel, 1880), pp. 65-96, on p. 93.

33. W. Preyer, *Darwin. Sein Leben und Wirken* (Berlin: Hoffmann, 1869), p. 169.

34. W. Preyer, *Über die Erforschung des Lebens* (Jena: Mauke, 1873), p. VI.

35. Preyer, *Tatsachen und Probleme*, p. 318.

36. See W. Preyer (ed.), *Wissenschaftliche Briefe von Gustav Theodor Fechner und William Preyer* (Hamburg: Voss, 1890), p. 123, where Fechner, in opposition to Hartmann, Zöllner, and Preyer, holds to the doctrine of the origin of consciousness by the reciprocal action of matter.

37. Preyer, *Tatsachen und Probleme*, p. 319.

38. Ibid., p. 327.

39. Preyer, "Die Aufgabe der Naturwissenschaft" (1876), in *Tatsachen und Probleme*, pp. 239-77, on p. 274.

40. Preyer, "Die fünf Sinne des Menschen" (1870), in *Natur- und Menschenleben*, pp. 131-89, on p. 186.

41. Preyer, "Psychogenesis" (1880), in *Tatsachen und Probleme*, pp. 199-238; *Die Seele des Kindes. Beobachtungen über die geistige Entwicklung des Menschen in den ersten Lebensjahren* (Leipzig: Grieben, 1882); cf., *The Mind of the child*, trans. H. W. Brown (New York: Appleton, 1889); *Die geistige Entwicklung in der ersten Kindheit nebst Anweisungen für die Eltern, dieselbe*

zu beobachten (Stuttgart, Berlin, Leipzig: Union Deutsche Verlagsanstalt, 1893), Cf. *The Mental Development of the Child*, trans. H. W. Brown (New York: Appleton, 1893).

42. W. Preyer, *Specielle Physiologie des Embryo. Untersuchungen über die Lebenserscheinungen von der Geburt* (Leipzig: Grieben, 1885).

43. Preyer, *Erforschung des Lebens*, p. 66.

44. Preyer, *Tatsachen und Probleme*, p. 203.

45. Preyer, *Seele des Kindes*, pp. VI–VII.

46. Ibid., p. IX.

47. Preyer, *Tatsachen und Probleme*, p. 230.

48. Preyer, *Seele des Kindes*, p. 384.

49. Preyer, *Die geistige Entwicklung*, p. 50.

50. Ibid., p. 50.

51. Preyer, *Tatsachen und Probleme*, p. 218.

52. Preyer, *Die geistige Entwicklung*, p. 136.

53. W. Preyer, *Naturforschung und Schule* (Stuttgart: Spemann, 1887), p. 37.

54. "Dekret gegen sozialdemokratische Umtriebe," reprinted in Berthold Michael and Heinz-Hermann Schepp (eds.), *Politik und Schule von der Französischen Revolution bis zur Gegenwart*, 2 vols. (Frankfurt: Fischer, 1973), vol. 1, p. 409.

55. *Die Neue Deutsche Schule* was the title of both the monthly magazine of the association for school reform and of a programmatic book by Goring; see W. H. Burnham, "The New German School," *The Pedagogical Seminary*, 1 (1891):13–18.

13

James McKeen Cattell and the Failure of Anthropometric Mental Testing, 1890–1901

Michael M. Sokal

James McKeen Cattell as a thinker does not rank with Kant and Fechner, Helmholtz and Wundt; he carried out no psychological studies cited today or even cited 50 years ago. Even his experimental procedures—on which he prided himself—have long since been abandoned. As the title indicates, his major enterprise of anthropometric mental testing, to which he devoted more than a dozen years, failed miserably. But despite the obsolescence of his laboratory work, the failure of his tests, and especially the shallowness of his ideas, Cattell is possibly the nineteenth-century psychologist with the greatest influence on the twentieth century, particularly in the United States. The man who coined the term "mental test" and who sold "science" to the public clearly did much to shape modern culture.

This paper could not have been written without the support of the Reading Room Staff of the Manuscript Division of the Library of Congress, Washington, D.C. A much earlier version of it was presented before the History of Science Society in Washington, D.C., December 1972. The current version owes much to the encouragement and stylistic judgment of the editors of this volume, and to the example of Raymond E. Fancher, Reese V. Jenkins, and James Reed.

Cattell was a child of the nineteenth century, and he remained rooted in it long after 1900. His famous series of directories, *American Men of Science*, clung to the genteel term used by those who avoided the neologism "scientist";[1] it continues today—suitably modified for our time—as *American Men and Women of Science*. The journal *Science*, which he owned and edited for the first half of the century, reflected many nineteenth-century views of science.[2] Most importantly, the way in which Cattell actually did science—from his first experiments with G. Stanley Hall at Johns Hopkins in the early 1880s, through his apprenticeship with Wundt at Leipzig in the mid-1880s, to his psychophysical experiments at Pennsylvania in the late 1880s—was based upon scientific methods already out of date by the time he learned them. Even his program of mental testing at Columbia in the 1890s, his studies of scientific eminence in the early 1900s, and his founding of The Psychological Corporation in the 1920s were based on passé conceptions of the social use and social organization of science.[3] If the legacy of Cattell and of the professionalization of science in America is to be understood, then his historical context will admirably serve the purpose.

CATTELL'S EDUCATION IN THE UNITED STATES, GERMANY, AND ENGLAND, 1876-1888

James McKeen Cattell was born in 1860 in Easton, Pennsylvania, where his father, William C. Cattell, was professor of ancient languages at Lafayette College.[4] Cattell's early life revolved around this college, especially after 1863, when his father became its president. He never attended public school, but read and was tutored in his father's library. He also traveled with his father, spending thirteen months in Europe during 1869-70. At fourteen, he began auditing classes at Lafayette, and in September 1876 he matriculated there as a freshman. Cattell studied hard and graduated with honors in 1880; what he learned at college shaped his later scientific career.

Lafayette, like many American colleges of the period, sought to develop "discipline and piety" among its students within a Presbyterian religious framework of improving their mental faculties.[5] By the late 1870s, however, this Scottish realist approach to higher education was elsewhere losing its hold, and Lafayette was clearly not on the "cutting edge" of educational innovation. Its faculty did include several distinguished scholars, most notably Francis A. March, an outstanding philologist and contributor to the *Oxford English Dictionary*. But even he worked within the older tradition and, by doing so, influenced many generations of Lafayette students.

March was especially influential on Cattell, who took several courses with him and later praised him as "the great teacher, the great scholar, and the great man."[6] March admired Francis Bacon's philosophy, which he reduced to an empiricism based upon exhaustive collection of data without regard to hypotheses. His greatly oversimplified understanding of Baconianism and his "vulgar utilitarianism" was widespread in the United States at the time.[7] His early essay "The Relation of the Study of Jurisprudence to the Origin and Progress of the Baconian Philosophy"[8] made this debt explicit. His greatest philological work was described by one of his students as built of "thousands of interrelated details": *A Comparative Grammar of the Anglo-Saxon Language: In which its Forms are Illustrated by those of the Sanskrit, Greek, Latin, Gothic Old Saxon, Old Norse, and Old High Gothic.*[9] In his lectures, March honored Bacon as "the prophet of inductive science," echoing that "we should seek the truth, says Bacon, for generation, for fruit, and for comfort."[10] In 1878–79, March took the junior class, with Cattell in it, through the annual exegesis of Bacon's essays. In later life, Cattell became March's kind of Baconian: empirical, inductive, and utilitarian.[11]

Formal philosophy was also part of the curriculum; March taught mental philosophy too, and the professor of rhetoric taught moral philosophy. Both courses introduced Scottish common-sense realism, deriving from Thomas Reid, which had close ties with Presbyterianism and the goals of the college. In Scotland, this philosophy was developed subtly, often in conjunction with a sophisticated understanding of Baconianism.[12] In the United States however, this faculty psychology had deteriorated by the 1860s into mere scholastic disputation over precise terminologies; for example, the classification of human desires under the headings of hunger, thirst, and sex.[13] Neither of the two most distinguished textbooks of the period satisfied Cattell: Joseph Haven's *Mental Philosophy* and, for moral philosophy, Mark Hopkins's *An Outline Study of Man*.[14] In March's class, students had to write essays on such topics as "Is there any such thing as immediate perception?" Cattell's essay began, "I do not know, and I doubt if anyone else knows." Cattell also questioned Hopkins's classification of human desires, and, when informed of Cattell's objections, Hopkins responded: "Young Cattell is sharp, and the President is to be congratulated on having such a son. I agree with the suggestion he makes."[15]

Cattell's dissatisfaction with Scottish realism reflected the feelings of many other young Americans of the period. Cattell had access to the post-Darwinian literature through the excellent libraries that Lafayette and his father had been building since the 1850s. By 1880 he was studying the positivism of Auguste Comte, and his honorary philosophy oration at the commencement that year treated "The Ethics of Positivism." No copy of the talk has been found, but Cattell would have known that Comte stressed the authority of scientific (or positive) thought, meaning that each science should be as mathematical as its practitioners could make it. But Comte knew that not all disciplines could be reduced to mathematical formulation, and he left a major role for empiricism. This emphasis on both quantification and empiricism meshed well with Cattell's Baconianism, though he would add his own experimentalist and utilitarian twist.[16] This scientistic philosophy was the basis for Cattell's 60-year career.

Soon after graduation from Lafayette, Cattell traveled to Europe, toured for a while, and spent the 1880–81 winter semester at the University of Göttingen, where he heard Hermann Lotze lecture. Lotze impressed him greatly, as he saw in his philosophical system a way of combining the ethical concerns of his father's Presbyterianism with his own belief in the value of scientific forms of thought. He planned to follow Lotze when he accepted a call to Berlin, but Lotze's death and Cattell's family concerns led him to Leipzig, where he heard Wilhelm Wundt lecture on psychology. Wundt was clearly a second choice for him, and he did not impress Cattell at this time. He prepared an essay on Lotze's moral philosophy, which helped him to win a fellowship in philosophy at Johns Hopkins for the 1882–83 academic year, and he returned to the United States looking forward to a year (at least) at America's premier research university.[17]

At Johns Hopkins, Cattell thrived.[18] He had been subject to fits of depression in Europe, but these dissipated in Baltimore. More importantly, he began to experience nineteenth-century scientific empiricism. In October 1882 he conducted his first experiments in the Johns Hopkins physiological laboratory under the direction of H. Newell Martin, professor of biology. He also began taking hashish, morphine, opium, and other psychoactive drugs, in part for the sensation and in part out of interest in what they do to the mind. One of the first notations he made under the influence of hashish expressed his commitment to experimental science: "I seemed to be two persons, one of whom could observe and even experiment on the other." In February 1883 he entered G. Stanley Hall's brand-new psychological laboratory and soon had results: he had measured, in milliseconds, the time to recognize the letters of the Latin alphabet for each of nine subjects. This quantitative data was followed by a utilitarian recommendation, that the least distinct letters be modified in certain ways to make them easier to read.[19] Despite this work, his fellowship was given to John Dewey in May 1883 for the following year, in part because of his constant bickering with the university's faculty and administration, and in part because of his competitor's superiority as a philosopher.

Cattell decided to return to Europe to earn the equivalent of a doctorate with Wundt in experimental psychology. He spent almost three full years at Leipzig, from November 1883 through June 1886.[20] He carried out numerous reaction-time experiments, and when he came to disagree with Wundt's views he modified the procedures extensively and adopted Sigmund Exner's interpretation of mental chronometry.[21] Contrary to the remarks of history of psychology textbooks, Cattell showed little interest in individual differences between the two experimental subjects whose reaction times he measured.[22] He directed his effort to the collection of exclusively mathematical data, measuring the reaction times under different conditions of, for instance, attention, practice, and fatigue, without concern for the meaning of these data. Wundt tried to force him to interpret his experiments psychologically; for instance, his doctoral dissertation was appropriately titled "Psychometrische Untersuchungen" whereas he called the report in English "The Time Taken up by Cerebral Operations."[23] He preferred a physicalistic interpretation of his results.[24]

Cattell initially looked to a career in neurology as a means of capitalizing on this early work. Thus from Leipzig he went to St. John's College, Cambridge, to study medicine. However, his father soon arranged for him a lectureship in psychology at the University of Pennsylvania, and he quickly abandoned his medical studies. He matured socially during twenty-four months at Cambridge, from October 1886 through December 1887, and from April through December 1888;[24] he became engaged to a young Englishwoman whom he had met while she studied music at Leipzig, and he spent much time making acquaintances among the intellectual aristocracy.[25] Most importantly, he fell under the direct influence of one of the members of the group, Francis Galton. Although he never studied with Galton, the rest of his career reflected in many ways Galton's understanding of science.

Galton's interests were wide-ranging.[26] By the 1860s, he was devoting most of his attention to the study of individual and racial differences. Biological variation was an important basis for the theory of natural selection developed by his cousin, Charles Darwin. Galton's emphasis on the heredity of human traits led him to develop the concept (and ideology) of eugenics, the systematic biological improvement of the human race.[27] In order to collect data about the differences between people, he established his Anthropometric Laboratory at the International Health Exhibition in 1884.[28] When the exhibition had closed, he transferred the Laboratory to the South Kensington Museum, from which evolved the later Science Museum. At the Laboratory, for a fee of three pence, individuals could have a full range of bodily measurements taken, as well as measures of their abilities to perform certain physical tasks (see Figure 13-1). His final schema for anthropological measurements in fact included two reaction-time determinations, showing that he had the idea of using reaction times before he met Cattell, although Cattell introduced him to some particular procedures.

Despite the fact that Cattell had read Galton's articles as early as January 1884, it was Galton who seems to have made the first contact between the two men.[29] His earliest anthropometric work had concentrated on physical and physiological characteristics, and he soon looked beyond these for a way to investigate psychological differences. For several years he had considered the reaction-time experiment as such a technique.[30] Perhaps Galton found Cattell's name in the literature, or perhaps mutual acquaintances such as Alexander Bain mentioned the young American to him. In any event, by October 1885 the two men had met in England and by February 1886 Galton was quoting Cattell's letters to him about reaction-time apparatus at the Anthropological Institute.[31]

Despite Galton's use of Cattell's apparatus, he was not greatly influenced by the young American. But his influence on Cattell was unbounded. Cattell later wrote that Galton had been "the greatest man I have ever known"; he is reputed to have remarked that his career had been shaped by three men named Francis: Bacon, March, and Galton.[32] Galton provided him with a scientific goal—the measurement of the psychological differences between people—that made use of the experimental procedures he had developed at Leipzig. Cattell could collect quantitative data that might eventually be useful without relying upon any systematic view of the mind; curiously, he showed little interest in the statistical foundation of Galton's work, the law of normal distribution.

MR. FRANCIS GALTON'S ANTHROPOMETRIC LABORATORY.

The Laboratory communicates with the Western Gallery containing the Scientific Collections of the South Kensington Museum. Admission to the Gallery is free. It is entered either from Queen's Gate or from Exhibition Road.

Date of Measurement.	Initials.	Birthday. Day.	Month.	Eye Color.	Sex.	Single, Married, or Widowed ?	Page of Register.
11 August 88	JMcK	25	5 · 62	Grey	m	Single	626

Head length, maximum from root of nose.		Head breadth maximum.		Height standing, less heels of shoes.		Span of arms from opposite finger tips.		Weight in ordinary clothing.	Strength of squeeze. Right hand.	Left hand.	Breathing capacity.	Keenness of Eyesight. Distance of reading diamond numerals. Right eye.	Left eye.	Snellen's type read at 20 feet.	Color Sense.
Inch.	Tenths.	Inch.	Tenths.	Inch.	Tenths.	Inch.	Tenths.	lbs.	lbs.	lbs.	Cubic inches.	Inches.	Inches.	No. of Type	? Normal.
7	5	8½	66	7	68 · 9	144	89	82	238	16	12	218		Yes

Height of top of knee, when sitting, less heels.		Length of elbow to finger tip left arm.		Length of middle finger of left hand.		Height sitting above seat of chair.		Keenness of hearing. Highest audible note.		? Normal.	Reaction time. To sight.	To sound.	Judgment of Eye. Error in dividing a line of 10 inches in half	Error in degrees, estimating an angle of
Inch.	Tenths.	Inch.	Tenths.	Inch.	Tenths.	Inch.	Tenths.	Vibrations per second.			Hundredths of a second.	Hundredths of a second.	Per cent. in half	Per cent. in thrds	90°	60°
34	8	21	1	17.7	4 · 3			19,000	Yes		30	20	0	3	1	10

One page of the Register is assigned to each person measured, in which his measurements at successive periods are entered in successive lines. No names appear on the Register. The measurements that are entered are those marked with an asterisk (*). Copies of the entries can be obtained through application of the persons measured, or by their representatives, under such conditions and restrictions as may be fixed from time to time.

Figure 13-1. Cattel's record at Francis Galton's anthropometric laboratory. (From Cattell papers, Library of Congress.)

To be sure, a native American anthropometric tradition had grown out of phrenology and craniometry. In post-Civil-War America this older tradition had become an important part of the emerging physical education movement.[33] Despite Cattell's interest in athletics and his acquaintanceship at Johns Hopkins with Edward M. Hartwell, a leading American physical educator, he appears not to have drawn on this tradition.[34] His collection of physical data about hundreds of individuals was an essentially Baconian endeavor, as was Galton's work. Thus, from 1889, when he left England, to the end of the century, Cattell devoted himself to an extension of Galton's program into what he called mental testing.

CATTELL'S PROGRAM FOR ANTHROPOMETRIC MENTAL TESTING

On January 1, 1889, Cattell was appointed to a professorship of psychology at the University of Pennsylvania that he later claimed (erroneously) to be the world's first. His father's advocacy and his European scientific pedigree played a part in this high honor to a twenty-nine-year-old youth. Within a year, he had established a laboratory, begun to train students, and sketched out a research program on "mental tests and measurements," which coined the term now in common use.[35] He explicitly ignored the simple measurements of bodily dimensions that had been so much a part of Galton's program; instead, he concentrated on procedures to examine both physiological and psychological characteristics. These tests, carried out sporadically on his students at the University, were dynamometer pressure, rate of movement, sensation areas, pressure causing pain, least noticeable difference in weight, reaction time to sound, time for naming colors, bisection of a 50 cm line, judgment of 10 seconds' time, and number of letters remembered on one hearing.

Cattell was clearly skillful in parlaying this simple program into a major institutional and eventually public commitment. He effectively alluded to Helmholtzian science with the term "mental energy," flimsily applied to the tasks measuring strength of squeeze and rate of arm movement in the first two tests above. The ideology of evolution was also invoked by his claim that the tests "would be of considerable value in discovering the constancy of mental processes, their interdependence, and their variation under different circumstances." Galton himself amplified this point in a series of comments, comparing Cattell's testing to "sinking shafts . . . at a few critical points." He admitted that one goal of Cattell's procedures was exploratory, to determine "which of the measures are the most instructive."[36] Cattell also hinted at a public need when he commented that the tests might "perhaps [be] useful in regard to training, mode of life or indication of disease."

Cattell was not the only American to sense a public need to be tapped by mental testing in the 1890s. By that decade, scientists working in physical anthropometry began to claim that they could measure "The Physical Basis of Precocity and Dullness," and though their claim was disputed,[37] their studies continued throughout the decade.[38] Within the discipline just beginning to identify itself as psychology, testing boomed. At Clark University, for example, Edmund C. Sanford extended his colleague Franz Boas's anthropometric studies of school children.[38] At the University of Nebraska, Harry K. Wolfe, the second American doctoral student of Wundt in experimental psychology, urged the adoption of mental tests in the local public schools. Like Cattell, he admitted that he was not sure what he was studying, and he reminded teachers "not [to] be uneasy because the meaning of any peculiarities is obscure."[39] At Yale, another of Wundt's students, Edward Wheeler Scripture, tried out various mental testing procedures and even published a paper on fencing as an indication of mental ability.[40]

Most important from the viewpoint of legitimating the new discipline in the public eye was the work of Joseph Jastrow. He had earned a Ph.D. with G. Stanley Hall at Johns Hopkins in 1886. He began corresponding with Francis Galton about his anthropometric interest in 1887, and he became professor of psychology at the University of Wisconsin in 1888. By 1890, his concern with mental testing paralleled Cattell's; early in 1892 he published a proposal for "Some Anthropological and Psychological Tests on College Students" based almost completely on Galton's program.[41] He also used tests to investigate sex differences and clashed with Mary Whiton Calkins, the distinguished Wellesley psychologist, as to the meaning of the differences his tests revealed.[42]

Under Jastrow's direction in 1893, the two streams of interest in anthropometric mental testing converged at the World's Columbian Exposition in Chicago. At this World's Fair, Frederic Ward Putnam, Curator of the Peabody Museum of American Archaeology and Ethnology at Harvard University, planned a Department of Ethnology to include a Section on Physical Anthropology under the direction of Franz Boas. Part of Boas's plan was to carry out a program of anthropometric measurements on the visitors to the Fair, including as many foreign visitors as possible, and the members of the Indian tribes brought to Chicago for the occasion. Jastrow, Boas, and Putnam saw no reason why the program should be limited to phsyical anthropometry and extended it to include mental tests.[43] The result was to be an outgrowth of Galton's Anthropometric Laboratory, and Jastrow wrote to Galton in 1892, asking for suggestions as to procedures and apparatus. He even went before the preliminary meeting of the American Psychological Association and "asked the cooperation of all members for the Section of Psychology at the World's Fair and invited correspondence on the matter."[44] Using a schedule of tests that resembled Galton's and Cattell's, Jastrow tested thousands of individuals with the help of the army of graduate student volunteers he had assembled for the occasion.

Despite this flurry of interest in testing that he had in large part set off, Cattell was unable to devote much time to this work between 1891 and 1894. About the time he published his "Mental Tests and Measurements" paper, he began to commute to New York from Philadelphia to lecture a day or so a week at Columbia College. In 1891, Cattell moved to Columbia and so had to give up his program of testing at Pennsylvania. He devoted the next three years to establishing the psychological laboratory at Columbia, completing two major experimental studies[45] and planning the *Psychological Review*. He did find time to review books on anthropometry of interest to psychologists and to prepare a popular article on mental testing at the invitation of the editor of the *Educational Review*.[46]

In January 1893, Cattell wrote to the President of Columbia "concerning the possibility of using tests of the senses and faculties in order to determine the condition and progress of students, the relative value of different courses of study, etc." Beneath his rationale for educational efficiency, he had to admit that he did not have specific tests designed for specific purposes; he compared his program of testing with the work of researchers in electricity 50 years earlier: "they believed that practical applications would be made, but knew that their first duty was to obtain more exact knowledge." He carried this argument to its Baconian conclusion: "The best way to obtain the knowledge we need is to make the tests, and determine from the results what value they have."[47]

It was not, however, until September 1894 that Cattell finally received authorization for the testing program he wanted. He was granted permission to examine every student on entering Columbia College and the Columbia School of Mines for the next four years, and in fact he tested students throughout the 1890s and into the twentieth century. Cattell, his junior colleague Livingston Ferrand, and all their graduate students were deeply involved in the testing program, which soon began to attract national attention. The scope of their reputation may be appreciated from the diversity of their audiences. Cattell and Ferrand described their work in papers presented at meetings of the New York Schoolmasters' Association, The New York Academy of Sciences, the American Psychological Association, and the American Association for the Advancement of Science.[48] The day had yet to come when errors in the Scholastic Aptitude Test were front-page news, but the clipping service to which Cattell subscribed certainly kept busy.

The schedule of tests that Cattell prepared at Columbia was explicitly concerned with both physical and mental measurements. Cattell stressed again that he did not "wish to draw any definite conclusions from the results of the tests made so far" because they were "mere facts." However, like the positivist he was, he noted that "they are quantitative facts and the basis of science." He concluded with the pragmatic resolution that "there is no scientific problem more important than the study of the development of man, and no practical problem more urgent than the application of our knowledge to guide this development." The questions he hoped to answer were:

> To what extent are the several traits of body, of the senses and of mind interdependent? How far can we predict one thing from our knowledge of another? What can we learn from the tests of elementary traits regarding the higher intellectual and emotional life?[49]

Within a few years, Cattell's testing program provided answers to at least the last two of these questions, but these were to be extremely disappointing to him.

Perhaps the weakness of his testing program stemmed from the ad hoc manner in which Cattell adapted Wundt's reaction-time experiment into a testing instrument. The technical details are of interest in appreciating just what he was offering to society. The experimenter, now called a tester, sits at the left in front of a Hipp chronoscope, which measures time intervals accurately to milliseconds (see Figure 13-2). The subject or person being tested sits at the right in front of a Cattell gravity chronograph, with a Cattell lip key in his mouth. The experiment or test begins when the experimenter, or tester, pulls the string in his left hand to start the mechanism of the chronoscope and then closes the switch to his left. The closing of the switch completes an electric circuit that starts the hands of the chronoscope revolving and allows the screen of the chronograph to fall, thus revealing a card to the subject, on which

Figure 13-2. A reaction-time experiment, 1893. See Note 50. (From Clark University Archives.)

is printed a stimulus. He then responds verbally in a previously agreed-upon way, thus opening the lip key and breaking the electric circuit, which stops the hands of the chronoscope. The experimenter, or tester, then reads the reaction time directly from the chronoscope dials.[50]

The transformation of an experimental situation into a testing one brought with it several major innovations. Wundt required that his subjects introspect while carrying out the reaction, while Cattell arranged his tests so that those being tested did not have to introspect at all. To be sure, Wundt's use of this technique did not resemble the systematic introspection developed by Edward B. Titchener, and both he and Cattell were concerned primarily with the reaction time itself as a self-contained datum, rather than as an adjunct to a subject's mental observations. Titchener, in fact, complained in print when Jastrow adopted Cattell's approach to the reaction-time experiment at the Chicago World's Fair.[51] In any event, by adopting only the mechanics of Wundt's procedures while ignoring his broader concerns, Cattell was acting no differently with respect to his German teacher than did the American historians who studied with Ranke or the American chemists who studied with Liebig.[52] Paradoxically, what they lost by oversimplifying their European models the Americans gained back in social usefulness.

PROFESSIONAL JUDGMENTS ABOUT MENTAL TESTING

Interest in mental testing in the United States reached a peak in December 1895, when the American Psychological Association, meeting under Cattell's presidency, appointed a committee "to consider the feasibility of cooperation among the various psychological laboratories in the collection of mental and physical characteristics." The committee took upon itself the task to "draw up a series of physical and mental tests which are regarded as especially appropriate for college students."[53] It consisted of Cattell, Jastrow, Sanford, and two other psychologists: James Mark Baldwin of Princeton University and Lightner Witmer of the University of Pennsylvania. Witner had been Cattell's student at Pennsylvania and had earned a Ph.D. with Wundt, at Cattell's insistence. He then succeeded Cattell to the chair of psychology at Pennsylvania, and in many ways his approach to psychology was similar to Cattell's.[54]

Baldwin, by contrast, was broadly educated in philosophy and, though he had experimented, was not convinced that the laboratory provided the best approach to an understanding of individuals. Instead, he worked on broader questions and in 1895 had published his *Mental Development in the Child and the Race*.[55] As such, he was the only member of the committee to come to the problem of testing without a commitment to an anthropometric approach to the study of human differences.

The committee presented a preliminary report in December 1896 and a detailed report in December 1897, and both accounts stressed mental anthropometry as a preferred method. Sanford, for example, wrote that he "approved the Columbia schedule as it stands." Jastrow did recognize that at least three categories of tests could be developed, namely, those of "(a) the senses, (b) the motor capacities, and (c) the more complex mental processes." But he argued that the last category should be ignored and that "it is better to select, even if in part arbitrarily, on part of a certain sense capacity" than a broader aspect of mental life.[56]

But the report of the committee was not unanimous. Baldwin presented a minority report in which he agreed that tests of the senses and motor abilities were important, but he argued that such essentially physiological tests had received too great a place in a schedule developed by a committee of the American Psychological Association. He asked for additional tests of the higher mental processes and discussed several possible approaches that could be used in testing memory. He concluded by arguing for "giving the tests as psychological a character as possible."[57]

Baldwin's criticisms of the anthropometric tests were the first, but not the last. Some of the critiques took the form of attacks on the assumptions made by the testers. Hugo Münsterberg, for example, director of the psychological laboratory at Harvard, wrote about the "danger" of believing that psychology could never help educators. More directly, he attacked Scripture's work and the scientific assumptions that underlay much of the test, claiming that "I have never measured a psychical fact, I have never heard that anyone has measured a psychical fact, I do not believe that in centuries to come a psychical fact will ever be measured."[58] To be sure, there were other reasons for Münsterberg's attack,[59] and it went beyond the criticisms that most psychologists would make of what the testers were doing. Furthermore, it was not directed at Scripture solely as a tester and, if Baldwin's criticisms were taken seriously, it was not clear that the testers were trying to measure psychological quantities. But to deny that psychological processes were in principle measureable was to undercut the positivistic assumption of Cattell that quantifiable data was the only type worthy of scientific attention.

Other critics were to compare Cattell's tests then being developed in France by Alfred Binet and his collaborators, which were explicitly concerned with the higher mental processes.[60] Cattell knew of Binet—who was a cooperating editor of the *Psychological Review*— and of his work. He even cited Binet's work in his major paper on anthropometric tests. There he noted that he and his coauthor "fully appreciate the arguments urged by . . . M M. Binet and Henri in favor of making tests of a strictly psychological character," but he stressed that "measurements of the body and of the senses come as completely within our scope as the higher mental processes." They went even further, noting that "if we undertake to study attention or suggestibility we find it difficult to measure definitely a definite thing."[61] In other words, Cattell's stress on quantification led him to avoid investigating that which was difficult to quantify and to concentrate on what he could measure. His positivistic Baconianism therefore had him avoid what he knew was more important, or at least what his colleagues told him was more important, to focus on that which he could work with easily. He was like a man who lost a quarter one night in the middle of the block, but who looked for it at the corner, because that was where the light was better.

One psychologist who compared Cattell's work with Binet's was Stella Emily Sharp, a graduate student of Edward Bradford Titchener at Cornell. In 1898, she published her doctoral dissertation in which she compared the theories of "individual psychology"—the phrase is Binet's—of the American and French testers. In it, she stressed that "the American view is founded upon no explicit theory," a conclusion with which Cattell would have agreed entirely, and presented Binet's view as the belief that "the complex mental processes . . . are those the variations of which give most important information in regard to those mental characteristics whereby individuals are commonly classed." She did not describe her classification scheme but informally tried out some of Binet's suggested procedures on several of her graduate student classmates. For example, she asked them to remember sentences (rather than Cattell's series of letters) and to describe a picture that they had seen sometime before (rather than reproduce the length of a line seen earlier). Her results for some tests seemed to form "a basis of a general classification of the individuals," but she also found that "a lack of correspondences in the individual differences observed in the various tests was quite as noticeable as their presence." She therefore concluded that she had demonstrated the "relative independence of the particular mental activities under investigation" and hence the uselessness of Binet's procedures. But she went further. If Binet's tests did not give a good picture of the variations among individuals, she argued, then "mental anthropometry," which lacked any theoretical superstructure, could not yield results of any value either.[62]

Sharp's results are still quoted today,[63] but other events of the late 1890s had more to do with the failure of anthropometric mental testing. At least two were personal. At Yale, Scripture's personality had led him into conflicts with most of his colleagues and in the last years of the decade he was too busy fighting for his academic life to continue testing. Jastrow, meanwhile, had given up his struggle to publish the results of his testing program; this effort had led to conflicts with the officials at the Exposition and contributed to his nervous breakdown in the mid-1890s.[64] Scripture's and Jastrow's abandonment of anthropometric mental testing left Cattell and Witmer the only prominent psychologists working in the area, and Witmer's attention was soon focused on narrow applications of tests in his clinical psychology. Cattell was therefore left alone with his tests, which he continued throughout the decade, and by the late 1890s he was able to subject the data he collected to a new form of analysis. And this analysis, carried out by one of his graduate students, led most directly to the failure of his testing program.

Clark Wissler was an 1897 graduate of Indiana University who had come to Columbia as a graduate student primarily to work with Cattell on his anthropometric testing program. At Columbia, he was especially impressed by Franz Boas, the distinguished anthropologist whom Cattell had brought to the University, and soon grew interested in the anthropological implications of Cattell's work. He later had an important career as an anthropologist, but his studies with Boas in the late 1890s had a more immediate effect. Cattell was mathematically illiterate—his addition and subtraction were often inaccurate—but Boas, with a Ph.D. in physics, was mathematically sophisticated. Cattell knew that Galton had developed mathematical techniques to measure how closely two sets of data were related, or were correlated, and he made sure that Wissler learned these procedures from Boas. He then had Wissler apply these techniques to the data collected during his decade-long testing program at Columbia.[65]

Wissler calculated the correlation between the results of any one of Cattell's tests and the grades the students tested earned in their classes; and between the grades earned in any class and those earned in any other. His results showed that there was almost no correlation among the results of the various tests. For example, in calculating the correlation between the results of the reaction-time test and the marking-out-A's test,[66] Wissler found that 252 students took both tests, and he measured the correlation between the results of the two tests as -0.05. Consequently, despite the fact that the two tests might appear to be closely related "an individual with a quick reaction-time [was] no more likely to be quick in marking out the A's than one with a slow reaction-time." Furthermore, Wissler's analysis showed that there was no correlation between the results of any of Cattell's tests and the academic standing of any of the students tested. In contrast, Wissler found that academic performance in most subjects correlated very well with that in other subjects. Even "the gymnasium grade, which [was] based chiefly on faithfulness in attendance, correlated with the average class standing to about the same degree as one course with another."[67] In all, Wissler's analysis struck most psychologists as definitive and, with it, anthropometric mental testing, as a movement, died.

Cattell, of course, abandoned his career as an experimental psychologist, but he continued his activity within the American psychological community. For example, in the 1920s he founded The Psychological Corporation. From about 1900 on, he was better known as an editor and as an entrepreneur of science than he was as a psychologist. In many ways, his later career is more interesting than his earlier one, though as his experience with The Psychological Corporation shows, it may not have been any more successful.[68]

THE INFLUENCE
OF THE MENTAL TESTING MOVEMENT

But despite the death of the anthropometric movement as such, anthropometric testing itself—in many ways a product of nineteenth-century philosophy of science—continued into the first years of the twentieth century. America at that time was engaged in what has been called "The Search for Order."[69] Millions of new immigrants— most with cultural backgrounds totally different from those of the early nineteenth century—were flocking to the New World. The rapid industrialization of the period and the rise of the new professions placed a heavy premium on a standardized work style and on the development of formalized criteria for judging applicants for universities and jobs. Many citizens looked to education as an ordering, and Americanizing, process, and compulsory education laws were enacted by 1900. The rising concern for the welfare, and evil influence, of the delinquent, dependent, and defective classes led to the rapid growth of institutions to serve their needs and to protect the public from them.[70]

In such an atmosphere of social concern, mental testing was seen to be too valuable a tool to be completely abandoned, even if anthropometric mental testing was shown to have extreme limitations. On one level, specialized anthropometric tests, designed for specialized uses, were found to be useful. Even one of Titchener's students, who was studying the sense of hearing and techniques for evaluating it, had to admit that they served "practical purposes" when designed carefully. In many ways, the clinical psychology developed by Witmer in the late 1890s illustrates the point perfectly. After all, in diagnosing what are today called sensory disorders and learning disabilities, Witmer applied the tests developed by Cattell and others in particularly appropriate ways. Similarly, Scripture's best-known student—Carl E. Seashore—merely developed a set of specialized tests relating to the sense of hearing when he constructed his widely used tests of musical talent.[71] In these ways anthropometric mental tests, especially designed to focus on specific sensory problems, played (and continue to play) a major role in bringing order to American society and, especially to American education.

On another level, however, the continued use of anthropometric tests in the early twentieth century was much less successful. Though testing worked when applied narrowly, it yielded essentially useless results when the testers set larger goals. One can readily see eugenical implications in Cattell's goals for his early tests. Similarly, Jastrow believed that his tests demonstrated the proper spheres of activity for each of the sexes. Others used anthropometric tests to justify, and argue for, their own ideas as to the proper relations between the races.[72] More prosaically, though still on a large scale, Frank Parsons in the early 1900s established a vocational guidance bureau in Boston with a goal of helping young men find the profession for which they were best suited. Here he used tests of the "delicacy of touch, nerve, sight and hearing reactions, association time, etc." And as late as 1908, Parsons argued that reaction-time tests had a great value for judging an "individual's probable aptitudes and capacities."[73]

More important for psychology was the work of Henry H. Goddard, a Clark Ph.D. and student of G. Stanley Hall. In 1906, after several years of teaching psychology at a small state college, he became director of the psychological laboratory at the Vineland,

New Jersey, Training School for the Feeble-Minded. There he worked with children who would today be called retarded or developmentally disabled. To obtain some estimate of the children's abilities, he used various anthropometric techniques—more than five years after Wissler's analysis was published. Although he did not find this approach very helpful, he continued to employ it for lack of another. Finally, in the last years of the decade, he traveled to France and there discovered in detail the full range of the work of Binet and his colleagues. When he brought this knowledge back to America, his English version of Binet's tests finally supplanted anthropometric mental testing, at least outside its narrower applications.[74] Thereby, Goddard introduced a new testing movement, which has done much to shape modern America. But that is another story, more appropriate to a volume on psychology in the twentieth century.

NOTES

1. See C. P. Snow, *The Masters* (New York: Charles Scribner's Sons, 1951), p. 185.

2. Michael M. Sokal, "*Science* and James McKeen Cattell, 1894 to 1945," *Science* 209 (1980):43–52.

3. Michael M. Sokal, "The Origins of the Psychological Corporation," *Journal of the History of the Behavioral Sciences* 17 (1981):54–67.

4. Most of the discussion of Cattell's early education here is paraphrased from the Introduction of Michael M. Sokal (ed.), *An Education in Psychology: James McKeen Cattell's Journal and Letters from Germany and England, 1880–1888* (Cambridge: MIT Press, 1981), pp. 1–12.

5. David Bishop Skillman, *The Biography of a College: Being a History of the First Century of Lafayette College*, 2 vols. (Easton, Pa.: Lafayette College, 1932). Cf. Laurence R. Veysey, *The Emergence of the American University* (Chicago: University of Chicago Press, 1965), pp. 21–56.

6. James McKeen Cattell, "The American College," *Science* 26 (1907): 368–73.

7. George H. Daniels, *American Science in the Age of Jackson* (New York: Columbia University Press, 1968); Theodore Dwight Bozeman, *Protestants in an Age of Science: The Baconian Ideal and Antebellum American Religious Thought* (Chapel Hill: University of North Carolina Press, 1977).

8. Francis Andrew March, "The Study of Jurisprudence," *The New Englander* 5 (1848):543–48.

9. Francis Andrew March, *A Comparative Grammar* (New York: Harper, 1869); James Wilson Bright, "Address in Commemoration of Francis Andrew

March, 1825-1911," *Publications of the Modern Language Assocation* 29 (1914):1-24.

10. Francis Andrew March, "The Future of Philology," *The Presbyterian Quartery* n.s. 33 (1894):698-714.

11. Seldon J. Coffin (ed.), *The Men of Lafayette, 1826-1893: Lafayette College, Its History, Its Men, Their Record* (Easton, Pa.: George W. West, 1892), pp. 63-68.

12. J. C. Robertson, "A Bacon-Facing Generation: Scottish Philosophy in the Early Nineteenth Century," *Journal of the History of Philosphy* 14 (1976): 37-50.

13. Frank M. Albrecht, Jr., "A Reappraisal of Faculty Psychology," *Journal of the History of the Behavioral Sciences* 6 (1970):36-38.

14. Joseph Haven, *Mental Philosophy: Including the Intellect, Sensibilities and Will* (Boston: Gould and Lincoln, 1857): Mark Hopkins, *An Outline Study of Man: Or the Mind and Body in One System, with Illustrative Diagrams, and a Method for Blackboard Teaching* (New York: Scribner, Armstrong, 1873).

15. James McKeen Cattell, manuscript undergraduate essays, James McKeen Cattell papers, Manuscript Division, Library of Congress, Washington, D.C.; "Extracts from Testimonials of the Faculty of Lafayette College to Accompany the Thesis of James M. Cattell, an Applicant for a Fellowship in Philosophy in Johns Hopkins University, May 1882," Cattell papers.

16. See Sokal, *An Education in Psychology*, pp. 16-17.

17. Ibid., pp. 19-46.

18. Ibid., pp. 47-82.

19. James McKeen Cattell, "Uber die Zeit der Erkennung und Benennung von Schriftzeichen, Bildern und Farben," *Philosophische Studien* 2 (1885): 635-50; James McKeen Cattell, "Uber die Tragheit der Netzhaut und des Sehcentrums," *Philosophische Studien* 3 (1886):94-127.

20. Sokal, *An Education in Psychology*, pp. 83-105, 121-217; Michael M. Sokal, "Graduate Study with Wundt: Two Eyewitness Accounts," *Wundt Studies: A Centennial Collection*, ed. Wolfgang G. Bringmann and Ryan D. Tweney (Toronto: C. J. Hogrefe, 1980), pp. 210-25.

21. Sokal, *An Education in Psychology*, pp. 96-105, 151-52, 156.

22. Ibid., pp. 132-35, 179. Cf. Franz Samelson, "Cattell: The Beginnings of a Career," *Science* 212 (1981):777-78.

23. James McKeen Cattell, "Psychometrische Untersuchungen," *Philosophische Studien* 3 (1886):305-35, 452-92; James McKeen Cattell, "The Time Taken up by Cerebral Operations," *Mind* II (1886):220-42, 377-92, 524-38. Cf. Sokal, *An Education in Psychology*, 202-3, 206.

24. Sokal, *An Education in Psychology*, pp. 218-313.

25. Noel G. Annan, "The Intellectual Aristocracy," *Studies in Social History: A Tribute to G. M. Trevelyan*, ed. J. H. Plumb (London: Longmans, Green, 1955), pp. 241-87.

26. Raymond E. Fancher is preparing what promises to be an insightful and revealing biography of Galton. Meanwhile, the most complete review of Galton's career is Karl Pearson, *The Life, Letters, and Labours of Francis Galton*, 3 vols. in 4 (Cambridge: Cambridge University Press, 1914-30).

27. Pearson, *Galton*, vol. 1, pp. 70-215; Francis Galton, *Hereditary Genius* (London: Macmillan 1869); Francis Galton, *English Men of Science: Their Nature and Nurture* (London: Macmillan, 1874).

28. Pearson, *Galton*, vol. 2, pp. 357-86; Francis Galton, "The Anthropometric Laboratory," *Fortnightly Review* n.s. 31 (1882):332-38; Francis Galton, "On the Anthropometric Laboratory of the Late International Health Exhibition," *Journal of the Anthropological Institute* 14 (1885):205-21; Francis Galton, *Inquiries into Human Faculty and Its Development* (London: Macmillan, 1883).

29. Sokal, *An Education in Psychology*, pp. 89-90.

30. Francis Galton, "Notes and Calculations about Reaction Time, 1878-83," unpublished notes, Francis Galton papers, D. M. S. Watson Library, University College, London. See also Galton to John Shaw Billings, November 13, 1884, Billings papers, New York Public Library, New York, N.Y.

31. Sokal, *An Education in Psychology*, pp. 191-92, 218, 222-23; Francis Galton, "On Recent Designs of Anthropometric Instruments," *Journal of the Anthropological Institute* 16 (1887):2-11.

32. James McKeen Cattell, "Psychology in America," *Science* 70 (1929): 335-47.

33. See Michael M. Sokal, "Anthropometric Mental Testing in Nineteenth-Century America," unpublished Sigma Xi National Lecture, 1979-81.

34. Michael M. Sokal, "The Unpublished Autobiography of James McKeen Cattell," *American Psychologist* 26 (1971):626-35.

35. James McKeen Cattell, "Mental Tests and Measurements," *Mind* 15 (1890):373-81.

36. Ibid., pp. 373, 379-81.

37. William T. Porter, "The Physical Basis of Precocity and Dullness," *Transactions of the Academy of Science of St. Louis* 6 (1893):161-81; Franz Boas, "On Dr. William Townsend Porter's Investigation of the Growth of School Children of St. Louis," *Science* 1 (1895):225-30.

38. For example, Arthur MacDonald, "Mental Ability in Relation to Head Circumference, Cephalic Index, Sociological Conditions, Sex, Age, and Nationality," unpublished paper, Arthur MacDonald files, U.S. Office of Education papers, U.S. National Archives, Washington, D.C. See also Michael M. Sokal, "Anthropometric Mental Testing in Nineteenth-Century America," James Allen Young, "Height, Weight, and Health: Anthropometric Study of Human Growth in Nineteenth-Century American Medicine," *Bulletin of the History of Medicine* 53 (1979):214-43; Elizabeth Lomax, "Late Nineteenth-Century American Growth Studies: Objectives, Methods and Outcomes," unpublished paper, Fifteenth International Congress of the History of Science, Edinburgh, Scotland, August 1977.

39. Sokal, "Anthropometric Mental Testing," Harry K. Wolfe, "Simple Observations and Experiments: Mental Tests and Their Purposes," *North-Western Journal of Education* 7 (1896):36-37.

40. Edward W. Scripture, "Tests of Mental Ability as Exhibited in Fencing," *Studies from the Yale Psychological Laboratory* 2 (1894):114-19; Michael M. Sokal, "The Psychological Career of Edward Wheeler Scripture," *Historiography of Modern Psychology: Arms, Resources, Approaches*, ed. Josef Brozek and Ludwig J. Pongratz (Toronto: C. J. Hogrefe, 1980), pp. 255-78.

41. For example, Joseph Jastrow to Galton, August 19, 1887, Galton papers; Joseph Jastrow, "Some Anthropometric and Psychologic Tests on College Students; A Preliminary Survey," *American Journal of Psychology* 4 (1892):420-28.

42. Joseph Jastrow, "A Study in Mental Statistics," *New Review* 5 (1891):559-68; Mary Whiton Calkins, "Community of Ideas of Men and Women," *Psychological Review* 3 (1896):426-30. Cf. Laurel Furumoto, "Mary Whiton Calkins (1863-1930),"*Psychology of Women Quarterly* 5 (1980):55-68.

43. World's Columbian Exposition, *Official Catalogue, Department M Ethology: Archaeology, Physical Anthropology, History, Natural History, Isolated and Collective Exhibits* (Chicago: W. B. Conkey, 1893).

44. Jastrow to Galton, July 17, 1892, Galton papers; Michael M. Sokal (ed.), "APA's First Publication: Proceedings of the American Psychological Association, 1892-1893," *American Psychologist* 28 (1973):277-92.

45. James McKeen Cattell and George S. Fullerton, *On the Perception of Small Differences, with Special Reference to the Extent, Force and Time of Movement*, Publications of the University of Pennsylvania, Philosophical Series, no. 2 (Philadelphia: University of Pennsylvania, 1892): James McKeen Cattell and Charles S. Dolley, "On Reaction-Times and the Velocity of the Nervous Impulse," *Proceedings of the National Academy of Sciences* 7 (1896):393-415.

46. James McKeen Cattell, "Psychological Literature: Anthropometry," *Psychological Review* 2 (1895):510-11; James McKeen Cattell, "Tests of the Senses and Faculties," *Education Review* 5 (1893):257-65.

47. Cattell to Seth Low, January 30, 1893, James McKeen Cattell collection, Columbia University Archives, New York, N.Y.

48. Sokal, "Anthropometric Mental Testing."

49. James McKeen Cattell and Livingston Farrand, "Physical and Mental Measurements of the Students of Columbia University," *Psychological Review* 3 (1896):618-48.

50. Michael M. Sokal, Audrey B. Davis, and Uta C. Merzbach, "Laboratory Instruments in the History of Psychology," *Journal of the History of the Behavioral Sciences* 12 (1976):59-64.

51. Edward B. Titchener, "Anthropometry and Experimental Psychology," *Philosophical Review* 2 (1893):187-92.

52. George G. Iggers, "The Image of Ranke in American and German Historical Thought," *History and Theory* 2 (1962):17-33; Margaret W. Rossiter, *The Emergence of Agricultural Science: Justus Liebig and the Americans, 1840-1880* (New Haven, Conn.: Yale University Press, 1975). Cf. Sokal, "Foreign Study Before Fulbright: American Students at European Universities in the Nineteenth Century," unpublished Sigma Xi National Lecture, 1979-81.

53. Edward C. Sanford, "The Philadelphia Meeting of the American Psychological Association" *Science* 3 (1896):119-21.

54. John O'Donnell, "The Clinical Psychology of Lightner Witmer: A Case Study of Institutional Innovation and Intellectual Change," *Journal of the History of the Behavioral Sciences* 15 (1979):3-17.

55. James Mark Baldwin, *Mental Development in the Child and the Race: Methods and Processes* (New York: Macmillan, 1895).

56. Sanford to Baldwin, December 7, 1896, Cattell papers; James Mark Baldwin, James McKeen Cattell, and Joseph Jastrow, "Physical and Mental Tests," *Psychological Review* 5 (1898):172-79.

57. Baldwin et al., "Physical and Mental Tests."

58. Hugo Munsterberg, "The Danger from Experimental Psychology," *Atlantic Monthly* 81 (1898):159-67.

59. Matthew Hale, Jr., *Human Science and Social Order: Hugo Munsterberg and the Origins of Applied Psychology* (Philadelphia: Temple University Press, 1980); Sokal, "The Psychological Career of Edward Wheeler Scripture."

60. Alfred Binet and Victor Henri, "La psychologie individuelle," *L'Annee psychologique* 2 (1895):411-15.

61. Cattell and Farrand, "Physical and Mental Measurements."

62. Stella Emily Sharp, "Individual Psychology: A Study in Psychological Method," *American Journal of Psychology* 10 (1898):329-91.

63. See Richard J. Herrnstein and Edwin G. Boring (ed.), *A Source Book in the History of Psychology* (Cambridge: Harvard University Press, 1965), pp. 438-42.

64. Sokal, "The Psychological Career of Edward Wheeler Scripture," Joseph Jastrow, autobiography, *A History of Psychology in Autobiography*, vol. 1, edited by Carl Murchison (Worcester: Clark University Press, 1930), pp. 135-62. Cf. Jastrow, correspondence with Frederic Ward Putnam, 1891-1900, Frederic Ward Putnam papers, Harvard University Archives, Cambridge, Massachusetts.

65. Clark Wissler, "The Contribution of James McKeen Cattell to American Anthropology," *Science* 99 (1944):232-33; James McKeen Cattell, "Memorandum for Miss Helen M. Walker," undated note, Cattell papers.

66. Individuals were presented with a ten-by-ten array of one hundred letters in which were scattered ten A's. The time required to strike out all A's was measured.

67. Clark Wissler, "The Correlation of Mental and Physical Tests," *Psychological Review Monography Supplements* 3, no. 6 (1901).

68. Sokal, "The Origins of The Psychological Corporation."

69. Robert H. Wiebe, *The Search for Order, 1877-1920* (New York: Hill and Wang, 1967).

70. This paragraph summarizes many years of scholarship in the social history of American ideas. See Wiebe, *The Search for Order;* Henrika Kuklick, "The Organization of Social Science in the United States," *American Quarterly* 28 (1976):124-41; Burton J. Bledstein, *The Culture of Professionalism: The Middle Class and the Development of Higher Education in America* (New York: Norton, 1978).

71. Benjamin Richard Andrews, "Auditory Tests," *American Journal of Psychology* 15 (1904):14-56; O'Donnell, "The Clinical Psychology of Lightner Witmer;" Audrey B. Davis and Uta C. Merzbach, *Early Auditory Studies: Activities in the Psychology Laboratories of American Universities*, Smithsonian Studies in History and Technology, no. 31 (Washington: Smithsonian Institute Press, 1975).

72. R. Meade Bache, "Reaction Time with Reference to Race," *Psychological Review* 2 (1895):475-86; Anna Tolman Smith, "A Study of Race Psychology," *Popular Science Monthly* 50 (1896):354-60; Arthur MacDonald, "Colored Children—A Psycho-Physical Study," *Journal of the American Medical Association* 32 (1899):1140-44. Cf. Charles S. Johnson and Horace M. Bond, "The Investigation of Racial Difference Prior to 1910," *Journal of Negro History* 3 (1934):328-39.

73. Frank Parson, "The Vocation Bureau: First Report to Executive Committee and Trustees, May 1st, 1908," as reprinted in John M. Brewer,

History of Vocational Guidance: Origins and Early Development (New York: Harper and Brothers, 1942), pp. 303–8.

74. Henry H. Goddard, *The Research Department: What It Is, What It Is Doing, What It Hopes To Do* (Vineland, New Jersey: The Training School, 1914).

Epilogue

Reflections on Psychology
in History

Mitchell G. Ash

What connects the contributions in this volume to one another more than anything else is the shared conviction of their authors that the history of psychology cannot be presented in isolation from the historical reconstructions of other disciplines or from the general history of thought and society. At the beginning of the nineteenth century, psychological thinking was embedded in categories drawn from a wide variety of intellectual concerns and social contexts. The period is conventionally treated by historians of psychology as the time in which the field was liberated from such bondage. But the liberation of psychology, such as it was, was nowhere a simple matter of one part of philosophy, or of medicine, reaching a certain stage of development and then splitting off more-or-less inevitably and developing further on its own, supported by independent institutions. Instead, we are dealing here with complex processes of conceptual construction, reconstruction, and transformation, which took place in various historical settings. The successful institutionalization of some kinds of psychological thinking was only one of these processes; it did not end psychology's intellectual and social embeddedness, but only changed its structure.[1]

The essays appearing here are part of a growing literature in which the implications of these statements are being worked out. The time is not yet ripe for a synthesis of all these efforts. Instead, the purpose of these concluding remarks is to draw out and expand upon some of the significant themes linking the essays, indicating directions in which further research might proceed, and providing additional information where this seems appropriate in order to place this material in broader historical context.

The perspective from which this attempt will be made is that of the social history of ideas. This subject area has been undergoing redefinition for some time, as the notorious problem of the role of "external" and "internal" factors ceases to be an issue fought out by rival camps and becomes a subject of concrete research. The project has become not to depict ideas as one-dimensional reflections of social attitudes, or of abstractions like "the rise of capitalism" or "the industrial revolution," but to describe and analyze the middle level situations in which ideas are actually produced, propagated, or applied.[2] Recent calls for a "sociology of psychological knowledge" or for a "social history of psychology" may be seen as part of this trend.[3] In many respects the contributions to this volume can be read as attempts to develop a suitable vocabulary for such a project.

Of course there are fundamental theoretical and empirical issues in psychological thought that persist over time; but the relevance or even the existence of many problems, and the way in which persistent problems are treated, are related in important ways to concrete sociocultural and political circumstances. The first section of these reflections treats the influence of such circumstances upon conceptual continuities of psychology in the German- and English-speaking cultural regions. The discussion is then extended to other cultural contexts and to the influence of more narrowly defined settings such as the scientific school. The final section addresses the issue of the institutionalization of psychology as an academic discipline in Germany and the United States, where that process had advanced the farthest by the end of the century. Though the emphasis in each section may be upon conceptual, social, and institutional history, respectively, it will become clear soon enough that these cannot be separated.

CONCEPTUAL CONTINUITIES IN
SOCIOCULTURAL CONTEXT:
GERMANY AND ENGLAND

In both the English and the German-speaking cultural regions, psychology was located at the center of the major challenge faced by scientific thought in the nineteenth century—to establish criteria for objective knowledge, while at the same time leaving room for intellectual freedom and moral values. However, the ways in which that challenge was met were closely related to differences in the social structure of intellectual discourse in the two realms.

At the beginning of the nineteenth century, the German states had long possessed an extensive array of universities, the primary purpose of which was to train an educated elite for positions in the state administration or the so-called "academic" professions, such as medicine and law.[4] Traditionally, each university retained a single professor in each subject, whose obligation was to cover a prescribed syllabus of examination topics set by the state, but who was free to teach other subjects in addition to this. The books these professors wrote naturally tended to be systematic treatises or compendia treating entire fields of knowledge according to fixed principles of organization. Immanuel Kant's philosophical system was arguably the most outstanding product of this institutional milieu. Within this system Kant answered questions about mind, its relationship to nature, and its accessibility to scientific investigation, and offered a powerful, unified synthesis of thought, feeling, and will.

However, both Kant's philosophical system and his psychological synthesis proved difficult to sustain. In early nineteenth-century German culture, the response was either to emphasize one aspect at the expense of the others or to attempt to transcend Kant's self-imposed limits to reason in the interests of a romantic ideal of the unity of mind and nature. Especially interesting from this point of view, and worth pursuing in greater detail, are the intellectual lineages that David Leary presents at the end of his contribution. By indicating the variety of ways in which Kantian ideas were taken up and transformed in the conceptual development of psychology, they also raise the issue of which "uses" of Kant were accepted, and which rejected.

Such decisions were not made at the level of philosophy alone, however. When Prussian officials responded to their country's defeat by Napoleon with far-reaching reforms, especially in secondary and higher education, they faced anew the problem of deciding who was best qualified intellectually and morally to assume positions requiring this training. The acceptance in many elite secondary schools (humanistic *Gymnasien*) of pedagogical theories derived from the psychology of Herbart, which subordinated will to intellect, may have helped them to solve this problem.[5] Set against this background, the popularity outside the academic establishment of the extreme voluntarism symbolized by the names of Arthur Schopenhauer, Eduard von Hartmann, and Friedrich Nietzsche becomes all the more significant. In their essays both David Leary and William Woodward refer in passing to points of tangency between Wilhelm Wundt's voluntarism and that of Schopenhauer. But it cannot be said that the relations of this highly influential thinker and his successors to academic psychology have been thoroughly studied as yet.[6] Such an exploration might teach us much about the growing separation between academic culture and that of the broader educated public in German lands and its shaping influence on psychological thinking.[7]

Within the university, the Prussian reformers fixed the academic status and social function of psychological thinking in 1810 by requiring courses in philosophy for both state teachers' and doctoral examinations in "philosophical" (arts and sciences) faculties, a move soon widely imitated in the other German states. In the belief that both university and Gymnasium teachers should be capable of independent research, they prescribed philosophy to give these future educators an idea of pure science, or *Wissenschaft*. Here they were guided by the post-Kantian idealism of Fichte and Schelling; for in that world-view it was the task of philosophy as *Wissenschaft* to elevate the results of both the humanistic disciplines and the natural sciences to the highest level of theoretical generality. The twin ideals of pure science and the unity of teaching and research soon became the ideological bases for the professionalization of research in German universities.[8] Gustav Theodor Fechner was one of many scholar–scientists who faced the difficulty of reconciling this expansive conception of science, and the socially sanctioned romantic ideal on which it was based, with the task of subjecting psychological processes to measurement.

Like others before her, Marilyn Marshall recognizes the fundamentally philosophical and religious roots of Fechner's psychophysics; but she also shows that his philosophical hopes and his allegiance to a "modern," that is, ametaphysical, conception of physical science were consistently interwoven throughout his career. The idea, now gaining currency among historians of nineteenth-century science, that such a productive tension was characteristic of scientific thought in general at mid-century receives support of another kind from Kurt Danziger's essay. The ideals of *Naturphilosophie*, brought by Thomas Laycock from Göttingen, were developed in England by his student, John Hughlings Jackson, into an evolutionary view of mind in nature which would prove important to the construction of a conceptual framework for scientific psychology.[9]

It would be very important to pursue the effects of this tension by looking at the way experimenting psychologists such as Wundt, G. E. Müller, and Carl Stumpf, along with logicians like Christian Sigwart and physicists like J. L. R. Delboeuf, distanced themselves from Fechner's interpretation of the measurement of sensation after 1870, while the experimentalists made use of his techniques. Were they defending the "hallowed cultural concept" of the primacy of mind and its inaccessibility to causal law when they argued that Fechner's law was a measure of judgment, not sensation? Or were some of them seeking an empirically based way of attacking the problem, which could also secure the status of experimental psychology as a subspecialty of philosophy?

Actually, these alternatives were not mutually exclusive, as the essays by Woodward and by R. Steven Turner show. The physiologist Helmholtz openly rejected *Naturphilosophie;* but he accepted Fechner's law as quite consistent with his simplifying physicalistic assumptions about sensation and his separation of the laws of sense from those of mind. Wundt, the physiologist turned philosopher incorporated his modification of Fechner's law into his "law of relativity" and thus took a major step toward making psychology an experimental discipline. But since this positing of independent psychological laws was not consistent with the conservation of energy, Wundt's step also rested implicitly on a dualistic basis. Seen in this light, the "reconstruction of psychophysics," or Wundt's version of it, may have been an important step on the road to a conceptually independent psychology; but it was not in itself an answer to the tension between dualistic restrictions and monistic hopes characteristic of psychological thinking in its German cultural context.

The continuity of another solution to that problem is implied by Marshall's far-reaching suggestion that Fechner's "public positivism," his commitment to an ametaphysical view of physical science, had more in common with the views of Ernst Mach and his successors than with those of Wundt and his generation. Mach was, in fact, deeply influenced by Fechner in the 1860s.[10] Though he took care to distance himself from panpsychism in *The Analysis of Sensations,* the romantic hope of the unity of knowledge lived no more vibrantly than in Mach's neutral monism. Lorraine Daston reminds us at the end of her essay of the fundamental importance of Mach's psychological research in the development of his philosophy of science, especially his rejection of physical atomism and of absolute space and time. But the relationship of the "phenomenalogical physics" of Mach, Kirchhoff, and others to the subsequent development of experimental psychology as a discipline is only beginning to be explored in detail.[11] Perhaps the answer to psychology's conceptual location problem was not to change its concept of mind, but to participate in the redefinition of nature. As will be shown, below, however, neither this solution nor Wundt's helped to solve psychology's institutional location problem.

We have begun to see that the emergence of the German university as a research and teaching establishment added an important dimension to the social context of psychological thinking. In the Anglo-Saxon world, on the other hand, the relative weakness of state administration and the professions put less of a premium upon academic qualification. This situtation changed somewhat in Britain, and rather more drastically in the United States, later in the century. But in Britain, at least, philosophical and scientific discussion continued to take place among an elite that perpetuated itself by the cultivation not so much of academic credentials as of social virtues.[12] The reform of secondary and university education from which the English "public" schools arose in the latter half of the century did not end this genteel tradition but revitalized it.

A good example of the genteel tradition at work is the genesis of Darwin's conception of the "moral sense." As Robert Richards shows, the inputs here came as much from Darwin's upbringing and from discussions with intellectual relatives and friends as from his studies of natural theology, or his travels and wide reading. Although utilitarianism was certainly part of that discussion context, Darwin's answer in *The Descent of Man* to the moral issues posed by his theory of evolution was no mere application of that theory, but an attempt to express in scientific terms the values of moral and social responsibility according to which he and his compeers had been raised. Of course, a theory erected on such a basis is especially vulnerable to the charge of being unable to justify its major premise, namely, that there is such a thing as the "community good," which the "moral sense" could perceive. As Europe entered the age of mass democracy in the late nineteenth century, politically sensitive readers were bound to ask the nagging question of who defines "the community good" in complex human societies, as opposed to populations in the wild. It is not surprising, then, that others with different intellectual and social interests drew rather different psychological, moral, and political conclusions from evolutionary theory.[13]

Particularly noteworthy in William Preyer's thinking, for example, is the nearly complete absence of social sensibility, altruism, or an inherited sense of the community good, despite his support for specific welfare measures. His use of Darwin, as Siegfried Jaeger shows, was governed as much by his opposition to working-class politics in Germany as by a strict application of Darwinian principles to child psychology. The fact that he ignored or disparaged Darwin's later work, especially *The Descent of Man*, is telling in this regard. For Sigmund Freud, too, altruism can hardly be said to be an instinct. Though he took over and transformed Haeckel's idea that the species lives in the individual, as Frank Sulloway writes, he supported the reform of sexual mores from a liberal–individualistic viewpoint. In this way he sought to defend the liberal ideals that had been dominant in the Austria of his youth against the encroachments of mass politics, in this case the right-wing, antisemitic "Christian Socialist" party of Karl Leuger.[14]

Nonetheless, the basic challenge to genteel values posed by the idea that behavior, even moral behavior, is a product of evolution, remained. In Britain, the rise of professionally organized medicine from mid-century onward set that challenge in a different context. Some aspects of the professional framework came to England far later than to Germany, especially the institutionalization of basic research in physiological laboratories.[15] British psycho-physiologists were nonetheless quick to make use of a new source of legitimating authority by adding naturalistic concepts, including the theory of evolution, to the essentially moralistic vocabulary that Daniel Hack Tuke and others had used up to that time to discuss psychopathological problems.

There was no single formula for the use of naturalistic concepts. But as Kurt Danziger shows, it was Henry Maudsley who exemplified the long-range implications of the new situation most clearly when he sought to fulfill the practical requirements of asylum psychiatrists for a systematic psychology that went beyond the classification of conscious processes and devalued consciousness itself in doing so. This interweave between the gradual development of the asylum into a custodial institution and the use of organicist language in medical psychology can be seen in France earlier in the century. Similar developments in the United States, roughly contemporaneous with Maudsley's work in England, were closely connected with the search for social order in industrializing America.[16]

Such institutionally connected conceptual shifts contributed to the urgency of the debate on will that dominated English-language discussion of the New Psychology. Lorraine Daston's essay reveals that common political and social ideologies, in particular the view that science equals progress, covered widely differing metaphysical and methodological assumptions—ideologies of science, we could call them. But the violence of the reaction to the ideas of associationists such as Bain, reductionists such as Maudsley, and especially to Huxley's epiphenomenalism makes it clear that this is one case where the two kinds of ideology can be distinguished, but not separated. At stake were both the identity of psychology as a science and ideas essential to the self-definition of genteel intellectuals, values so cherished that participants like William James were willing to "save" will by removing it from science altogether.

By the end of the century, however, another kind of solution came to the fore in Britain, in the form of theories of emergent evolution like those of C. Lloyd Morgan and Leonard Trelawney Hobhouse, which indirectly supported the subsequent research of Charles Scott Sherrington on neural hierarchies. This way of "saving" mind and will for science by skilfully reformulating teleological metaphors proved to be highly productive, especially in the development of comparative psychology. But the organized pursuit of their implications in institutional research settings occurred mainly elsewhere. Perhaps the explanation for this lies in the educational reforms referred to above. Instead of replacing the classics with more modern subjects, the reformers of the "public" schools added character building and sports. Psychologies closely connected to moral philosophy, like those of James Ward and G. F. Stout, were well suited to such an educational approach. It was not the associationists, but Ward and Stout, along with other ethically oriented philosophers like Henry Sidgwick and T. H. Green, who were behind the proclamation of the New Psychology in Britain, chiefly in the journal *Mind*. Perhaps theories like those of emergent evolution, too, can be seen as expressions of the continuing integrative action of the genteel tradition in English culture. Hobhouse, for example, relied extensively upon Ward and Stout's ideas in *Mind in Evolution*.[17] But this requires further research.

CONCEPTUAL TRANSFORMATIONS IN SOCIAL SETTINGS: SOME EUROPEAN EXAMPLES

Whether the issue was that of defining a legitimate place inside or outside an academic establishment, or of recasting philosophical, political, or moral opinions in scientific language, the fundamental problem was the same: the orientation of nineteenth-century psychological thinking in specific sociocultural settings. Outside the German- and English-speaking cultural regions, too, social structures of intellectual discourse served as middle levels at which psychological thinking and societal reality met. In all of these settings, moreover, other mediating structures, from university research institutes to nonacademic organizations and small groups such as coteries of disciples, played a variety of transforming roles in the development and propagation of psychological thought.

The case of psychology in France is an example of the fundamental continuities involved here. Alexandre Métraux demonstrates both the ideological character of crowd psychology and the explicit political linkages of its leading practitioners. Their views on democracy in general and the Third Republic in particular placed them in opposition to the liberal and socialist academics who held the key positions in the universities, at least in the social sciences and the humanities.[18] Yet the requirements for success in French intellectual life remained the same for both: affiliation with powerful social groups, maintained by Gustave Le Bon, for example through his weekly *salon*, and above all connections in the appropriate ministries of the centralized state, for Alfred Binet and Émile Durkheim in the ministry of education, for Le Bon with the military.

In France, then, what could be called academic politics—intellectual, institutional, or personal allegiances within university or research establishments—and the politics of academics were often inseparable. Nonetheless, one important distinction should be made. Binet was interested in and committed primarily to science; after his decisive defeat by J. L. R. Delbeouf, he stopped advocating the so-called "psychiatric paradigm" of suggestion analyzed by Métraux, though he did work later on the "suggestibility" of normal subjects. The crowd psychologists, on the other hand, continued to evoke that paradigm, or at least the metaphor of suggestion, for their own ideological purposes. Perhaps the notions of useful but politically neutral expertise characteristic of U.S., now of world, psychology are intended to function as a form of insulation from the sorts of overtly political linkages we find here. Whether that purpose has been or ever could be achieved, especially in fields like social or mass psychology, is another matter.

The connections between scientific ideas in psychology, or the idea of a scientific psychology, and political ideology may have been more subtle in nineteenth-century Spain than they were in France; explicit political affiliation does not seem to have played a direct role. But they existed nonetheless. As Helio Carpintero portrays them, the battle lines were often drawn between intellectuals like Francisco Giner de los Ríos, who espoused liberal, "modern," and "European" ideas, and conservative and clerical forces, with occasional liberal clerics in between. Important here was the fact that in the Spanish universities, as opposed to the French, the conservatives were the in group and the liberals were the out group. The institutional difficulties of scientific psychology, as a foreign import, were thus probably not very different from those of the social or even the natural sciences in Spain.

Of interest in this context are the ways in which ideas from European "centers" were propagated in the new setting, especially the establishment of independent pedagogical societies like the Athenaeum and the "Free Institution of Education," both in Madrid. The emergence of such organizations in Germany has been portrayed as a sign of psychology's emergence as a discipline.[19] Here, however, they functioned as an alternative to the absence of institutionalization, or to the already institutionalized, Catholic psychology. Institutionalized research on psychological issues came to Spain only at the end of the century, and then primarily in physiology. When we recall that in Britain, too, physiological laboratories were not established until late in the century, and note the achievements of figures like Santiago Ramon y Cajal, then we can see that it is incorrect to speak here of derivative or "peripheral" science. Instead, it would be more accurate to speak of the transformation of ideas and their propagation in an environment different from the one in which they were produced. Such language might provide a basis for comparative studies.

An important instance of the transformation of scientific ideas in a new social setting is the fundamental revision of reflex physiology begun by Ivan M. Sechenov and his students. Here, as in Spain, the basic ideas were brought from Germany, a "center" of physiological research, to what was then a "peripheral" location in St. Petersburg. Here, too, we have a small, cohesive group of workers who drew strength in the 1860s—an era of liberal reform in Russia—from their identification with progressive, West-European ideas against clerical and conservative, in this case Orthodox and slavophile, opposition.[20] However, Sechenov and his students were not a group of free intellectuals and professionals organizing alternative institutions, but a scientific school working within the university system, making full use of the relative freedom allowed them by the Czarist state because of the value of their work for medical practice—a point Sechenov took care to emphasize very early on.

The benefits of this relatively privileged position were clear. While in Spain the exchange of knowledge was nearly entirely one-way, consisting mainly of translations and expositions until the end of the century, Sechenov and his students published in West-European journals from the beginning; and his and Nadeshda Suslova's final resolution of the controversy with Moritz Schiff and Alexander A. Herzen on central inhibition occurred in Austria, not Russia. Although Mikhail Yaroschevskii is right to speak of national "schools" or traditions in physiology, they were clearly interacting parts of a complex whole. Whether such benefits were enjoyed by academic psychology in Russia, however, is an open question. The ideological significance of the mother discipline, philosophy, and the different legitimating basis provided by the regime, which was not committed to scientific research to the same extent as in Germany, may be the reasons why we identify Russian contributions to psychological thinking in the nineteenth century mainly with the work of physiologists; but more research is clearly needed here to clarify the issue.

Although it was obviously not located within a scientific establishment, the group that developed around the powerful intellect and personality of Sigmund Freud certainly possessed many of the features that Yaroschevskii attributes to the scientific school as research collective. Freud's sense of his role as teacher and leader was, if anything, even stronger than Sechenov's; and he, too, participated directly in the intellectual and methodological initiation of his students, above all in the training analysis, treating his followers as coworkers in a great cause to be defended against outside opposition. The most important difference, of course, was Freud's claim to have established an independent science not subject to intersubjective confirmation by outsiders. A major part of the support for Freud's scientific claims came from his transformation of the biological ideas he had learned in his medical training into psychological theory, as Frank Sulloway shows.

But the biologization of the unconscious was not in itself a basis for therapy, at least not for the patients Freud and his followers had. The unity of theory and therapy was not only a core principle of mature psychoanalytic doctrine, but also the basis of the psychoanalytic movement's cohesiveness as a group. Here is where we might look for the "psychologization" at the basis of what Sulloway calls the "Freud legend." What that legend obscured, however, was the role of a socially transmitted intellectual tradition (Haeckelian biogenesis) in the development of psychoanalysis. This then, is a case in which the theoretical and practical requirements of a school in the narrower sense came into conflict with those of a school in the larger sense.

With William Preyer's use of child psychology in the cause of the German school reform movement, we return to the location of psychological thinking in larger social contexts. Again we encounter a close connection between academic culture and politics; in this case, however, the central issue was not access to academic establishments for intellectuals or scientists, but educational opportunities for members of the so-called "new middle classes" generated by Germany's rapid industrialization in the late nineteenth century. Science and technology were central in Germany's economic upswing, in which the chemical, electrical, and machine tool industries were leading sectors. Correspondingly prominent in the struggle for educational reform were demands for additional secondary instruction in the natural sciences and the modern languages, and the battle of technical schools for equal academic standing with the universities.[21]

Given his own commitment to natural-scientific methods in physiology, Preyer's support of these demands was logical enough. His combination of an individualistic version of Darwinism, already mentioned, and his praise of competition as progress with fervent nationalism, which implied subordination of the individual, was no paradox but a typical reflection of the increasing *rapprochement* of the leaders of the newly unified German Empire and the new middle classes against the threat of social democracy.[22] Thus it was Kaiser Wilhelm II's personal endorsement that finally brought the educational reforms Preyer and his cohorts sought in 1890, and which also led to the upgrading of the technical schools in 1899.

However, the content of Preyer's "physiological" pedagogy— more room for physical activity and character development and less of the intellectual drill required by the classically oriented Herbartian Gymnasium—is reminiscent not only of the position of educational reformers in the United States in the same period, but also of the program of the reformed English "public" school. Here, apparently, is an excellent example of the very different ways in which an idea derived from psychological thinking can be used in different settings: in England to revitalize elite education, in Germany to expand and at least partially modernize it, and in America to help organize mass education, thus creating professional roles for experts in child development. Clearly, Siegfried Jaeger's call for comparative studies is highly appropriate. Such work could be at least as important for general social history as for the history of psychology and of education.

In Germany, however, the pressure of movements like that for school reform led to deep divisions within the established elite of the humanistically educated. We shall see that the bitter resistance of a part of this group to social change posed a direct threat to the status of experimental psychology in that country.

PROBLEMS OF ACADEMIC INSTITUTIONALIZATION: GERMANY AND THE UNITED STATES

Now that various examples have been presented in this book of significant and historically influential psychological thinking outside the academy, the reader might well ask whether its institutionalization there was either inevitable or necessary. The answer is that it was neither. Not psychological thinking *per se* required institutional support, but psychological research, the transformation of theoretical issues into research problems, and the transfer of results to others for confirmation, further development, or application. The form that support took, and the fact that it was forthcoming at all on an appreciable scale, depended on the interaction of various historical circumstances; of these the conceptual and methodological development of psychology was only one, perhaps not even the most important. We have seen that in Britain significant theoretical changes could and did occur without the extensive institutionalization of research. In Germany and the United States, however, the vicissitudes of academic institutionalization shaped the emerging discipline in important ways as it entered the twentieth century.

During the Wilhelminian period (1871–1914) and especially after 1890, German universities expanded rapidly, partly in order to meet the rising demand in industry for scientifically trained personnel, mentioned above. New fields seeking entry into this growing matrix were required, as before, both to earn recognition as *Wissenschaft*, or pure research, in the eyes of peers, and to demonstrate their social usefulness to state officials. The university reformers of the early nineteenth century had already squared this circle in the case of philosophy by making theory a practical requirement for Gymnasium teachers. But the rise of empirical research on psychological issues made the position of that branch of philosophy increasingly anomalous. The dilemma of experimenting psychologists, then, was to find ways of realizing the research potential of the new methods while retaining their place in the established order.

The work of Hermann Helmholtz and his cohorts seemed at first to offer a solution to this problem of academic legitimation. By the 1870s their assumptions about science, and the experimental and mathematical methods connected with them, had become the defining features of German physiology; and the usefulness of their results in medical practice seemed evident. Helmholtz was by no means as skeptical about the possibility of extending these methods to psychology as his colleague Emil Du Bois-Reymond, who declared mental processes "outside the realm of causal law."[23] We have seen that he accepted Fechner's law as consistent with his simplifying physicalistic assumptions about sensation; and he could easily claim to have reduced one of Kant's *a priori* categories, that of space, to an empirical research problem. However, as R. Steven Turner demonstrates, he succeeded in doing this only by invoking "psychological" processes, such as unconscious inductive reasoning, which were dependent in the last analysis upon a Fichtean philosophy of mind. Experimenting psychologists employed Helmholtz's methods and observations; but his assumptions about science proved to be better suited to defining a conceptual basis for sensory physiology than to establishing the intellectual autonomy of psychology.

It was Helmholtz's former assistant Wilhelm Wundt who most eagerly and fully accepted the master's implied invitation to put speculative philosophy on an empirical basis. He did this, however, at the cost of replacing Helmholtz's simpliyfing assumptions about sensation with complicating ones about entities like his hypothetical "apperception center." As William Woodward's synthesis of the recent flood of Wundt literature indicates, Wundt's "apostasy"—to use Turner's term—was part of a broad philosophical trend, not limited to experimenting psychologists, toward what would later be called "psychologism"—the attempt to base philosophy upon the facts of conscious experience. His establishment of the Leipzig laboratory and the journal *Philosophische Studien*, his elaboration of the "law of relativity," his increasing emphasis on emergent principles like that of the "heterogeny of ends," and his growing concentration on language, logic, and culture in his extraordinary effort to develop a comprehensive psychophilosophical system were all of a piece. The aim was to establish psychology as a fundamental philosophical discipline, within which experimental psychology could have a secure, if limited, place.

Though most experimenting psychologists in Germany shared this aim, they paid little heed to Wundt's system. Instead, they used the institutional innovations he imported from physiology, especially the research laboratory, to establish themselves as specialists within philosophy. Carl Stumpf, another participant in the "reconstruction of psychophysics," provided one important rationale for this effort when he reminded neo-Kantian opponents of empirical psychology that no discussion of *a priori* judgment or "forms of understanding" can be developed without presupposing some kind of psychology. Given this, he argued, careful analysis of the phenomena of consciousness is surely preferable to relying on speculation.[24] As Turner shows, Stumpf criticized Helmholtz's theory of perception from the same viewpoint, by demonstrating that it ignored or denied the reality of important data from immediate experience. Thus, though Stumpf and his colleagues aligned themselves with physiologists, including Helmholtz, for purposes of scientific legitimation, they soon turned away from Helmholtz's way of thinking, if not always from physiological speculation. At the same time, they used phenomenological and other methods to expand the realm of experimentation far beyond the limits originally set by Wundt.

Advantageous as it seemed, however, its location within philosophy limited the growth potential of the field. The new generation of experimenting psychologists and their students thought that their work could solve philosophical problems, but the actual result was a mutual parting of the ways. The work of the laboratory left them with little time for philosophical discussion; at the same time, voices were raised calling for a return to "pure" philosophy. Rooted partly in idealistic and logicistic reactions to "psychologism" and partly in the resentment of the humanistically educated against the growing status and power of the technically trained, such calls found a ready target in the experimenting psychologists.[25] These attacks also posed questions about the field's social function. Why, after all, should future Gymnasium teachers need to hear about experimental psychology in required philosophy lectures, when their role in life was to communicate higher values, a metaphysical world view?

Despite the increasing theoretical and methodological sophistication of its practitioners, experimental psychology in Germany was caught in an academic impasse: both the intellectual and the social bases of its legitimacy were in doubt. Many experimenting psychologists sought to apply their methods to social problems, both in education and in industry.[26] But to base the legitimacy of the field upon such work would have threatened its philosophical status still more. By the 1920s, as Turner states, the field had achieved a certain level of institutional security; but it remained limited mainly to single chairs of philosophy in the German universities until after the Second World War.[27] The thesis advanced by the sociologists Joseph Ben-David and Randall Collins 15 years ago, that

Wundt's institutional innovation led to experimental psychology's "take-off into sustained growth," requires significant modification. That growth happened, but only after Wundt's innovation was taken out of the context he had set for it and transplanted into a very different social and intellectual milieu in the United States.

The contrast with the German situation could hardly be greater. By 1900, there were already more psychological laboratories in the United States than there were universities in Germany. Such growth was possible in a rapidly growing university network with no direct connections to any state bureaucracy. But this situation, combined with the lower status of academics in America, also made the pressure to show some kind of social usefulness more direct in the American case.[28] The way to intellectual legitimation was prepared by the teaching and writing of thinkers like James Mark Baldwin, William James, and John Dewey, who tried to forge a practical philosophy of education based on a synthesis of Continental and Scottish philosophy and evolutionary theory.[29] These philosopher-psychologists supported laboratory work, as well; but the institutionalization effort was driven forward primarily by figures such as G. Stanley Hall, James McKeen Cattell, Edward Thorndike, and Hugo Münsterberg. Thanks to them and others, scientific psychology soon found a place in American life, primarily because of its potential usefulness in the organization and rationalization of education and personnel selection in an industrializing society.[30]

The career of James McKeen Cattell and anthropometric mental testing was an important part of this story. Like many others of his generation, Cattell was educated according to an American version of the genteel tradition, characterized by philosophical realism, loyalty to facts over explicit theory, and a strong pragmatic orientation. His work was a counterpart at the technical level of contemporary efforts to synthesize contributions from European sources, often gathered personally, and to transform them for use in this American context. We might almost say that his and others' know-nothing worship of the facts was a highly truncated sort of "radical empiricism." In more philosophically sophisticated hands it provided scientific psychology with an alternative metaphysical foundation and methodological openness; in Cattell's it resulted in a hopeless adulteration of the ideas and techniques of both his masters, Wundt and Galton.

The weaknesses of his effort were exposed by other scientists, not by public outcry; and the work of his student Clark Wissler, which actually ended his program, employed the substance, not only the appearance, of Galton's methods. But the framework of overly simple assumptions about science, combined with beliefs in its ability to accomplish great things in education and other areas of life, persisted. The tests that superseded Cattell's were also conducted with large-scale social applications in mind; and when Alfred Binet's far more sophisticated mental tests were adopted in America, the assumptions behind their use were hardly more profound than Cattell's had been.[31]

The status of experimental psychology in the German universities was the social problem faced by Wundt, Stumpf, and others, to which they responded with attempts to define their field as an experimentally based but still philosophical discipline. In the United States, the academic establishment of psychology was achieved with a potent mixture of naturalistic and technocratic legitimation, with emphasis on the latter. John B. Watson's proclamation of a new goal for psychology, "the prediction and control of behavior," only gave a name to this development. Of course this did not occur without resistance; but the turn to technocracy was so far advanced by the 1920s that its opponents apparently felt called upon to write, or rather rewrite, the history of the discipline to legitimate themselves more effectively.[32]

* * *

The contributions to this volume obviously do not constitute a comprehensive survey of psychological thinking in the nineteenth century; but they do show that it was embedded in a wide variety of philosophical, scientific, and social concerns. Nontheless, we can say that the nineteenth century was the time in which psychology began to become not a set of questions raised on the way to solving other problems, but itself a problem—a subject of intellectual inquiry and of scientific and technical expertise in its own right. It was precisely because this was happening that psychological concepts figured so prominently in the use of naturalistic vocabulary for ideological purposes. By the end of the century, the process of conceptual construction had begun to develop a momentum of its own, and a rich variety of research techniques had been developed. But a heavy price had been paid: the loss of a view of the person in society.

At the same time, developments had occurred, primarily, though not exclusively, in the United States, which shaped the discipline as we know it today. Perhaps we can call these the turn to technocracy without much danger of exaggeration. It was against this tendency that Wundt warned in his 1913 polemic, "Psychology in the Struggle for Existence." Pointing to the increasing dominance of educational psychology in America, he predicted that if psychology ceased to be primarily a theoretical discipline closely linked to philosophy, its practitioners would become "artisans, but not exactly artisans of the most useful sort."[33]

We may not agree about whether Wundt's prediction has come true, or whether psychology has genuinely freed itself from its former linkages to philosophy. But inasmuch as the discipline lives in or with the tension between imperatives of science and those of technological society, it has become much like any other discipline. With or without a unifying paradigm, its problematic social situation is no different in its essential features from that of physics. Its history should be written accordingly, not like the story of a child perpetually knocking at the door of true science, but like that of any individual or group struggling for orientation in an increasingly complicated world.

NOTES

1. This holds as well for other disciplines that were institutionalized in this period, for example the social sciences. Cf. Anthony Oberschall (ed.), *The Establishment of Empirical Sociology: Studies in Continuity, Discontinuity, and Institutionalization* (New York: Harper & Row, 1972). For the need to expand the history of science beyond the history of individually constructed disciplines, see Wolf Lepenies, "Problems of a Historical Study of Science," in Everett Mendelsohn, Peter Weingart and Richard Whitley (eds.), *The Social Production of Scientific Knowledge* (Dordrecht and Boston: Reidel, 1977), pp. 55-67.

2. On the social history of science in particular, see Roy MacLeod, "Changing Perspectives in the Social History of Science," in Ina Spiegel-Rosing and Derek de Sola Price (eds.), *Science, Technology and Society* (London & Beverly Hills: Sage Publications, 1977), pp. 149-95; and Everettt Mendelsohn, "The Social Construction of Scientific Knowledge," in Mendelsohn et al., *Social Production*, pp. 3-21.

3. Alan Buss, "The Emerging Field of the Sociology of Psychological Knowledge," in Alan Buss (ed.), *Psychology in Social Context* (New York: Irvington, 1979), pp. 1-24; Hans Thomae, *Psychologie in der modernen Gesellschaft* (Hamburg: Hoffmann & Campe, 1977); and Hans Thomae, "Social Approach: The Rise of Psychology as an Independent Discipline," in Josef Brozek and Ludwig Pongratz (eds.), *Historiography of Modern Psychology* (Toronto: Hogrefe, 1980), pp. 302-14. East European scholars have also begun to speak of "mediating links" between psychology and larger social developments. Cf. Georg Eckardt, "Einleitung: Bemerkungen zum Anliegen psychologie-historischer Forschung," in Georg Eckardt (ed.), *Zur Geschichte der Psychologie* (Berlin, G.D.R.: VEB Deutscher Verlag der Wissenschaften, 1979), pp. 7-20.

For an excellent discussion of these and other recent approaches to the history of psychology, see Ulfried Geuter, "Psychologiegeschichte" in Gunther Rexilius and Siegfried Grubitzsch (eds.), *Handbuch psychologischer Grundbegriffe* (Reinbek bei Hamburg: Rowohlt, 1981), pp. 824-38.

4. For a comprehensive historical treatment of the German universities in the eighteenth and nineteenth centuries, see Charles E. McClelland, *State, Society and University in Germany 1700-1914* (Cambridge: Cambridge University Press, 1980).

5. Cf. Siefried Jaeger and Irmingard Staeuble, *Die Gesellschaftliche Genese der Psychologie* (Frankfurt am Main: Campus Verlag, 1978), chap. 5. For a discussion of the Prussian educational reforms, see Fritz K. Ringer, *Education and Society in Modern Europe* (Bloomington: Indiana University Press, 1979), chap. 2.

6. For some first steps in this direction, see Nicolas Pastore, "Reevaluation of Boring on Kantian Influence, Nineteenth Century Nativism, Gestalt Psychology and Helmholtz," *Journal of the History of the Behavioral Sciences* 10 (1974):375-90.

7. On the roots of the bifurcation of cultures in Germany, see Hugh West, "Gottingen and Weimar: The Organization of Knowledge and Social Theory in Eighteenth Century Germany," *Central European History* 11 (1978): 150-61. A sharply critical account of the effects of this separation on psychological thinking is Werner Obermeit, *'Das unsichtbare Ding, das Seele heisst': Die Entdekkung der Psyche im burgerlichen Zeitalter* (Frankfurt am Main: Syndikat, 1980).

8. See R. Steven Turner, "The Growth of Professorial Research in Prussia 1818 to 1848: Causes and Context," *Historical Studies in the Physical Sciences*, 3 (1971):137-82.

9. Laycock's transfer of ideas was not unique, but part of an important cultural trend of the time. Cf. Rosemary Ashton, *The German Idea: Four English Writers and the Reception of German Thought 1800-1860* (Cambridge: Cambridge University Press, 1980).

10. John Blackmore, *Ernst Mach: His Life, Work and Influence* (Berkeley, Calif.: University of California Press, 1972), pp. 14-15, 30-31.

11. Cf. Kurt Danzier, "The Positivist Repudiation of Wundt," *Journal of the History of the Behavioral Sciences* 15 (1979):205-30. For a discussion of "phenomenological physics," see Ernst Cassirer, *The Problem of Knowledge: Philosophy, Science and History Since Hegel*, trans. William H. Woglom & Charles W. Hendel (New Haven: Yale University Press, 1950), pp. 93ff.

12. See, for example, M. Berman, " 'Hegemony' and the Amateur Tradition in British Science," *Journal of Social History* 8 (1975):30-50; cf. S. F. Cannon, *Science in Culture* (New York: Neale Watson Publications, 1978), especially chaps. 5, 8, and 9. For a full discussion of this elite in American culture and its roots in Britain, see Stow Persons, *The Decline of American Gentility* (New York: Columbia University Press, 1973).

13. On the reception of Darwinian theory in Anglo-Saxon science and social thought, see Michael Ruse, *Science Red in Tooth and Claw: The Darwinian Revolution* (Chicago: University of Chicago Press, 1979), especially chaps. 8-9.

14. A brilliant interpretation of Freud's thought as at least partly a response to the crisis of liberalism in turn-of-the-century Vienna is Carl E. Schorske, *Fin-de-Siècle Vienna* (New York: Alfred A. Knopf, 1980), chap. 4.

15. Cf. Gerald L. Geison, *Michael Foster and the Cambridge School of Physiology: The Scientific Enterprise in Late Victorian Society* (Princeton: Princeton University Press, 1978).

16. Michael Foucault, *The Birth of the Clinic: An Archeology of Medical Perception*, trans. A. M. Sheridan Smith (New York: Vintage Books, 1975); David J. Rothman, *The Discovery of the Asylum* (Boston: Little, Brown, 1971), and *Conscience and Convenience: The Asylum and its Alternatives in Progressive America* (Boston: Little, Brown, 1980). The American situation was complicated by the fact that asylum superintendents, who were not necessarily medical men and had their own professional association, were in constant conflict with the psychiatrists.

17. Leonard Trelawney Hobhouse, *Mind in Evolution* (1901), 2nd ed. (reprint: New York: Arno Press, 1973), for example p. 103, n. 1.

18. On the political affiliations of French university professors, see Terry N. Clark, *Prophets and Patrons: The French University and the Emergence of the Social Sciences* (Cambridge, Mass.: Harvard University Press, 1973).

19. Frank R. Pfetsch, *Zur Entwicklung der Wissenschaftspolitik in Deutschland 1750–1914* (Berlin: Duncker & Humbolt, 1974), p. 233ff.

20. Cf. Alexander Vucinich, *Science in Russian Culture, 1861–1917* (Stanford: Stanford University Press, 1970), especially chap. 1.

21. On the struggle of the technical fields for equal status, see Karl-Heinz Manegold, *Universität, Technische Hochschule und Industrie: Ein Beitrag zur Emanzipation der Technik im 19. Jahrhundert unter besonderer Berücksichtigung der Bestrebungen Felix Kleins* (Berlin: Duncker & Humblot, 1970).

22. Cf., for example, Gerd Hortleder, *Das Gesellschaftsbild des Ingenieurs: Zum politischen Verhalten der Technischen Intelligenz in Deutschland*, 2nd ed. (Frankfurt am Main: Suhrkamp, 1970).

23. Emil Du Bois-Reymond, *Über die Grenzen des Naturerkennens* (1872), 11th ed. (Leipzig: Veit, 1916), p. 41.

24. Carl Stumpf, "Psychologie und Erkenntnistheorie," *Abhandlungen der königlich bayrischen Akademie der Wissenschaften*, I. Kl., 19 (1891):467–516.

25. For the background of these attacks, see Fritz K. Ringer, *The Decline of the German Mandarins: The German Academic Community, 1890-1933* (Cambridge, Mass.: Harvard University Press, 1969), especially pp. 295-304.

26. On the development of applied psychology in this period, especially in Germany, see Siegfried Jaeger and Irmingard Staeuble, "Die Psychotechnik und ihre gesellschaftlichen Entwicklungsbedingungen," in *Die Psychologie des 20. Jahrhunderts*, vol. 13, ed. Francois Stoll (Zurich: Kindler Verlag, 1981), pp. 53-95.

27. For more detailed accounts of these developments, see Mitchell G. Ash, "Wilhelm Wundt and Oswald Kulpe on the Institutional Status of Psychology: An Academic Controversy in Historical Context," in Wolfgang G. Bringmann and Ryan D. Tweney (eds.), *Wundt Studies* (Toronto: Hogrefe, 1980), pp. 396-431, and "Academic Politics in the History of Science: Experimental Psychology in Germany, 1879–1941," *Central European History* 13 (1980), 255-86.

28. For this point see Kurt Danziger, "The Social Origins of Modern Psychology," in Alan Buss (ed.), *Psychology in Social Context* (New York: Irvington, 1979), pp. 27-46.

29. Cf. William R. Woodward, "William James' Psychology of Will: Its Revolutionary Impact on American Psychology," in Josef Brozek (ed.), *Explorations in the History of Psychology* (Lewisburg, Pa.: Bucknell University Press, in press); Robert H. Wozniak, "Metaphysics and Science, Reason and Reality: The Intellectual Origins of Genetic Epistemology," in John Broughton and John Freeman-Moir (eds.), *The Cognitive Developmental Psychology of James Mark Baldwin: Current Theory and Research in Genetic Epistemology* (New York: Ablex Press, in press).

30. See John M. O'Donnell, "The Origins of Behaviorism: American Psychology, 1880-1920," Ph.D. dissertation, University of Pennsylvania, Xerox University Microfilms Order No. 7928159. See also Matthew Hale, Jr., *Human Science and Social Order: Hugo Münsterberg and the Origins of Applied Psychology* (Philadelphia: Temple University Press, 1980). An attempt to set these developments in a broader social and intellectual context is Dorothy Ross, "The Development of the Social Sciences," in Alexandra Oleson and John Voss (eds.), *The Organization of Knowledge in Modern America, 1860-1920* (Baltimore: Johns Hopkins University Press, 1979): pp. 107-38.

31. Cf. Hamilton Cravens, *The Triumph of Evolution: American Scientists and the Hereditary-Environment Controversy 1900-1941* (Philadelphia: University of Pennsylvania Press, 1979), chap. 2.

32. John M. O'Donnell, "The Crisis of Experimentation in the 1920s: E. G. Boring and His Uses of History," *American Psychologist* 34 (1979):289-95. On the resistance especially to Watsonian behaviorism, see Franz Samelson, "Struggle for Scientific Authority: The Reception of Watson's Behaviorism, 1913-1921," *Journal of the History of the Behavioral Sciences* 17 (1981): 399-425.

33. Wilhelm Wundt, "Die Psychologie im Kampf ums Dasein," (1913), in *Kleine Schriften*, vol. 3, ed. Max Wundt (Stuttgart: Kroner, 1921), pp. 515-43, on p. 533.

NAME INDEX

SUBJECT INDEX

ABOUT THE AUTHORS

MITCHELL G. ASH is Research Associate at the Psychological Institute of the University of Mainz, Federal Republic of Germany. He is currently working on a project "Psychology in Exile" supported by the German Research Council. He was a Fulbright Scholar in history at the Free University of Berlin between 1978 and 1980.

His articles have appeared in *Central European History*, *Psychological Research*, and in *Wundt Studies* (edited by Wolfgang G. Bringmann and Ryan D. Tweney, Toronto, 1980).

Dr. Ash holds a B.A. from Amherst College and the A.M. and Ph.D. degrees in history from Harvard University.

HELIO CARPINTERO is Professor of Psychology and Director of the Department of General Psychology at the University of Valencia.

Among his many publications are *Historia de la Psicologia* (1976) and *Psicologia contemporanea: teoria y metodos para el estudio de su literatura cientifica* (coedited with Jose Peiro, 1981). He is codirector of the new journal *Revista de Historia de la Psicologia* and associate director of *Analisis y Modificacion de Conducta*.

Professor Carpintero holds the doctorate in philosophy and letters from the Universidad Complutense in Madrid.

KURT DANZIGER is Professor of Psychology at York University, Toronto, Canada.

Dr. Danziger is the author of several books and journal articles in the areas of social and developmental psychology as well as the history of psychology and the sociology of knowledge.

He is a graduate of the University of Oxford.

LORRAINE J. DASTON is Assistant Professor of the History of Science at Harvard University, Cambridge, Massachusetts. In 1979/80 she was a member of the Society of Fellows in the Humanities at Columbia University.

Dr. Daston has published in the areas of the history of mathematics, of psychology, and of natural history. Her articles and reviews have appeared in *Isis, Historia Mathematica,* and *Past and Present.*

Dr. Daston holds a B.A. from Harvard University and a Dipl. from the University of Cambridge. She took her Ph.D. in history of science from Harvard University.

SIEGFRIED JAEGER is Research and Teaching Associate of the Psychological Institute of the Free University of Berlin.

Dr. Jaeger is coauthor, with Irmingard Staeuble, of *Gesellschaftliche Genese der Psychologie* (Frankfurt: Campus Verlag, 1978).

He holds a diploma in psychology from the University of Marburg and a Ph.D. in psychology from the Free University of Berlin.

DAVID E. LEARY is Associate Professor of Psychology and the Humanities at the University of New Hampshire. He is codirector of the graduate program in the History and Theory of Psychology, which is one of the specialty areas within the Department of Psychology.

Dr. Leary's publications have appeared in the *Journal of the History of Ideas, Journal of the History of Philosophy, Psychological Research, Journal of General Psychology,* and *Journal of the History of the Behavioral Sciences.* He is coeditor, with Sigmund Koch, of *A Century of Psychology as Science: Retrospections and Assessments* (New York: McGraw-Hill, 1982).

He holds a B.A. degree from San Luis Rey College, a M.A. in psychology from San Jose State College, and a Ph.D. in history of science from the University of Chicago.

MARILYN E. MARSHALL is Professor of Psychology at Carleton University, Ottawa, Canada.

Dr. Marshall has published in the area of experimental psychology and in the history of psychology. Her articles have appeared in *Perceptual and Motor Skills*, *Canadian Journal of Psychology*, the *Journal of the History of the Behavioral Sciences*, and *Wundt Studies*.

She holds a B.A. Degree from Lake Erie College, a M.A. from Bowling Green State University, and a Ph.D. from the State University of Iowa.

ALEXANDRE MÉTRAUX works at the Psychological Institute of the University of Heidelberg in the Federal Republic of Germany. During 1974/75 he was Visiting Assistant Professor of Philosophy at the Graduate Faculty of the New School for Social Research in New York City.

Dr. Metraux has published in the area of philosophy, the history of psychology, the theoretical foundations of the social sciences, and the philosophy of law. His publications include *Max Scheler ou la phenomenologie des valeurs* (Paris: Seghers, 1973) and *Kurt Lewin, Wissenschaftstheorie I* (1981). He is coeditor, with Horst Gundlach, of *Kinesis—Studies in the Theory and in the History of Psychology*.

He received his Ph.D. in philosophy from the University of Basel in Switzerland.

ROBERT J. RICHARDS is Assistant Professor in History of Science, Conceptual Foundations of Science, and Biopsychology at the University of Chicago.

Dr. Richards has published in the *British Journal of the History of Science*, the *Journal of the History of Ideas*, the *Journal of the History of the Behavioral Sciences*, *Wundt Studies*, and the *Proceedings of the American Philosophical Society*. His current research focuses on evolutionary theories of mind and behavior in the nineteenth century.

He holds a M.A. in biological psychology from the University of Nebraska, a Ph.D. in philosophy from St. Louis University, and a Ph.D. in history of science from the University of Chicago.

MICHAEL M. SOKAL is Professor of History in the Department of Humanities, Worcester Polytechnic Institute, Worcester, Massachusetts.

Dr. Sokal's work has appeared in *Science*, the *American Psychologist*, *Isis*, the *Proceedings of the American Philosophical Society*, and the *Journal of the History of the Behavioral Sciences*. His book, *An Education in Psychology: James McKeen Cattell's Journal and Letters from Germany and England, 1880–1888*, was published in 1981 by The MIT Press. During the 1979/80 and 1980/81 academic years he was a National Lecturer for Sigma Xi, the Scientific Research Society. Dr. Sokal is now preparing a full biography of Cattell with the support "without restriction" from the James McKeen Cattell Fund.

He holds a Ph.D. in history of science and technology from Case Western Reserve University.

FRANK J. SULLOWAY is a Visiting Scholar at Harvard University in the Department of Psychology and Social Relations.

Dr. Sulloway's publications include films and articles on the life and scientific work of Charles Darwin. His intellectual biography of Sigmund Freud *(Freud, Biologist of the Mind: Beyond the Psychoanalytic Legend)* won the Pfizer Award of the History of Science Society for the best book published in the field in 1979.

Dr. Sulloway received his B.A. from Harvard, summa cum laude, in 1969. From 1974 to 1977 he was a Junior Fellow in the Harvard Society of Fellows, receiving his doctorate from Harvard in 1978. He has been a member of the Institute for Advanced Study (1977/78); a Research Fellow at the Miller Institute for Basic Research in Science, University of California, Berkeley (1978/80); and a Visiting Scholar at M.I.T. in the Program in Science, Technology, and Society (1980/81).

R. STEVEN TURNER is Associate Professor for the History of Science and Technology at the University of New Brunswick in Fredericton, New Brunswick, Canada.

Dr. Turner's main research interest is the development of the German university system during the nineteenth century and the role of the professorial career in the professionalization of German learning. His work has appeared in *Historical Studies in the Physical*

Sciences, the *Dictionary of Scientific Biography*, the *British Journal of the History of Science*, and *Journal of the History of the Behavioral Sciences*, and in Lawrence Stone, ed., *The University in Society* (Princeton, 1974).

He received his Ph.D. from the Program in the History and Philosophy of Science at Princeton University.

WILLIAM R. WOODWARD is Associate Professor of Psychology at the University of New Hampshire and codirector of the graduate program in History and Theory of Psychology.

He is currently working on an intellectual biography of the German philosopher and psychologist, Rudolph Hermann Lotze; his publications have appeared in the *American Psychologist*, *Genetic Psychology Monographs*, *Isis*, *Medical History*, *Social Studies of Science*, and the *Journal of the History of the Behavioral Sciences*.

Dr. Woodward holds a B.A. from Harvard University in history and science, a M.A. in psychology from Princeton University, and a Ph.D. in history of science and medicine from Yale University.

MIKHAIL GRIGOREVICH YAROSCHEVSKII is Professor and Assistant Director at the Institute for the History of Science and Technology of the Academy of Sciences of the U.S.S.R., Moscow.

Among his publications in the history of science and the history of psychology are *Ivan Mikhailovich Sechenov* (1968) and *Psichologia v XX stoletti* [Psychology in the Twentieth Century], which has also appeared in German translation (1975).